Lecture Notes in Computer Science 1207

Edited by G. Goos, J. Hartmanis and J. van Leeuwen

Advisory Board: W. Brauer D. Gries J. Stoer

Springer
Berlin
Heidelberg
New York
Barcelona
Budapest
Hong Kong
London
Milan
Paris
Santa Clara
Singapore
Tokyo

John Gallagher   (Ed.)

Logic Program Synthesis and Transformation

6th International Workshop, LOPSTR'96
Stockholm, Sweden, August 28-30, 1996
Proceedings

 Springer

Series Editors

Gerhard Goos, Karlsruhe University, Germany

Juris Hartmanis, Cornell University, NY, USA

Jan van Leeuwen, Utrecht University, The Netherlands

Volume Editor

John Gallagher
University of Bristol, Department of Computer Science
Woodland Road, Bristol BS8 1UB, UK
E-mail: jpg@compsci.bristol.ac.uk

Cataloging-in-Publication data applied for

Die Deutsche Bibliothek - CIP-Einheitsaufnahme

Logic program synthesis and transformation : 6th international
workshop ; proceedings / LOPSTR '96, Stockholm, Sweden,
August 28 - 30, 1996. John Gallagher (ed.). - Berlin ;
Heidelberg ; New York ; Barcelona ; Budapest ; Hong Kong ;
London ; Milan ; Paris ; Santa Clara ; Singapore ; Tokyo :
Springer, 1997
  (Lecture notes in computer science ; Vol. 1207)
  ISBN 3-540-62718-9
NE: Gallagher, John [Hrsg.]; LOPSTR <6, 1996, Stockholm>; GT

CR Subject Classification (1991): D.1.2, I.2.2, D.1.6, F.4.1, F.3.1

ISSN 0302-9743
ISBN 3-540-62718-9 Springer-Verlag Berlin Heidelberg New York

© Springer-Verlag Berlin Heidelberg 1997
Printed in Germany

Typesetting: Camera-ready by author
SPIN 10550413   06/3142 - 5 4 3 2 1 0   Printed on acid-free paper

Preface

This volume contains the papers from the Sixth International Workshop on Logic Program Synthesis and Transformation (LoPSTr-96), August 28–30, 1996. LoPSTr has developed a tradition of co-locating with other related workshops and conferences, in order to encourage the cross-fertilisation of ideas. In 1996 LoPSTr-96 was held in conjunction with the Sixth Inductive Logic Programming Workshop (ILP'96). LoPSTr/ILP-96 was held on board a ship which sailed from Stockholm to Helsinki and back during the workshop.

ILP-96 and LoPSTr-96 shared invited speakers, namely Michael Lowry from NASA Ames (invited by LoPSTr-96) and Ray Mooney from the University of Texas, Austin (invited by ILP-96). Both gave accounts of impressive practical applications of the state of the art in their fields. Lowry described the Meta-Amphion program synthesis system, which generates domain-specific program synthesizers using knowledge about algebraic structures and decision procedures for the domain of interest. Mooney gave an account of an inductive logic programming system called CHILL which learns grammar rules by induction from a corpus of parsed sentences. Tutorials on logic program synthesis and transformation and on inductive logic programming were given by Alberto Pettorossi and Luc De Raedt respectively.

The common ground between LoPSTr and ILP, explored in a joint discussion session, concerns program synthesis from concise declarative specifications. In inductive logic programming, the specifications are incomplete, consisting of examples and background knowledge. A natural division of labour (regarding program construction) between ILP and LoPSTr is for inductive logic programming to focus on deriving complete specifications from examples, and for program transformation to develop efficient programs from those specifications. Another area in which to seek common problems is the use of syntactic structure in the form of program schemata, already studied in different forms in both communities.

There were 19 technical papers accepted for presentation at LoPSTr-96, out of 27 submissions. Of these, 17 appear in this volume. The topics ranged over the areas of synthesis of programs from specifications, verification, transformation, specialisation, and analysis of programs, and the use of program schemata in program development. The increasing interdependence of program analysis with transformation, verification, and specialisation of programs was visible in several papers. The use of constraints in program analysis was also a strong theme.

My thanks are due to the local organiser, Carl Gustaf Jansson, and his team at Stockholm for efficiently organising the event, and to the chairman of ILP-96, Stephen Muggleton. I am also grateful to the programme chairman of LoPSTr-95, Maurizio Proietti for his helpful advice. LoPSTr-96 received sponsorship from the Network for Computational Logic (CompuNet) which is gratefully acknowledged. Laura Lafave assisted in preparing the final proceedings. Finally I wish to thank the LoPSTr-96 programme committee for their prompt and thorough work.

December 1996   John Gallagher

Programme Committee

W. Bibel, Germany
A. Bossi, Italy
N. Fuchs, Switzerland
J. Gallagher, UK
T. Gegg-Harrison, USA
A. Hamfelt, Sweden
P. Hill, UK
B. Martens, Belgium
U. Nilsson, Sweden
A. Pettorossi, Italy
L. Sterling, Australia

Local Organising Committee

Chair: Carl Gustaf Jansson, University of Stockholm
Workshop Secretariat: Helene Karlsson, University of Stockholm

Sponsorship

European Commission: ESPRIT Compulog Net

Referees

The referees for papers submitted to LoPSTr-96 were as follows:

W. Bibel, A. Bossi, M. Bruynooghe, N. Cocco, A. Cortesi,
D. De Schreye, S. Decorte, B. Demoen, S. Etalle, N. Fuchs,
J. Gallagher, T. Gegg-Harrison, A. Hamfelt, A. Heaton, P. Hill,
E. Kazmierczak, A. King, D. Korn, C. Kreitz, M. Leuschel,
M. Marchiori, B. Martens, L. Naish, U. Nilsson, S-O. Nyström,
J. Otten, S. Padelis, A. Pettorossi, M. Proietti, S. Schmitt,
H. Søndergaard, L. Sterling, M. Thielscher, A. Yamamoto

Contents

Refining Specifications to Logic Programs

I. J. Hayes, R. G. Nickson and P. A. Strooper

Department of Computer Science, The University of Queensland,
Brisbane, 4072, Australia.

Abstract. The refinement calculus provides a framework for the stepwise development of imperative programs from specifications. In this
paper we study a refinement calculus for deriving logic programs. Dealing with logic programs rather than imperative programs has the dual
advantages that, due to the expressive power of logic programs, the final
program is closer to the original specification, and each refinement step
can achieve more. Together these reduce the overall number of derivation
steps.
We present a logic programming language extended with specification
constructs (including general predicates, assertions, and types and invariants) to form a wide-spectrum language. General predicates allow
non-executable properties to be included in specifications. Assertions,
types and invariants make assumptions about the intended inputs of a
procedure explicit, and can be used during refinement to optimize the
constructed logic program. We provide a semantics for the extended logic
programming language and derive a set of refinement laws. Finally we
apply these to an example derivation.

1 Introduction

The refinement calculus [3, 12, 13, 14] provides a framework for the stepwise
development of imperative programs from specifications. It makes use of a wide-
spectrum language which includes both specification and programming language
constructs. That allows a specification to be refined, step by step, to program
code within a single language. The *programs* produced during intermediate steps
of this process may contain specification constructs as components, and hence
may not be *code* suitable for input to a compiler for the programming language.

A logic program in a language such as Prolog [22] consists of a set of procedures. A call on one of these procedures may result in any of the non-ground
variables in the call being further instantiated. Each procedure of a logic program
is a predicate written in a restricted language (Horn clauses) that is amenable to
efficient execution. Unlike an imperative procedure, where only a single value of
the output variables that satisfies its postcondition is required, with a logic procedure all instantiations that satisfy the procedure are (successively) required. For
example, consider the procedure $append(X, Y, Z)$, where Z is the concatenation
of X and Y. For the call $append(X, Y, [1, 2])$ there is no unique instantiation of
the variables X and Y. The call results in the following instantiations:

$$X = [\,], Y = [1, 2] \qquad X = [1], Y = [2] \qquad X = [1, 2], Y = [\,]$$

A logic specification is also a set of procedures, but in this case it is not necessary to restrict the language to an executable subset. The process of refinement replaces (non-executable) general predicates in specifications by equivalent (executable) Horn clauses in programs.

Viewed at the programming language level, any refinement of a logic procedure must be another logic procedure that returns an equivalent set of instantiations of variables, for all initial (partial) instantiations of variables in the call. Viewing the logic procedures as characteristic predicates, they must be logically equivalent. However, requiring logical equivalence of logic procedures is too restrictive, because it does not take into account the intended purpose of a procedure. It is common that a procedure will only ever be used with its variables instantiated in restricted ways. It is our intention to take advantage of this to provide for more flexible refinement. There are two separate mechanisms we employ to do this:

- *assertions* allow assumptions about the values of the variables prior to execution of a procedure to be stated, and
- *types*, and their generalization *invariants*, allow restrictions on the intended types of variables to be specified; variables may be instantiated to the specified type after the procedure is executed.

Refinement is relaxed to be equivalence, under the assertions and invariants, of the specification procedure and the implementation procedure. The implementation only needs to meet the specification when the assertions and invariants hold, so during refinement one may perform optimizations that depend on these assumptions. Of course, calls of the procedure now have to ensure that the assertions hold prior to execution, and that the invariants are upheld.

In this paper we investigate adapting the refinement approach to developing pure logic programs. In Section 2 we present a wide-spectrum logic programming language and in Section 3 we provide its semantics and a theory of logic program refinement. Section 4 lists laws which have been justified with respect to the semantics, and Section 5 gives an example of the development of a logic program in this style. Section 6 discusses related work.

2 Wide-spectrum language

We define a pure logic programming language, which is extended with specification and assertion constructs. Throughout the remainder of the paper we use the notational conventions shown in Figure 1.

The language is similar to a pure subset of Prolog, without cuts, negation, or extra-logical procedures. Programs compute sets of answers, so the order in which answers are found is irrelevant. The potential for nontermination can arise explicitly via assertions, or due to ill-founded recursions. No assumption is made about the search strategy, so if a program has the potential to fail to terminate, we consider it equivalent to the program **abort**, which never terminates.

$A, B, \ldots$ – predicate (assertion)
$G, H, \ldots$ – predicate (goal)
$P, Q, \ldots$ – predicate (specification)
$S, T, \ldots$ – program fragment
$X, Y, \ldots$ – variable or list of variables
$F, F', \ldots$ – formal parameter or list of formal parameters
$K, L, \ldots$ – actual parameter or list of actual parameters

Fig. 1. Notational conventions

2.1 Specifications

The specification construct is of the form

$$\langle P \rangle$$

where P is a predicate. It represents a set of instantiations of free variables of P that satisfy P: these instantiations are the answers computed by the program. As usual, the answer set may be finite or infinite; infinite answer sets arise if a program leaves some variables completely unconstrained.

The specification $\langle false \rangle$ always computes an empty answer set: it is like Prolog's **fail**.

2.2 Assertions

An assertion is of the form

$$\{A\}$$

where A is a predicate. Assertions are introduced primarily to allow the assumptions a program fragment makes about the context in which it is used to be stated formally. If these assumptions do not hold, the program fragment may abort. Aborting includes program behaviour such as nontermination and abnormal termination due to exceptions like division by zero (the latter being distinct from a procedure that fails if the divisor is zero), as well as termination with arbitrary results. An assertion, $\{A\}$, is equivalent to $\langle true \rangle$ if A holds, but aborts if A is false. We define the (worst possible) program **abort** by

$$\textbf{abort} \,\hat{=}\, \{false\}$$

Note that **abort** is quite different from the program $\langle false \rangle$, which never aborts, but always fails.

2.3 Propositional operators

There are two forms of conjunction: a sequential form (S, T) where S is evaluated before T; and a parallel version $(S \wedge T)$ where S and T are evaluated independently and the intersection of their respective results is formed on completion. When forming the sequential conjunction of an assertion and a program construct, we sometimes follow the convention of omitting the comma, i.e., we write '$\{A\}, S$' as '$\{A\}S$'.

The disjunction of two programs $(S \vee T)$ computes the union of the results of the two programs.

2.4 Quantifiers

Disjunction is generalized to an existential quantifier $(\exists X \bullet S)$, which computes the union of the results of S for all possible values of X. Similarly, the universal quantifier $(\forall X \bullet S)$ computes the intersection of the results of S for all possible values of X.

2.5 Types and invariants

When specifying a procedure, one would like the ability to specify the types of its parameters. A procedure is only required to work correctly with respect to parameters consistent with those types. One approach to handling type constraints is to simply conjoin them with the specification. For example, a specification of $append(X, Y, Z)$ may be written

$$\langle X, Y, Z \in list \rangle \wedge \langle X \frown Y = Z \rangle$$

where $X \frown Y$ stands for the concatenation of X and Y. In this specification, the first conjunct is a type constraint and the second conjunct is the desired property of $append$ for parameters satisfying that constraint.

One way to refine the specification is to include the type constraint in the relation computed by $append$. For example, $append([1], 5, Z)$ must fail since 5 is not a list, as must $append([1], Y, Z)$, $Y = 5$. While this is a valid approach to refining $append$, it can lead to unnecessary checks in the implementation. When $append$ is called in a context where the type constraints are satisfied (as is usually the case), the check is redundant. In some cases, explicit checks of type constraints may be expensive operations that should be avoided if they are unnecessary.

An alternative is to refine the second conjunct of $append$ using the first conjunct as a type context. For example, the body of $append$ may be refined to

$$\langle X, Y, Z \in list \rangle \wedge$$
$$(X = [], Y = Z \vee$$
$$(\exists H, T, V \bullet X = [H \mid T], Z = [H \mid V], append(T, Y, V)))$$

where the typing conjunct remains unchanged, but has been assumed to hold during the refinement of the second conjunct. The second conjunct is intended to

$\langle P \rangle$ — a specification

$\{A\}$ — an assertion

(S, T) — sequential conjunction

$(S \wedge T)$ — (parallel) conjunction

$(S \vee T)$ — disjunction

$(\exists X \bullet S)$ — existential quantification

$(\forall X \bullet S)$ — universal quantification

$pc(K)$ — procedure call

Fig. 2. Summary of language

be the actual implementation that is used. The typing conjunct may be removed in certain cases, using a technique suggested by Naish [15]. For a program using *append*, if one can show that the parameters to every call of *append* are lists, assuming only the second conjunct of *append*, the first conjunct is redundant and may be removed. In general, if the context of every call on a procedure together with the implemented part of the procedure guarantees the type constraints of the procedure, those constraints may be eliminated.

Because type constraints are expressed using specifications, it is natural to generalize them to arbitrary predicates, called *invariants*, that can impose constraints relating multiple variables. The calculus described in this paper supports types and invariants expressed as specifications, and there are laws that allow the effect of an invariant specification to be assumed as context. In earlier work [7] we had explicit notation for invariants in the language.

2.6 Procedures

A procedure definition has the form

$$pc(F) = S.$$

It defines the procedure called *pc* with a list of formal parameters F and body S. The free variables of S should be a subset of the free variables of F. A call on the procedure *pc* is of the form $pc(K)$ where K is a list of actual parameters. The procedure definition extends the language so that the call $pc(K)$ is a command of the extended language.

2.7 Summary

A summary of the language constructs is given in Figure 2. Some primitive procedures are considered part of the executable subset of the programming language, e.g., Herbrand equality. A program is executable if each of its defined procedures is a disjunction of clauses, each of which is a (possibly existentially quantified) sequential conjunction of calls on primitive and defined procedures.

$$ef.\langle P\rangle \cong P \qquad\qquad ok.\langle P\rangle \cong true$$
$$ef.\{A\} \cong true \qquad\qquad ok.\{A\} \cong A$$
$$ef.(S,\,T) \cong ef.S \wedge ef.T \qquad ok.(S,\,T) \cong ok.S \wedge (ef.S \Rightarrow ok.T)$$
$$ef.(S \wedge T) \cong ef.S \wedge ef.T \qquad ok.(S \wedge T) \cong ok.S \wedge ok.T$$
$$ef.(S \vee T) \cong ef.S \vee ef.T \qquad ok.(S \vee T) \cong ok.S \wedge ok.T$$
$$ef.(\exists\, X \bullet S) \cong (\exists\, X \bullet ef.S) \qquad ok.(\exists\, X \bullet S) \cong (\forall\, X \bullet ok.S)$$
$$ef.(\forall\, X \bullet S) \cong (\forall\, X \bullet ef.S) \qquad ok.(\forall\, X \bullet S) \cong (\forall\, X \bullet ok.S)$$

Fig. 3. Effects and non-aborting conditions for program constructs

3   Semantics

To define the semantics of the extended language we first define the effect of a program if assertions are ignored; then we define the condition under which programs are guaranteed not to abort. We give the semantics for the basic constructs first; procedures are covered later.

3.1   Program effect

We define a function, ef, that gives the effect of a program as a characteristic predicate of the results computed by the program, ignoring assertions. The effect function for the basic constructs in our language is detailed in Figure 3.

3.2   No abort

We define a function, ok, which defines under what circumstances a program is guaranteed not to abort. A specification can never abort; an assertion aborts when its predicate is false; a parallel conjunction or a disjunction aborts if either branch aborts. The sequential conjunction $(S,\,T)$ aborts either if S aborts, or if S succeeds and T aborts (if S fails, T is not executed at all). The details of ok for basic constructs are given in Figure 3.

This definition handles explicit nontermination due to assertions; later we extend it to handle recursive programs with the potential to fail to terminate. The definition does not handle exceptional situations that might arise due to partial functions within specifications evaluated outside their domains. Explicit assertions can be used to make procedures containing such specifications abort in exceptional circumstances. For example, a division procedure that aborts on division by zero may be specified by

$$div(X,\,Y,\,Z) = \{Y \neq 0\}, \langle X = Z \times Y\rangle$$

which is equivalent (Law 11, Section 4) to

$$div(X,\,Y,\,Z) = \{Y \neq 0\}, \langle X/Y = Z\rangle$$

3.3 Procedures

Suppose we have a non-recursive procedure definition

$$pc(F) = S$$

and let V be the set of free variables of F. A call of the form $pc(K)$ is by definition equivalent to $(\exists\, V \bullet \langle F = K \rangle, S)$. The bound variables V are renamed if necessary, to avoid capturing occurrences in K. The effect and non-aborting condition for the procedure call are thus:

$$ef.pc(K) = (\exists\, V \bullet (F = K) \wedge ef.S)$$
$$ok.pc(K) = (\forall\, V \bullet (F = K) \Rightarrow ok.S)$$

Thus, a non-recursive procedure behaves like the right-hand side of its definition, with appropriate parameter substitution.

3.4 Recursion

Suppose we have a procedure definition

$$pc(F) = S[pc(K)]$$

where $pc(K)$ is a recursive call on pc occurring within the body S.

The effect of a call $pc(A)$ is defined by a sequence of approximations:

$$ef_0.pc(A) \mathrel{\widehat{=}} false$$
$$ef_{i+1}.pc(A) \mathrel{\widehat{=}} (\exists\, F \bullet F = A \wedge ef.S[\langle ef_i.pc(K) \rangle])$$

We define $ef.pc(A)$ to be the limit of the disjunction

$$ef_0.pc(A) \vee ef_1.pc(A) \vee \cdots$$

To define the termination condition of the call, we make the sequence of approximations:

$$ok_0.pc(X) \mathrel{\widehat{=}} false$$
$$ok_{i+1}.pc(X) \mathrel{\widehat{=}} (\exists\, F \bullet F = X \Rightarrow ok.S[\{ok_i.pc(K)\}])$$

We define $ok.pc(A)$ to be the limit of the disjunction

$$ok_0.pc(A) \vee ok_1.pc(A) \vee \cdots$$

Intuitively, $ok_n.pc(X)$ is the condition that $pc(X)$ would terminate after exactly n iterations, in which case $ef_n.pc(X)$ is the effect of $pc(X)$. Thus, a recursive procedure terminates if there is some finite number n of iterations after which no further recursion takes place, and if every individual iteration terminates.

3.5 Declarative and operational semantics

We can relate the above denotational semantics to the kind of declarative and operational semantics that are more traditionally given for logic programs. The Herbrand universe is formed in the usual way, from the constant and function symbols in the program. A term (which may contain variables) denotes some subset of the Herbrand universe. The meaning of a program is given by mapping each procedure pc in the program to a pair of subsets of the Herbrand universe[1]:

$$EF.pc \mathbin{\widehat{=}} \{K \mid ef.pc(K)\}$$
$$OK.pc \mathbin{\widehat{=}} \{K \mid ok.pc(K)\}$$

A call $pc(A)$ also represents a subset of the Herbrand universe, namely the set of all ground terms covered by A. The call is acceptable if $pc(A) \subseteq OK.pc$; that is, if the program promises to terminate for every possible instantiation of the call. The answer set computed by an acceptable call is given by $pc(A) \cap EF.pc$.

3.6 Refinement

Refinement between programs is given by reducing the circumstances under which abortion is possible — that is, by weakening ok — while maintaining the effect in those cases where abortion is not possible.

$$S \sqsubseteq T \mathbin{\widehat{=}} ok.S \Rightarrow (ok.T \wedge (ef.S \Leftrightarrow ef.T)) \tag{1}$$

Equivalence between programs is defined as refinement in both directions.

$$S \mathbin{\underline{\sqcup}} T \mathbin{\widehat{=}} S \sqsubseteq T \wedge T \sqsubseteq S \tag{2}$$

From (1) and (2) we can readily deduce the following theorems, which are used in the proofs of refinement laws:

$$(S \sqsubseteq T) \equiv (ok.S \Rightarrow ok.T) \wedge (ok.S \Rightarrow (ef.S \Leftrightarrow ef.T)) \tag{3}$$
$$(S \mathbin{\underline{\sqcup}} T) \equiv (ok.S \Leftrightarrow ok.T) \wedge (ok.S \Rightarrow (ef.S \Leftrightarrow ef.T)) \tag{4}$$

3.7 Alternative semantics

An alternative semantics of programs can be given using the *weakest assumption* [7] (cf. weakest precondition [6]):

$$wa.S.G \mathbin{\widehat{=}} ok.S \wedge (ef.S \Leftrightarrow G)$$

Refinement between programs can be defined in terms of weakest assumptions similarly to the way imperative refinement is defined in terms of weakest preconditions [12]:

$$S \sqsubseteq T \mathbin{\widehat{=}} (\forall G \bullet wa.S.G \Rightarrow wa.T.G)$$

The present semantics, with ef and ok, is simpler, and the notion of refinement is close to that used in Z and VDM [25, 10] (but note the '$\Leftrightarrow$' between the effects).

---

[1] For technical reasons it is necessary to consider an extended Herbrand universe that includes infinite terms; we do not pursue this in the present paper.

3.8 Refinement of procedures

Given two procedures pa and pc we say that pa is refined by pc if for all arguments K

$$pa(K) \sqsubseteq pc(K).$$

When reasoning about calls on a procedure, the specification of the procedure can be used, since it is assured that any refinement is a valid implementation of the specification.

In the refinement of the body of a recursive procedure with specification

$$pc(F) = S$$

where F is a list of distinct variables, we may make use of recursive calls on the procedure provided that we can find a well-founded relation '$<$' such that the arguments to all of the recursive calls are less than F according to the well-founded relation. Introduction of a recursive call with actual parameter K can be achieved via the refinement

$$\{K < F\}, S\left[\tfrac{K}{F}\right] \sqsubseteq pc(K)$$

It should be possible to justify this refinement using the fixpoint semantics for recursive procedures; we have not yet done so.

4 Refinement laws

In this section we examine some sample refinement laws that may be proved correct from the semantics above. Each law is a theorem of the form $S \sqsubseteq T$ or $S \sqsupseteq T$, or an inference rule whose conclusion has one of those forms.

We supply several proofs for illustration. All laws presented here have been proven, and the proofs checked mechanically, but most proofs are omitted from this paper. The proof of a theorem or inference rule is by appeal to theorems (3) and (4); assuming that any premises are true, the following must hold:

1. $ok.S \Rightarrow ok.T$ ($ok.S \equiv ok.T$, in the case of a rule with conclusion $S \sqsupseteq T$), and
2. $ef.S \equiv ef.T$, under the further assumption $ok.S$.

4.1 Algebraic laws

Parallel conjunction and disjunction form a distributive lattice: they are associative, commutative and idempotent, and each operation distributes over the other. Sequential conjunction is associative but not commutative. It is distributive on the left over both parallel operators, but only semi-distributive on the right. Universal quantification distributes through parallel conjunction, and existential quantification distributes through disjunction.

Three of the above algebraic laws that we need for the example (Section 5) are as follows.

Law 1 (Associativity of sequential conjunction)

$$(S, T), U \sqsubseteq S, (T, U)$$

Proof.

$$
\begin{aligned}
& ok.((S, T), U) \\
\equiv\ & ok.(S, T) \wedge (ef.(S, T) \Rightarrow ok.U) \\
\equiv\ & ok.S \wedge (ef.S \Rightarrow ok.T) \wedge (ef.S \wedge ef.T \Rightarrow ok.U) \\
\equiv\ & ok.S \wedge (ef.S \Rightarrow ok.T) \wedge (ef.S \Rightarrow (ef.T \Rightarrow ok.U)) \\
\equiv\ & ok.S \wedge (ef.S \Rightarrow ok.T \wedge (ef.T \Rightarrow ok.U)) \\
\equiv\ & ok.S \wedge (ef.S \Rightarrow ok.(T, U)) \\
\equiv\ & ok.(S, (T, U))
\end{aligned}
$$

$$
\begin{aligned}
& ef.((S, T), U) \\
\equiv\ & ef.(S, T) \wedge ef.U \\
\equiv\ & (ef.S \wedge ef.T) \wedge ef.U \\
\equiv\ & ef.S \wedge (ef.T \wedge ef.U) \\
\equiv\ & ef.S \wedge ef.(T, U) \\
\equiv\ & ef.(S, (T, U))
\end{aligned}
$$

Law 2 (Left-distribution of sequential conjunction over disjunction)

$$S, (T \vee U) \sqsubseteq (S, T) \vee (S, U)$$

Proof.

$$
\begin{aligned}
& ok.(S, (T \vee U)) \\
\equiv\ & ok.S \wedge (ef.S \Rightarrow ok.(T \vee U)) \\
\equiv\ & ok.S \wedge (ef.S \Rightarrow ok.T \wedge ok.U) \\
\equiv\ & ok.S \wedge (ef.S \Rightarrow ok.T) \wedge (ef.S \Rightarrow ok.U) \\
\equiv\ & (ok.S \wedge (ef.S \Rightarrow ok.T)) \wedge (ok.S \wedge (ef.S \Rightarrow ok.U)) \\
\equiv\ & ok.((S, T) \vee (S, U))
\end{aligned}
$$

$$
\begin{aligned}
& ef.(S, (T \vee U)) \\
\equiv\ & ef.S \wedge (ef.T \vee ef.U) \\
\equiv\ & (ef.S \wedge ef.T) \vee (ef.S \wedge ef.U) \\
\equiv\ & ef.((S, T) \vee (S, U))
\end{aligned}
$$

Law 3 (Distribution of existential over disjunction)

$$(\exists X \bullet (S \vee T)) \sqsubseteq (\exists X \bullet S) \vee (\exists X \bullet T)$$

4.2 Assertions and specifications

The following are typical laws relating assertions, specifications and commonly-occurring compositions thereof.

Law 4 (Conjunction of specifications)

$$\langle P \rangle \wedge \langle Q \rangle \sqsubseteq \langle P \wedge Q \rangle$$

Law 5 (Disjunction of specifications)

$$\langle P \rangle \vee \langle Q \rangle \sqsubseteq \langle P \vee Q \rangle$$

Law 6 (Existential of specification)

$$\exists X \bullet \langle P \rangle \sqsubseteq \langle \exists X \bullet P \rangle$$

Law 7 (Remove assertion)

$$(\{A\}, S) \sqsubseteq S$$

Proof.

$$ok.(\{A\}, S)$$
$$\equiv ok.\{A\} \wedge (ef.\{A\} \Rightarrow ok.S)$$
$$\equiv A \wedge ok.S$$
$$\Rightarrow ok.S$$

$$ef.(\{A\}, S)$$
$$\equiv ef.\{A\} \wedge ef.S$$
$$\equiv true \wedge ef.S$$
$$\equiv ef.S$$

Law 8 (Weaken assertion)

$$\frac{A \Rightarrow B}{\{A\} \sqsubseteq \{B\}}$$

Law 9 (Combine assertions)

$$\{A\}, \{B\} \sqsubseteq \{A \wedge B\}$$

Law 10 (Augment weakened assertion)

$$\frac{A \Rightarrow B}{\{A\}, S \sqsubseteq \{A\}, (\langle B \rangle \wedge S)}$$

Theorem 4 allows one to assume $ok.(\{A\}, S)$ during the proof of the equivalence of the left- and right-hand sides, in addition to the premiss $A \Rightarrow B$.

Proof.

$ok.(\{A\}, S)$

$\equiv A \wedge ok.S$

$\equiv ok.(\{A\}, (\langle B \rangle \wedge S))$

$ef.(\{A\}, S)$

$\equiv ef.S$

$\equiv A \wedge ef.S$ [Assumption: $ok.(\{A\}, S)$]

$\equiv A \wedge B \wedge ef.S$ [Assumption: $A \Rightarrow B$]

$\equiv B \wedge ef.S$ [Assumption: $ok.(\{A\}, S)$]

$\equiv ef.(\{A\}, (\langle B \rangle \wedge S))$

Law 11 (Equivalent under assumption)

$$\frac{A \Rightarrow (P \Leftrightarrow Q)}{\{A\}, \langle P \rangle \sqsubseteq \{A\}, \langle Q \rangle}$$

Law 12 (Establish assertion)

$$\langle P \rangle \sqsubseteq \langle P \rangle, \{P\}$$

Law 13 (Parallel to sequential)

$$(S \wedge T) \sqsubseteq (S, T)$$

4.3 Monotonicity of refinement

Each of the language constructs is monotonic with respect to the refinement relation. Monotonicity guarantees that the result of replacing a component of a program by its refinement is itself a refinement of the original program.

Law 14 (Monotonicity)

$$\frac{S \sqsubseteq T}{C[S] \sqsubseteq C[T]} \quad \textit{for any context } C.$$

Law 15 (Monotonicity call) *If we have two procedures*

$pa(F) = S$

$pb(F) = T$

such that $S \sqsubseteq T$ then any call on pa can be replaced by a call on pb:

$$pa(K) \sqsubseteq pb(K)$$

4.4 Distribute assertions

It is often necessary to distribute an assertion into a complex program, so the assertion may be used to justify a refinement within the program.

Law 16 (Distribute assertion)

$$\{A\}, C[S] \sqsubseteq \{A\}, C[\{A\}, S]$$

provided the context C does not capture any variables in A.

5 An example

Consider the procedure *isin*, which determines the elements in a strictly ordered tree (or tests whether an element is in a tree). The specification is

$$isin(Y, T) = \{isordered(T)\}, \langle Y \in members(T) \rangle$$

where the auxiliary predicate *isordered* and function *members* are defined as follows.

$$members(empty) \mathrel{\hat{=}} \{\}$$
$$members(tree(L, X, R)) \mathrel{\hat{=}} members(L) \cup \{X\} \cup members(R)$$
$$isordered(T) \mathrel{\hat{=}} (T = empty) \vee$$
$$(\exists L, X, R \bullet T = tree(L, X, R) \wedge isordered(L) \wedge isordered(R) \wedge$$
$$(\forall Y : members(L) \bullet Y < X) \wedge (\forall Y : members(R) \bullet X < Y))$$

This use of auxiliary predicates and functions deserves comment. The auxiliary definitions introduce interpreted constant, function and predicate symbols; rather than contributing to the Herbrand universe and base, they merely introduce alternative notation for objects already in those domains. For example, the specification terms *empty* and {} denote distinct objects in the Herbrand universe, as usual, but the term *members(empty)* denotes (by definition) the same object as {}.

It is possible to express the specification entirely in a more traditional logic programming style, with a procedure *members(Tree, Set)* in place of the auxiliary function *members(Tree)*. The recursive specification of this procedure involves {} and ∪ operations, which can be represented by uninterpreted constant and function symbols in the usual style of logic programs. We present the 'functional' version here as it is shorter and less tedious.

We refine the specification of *isin* to a recursive procedure. During the refinement we may assume calls on the procedure *isin* with a smaller argument satisfy the specification, that is, for all U

$$\{U \prec T\}, \{isordered(U)\}, \langle Y \in members(U) \rangle \sqsubseteq isin(Y, U)$$

where '$\prec$' is the 'proper subtree' relation on finite trees, which is well-founded. Note that when reasoning about the procedure call, only the specification needs to be considered, not any refinements.

The example illustrates the use of an assertion ($\{isordered(T)\}$) to establish various equivalences (via law 11). The assertion itself is not implemented, and is removed (law 7) once it is no longer needed in the refinement. Several applications of the associativity and monotonicity laws, used to justify refinement of subcomponents, have not been explicitly mentioned.

$\{isordered(T)\}, \langle Y \in members(T) \rangle$

$\sqsupseteq$ [from $isordered$ using law 10; law 4]

$\{isordered(T)\},$

$\langle (T = empty \vee (\exists L, X, R \bullet T = tree(L, X, R))) \wedge Y \in members(T) \rangle$

$\sqsupseteq$ [law 11]

$\{isordered(T)\},$

$\langle (T = empty \wedge Y \in members(empty)) \vee$

$(\exists L, X, R \bullet T = tree(L, X, R) \wedge Y \in members(tree(L, X, R)))) \rangle$

$\sqsupseteq$ [unfolding the definition of $members$; law 11]

$\{isordered(T)\},$

$\langle false \vee$

$(\exists L, X, R \bullet T = tree(L, X, R) \wedge Y \in members(L) \cup \{X\} \cup members(R))) \rangle$

$\sqsupseteq$ [law 11; law 6]

$\{isordered(T)\},$

$(\exists L, X, R \bullet \langle T = tree(L, X, R) \wedge$

$(Y \in members(L) \vee Y = X \vee Y \in members(R)))) \rangle$

$\sqsubseteq$ [law 16; law 4; law 7]

$(\exists L, X, R \bullet$

$\{isordered(T)\}, \langle T = tree(L, X, R) \rangle \wedge$

$\langle Y \in members(L) \vee Y = X \vee Y \in members(R) \rangle)$

$\sqsubseteq$ [law 16; law 7]

$(\exists L, X, R \bullet \langle T = tree(L, X, R) \rangle \wedge \{isordered(T)\},$

$\langle Y \in members(L) \vee Y = X \vee Y \in members(R) \rangle)$

$\sqsubseteq$ [law 13; law 12; law 9]

$(\exists L, X, R \bullet \langle T = tree(L, X, R) \rangle, \{T = tree(L, X, R) \wedge isordered(T)\},$

$\langle Y \in members(L) \vee Y = X \vee Y \in members(R) \rangle)$

$\sqsubseteq$ [2× law 5; law 16; law 7]

$(\exists L, X, R \bullet \langle T = tree(L, X, R) \rangle,$

$(\{T = tree(L, X, R) \wedge isordered(T)\}, \langle Y \in members(L) \rangle$

$\vee \{T = tree(L, X, R) \wedge isordered(T)\}, \langle Y = X \rangle$

$\vee \{T = tree(L, X, R) \wedge isordered(T)\}, \langle Y \in members(R) \rangle))$

$\sqsubseteq$ [2×(law 8; definition of *isordered*); law 7]

$(\exists\, L, X, R \bullet \langle T = tree(L, X, R)\rangle,$

$\quad (\{L \prec T \wedge isordered(L) \wedge (\forall\, Z : members(L) \bullet Z < X)\},$

$\qquad \langle Y \in members(L)\rangle$

$\quad \vee \langle Y = X \rangle$

$\quad \vee \{R \prec T \wedge isordered(R) \wedge (\forall\, Z : members(R) \bullet X < Z)\},$

$\qquad \langle Y \in members(R)\rangle))$

$\sqsupseteq$ [2×law 11]

$(\exists\, L, X, R \bullet \langle T = tree(L, X, R)\rangle,$

$\quad (\{L \prec T \wedge isordered(L) \wedge (\forall\, Z : members(L) \bullet Z < X)\},$

$\qquad \langle Y < X \wedge Y \in members(L)\rangle$

$\quad \vee \langle Y = X \rangle$

$\quad \vee \{R \prec T \wedge isordered(R) \wedge (\forall\, Z : members(R) \bullet X < Z)\},$

$\qquad \langle X < Y \wedge Y \in members(R)\rangle))$

$\sqsubseteq$ [2×(law 4; law 16; law 8; law 7; law 13)]

$(\exists\, L, X, R \bullet \langle T = tree(L, X, R)\rangle,$

$\quad ((\langle Y < X\rangle \wedge \{L \prec T\}, \{isordered(L)\}, \langle Y \in members(L)\rangle$

$\quad \vee \langle Y = X \rangle$

$\quad \vee \langle X < Y \rangle \wedge \{R \prec T\}, \{isordered(R)\}, \langle Y \in members(R)\rangle))$

$\sqsubseteq$ [2×recursive call; L and R proper subtrees of T]

$(\exists\, L, X, R \bullet \langle T = tree(L, X, R)\rangle,$

$\quad ((\langle Y < X\rangle \wedge isin(Y, L)$

$\quad \vee \langle Y = X \rangle$

$\quad \vee \langle X < Y \rangle \wedge isin(Y, R)))$

$\sqsubseteq$ [2×law 13]

$(\exists\, L, X, R \bullet \langle T = tree(L, X, R)\rangle,$

$\quad ((\langle Y < X\rangle, isin(Y, L)$

$\quad \vee \langle Y = X \rangle$

$\quad \vee \langle X < Y \rangle, isin(Y, R)))$

$\sqsupseteq$ [law 2, law 3]

$\quad (\exists\, L, X, R \bullet \langle T = tree(L, X, R)\rangle, \langle Y < X\rangle, isin(Y, L))$

$\vee (\exists\, L, X, R \bullet \langle T = tree(L, X, R)\rangle, \langle Y = X\rangle)$

$\vee (\exists\, L, X, R \bullet \langle T = tree(L, X, R)\rangle, \langle X < Y\rangle, isin(Y, R))$

The step from the last predicate to a program in a language like Prolog is a mechanical translation.

6 Related work

Traditionally, the refinement calculus has been used to develop imperative programs from specifications [3, 12, 13, 14]. The increase in expressive power of logic programming languages, when compared with imperative languages, leads to a reduced conceptual gap between a problem and its solution, which means that fewer development steps are required during refinement. An additional advantage of logic programming languages over procedural languages is their simpler, cleaner semantics, which leads to simpler proofs of the refinement steps. Finally, the higher expressive level of logic programming languages means that the individual refinement steps typically achieve more.

There have been previous proposals for developing a refinement calculus for declarative languages. A refinement calculus for functional programming languages is discussed in [24]. Kok [11] has applied the refinement calculus to logic programming languages, but his approach is quite different from ours. Rather than defining a wide-spectrum logic programming language, Kok embeds logic programs into a more traditional refinement calculus framework and notation.

There have been several proposals for the constructive development of logic programs (for example, see [9]). This work has focused on program transformations or equivalence transformations from a first-order logic specification [4, 8]. Read and Kazmierczak [20] propose a stepwise development of modular logic programs from first-order specifications, based on three refinement steps that are much coarser than the refinement steps proposed in this paper. This leaves most of the work to be done in discharging the proof obligations for the refinement steps, for which they provide little guidance. A key aspect of the refinement calculus that differentiates it from these other proposals, is the use of specifications involving assertions, types, and invariants. This type of specification allows refinements to be proved correct with respect to the context in which they appear. To our knowledge, such *refinements in context* are novel in the logic programming community.

In [5], Deville introduces a systematic program development method for Prolog that incorporates assertions and types similar to ours. The main difference is that Deville's approach to program development is mostly informal, whereas our approach is fully formal. A second distinction is that Deville's approach concentrates on the development of individual procedures. By using a wide-spectrum language, our approach blurs the distinction between a logic description and a logic program. For example, general predicates may appear anywhere within a program, and the refinement rules allow them to be transformed within that context. Similarly, programming language constructs may be used and transformed at any point.

The importance of types in the specification and verification of logic programs has also been noted by several authors [19]. For example, Naish notes that while most "specifications" of logic programs do take types into account, these types are often ignored in the corresponding Prolog programs, which may lead to incorrect answers [16]. He defines when a program is *type correct*, which ensures that all well-typed answers returned by such programs are correct. He also uses this notion of type correctness to compare the verification of logic programs with that of imperative programs [17]. Apt proposes a framework for logic program verification that includes both modes and types [1]. He studies the termination, partial correctness, occur-check freedom, and absence of errors and floundering for three classes of programs: Pure Prolog, Pure Prolog with arithmetic, and Pure Prolog with negation.

A different approach to program development, not based on logic programming, is the synthesis of programs based on a small number of strategies for deriving algorithms [2]. Although logic programming is suggested as one of the possible implementation languages for the resulting algorithms, no concrete proposal for how this can be achieved is presented. The KIDS system [21] also provides high-level tactics for algorithm design, and in addition it incorporates lower-level transformation rules for program simplification, partial evaluation, and finite differencing.

7 Conclusions

The wide-spectrum language introduced in this paper covers both purely logical constructs as well as efficiently executable programming constructs such as sequential conjunction. This allows a significant proportion of the refinement of a program to be carried out via the use of logical equivalence. The addition of assertions allows assumptions to be incorporated into specifications, and hence allows more flexible equivalence transformations under those assumptions. The incorporation of invariants (including types) allows the intended use of a procedure to be specified. The procedure need not work correctly for arguments that are not consistent with the assertions and invariants, so can be optimized for efficient execution in the case where these assumptions are satisfied. For example, in Section 5, the assumption that the tree was ordered was used to determine whether to traverse the left or right subtree, avoiding the need to search both subtrees.

We have not yet considered how to treat negation, and our treatment of recursive procedures is limited to those with only a single recursive call. Nor have we considered how to handle undefinedness arising from partial functions in specifications. We intend to address these omissions in future work.

We have developed a theory of logic program refinement for the Ergo theorem prover [23], and used it to prove most of the refinement laws. This theory forms the basis of a tool supporting refinement of logic programs, which has been used to check the example refinement from Section 5. We intend to adapt our *program window inference* technique [18] to logic program refinement. With this technique, assertions and invariants are managed separately from the specification being refined, and are always available as context in refinements. Explicit applications of monotonicity and distribution laws are then unnecessary. This may make refinements of more realistic programs feasible.

Acknowledgements We would like to thank Robert Colvin for completing the rigorous proofs of the refinement laws using Ergo, and for comments on earlier drafts of this paper. Yves Deville also provided valuable comments, as did three anonymous referees. The work reported in this paper has been supported by Australian Research Council grant number 96/ARCS181G: *Refinement calculus for logic programming*.

References

1. K. R. Apt. Program verification and Prolog. In E. Börger, editor, *Specification and Validation Methods*. Oxford University Press, 1995.
2. W. Bibel. Syntax-directed, semantics-supported program synthesis. *Artificial Intelligence*, 14:243–261, 1980.
3. R.-J. Back. Correctness preserving program refinements: Proof theory and applications. Tract 131, Mathematisch Centrum, Amsterdam, 1980.
4. K. Clark. The synthesis and verification of logic programs. Research report, Imperial College, 1978.
5. Yves Deville. *Logic Programming: Systematic Program Development*. Addison-Wesley, 1990.
6. Edsger W. Dijkstra. *A Discipline of Programming*. Prentice-Hall, 1976.
7. I. J. Hayes and P. A. Strooper. Refining specifications to logic programs. Fifth Australasian Refinement Workshop. Software Verification Research Centre, Department of Computer Science, The University of Queensland, April 1996.
8. C. J. Hogger. Derivation of logic programs. *Journal of the ACM*, 2:372–392, 1981.
9. J.-M. Jacquet. *Constructing logic programs*. John Wiley & Sons, 1993.
10. Cliff B. Jones. *Systematic Software Development using VDM*. Second edition. Prentice-Hall International, 1990.
11. Joost N. Kok. On logic programming and the refinement calculus: semantics based program transformations. Technical Report RUU-CS-90-39, Department of Computer Science, Utrecht University, 1990.
12. Carroll Morgan. *Programming from Specifications*. Prentice Hall, 1990. Second edition 1994.
13. C. C. Morgan and K. A. Robinson. Specification statements and refinement. *IBM Jnl. Res. Dev.*, 31(5), September 1987.
14. J. M. Morris. A theoretical basis for stepwise refinement and the programming calculus. *Science of Computer Programming*, 9(3):287–306, December 1987.
15. L. Naish. Specification = program + types. In *Proc. Seventh Conf. on the Foundations of Software Technology and Theoretical Computer Science, Pune, India*, volume 287 of *Lecture Notes in Computer Science*. Springer Verlag, 1987.
16. L. Naish. Types and the intended meaning of logic programs. In F. Pfenning, editor, *Types in Logic Programming*, pages 189–216. MIT Press, 1992.
17. L. Naish. Verification of logic programs and imperative programs. In J.-M. Jacquet, editor, *Constructing Logic Programs*. John Wiley & Sons, 1993.
18. Ray Nickson and Ian Hayes. Supporting contexts in program refinement. Technical Report 96-29, Software Verification Research Centre, Department of Computer Science, The University of Queensland, 1996.
19. F. Pfenning. *Types in logic programming*. MIT Press, 1992.
20. M. G. Read and E. A. Kazmierczak. Formal program development in modular Prolog: A case study. In T.P. Clement and K.-K. Lau, editors, *Proc. of LOPSTR'91*, 1991.

21. D. R. Smith. KIDS: A semi-automatic program development system. *IEEE Transactions on Software Engineering*, 16(9):1024–1043, 1990.
22. Leon Sterling and Ehud Shapiro. *The Art of Prolog*. MIT Press, 1986. Second edition 1994.
23. Mark Utting, Anthony Bloesch and Ray Nickson. Ergo 4.1 Reference Manual. Technical Report, Software Verification Research Centre, Department of Computer Science, The University of Queensland. In preparation.
24. Nigel Ward. *A Refinement Calculus for Nondeterministic Expressions*. PhD thesis, The University of Queensland, 1994.
25. J. B. Wordsworth. *Software Development with Z: A Practical Approach to Formal Methods*. Addison-Wesley, 1992.

Symbolic Verification with Gap-Order Constraints

Laurent Fribourg[1] & Julian Richardson[2]*

[1]Ecole Normale Supérieure/CNRS - 45 rue d'Ulm - 75005 Paris, France
email: fribourg@dmi.ens.fr,
[2]Department of Artificial Intelligence, Edinburgh University, 80 South Bridge,
Edinburgh EH1 1HN, Scotland
email: julianr@aisb.ed.ac.uk

Abstract. Finite state automata with counters are useful for modelling systems with discrete parameters. The calculation of *state invariants* is an important tool in the analysis of such systems. Previous authors have presented techniques for the calculation of state invariants based on their approximation by convex polyhedra or periodic sets.

In this paper we present a new method for the calculation of invariants for finite state automata with counters, based on their representation by *gap-order constraints*. This method differs from previous approaches by exploiting existing techniques for the calculation of least fixed points. The use of least fixed points reduces the need for approximation and allows the generation of non-convex invariants. We do not need to specify the initial inputs to the automaton, but can leave them as uninstantiated parameters, or partially specify them using gap-order constraints.

Our method not only provides a new tool for program analysis, but is also an interesting application of logic programming techniques.

1 Introduction

The extension of finite state automata with arithmetical variables has received recently considerable attention. Such automata are very useful for modeling systems which use parameters (e.g. time) taking values on an infinite (or very large) domain. The domain of the arithmetic variables is either dense (e.g. reals) as used in the model of timed automata [1, 7], discrete as used in the model of automata with (delay-) counters [6], or mixed (hybrid automata). Here we focus on automata with counters over a discrete domain.

In this paper we present a new method for determining state invariants for finite state automata with counters. Our method not only provides a new tool for program analysis, but is also an interesting application of logic programming techniques.

---

* This work was performed while the second author was a visiting research fellow at the Ecole Normale Supérieure, funded by EC HCM grants Compulog ERBCHBGCT 930365 and Logic Program Synthesis and Transformation CHRX.CT.93 0414.

Existing methods (e.g. [6, 9]) make use of an approximation operation called *widening*. One of the drawbacks of widening is that it decreases the accuracy of the resulting invariant. Our new method reduces the need for widening by exploiting two techniques for calculating precise fixed points.

As in [6], the automaton is divided into progressively larger cycles. The major difference from [6] is, however, that we can calculate least fixed points (i.e. *exact* invariants) for some of the cycles. The method of [3, 5] is used to calculate least fixed points for the innermost loops, and the method of [10] is used to calculate least fixed points for the outermost loops. This leads us to choose a different representation scheme to that used by Halbwachs.

A significant advantage of our method is that we do not need to specify the initial inputs to the automaton, but can leave them as uninstantiated parameters, or partially specify them using gap-order constraints.

After a few preliminary definitions (§2), we present the method in its basic form (§3). §4 goes through an example. Some approximation is needed, and this is discussed in §5. After a brief discussion of our implementation and a presentation of results (§6,7), we compare our technique with previous work in §8. We discuss the representation of invariants by periodic sets, and by convex hulls. Analysis of an example from [8] suggests that the methods and representations are complementary. The paper finishes by indicating our plans for further work, and drawing the conclusions.

2 Preliminaries

An automaton with counters is a finite-state automaton augmented by a certain number of integer variables: the counters. Transitions consist of a guard part and an operation part. The guard part is a linear relation over the counters. A transition $s_1 \xrightarrow{?\phi;\psi} s_2$ may be made from state s_1 with counter values $\overline{x}$ to state s_2 with counter values $\overline{x}'$ if the guard part evaluates to true when applied to $\overline{x}$, i.e. $\phi(\overline{x})$ holds. In this case, the operation part is executed, yielding new counter values $\overline{x}'$ such that $\psi(\overline{x}, \overline{x}')$ is satisfied. Such a transition can be encoded as a Prolog clause (with argument a tuple of counters, $\overline{x}$):

$$p(s_2, \overline{x}') :- p(s_1, \overline{x}), \phi(\overline{x}), \psi(\overline{x}, \overline{x}').$$

Operations $x' := x + k$ and $x' := k$, where k is a positive or negative integer, are called incrementation and reinitialisation respectively.

In our analysis, we distinguish between two kinds of transition:

1. Internal transitions: transitions which start and end in the same state s, whose operation parts may contain incrementation, but not reinitialisation.
2. External transitions: transitions which start in a state s and end in a distinct state t, incrementing or reinitialising the counters.

We distinguish accordingly three levels of *cyclic paths*, depicted in figure 1:

1. Internal cycles. These are paths starting from and ending in a state s using repeatedly a set of internal transitions. We use the notation s^* to signify a state s together with a set of internal transitions on s.

2. Simple circuits. A simple circuit (with two states) is a loop consisting of an internal cycle on a state s, an external transition from s to a state t, an internal cycle on t and another external transition back to s. Such a circuit is denoted $s^* \to t^* \to s^*$. More generally, a simple circuit consists of a number $n+1$ of internal cycles connected by $n+1$ external transitions. Such a circuit is denoted $s^* \to t_1^* \to ... \to t_n^* \to s^*$

3. General cyclic paths: these paths are obtained by composing simple circuits.

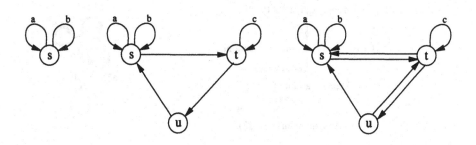

Fig. 1. The three levels of cyclic paths. From left to right: internal cycles, simple circuits and general cyclic paths.

Before analysis can proceed, the automaton must be checked (manually) for transitions of the form $s \xrightarrow{?\phi;\psi} s$, where ψ contains a reinitialisation. These 'illegal' internal transitions are removed by replacing the state s by two states, s_1 and s_2, linked by the external transition $s_1 \xrightarrow{?\phi;\psi} s_2$. Transitions into and out of s may then need to be duplicated, with one copy for each of the new states. In practice, many of these extra transitions can never be made and so can be eliminated.

Our method combines two methods for computing invariants, one for computing the invariants of internal cycles [3], and another for simple circuits [10]. Figure 2 shows how the various stages of the method fit together.

3 Method

The basis of the method (see figure 3) is the replacement of simple circuits in the automaton with *meta-transitions* on a single state, and then using bottom-up evaluation to calculate the state invariant.

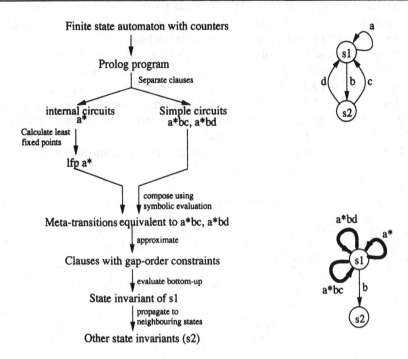

Fig. 2. The different stages of the method. The top right shows a small automaton, with one internal cycle in the initial state $s1$. Below this is shown the same automaton after the replacement of simple circuits by meta-transitions on $s1$.

More precisely, there are five steps to the method:

1. Identify the internal cycles in the automaton.
   We exploit the method of [3] to calculate least fixed points for the internal cycles. This allows us to calculate more accurate invariants than if, for example, we just treated internal cycles in the same way as we treat simple circuits below. The least fixed points can be seen as recurrence relations, relating values of the counters in a state before and after iterated application of its internal cycles.

2. Identify the simple circuits in the automaton.
   For each simple circuit, we derive a recurrence relation linking the values of the counters at the entry of a state s before and after the execution of the simple circuit.
   The recurrence relations are added as *meta-transitions* from s to s (see [2]), and the final transition $(t_n \rightarrow s)$ of each simple circuit is deleted. Meta-transitions can be expressed as Prolog clauses in the same way as ordinary transitions.

3. Approximate the meta-transitions as clauses with *gap-order constraints*. A

gap-order constraint is a total ordering of variables together with a "gap assignment" to each order relation where each gap assignment is a nonnegative integer subscript that denotes the minimal difference between two elements. The notation $X <_c Y$ means that $X + c < Y$. For example, the gap-order constraint $X <_0 5 <_3 Y <_2 Z = W$ is equivalent to $X < 5 \land 5 + 3 < Y \land Y + 2 < Z \land Z = W$.

Approximation is not always necessary, and need not result in a loss of accuracy in the invariant which is finally calculated (see §5).

4. Find a fixed point for the system of meta-transitions. Revesz's method [10] calculates the least fixed point of such a system of meta-transitions by bottom-up evaluation. The output constitutes the invariant at s.

5. Use the remaining transitions in the automaton to *propagate* the invariant at s to the other states.

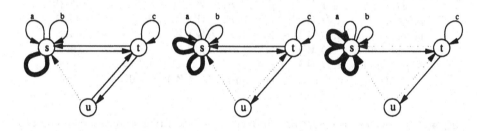

Fig. 3. From left to right, simple circuits are removed and replaced by meta-transitions (thick lines).

4 Example: A Read/Write File System

In this section we outline the analysis of an automaton describing a set of readers and writers. The behaviour to be verified is that no reads can take place when the system is writing.

The example is presented in [9] as a LOTOS specification in three parts: the reader, the writer, and the control process. A system with r_{max} readers and d_{max} writers is formed by synchronising the readers and the writers with the control process, which can then be seen as a single automaton. Unless the number of readers and writers is small, this quickly results in a large number of states. Here, we have simplified the problem somewhat. Instead of forming the parallel composition of r_{max} readers, d_{max} writers and a control process, we form the parallel composition of three processes: a reader which can perform up to r_{max}

reads simultaneously, a writer which can buffer up to d_{max} writes simultaneously, and a control process.

Kerbrat performs the analysis for a number of specific positive values of r_{max}, d_{max}. Here, we are able to compute the invariant parameterised by d_{max}, r_{max}.

The automaton is displayed in figure 5. In order to permit analysis by [3], state *resource* (left of diagram) must be split into two states, *res0* and *res1*, whose internal cycles contain no reinitialisation Once this has been done, we arrive at the rules in figure 4.

$$
\begin{align*}
& p(res0, 0, 0, 0). && (m0) \\
& p(res1, R, D, 0) : - p(res0, R, D, W). && (m1.1) \\
& p(res1, R, D, W) : - p(res1, R, D, W). && (m1.2) \\
& p(res0, R - 1, D, W) : - p(res0, R, D, W), R > 0. && (m2.1) \\
& p(res0, R - 1, D, W) : - p(res1, R, D, W), R > 0. && (m2.2) \\
& p(res1, R, D + 1, 0) : - p(res0, R, D, W), D < d_{max}. && (m3.1) \\
& p(res1, R, D + 1, W) : - p(res1, R, D, W), D < d_{max}. && (m3.2) \\
& p(not\_writing, R, D, W) : - p(res0, R, D, W), W = 0. && (m4.1) \\
& p(not\_writing, R, D, W) : - p(res1, R, D, W), W = 0. && (m4.2) \\
& p(res0, R + 1, 0, W) : - p(not\_writing, R, 0, W), R < r_{max}. && (m5) \\
& p(demands, R, D, W) : - p(not\_writing, R, D, W), D > 0. && (m6) \\
& p(res0, 0, D - 1, 1) : - p(demands, 0, D, W), D > 0. && (m7)
\end{align*}
$$

Fig. 4. The code for the read/write automaton, after splitting state *resource* into two.

4.1 Analysis

Internal Cycles The automaton contains two internal cycles:

1. $res0^*$. If the values at entry to $res0$ are r,d,w, then the values after n applications of rule (m2.1) are: $w' = w$, $r' = r - n$, $d' = d$. Applying (manually) the algorithm of [3] gives a least fixed point with bounds $0 \leq n \leq r$, which in turn gives constraints $w' = w, 0 \leq r' \leq r, d' = d$. This least fixed point can be encoded as a Prolog clause:

$$p(res0, R_1, D_1, W_1) : -p(res0, R, D, W), 0 \leq R_1, R_1 \leq R, D_1 = D, W_1 = W. \quad (1)$$

2. $res1^*$. In state $res1$, we apply rule (m1.2) k times and rule (m3.2) l times to get the following: $r' = r, d' = d + l, w' = w$. Again, we use the algorithm of [3] to manually produce a least fixed point with bounds $0 \leq l \leq d_{max} - d$, giving $r' = r, d \leq d' \leq d_{max}, w' = w$. This least fixed point can be encoded as a Prolog clause:

$$p(res1, R_1, D_1, W_1) : -p(res1, R, D, W), R_1 = R, D \leq D_1, D_1 \leq d_{max}, W_1 = W. \quad (2)$$

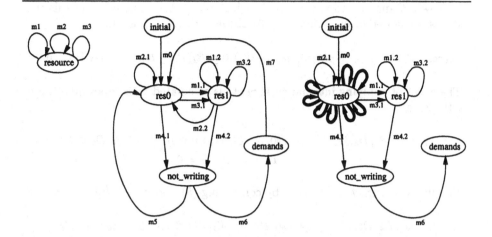

Fig. 5. State *resource* in the original rules is shown on the left of the diagram. The automaton, modified to split this into two, is shown in the middle. On the right, the simple circuits have been replaced by meta-transitions on *res0*.

Simple Circuits There are a total of 8 simple circuits:

1. *res0*-(m1.1)-res1*-res0**
2. *res0*-(m3.1)-res1*-res0**
3. *res0*-not_writing-demands- res0**
4. *res0*-not_writing-res0**
5. *res0*-(m1.1)-res1*- not_writing-demands-res0**
6. *res0*-(m3.1)-res1*- not_writing-demands-res0**
7. *res0*-(m1.1)-res1*- not_writing-res0**
8. *res0*-(m3.1)-res1*- not_writing-res0**

Note that the two transitions (given by rules (m1.1) and (m3.1)) from *res0* to *res1* each give rise to separate circuits.

Here, we only give the detailed analysis of one circuit. The other analyses are very similar.

Simple circuit *res0*-(m1.1)-res1*- res0**

Assume the counters have values r_0, d_0, w_0 at entry to *res0*. Clause (1) describes how the counter values change after an arbitrary number of applications of the internal cycle *res0**:

$$p(res0, R_1, D_1, W_1) : -p(res0, R_0, D_0, W_0), 0 \le R_1, R_1 \le R_0, D_1 = D_0, W_1 = W_0. \quad (3)$$

Now a transition to $res1$ is made using rule (m1.1). The effect of this transitions is calculated by composing (3) above with (m1.1), giving:

$$p(res1, R_2, D_2, W_2) : -p(res0, R_0, D_0, W_0), 0 \leq R_2, R_2 \leq R_0, D_2 = D_0, W_2 = 0. \quad (4)$$

The effect of applying internal cycle $res1^*$ is calculated by composing (4) above with (2), giving:

$$p(res1, R_3, D_3, W_3) : - p(res0, R_0, D_0, W_0), 0 \leq R_3, R_3 \leq R_0, D_0 \leq D_3, \quad (5)$$
$$D_3 \leq d_{max}, W_3 = 0.$$

Finally, we return to state $res0$ by composing (5) above with (m2.2), to give:

$$p(res1, R_4, D_4, W_4) : - p(res0, R_0, D_0, W_0), -1 \leq R_4, R_4 < R_0, D_0 \leq D_4, \quad (6)$$
$$D_4 \leq dmax, W_4 = 0.$$

We conjoin this with the domain constraint $r \geq 0$ and rename the variables to get the meta-transition:

$$p_{res0}^{entry}(r', d', w') \leftarrow p_{res0}^{entry}(r, d, w), 0 \leq r', r' < r, d \leq d', d' \leq d_{max}, w' = 0$$

The process of composing transitions to form meta-transitions can be automated. Sequential composition of two transitions is equivalent to partially evaluating the composition of the two Prolog clauses which encode them, followed by solving for the resulting inequalities. This has been implemented (see §6).

Similarly, we derive the following meta-transitions for each of these circuits (in the same order as above). Note that when the transitions and internal cycles which make up 8 are composed, the resulting meta-transition has unsatisfiable (i.e. *false*) constraints. It is therefore omitted.

$$p_{res0}^{entry}(r', d', w') \leftarrow p_{res0}^{entry}(r, d, w), 0 \leq r' < r, d \leq d' \leq d_{max}, w' = 0$$
$$p_{res0}^{entry}(r', d', w') \leftarrow p_{res0}^{entry}(r, d, w), 0 \leq r' < r, d < d' \leq d_{max}, r \leq r_{max}, w' = 0$$
$$p_{res0}^{entry}(r', d', w') \leftarrow p_{res0}^{entry}(d, r, w), r' = 0, 0 \leq d' = d - 1 < d_{max}\dagger, w' = 1, r \leq r_{max}$$
$$p_{res0}^{entry}(r', d', w') \leftarrow p_{res0}^{entry}(r, d, w), 0 < r' \leq r + 1\dagger, r' \leq r_{max}, d' = 0, d \leq d_{max}, w' = 0$$
$$p_{res0}^{entry}(r', d', w') \leftarrow p_{res0}^{entry}(d, r, w), r' = 0, 0 \leq d' < d_{max}, d' \geq d - 1\dagger, r \leq r_{max}, w' = 1$$
$$p_{res0}^{entry}(r', d', w') \leftarrow p_{res0}^{entry}(d, r, w), r' = 0, 0 \leq d' < d_{max}, r \leq r_{max}, w' = 1$$
$$p_{res0}^{entry}(r', d', w') \leftarrow p_{res0}^{entry}(r, d, w), 0 < r' \leq r + 1\dagger, r' \leq r_{max}, r \leq r_{max},$$
$$d \leq d_{max}, d' = 0, w' = 0$$

Replacing the simple circuits by their corresponding meta-transitions gives the rightmost part of figure 5.

Approximation The four constraints marked with a † cannot be translated to an equivalent gap-order form. They must be replaced by upper approximations: $r' \leq r + 1$ is approximated by $r' \leq r_{max}$, $d' = d - 1$ is approximated by $d' < d$. $d' \geq d - 1$ is equivalent to $d' \geq d \lor d' = d - 1$, which in view of the above approximation, is replaced by $d' \geq d \lor d' < d$, which is a tautology, and so omitted. We show in §5 that in this case, approximation does not affect the resulting invariant.

After these approximations, conversion to gap-order form is automatic.

Solution of Meta-transitions After making the necessary approximations described in §5 and converting to gap-order form, we can either substitute particular positive integers for r_{max} and d_{max}, or we can leave them as variables, with constraints $r_{max} > 0$ and $d_{max} > 0$. A great strength of Revesz's method is that the initial values of the counters need not be given specific values, but can be specified by a set of gap-order constraints.

We find an invariant describing the counter values at entry to state $s1$ which is a disjunction of 14 gap-order constraints:

$d = 0 \ \land \ r = 0 \ \land \ w = 0 \ \land \ 0 <_0 dmax \ \land \ 0 <_0 rmax$

$d = 0 \ \land \ r = 0 \ \land \ w = 0 \ \land \ 0 <_0 dmax \ \land \ 0 <_0 rmax \ \land \ d <_0 dmax \ \land \ r <_0 rmax$

$d = 0 \ \land \ r = 0 \ \land \ w = 1 \ \land \ 0 <_0 dmax \ \land \ 0 <_0 rmax \ \land \ d <_0 dmax$

$d = 0 \ \land \ r = rmax \ \land \ w = 0 \ \land \ 0 <_0 dmax \ \land \ 0 <_0 r \ \land \ 0 <_0 rmax$

$d = 0 \ \land \ r = rmax \ \land \ w = 0 \ \land \ 0 <_0 dmax \ \land \ 0 <_0 r \ \land \ 0 <_0 rmax \ \land \ d <_0 dmax$

$d = 0 \ \land \ w = 0 \ \land \ 0 <_0 r <_0 rmax \ \land \ 0 <_0 dmax \ \land \ 0 <_0 rmax \ \land \ d <_0 dmax$

$d = 0 \ \land \ w = 0 \ \land \ 0 <_0 r <_0 rmax \ \land \ 0 <_0 dmax \ \land \ 0 <_0 rmax$

$d = dmax \ \land \ r = 0 \ \land \ w = 0 \ \land \ 0 <_0 d \ \land \ 0 <_0 dmax \ \land \ 0 <_0 rmax \ \land \ r <_0 rmax$

$d = dmax \ \land \ r = 0 \ \land \ w = 0 \ \land \ 0 <_0 d \ \land \ 0 <_0 dmax \ \land \ 0 <_1 rmax \ \land \ r <_1 rmax$

$d = dmax \ \land \ w = 0 \ \land \ 0 <_0 r <_0 rmax \ \land \ 0 <_0 d \ \land \ 0 <_0 dmax \ \land \ 0 <_0 rmax$

$d = dmax \ \land \ w = 0 \ \land \ 0 <_0 r <_1 rmax \ \land \ 0 <_0 d \ \land \ 0 <_0 dmax \ \land \ 0 <_1 rmax$

$r = 0 \ \land \ w = 0 \ \land \ 0 <_0 d <_0 dmax \ \land \ 0 <_0 dmax \ \land \ 0 <_0 rmax \ \land \ r <_0 rmax$

$r = 0 \ \land \ w = 1 \ \land \ 0 <_0 d <_0 dmax \ \land \ 0 <_0 dmax \ \land \ 0 <_0 rmax$

$w = 0 \ \land \ 0 <_0 d <_0 dmax \ \land \ 0 <_0 r <_0 rmax \ \land \ 0 <_0 dmax \ \land \ 0 <_0 rmax$

These can be manually simplified to:

$$
p_{res0}^{entry}(r, d, w) \leftarrow \quad w = 0 \land \begin{cases} 0 \leq d \leq d_{max} \land 0 \leq r < r_{max} \\ \lor \\ d = 0 \land r = r_{max} \end{cases}
$$
$$
\lor
$$
$$
w = 1 \land r = 0 \land 0 \leq d < d_{max} \tag{7}
$$

Propagation The invariant in a single state s can be encoded as a set of clauses:

$$p_s(\overline{x}) \leftarrow \Phi_i(\overline{x})$$

Propagation is carried out by composing these clauses with the clauses for the remaining transitions in the automaton.

Here, we propagate the values at entry to $res0$ (equation (7)) to the other states in the automaton.

In $res0$, we can repeatedly apply (m2.1), but this does not change the invariant, giving:

$$p_{res0}(r, d, w) \leftarrow p_{res0}^{entry}(r, d, w)$$

Transferring to $res1$ using either (m1.1) or (m3.1), then repeatedly applying (m1.2) and (m3.2) gives:

$$p_{res1} \leftarrow w = 0 \ \wedge \ 0 \leq r \leq r_{max} \ \wedge \ 0 \leq d \leq d_{max}$$

The invariant in $not\_writing$ is the disjunction of the invariants formed by transferring from $res0$ using (m4.1) and from $res1$ using (m4.2). This ensures that $w = 0$, giving the same invariant as above:

$$p_{not\_writing} \leftarrow p_{res1}$$

Transfer to $demands$ using (m6), which ensures that $d > 0$, giving:

$$p_{demands} \leftarrow w = 0 \ \wedge \ 0 \leq r \leq r_{max} \ \wedge \ 0 < d \leq d_{max}$$

From these equations, we can readily verify, as required, that $w = 1 \rightarrow r = 0$, and $d + w \leq d_{max}$. Note that this invariant holds for *all values* of d_{max} and r_{max}, not just specific values.

5 Approximation by Gap-Order Constraints

The analysis of the previous section required four constraints to be replaced by upper approximations in order to ensure that the meta-transitions were in gap-order form and so could be solved by the method of Revesz. What are the effects of these approximations?

1. $r' \leq r + 1$. This is approximated by $r' \leq r_{max}$. This approximation can be safely made, because the extra values allowed by the approximation (i.e. those with $r + 1 < r' \leq r_{max}$) can all be achieved by multiple applications of the unapproximated rule, i.e. the approximated rule is equivalent to an iterated version of the unapproximated rule.

2. $d' = d - 1$. This is approximated by $d' < d$. Iteration of the original rule gives all values $d' < d$, so again, the approximated rule is equivalent to an iterated version of the unapproximated rule.

3. $d' \geq d - 1$. This is deleted entirely. The range of values allowed in the approximated rule can, however, be achieved by iterating the original rule: values of d' such that $d' < d$ can be achieved by repeatedly applying the original rule with $d' = d - 1$. The other values of d' are allowable by both rules. Therefore again we see that the approximated rule is equivalent to an iterated version of the unapproximated rule.

6 Revesz's Algorithm

Once the simple circuits (compositions of transitions) have been replaced by equivalent meta-transitions, an invariant is found by constructing a fixed point of the meta-transitions. This is a difficult process, and to obtain a practical algorithm, some kind of approximation is necessary.

Revesz's algorithm [10] provides us with a terminating algorithm for calculating the *least fixed point* of a set of datalog clauses, as long as they are in gap-order form. The approximation in our method takes place in the translation to gap-order form.

The essence of Revesz's algorithm is the following. At any point during the bottom-up evaluation process, the current solution set will be represented by a set (disjunction) $i = 0...n$ of constraints:

$$p(\overline{x}) \leftarrow \phi_i(\overline{x}).$$

The set of constraints is extended by applying the input gap-order constraints (rules) in every possible way to the existing set of constraints.[1] In order to apply an input rule (8) to an existing solution (9), the variables in $\overline{x}$ are renamed to match those in $\overline{x}_0$, $\phi(\overline{x}_0)$ and $\psi(\overline{x}_0, \overline{x}_1)$ are conjoined, the variables $\overline{x}_0$ are eliminated, and finally the new constraint is added to the solution set if it does not subsume an existing constraint.

$$p(\overline{x}_1) \leftarrow p(\overline{x}_0), \psi(\overline{x}_0, \overline{x}_1) \qquad (8)$$
$$p(\overline{x}) \leftarrow \phi(\overline{x}) \qquad (9)$$

In order for the algorithm to yield a least fixed point, elimination of the variables $\overline{x}_0$ from a conjunction $\phi(\overline{x}_0) \wedge \psi(\overline{x}_0, \overline{x})$ must yield an equivalent formula. Revesz's algorithm provides a way (the shortcut operation described below) of achieving this for gap-order constraints.

In Revesz's algorithm, gap-order constraints are represented as *gap graphs*. Each gap-graph represents a conjunction of gap-order constraints. Three operations are defined on gap-graphs:

1. Merge. Merging two gap-graphs produces a gap-graph which corresponds to the conjunction of the inputs. If the inputs are inconsistent, then the merge operation fails.
2. Shortcut. The shortcut operation is used to eliminate a variable from a gap-graph.
3. Subsumption checking.

These operations are depicted in figure 6.

Our implementation consists of Prolog predicates for the translation of meta-transitions into gap-order form, and their subsequent solution using Revesz's

---

[1] The clauses derived from meta-transitions define a single recursive predicate, p. Revesz's algorithm allows clauses with more than one recursive predicate.

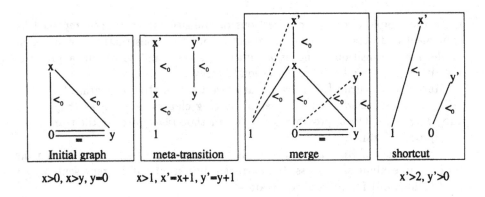

Fig. 6. The gap-graph operations.

algorithm. Occasionally, the user is required to supply an appropriate approximation of a meta-transition as a gap-order constraint.

Some optimisations have been made to Revesz's algorithm for efficiency reasons: an agenda keeps track of combinations of rules and database members which have yet to be processed, and the *merge* operation has been split into symmetric and asymmetric parts. Some simplification of the database is carried out during the execution of Revesz's procedure, by application of a number of equivalence-preserving normalisation rules, followed by removal of duplicate gap-graphs from the database. This is quite easily proved to preserve the correctness of the algorithm. Altogether, the optimisations have made the code roughly ten times faster. More sophisticated representations for gap-graphs (such as hash tables) would be expected to produce a further ten-fold improvement in code speed.

The procedures for composing transitions to form meta-transitions, translating the meta-transitions into gap-order form, solving them using Revesz's algorithm, and subsequently translating them back to meta-transitions, have been integrated into a workbench.

7 Results

This section provides a summary of the results. The fields in the table are respectively, the name of the problem, the number of states in the automaton, the number of transitions in the automaton, the number (M0) of meta-transitions before conversion to their gap-graphs, the number (M1) of meta-transitions after conversion to gap-graphs, the CPU time taken to evaluate the meta-transitions using Revesz's procedure in Sicstus Prolog on a Sparcstation-10 with 48M of memory, whether approximation was required to convert the meta-transitions to gap-order form (A?), the number (C) of gap-order constraints in the invariant found, and whether the desired invariants were found (Invts?).

Example	States	Counters	Transitions	M0	M1	CPU time	A?	C	Invts?
Subway[a]	5	3	13	4	10	4.1s	No	7	✓
Car[a]	3	3	5	2	3	0.8s	✓	5	✓
Reader/writer (5,3)[b]	3	5	12	8	53	38s	✓	12	✓
Reader/writer (n,m)	3	5	12	8	53	30s	✓	14	✓
Comparison §8.2	2	3	5	3	5	0.5s	✓	3	No
Comparison §8.2[c]	2	3	5	3	5	0.8s	✓	4	✓
Boolean circuit[d]	6	9	12	7	11	3.2s	✓	1-4	✓

[a] These examples are also treated in [6]. We present a detailed treatment of them in [4].

[b] The reader-writer example is discussed in §4. The parameters are d_{max} and r_{max} in that order.

[c] After addition of a new variable $z = x - y$ to the automaton. See §8.2.

[d] This automaton is a part of a larger example passed to us by an industrial collaborator. The invariants were calculated for several sets of initial values.

The results suggest that approximation is often necessary.

It is surprising that the reader/writer problem takes more time to solve when parameters d_{max} and r_{max} are set to specific values than in the abstract case. The order in which gap graphs are produced during bottom-up evaluation can effect the runtime, and that could be the cause of this phenomenon.

8 Comparison With Previous Work

Both [6, 2] apply abstract interpretation to the determination of state invariants. The primary difference lies in how the abstract domains are represented. Halbwachs represents domains as convex polyhedra, exploiting the efficient algorithms that are known for manipulating convex polyhedra, and making use of the operation of *widening* in order to avoid the generation of an infinite sequence of increasing sets of points.

8.1 Comparison With Periodic Sets

In [2], domains are expressed as *periodic sets*. This representation is chosen because if the state transitions are of a certain form, the invariants which result naturally have a periodic structure. Such periodic structures cannot be represented by gap-order constraints, as shown by the following example (the transitions from state a to b and b to a leave the counter x unchanged):

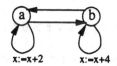

The simple circuit *a-b-a* can be represented by the following meta-transition:

$$p_a^{entry}(x') \leftarrow p_a^{entry}(x), x' = x + 2$$

The guard is not, however, a gap-order constraint. In order to make it so, we have to replace the equality on the right hand side with an inequality, $x' > x$. Now, the exact state invariant for state a is given by $x = x_0 + 2\lambda$ for $\lambda \in \mathbf{N}$, whereas that which we derive is simply $x \geq x_0$. Thus, we have lost the periodicity inherent in the system. Note, however, that if we replace $x := x + 4$ by $x := x + 3$ in the internal transition on b, then the system is no longer periodic and $x \geq x_0$ is almost the exact solution. [2] Commonly, periodic subsystems do not fit together, with the result that no periodicity appears when they are combined. The approximation by gap-order constraints seems appropriate in such cases. Furthermore, the use of gap-order constraints, rather than periodic sets or convex polyhedra, provides us with a formal explanation of two phenomena observed in [2, p.60]: first, the bottom-up evaluation procedure with a subsumption test often terminates in practice (without use of widening), second, the output may be not convex (due to the presence of disjunctions).

8.2 Comparison With Convex Hulls: An Example

Figure 7 shows an example used by Kerbrat [8, pp142–143] to illustrate the effect of different widening strategies on the invariants produced by his method. In this section, we shall see that using our techniques we arrive at quite different invariants to Kerbrat's. This suggests that the techniques are complementary.

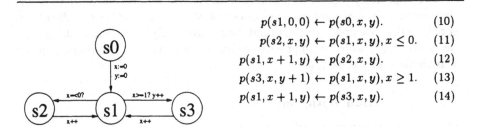

$$p(s1, 0, 0) \leftarrow p(s0, x, y). \quad (10)$$
$$p(s2, x, y) \leftarrow p(s1, x, y), x \leq 0. \quad (11)$$
$$p(s1, x + 1, y) \leftarrow p(s2, x, y). \quad (12)$$
$$p(s3, x, y + 1) \leftarrow p(s1, x, y), x \geq 1. \quad (13)$$
$$p(s1, x + 1, y) \leftarrow p(s3, x, y). \quad (14)$$

Fig. 7. Top: the automaton and its transition rules encoded in Prolog.

The *exact* invariant at $s1$ is:

$$\Omega_1 = \{x = y = 0 \lor x > 0 \land y = x - 1\}$$

---

[2] The exact solution is $x = x_0 \lor x \geq x_0 + 2$.

Kerbrat's Invariants Kerbrat determines the invariant in state $s1$ using three different widening strategies. The most accurate invariant, produced by "delayed widening", is:

$$\Phi_1 = \{x \leq y+1, 0 \leq y\}$$

Figure 8 depicts Kerbrat's invariant calculated using delayed widening, and the invariant calculated by our methods after introduction of the new counter.

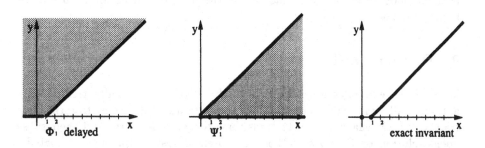

Fig. 8. Kerbrat's invariant, Φ_1, (left), ours, Ψ_1 (middle), and the exact invariant (right). Note that the intersection, $\Phi_1 \cap \Psi_1$, is a good approximation to the true invariant.

Our Invariants Using the techniques we have described, we arrive at the following invariant for state $s1$.

$$\Psi_1 = \{x \geq 0 \land y \geq 0\}$$

This invariant can be improved if we introduce a new counter $z = x - y$, and amend the automaton rules correspondingly, so that z is incremented when x is incremented or y is decremented, and decremented whenever x is decremented or y is incremented.

The new invariant is:

$$\Psi_1' = \{x \geq 0 \land y \geq 0 \land z = 0 \ \lor \ x > 1 \land y \geq 0 \land z > 0\}$$

Since $z = x - y$, we can incorporate its constraints into the diagrammatical representation of the state invariant Ψ_1'.

8.3 Discussion

A particular disadvantage of the convex hull method is that invariants which are composed of a number of disjoint regions must be approximated by a single convex hull. With gap-order constraints we can easily represent disjunctive invariants.

As we have seen, the invariants produced using our technique may be quite different from those produced using the convex hull technique. Having both techniques available in a single system will allow one method to be used when the other fails to produce a sufficiently accurate invariant.

In this example, the invariants calculated by our method and by the convex hull method are both quite gross over-approximations. Interestingly, the *intersection*[3] of Kerbrat's invariant with ours *is* a good approximation. This suggests that it would be useful to generate automaton invariants by applying *both* methods simultaneously and taking the intersection of the results as the final invariant.

9 Further Work

Most of the examples given in [6, 9, 2] have been successfully treated semi-automatically with our method. The composition of transitions to form meta-transitions, translation of meta-transitions to gap-order form and their subsequent solution by Revesz's method have been almost completely automated in Prolog. Once automation is complete, it is important to treat some large examples. At the same time, it will be necessary to carefully consider the complexity of our algorithms, and determine whether additional approximation operations are required.

10 Conclusion

In this paper we have presented a new method for the calculation of invariants for finite state automata with counters. This differs from previous methods by exploiting existing techniques for the calculation of least fixed points [3, 10]. The use of gap-order constraints allows the representation of non-convex invariants and often makes bottom-up evaluation terminate without the need for widening.

A significant advantage of our approach is that we can treat parameterised problems in which the initial values of the counters are not specified, or are partially specified by gap-order constraints.

Our technique has been implemented in Prolog, and may be used either on its own or in conjunction with other techniques. It not only provides a new tool for program analysis, but is also an interesting application of logic programming techniques.

11 Acknowledgements

We are grateful to the anonymous referees for their comments, and to the workshop delegates for providing stimulating discussion. The University of Edinburgh kindly funded the attendance of the second author at the workshop.

---

[3] Clearly the intersection of two invariants is also an invariant.

A A Short Session With the Workbench

```
| ?- workbench.
Welcome to the Invariant Workbench.
All user inputs and commands are appended to the
file ./tmp_gap_script.  Type help. for help.

>> load(kerbrat_extended).
Loaded rules from file lib/kerbrat_extended.
>> print.
Current ruleset is:

    [
        r6:(p1(s1,x_,y,z_)<--[p1(s3,x,y,z),x_=x+1,z_=z+1]),
        r5:(p1(s3,x,y_,z_)<--[p1(s1,x,y,z),y_=y+1,z_=z-1,x>=1]),
        r4:(p1(s1,x_,y,z_)<--[p1(s2,x,y,z),x_=x+1,z_=z+1]),
        r3:(p1(s2,x,y,z)<--[p1(s1,x,y,z),x=<0]),
        r2:(p1(s1,x,y,z)<--[x=0,y=0,z=0])
    ]
>> compose([r5,r6]).

Added rule v0:(p1(s1,x_,y_,z_)<--[p1(s1,x,y,z),x_=x+1,
z_=z-1+1,y_=y+1,x>=1]).
>> compose([r3,r4]).

Added rule v13:(p1(s1,x_,y_,z_)<--
[p1(s1,x,y,z),x_=x+1,z_=z+1,y_=y,x=<0]).
>> solve([r2,v0,v13]).
Meta transitions:
[(p1(x,y,z)<--[],[eq(x,0),eq(y,0),eq(z,0)]),
 (p1(x_,y_,z_)<--[p1(x,y,z)],[lt(0,x,x_),eq(z_,z),lt(0,y,y_),lt(0,0,x)]),
 (p1(x_,y_,z_)<--[p1(x,y,z)],[lt(0,x,x_),lt(0,z,z_),eq(y_,y),lt(0,x,0)]),
 (p1(x_,y_,z_)<--[p1(x,y,z)],[lt(0,x,x_),lt(0,z,z_),eq(y_,y),eq(x,0)])]

Rules contain the following free variables: [].

Agenda now contains 3 items... 5 items... 7 items... 5 items.

Result contains 4 gap graphs
```

$$p1(x,y,z) \leftarrow x = 0 \; \land \; y = 0 \; \land \; z = 0$$
$$p1(x,y,z) \leftarrow y = 0 \; \land \; 0 <_0 x \; \land \; 0 <_0 z$$
$$p1(x,y,z) \leftarrow z = 0 \; \land \; 0 <_0 x \; \land \; 0 <_0 y$$
$$p1(x,y,z) \leftarrow 0 <_0 y \; \land \; 0 <_0 z \; \land \; 0 <_1 x$$

```
>> quit.
Quitting. Saving rules in tmp_rules_.
Saved rules in file lib/tmp_rules_.
```

References

1. R. Alur, C. Courcoubetis, and D. Dill. Model-checking for real-time systems. In *Proceedings of 5th IEEE LICS*, pages 414–425. IEEE, 1990.

2. B. Boigelot and P. Wolper. Symbolic verification with periodic sets. In *Proceedings of conference on Computer-Aided Verification, 1994*, pages 55–67, 1994.

3. L. Fribourg and H. Olsén. Datalog programs with arithmetical constraints: hierarchic, periodic and spiralling least fixed points. Research report 95-26, Laboratoire Informatique, École Normale Supérieure, Paris, November 1995.

4. L. Fribourg and J. D. C. Richardson. Symbolic verification with gap-order constraints. Report LIENS - 96 - 3, Laboratoire d'Informatique, École Normale Supérieure (LIENS), Paris, February 1996. Available by ftp from host ftp.ens.fr in directory /pub/reports/liens.

5. L. Fribourg and M. Veloso Peixoto. Bottom-up evaluation of Datalog programs with arithmetic constraints. In Alan Bundy, editor, *12th Conference on Automated Deduction*, Lecture Notes in Artificial Intelligence, Vol. 814, pages 311–325, Nancy, France, 1994. Springer-Verlag.

6. N. Halbwachs. Delay analysis in synchronous programs. In *Proceedings of conference on Computer-Aided Verification, 1993*, pages 333–346, 1993.

7. T. A. Henzinger, X. Nicollin, J. Sifakis, and S. Yovine. Symbolic model checking for real-time systems. In *Proceedings 7th LICS Symposium, Santa Cruz*, pages 394 – 406, 1992.

8. A. Kerbrat. *Méthodes Symboliques pour la Vérification des Processus Communicants: étude et mise en oeuvre*. PhD thesis, L'Université Joseph Fourier - Grenoble I, November 1994. In French.

9. A. Kerbrat. Reachable state space analysis of LOTOS specifications. In *Proceedings of the 7th international conference on formal description techniques*, pages 161–176, 1994.

10. P. Z. Revesz. A closed-form evaluation for Datalog queries with integer (gap)-order constraints. *Theoretical Computer Science*, 1993. vol. 116, pages 117–149.

Specification-Based Automatic Verification of Prolog Programs*

Agostino Cortesi[1] and Baudouin Le Charlier[2] and Sabina Rossi[3]

[1] Dipartimento di Matematica e Informatica, via Torino 155, 30173 Venezia, Italy
[2] Institut d'Informatique, 21 rue Grandgagnage, B-5000 Namur, Belgium
[3] Dipartimento di Matematica, via Belzoni 7, 35131 Padova, Italy

Abstract. The paper presents an analyzer for verifying the correctness of a Prolog program relative to a specification which provides a list of input/output annotations for the arguments and parameters that can be used to establish program termination. The work stems from Deville's methodology to derive Prolog programs that correctly implement their declarative meaning. In this context, we propose an algorithm that combines, adapts, and sometimes improves various existing static analyses in order to verify total correctness of Prolog programs with respect to formal specifications. Using the information computed during the verification process, an automatic complexity analysis can be also performed.

1 Introduction

Logic programming is an appealing programming paradigm since it allows one to solve complex problems in a concise and understandable way, i.e., in declarative style. For efficiency reasons, however, practical implementations of logic programs (e.g., Prolog programs) are not always faithful to their declarative meaning. In his book [11], Deville proposes a methodology for logic program construction that aims at reconciling the declarative semantics with an efficient implementation. The methodology is based on four main development steps:

1. elaboration of a specification, consisting of a description of the relation, type declarations, and a set of behavioural assumptions;
2. construction of a correct logic description, dealing with the declarative meaning only;
3. derivation of a Prolog program;
4. correctness verification of the Prolog code with respect to the specification.

The FOLON environment [8, 12] was designed with the main goal of supporting the automatable aspects of this methodology. In this context, we propose a new analyzer for verifying total correctness of Prolog programs with respect to specifications.

* Partly supported by European Community "HCM-Network, Logic Program Synthesis and Transformation, Contract Nr. CHRX-CT93-00414", and by "MURST NRP, Modelli della Computazione e dei Linguaggi di Programmazione".

The new analyzer is an extension of the analyzers described in [7, 8, 12] which themselves automate part of the methodology described in [11]. The novelty is that we deal with total correctness, while [7, 8, 12] only deal with particular correctness aspects such as mode and type verification. At this aim, we extend the generic abstract domain Pat($\Re$) [5, 6, 19] to deal with multiplicity and size relations.

We adapt the framework for termination analysis proposed by De Schreye, Verschaetse and Bruynooghe in [10]: instead of proving termination based on the program code only, we use termination information given in the formal specification; this requires more information from the programmer but allows for more general termination proofs.

The analyzer computes information about the number of solutions using the notion of abstract sequence which was firstly introduced in [15]. This is related to the cardinality analysis described in [2]. However, we do not perform an abstract interpretation in the usual sense since we use the formal specification of the subproblems instead of their code; moreover, we allow the number of solutions to be expressed as a function of the input argument sizes. This enhances the expressiveness of cardinality analysis with respect to [2].

The information about size relations and number of solutions can be also used to perform, in an automatic way, complexity analysis of Prolog programs, in the spirit of the framework proposed by Debray and Lin in [9]. In this paper, we only sketch this application on examples. Notice that, in the context of program development, complexity analysis can be used to choose the most efficient version of a procedure.

The paper is organized as follows. In Section 2, we recall Deville's methodology. In Section 3, we introduce the abstract domains used by the analyzer. In Section 4, we describe the analyzer and give an example to illustrate the main operations. Section 5 contains a formal description of the operations. In Section 6, we discuss the complexity analysis and describe some examples of cost analysis which use information computed by the analyzer. Section 7 concludes the paper.

2 Program Synthesis Methodology Overview

Our work is based on and extends Deville's methodology for logic program development presented in [11]. Let us illustrate it with the construction of the procedure *select*/3 which removes an occurrence of X from the list L containing it and returns the list L_s.

2.1 Specification

The first step consists in specifying the procedure according to a standard specification format. Indeed, we extend the general specification form proposed by Deville in [11] with extra information which will be useful for proving termination of the derived procedures. Argument size relations are specified in the form of a set of inequations (see [9, 10]). They are used to prove termination of the recursive procedures in the spirit of [10]. Moreover, the number of solutions is allowed to be expressed in terms of the input argument sizes.

A specification for *select*/3 is depicted in Figure 1. First, the name and the formal parameters of the procedure are specified. The *type*, the *relation* and the *size relation* information express properties on the formal parameters which are intended to be satisfied after any successful execution. The *size measure* (see [10]) $\| \cdot \|_\lambda$ associates to each term t a natural number $\|t\|_\lambda$ by: $\|[t_1|t_2]\|_\lambda = 1 + \|t_2\|_\lambda$ and $\|t\|_\lambda = 0$ if t is not of the form $[t_1|t_2]$. The *size relation* is a set of linear (in)equations on the formal parameters expressing a relation between the corresponding sizes. In the example, after any successful execution, the size of L is required to be equal to the size of L_s plus 1.

Procedure: $select(X, L, L_s)$
Types: X : Term
$\qquad L, L_s$: Lists
Relation: X is an element of L and L_s is the list L without an occurrence of X
Size measure: $\| \cdot \|_\lambda$
Size relation: $\{L = L_s + 1\}$
Application conditions: $in(any, gr, any) :: out(gr, gr, gr)$ $\{0 \le sol \le L\}$ $\qquad L$
$\qquad\qquad\qquad\qquad\qquad$ $in(gr, any, gr) :: out(gr, gr, gr)$ $\{0 \le sol \le L_s + 1\}$ L_s

Fig. 1. Specification for *select*/3

The application conditions consist of three components namely, *directionality*, *multiplicity* and *size expression*. Each *directionality* specifies the allowed modes of the parameters before the execution (**in** part) and the corresponding modes after a successful execution (**out** part).

For any set of program variables V, we denote by $\mathbf{Exp}_V$ the set of all linear expressions with integer coefficients on variables in V. A *multiplicity* is a set E of (in)equations over $\mathbf{Exp}_{\{sol, X_1, \ldots, X_n\}} \cup \{\infty\}$ where $X_1, \ldots, X_n$ are the formal parameters of the procedure and *sol* is a new variable denoting the cardinality of the answer substitution sequence. For any call to the procedure satisfying the **in** part of the corresponding directionality and producing the sequence S of answer substitutions, the following property is expected to hold: the assignment $\{sol/|S|, X_1/\|t_1\|, \ldots, X_n/\|t_n\|\}$, where $t_1, \ldots, t_n$ are the input values corresponding to the formal parameters, satisfies the set of (in)equations E. The *size expression* is an expression from $\mathbf{Exp}_{\{X_1, \ldots, X_n\}}$[4] associating to each possible call, respecting the corresponding **in** part, a weight obtained by replacing the formal parameters with the size of the corresponding actual values. Such an expression is assumed to be a natural number for any instantiation of the parameters. In order to prove termination of a recursive call we need to prove

---

[4] It corresponds, in a sense, to the level mapping used by De Schreye *et al.* in [10].

that its weight is smaller than the weight for the initial one[5]. In the example, the weight for the calls of *select*/3 respecting the first (resp. the last) in part is given by the size of the actual value corresponding to L (resp. L_s).

2.2 Logic Description

Figure 2 provides a correct logic description for *select*/3, noted $LD(select/3)$.

$$select(X, L, L_s) \Longleftrightarrow L = [H|T] \wedge list(T) \wedge$$
$$((H = X \wedge L_s = T) \vee (L_s = [H_s|T_s] \wedge select(X, T, T_s))).$$

Fig. 2. $LD(select/3)$

The correctness of a logic description $LD(p/n)$ can be expressed as follows: for any ground n-tuple t, (1) $p(t)$ is a logical consequence of $LD(p/n)$ iff t belongs to the relation and respects the types; (2) $\neg p(t)$ is a logical consequence of $LD(p/n)$ iff either t does not belong to the relation or it does not respect the types.

2.3 Prolog Code Derivation

The next step consists in deriving a Prolog program from the logic description. First, the logic description $LD(p/n)$ is syntactically translated into a Prolog program $LP(p/n)$, in normalized form, whose completion [3] is the logic description again[6]. Figure 3, 4, and 5 depict three different translations of the logic description in Figure 2.

Among the derived procedures, we need to select the ones which are correct with respect to the initial specification. For instance, some of them may not terminate when executed following the left-to-right Prolog search rule.

Among the correct ones, some of them may be more efficient than others. Moreover, they can be simplified in order to gain efficiency. Atoms that surely succeed without instantiating their arguments can be removed; this is typically the case for type checking literals. For instance, procedure $LP_1(select/3)$ is not correct for the second directionality since the literal $list(T)$ could be called with its argument being a variable (e.g., when L is a variable) and then it would produce infinitely many solutions; procedure $LP_2(select/3)$ is correct with respect to the specification in Figure 1; and procedure $LP_3(select/3)$ is obtained from procedure $LP_2(select/3)$ by dropping the last atom $list(T)$. This transformation is made possible by the type information computed during the analysis.

Thus, the analyzer can play three different roles: finding correct permutations, selecting the most efficient one, and, finally, simplifying procedures to make them more efficient.

---

[5] For more details about these concepts the reader is referred to [1, 10].

[6] Actually, the translation process may produce more than one possible procedure. Different permutations of the clauses and of the literals in the bodies can be returned.

$select(X, L, L_s) : - L = [H|T], \; list(T), \; H = X, \; L_s = T.$
$select(X, L, L_s) : - L = [H|T], \; list(T), \; L_s = [H|T_s], \; select(X, T, T_s).$

Fig. 3. $LP_1(select/3)$

$select(X, L, L_s) : - L = [H|T], \; H = X, \; L_s = T, \; list(T).$
$select(X, L, L_s) : - L = [H|T], \; L_s = [H|T_s], \; select(X, T, T_s), \; list(T).$

Fig. 4. $LP_2(select/3)$

$select(X, L, L_s) : - L = [H|T], \; H = X, \; L_s = T, \; list(T).$
$select(X, L, L_s) : - L = [H|T], \; L_s = [H|T_s], \; select(X, T, T_s).$

Fig. 5. $LP_3(select/3)$

2.4 Correctness Verification

The last step, in Deville's methodology, is the verification of total correctness
of the derived program with respect to the specification. In order to be correct,
any procedure in the program must satisfy the following criteria: during any
execution (based on the SLDNF-resolution) called with arguments respecting at
least one **in** part of the corresponding specification and producing the sequence
S of answer substitutions,

1. the computation rule is safe, i.e., when selected, the negative literals are
   ground;
2. any subcall is called with arguments respecting at least one **in** part of its
   specification;
3. the arguments of the procedure after the execution respect the types, the
   size relation and the **out** part of each directionality whose **in** part is satisfied
   by the initial call;
4. S respects the multiplicity of each directionality whose **in** part is satisfied
   by the initial call;
5. completeness: every computed answer substitution in the SLDNF-tree belongs to S , i.e., it must eventually be caught by the analyzer according to
   the Prolog search rule;
6. termination: if S is finite then the execution terminates.

When S is finite, points 5 and 6 are satisfied if the execution of each clause
terminates. Termination of a clause is achieved when each literal in its body
which is not a recursive call terminates, and the weights for the recursive calls
are smaller than the weight for the initial call. When S can be infinite, then
only completeness has to be verified. A sufficient criterion for completeness is
the following: at most one literal in a clause of the procedure produces an infinite
number of answer substitutions and either this literal is in the last clause or the
following clauses are finitely failed (i.e., they terminate without producing any

result); moreover, if a clause contains a literal that produces an infinite number of answer substitutions, then none of the preceding literals in this clause produces more than one solution.

The main advantage provided by the analyzer that we present in this paper is the full automatization of the last step of Deville's methodology described so far, i.e., the verification of total correctness of synthesized programs with respect to the specification. Both the procedures $LP_2(select/3)$ and $LP_3(select/3)$ above can be proved to be correct wrt the specification depicted in Figure 1. In section 4 we will illustrate the behaviour of the analyzer by considering $LP_3(select/3)$.

3 Basic Notions

In this section we briefly describe the abstract domains used by the analyzer. Based on the notion of *abstract substitution*, the concept of *abstract sequence* is introduced to represent a sequence of answer substitutions. Finally, we formalize the program specification through the notion of *behaviour*.

In the following we call I_p the set of indices $\{1, \ldots, p\}$, denoting terms $t_1, \ldots, t_p$. Next notions are parameterized on p, and can be extended to the set of all I_p in the same way as in [16].

Definition 1 (Abstract substitution). An *abstract substitution* β is an element of the generic abstract domain $\mathbf{Pat}(\Re)$ described in [5, 6], i.e., a tuple $\langle sv, frm, \alpha \rangle$ where

1. the same-value component sv assigns an index from I_p to each program variable;
2. the pattern component frm associates with some of the indices in I_p a pattern $f(i_1, \ldots, i_q)$, where f is a q-ary function symbol and $\{i_1, \ldots, i_q\} \subseteq I_p$;
3. α is an element of a domain $\Re$ that gives information on term tuples $\langle t_1, \ldots, t_p \rangle$ about mode, sharing, types, or whatever else.

Example 1. Let $\Re$ be the abstract domain *Mode-Type*[7] described in [14], and consider the (concrete) substitution

$$\{X_1 \mapsto Y * a, X_2 \mapsto a, X_3 \mapsto []\}.$$

This substitution is represented, for instance, by the following abstract substitution:

$$
\begin{array}{lll}
sv\colon X_1 \mapsto 1 & frm\colon 1 \mapsto 4 * 2 & \alpha : 1/ngv \\
 X_2 \mapsto 2 & 2 \mapsto a & 2/gr \\
 X_3 \mapsto 3 & 3 \mapsto [] & 3/grlist \\
 & 4 \mapsto ? & 4/var
\end{array}
$$

---

[7] It consists of the elements *gr* denoting a ground term, *any* denoting any term, *var* denoting a variable, *nv* denoting a term which is not a variable, *ngv* denoting a term which is neither ground nor a variable, *grlist* denoting a ground list, *anylist* denoting either a variable or any list.

At each execution point, the analyzer computes (so-called) abstract sequences [2, 15] giving information about variables in the form of an abstract substitution, and also information about the number of solutions in terms of the input argument sizes. Thus, an abstract sequence can be seen as an extension of the abstract substitution notion, where an additional same-value component maintains the parameter assignments at clause entry, and a set of linear (in)equations represents information relative to the size relations among terms and the number of solutions.

Definition 2 (Abstract sequence). An *abstract sequence B* is a tuple of the form $\langle sv_{in}, sv, frm, \alpha, E \rangle$ where

1. $\langle sv_{in}, frm, \alpha \rangle$ and $\langle sv, frm, \alpha \rangle$ are abstract substitutions;
2. the domain of the same-value function sv_{in} is contained in the domain of sv;
3. the *size component E* is a (possibly empty) set of linear (in)equations over $\mathbf{Exp}_{\{sol, sz(1), \ldots, sz(p)\}}$.

The meaning of an abstract sequence is given in terms of the concretization function γ on abstract substitutions defined in [16]. Given a size measure $\| \cdot \|$, an abstract sequence $B = \langle sv_{in}, sv, frm, \alpha, E \rangle$ represents the set of all pairs (σ_{in}, S) where $\sigma_{in} \in \gamma(\langle sv_{in}, frm, \alpha \rangle)$ is a concrete substitution and S is a possibly infinite sequence of substitutions such that for all $\sigma \in S$, σ is an instance of σ_{in}, $\sigma \in \gamma(\langle sv, frm, \alpha \rangle)$, and S respects the size and the multiplicity relations expressed in E. The latter condition means that for every $\langle t_1, \ldots, t_p \rangle \in \gamma(\alpha)$ defining a substitution[8] $\sigma \in S : (sz(1)/\|t_1\|, \ldots, sz(p)/\|t_p\|, sol/|S|)$ satisfies the set of (in)equations E.

A behaviour for a procedure is a formalization of its specification (excluding the relation part which is formalized by the logic description).

Definition 3 (behaviour). A *behaviour* for a procedure p/n is a triplet of the form $(p, [X_1, \ldots, X_n], Prepost)$ where

1. $X_1, \ldots, X_n$ are distinct variables representing the formal parameters of the procedure p/n;
2. *Prepost* is a set of pairs $\langle B, Se \rangle$ where $B = \langle sv_{in}, sv_{out}, frm, \alpha, E \rangle$ is an abstract sequence and Se is a size expression from $\mathbf{Exp}_{\{X_1, \ldots, X_n\}}$.

Example 2. A behaviour for *select/3* formalizing the specification depicted in Figure 1 has the form

$$(select, [X_1, X_2, X_3], Prepost = \{\langle B^1, X_2 \rangle, \langle B^2, X_3 \rangle\})$$

where B^2 (corresponding to the second application condition) is equal to

---

[8] To be more precise, let $dom(sv) = \{X_1, \ldots, X_n\}$, $\langle t_1, \ldots, t_p \rangle$ is the (unique) tuple of terms such that $\sigma = \{X_1/t_{sv(X_1)}, \ldots, X_n/t_{sv(X_n)}\}$ and $\langle t_1, \ldots, t_p \rangle \in Cc(frm)$, see [16].

$$sv_{in}\colon X_1 \mapsto 1 \quad sv_{out}\colon X_1 \mapsto 4 \quad frm\colon 1 \mapsto? \quad \alpha\colon 1/gr \quad E\colon 0 \leq sol \leq sz(3)+1$$
$$X_2 \mapsto 2 \qquad\qquad X_2 \mapsto 5 \qquad\quad 2 \mapsto? \qquad 2/any \qquad sz(5) = sz(6)+1$$
$$X_3 \mapsto 3 \qquad\qquad X_3 \mapsto 6 \qquad\quad 3 \mapsto? \qquad 3/gr$$
$$4 \mapsto? \qquad 4/gr$$
$$5 \mapsto? \qquad 5/grlist$$
$$6 \mapsto? \qquad 6/grlist$$

and the abstract sequence B^1 (corresponding to the first application condition) can be defined in a similar way.

4 The Analyzer

In this section we first present a clause analyzer for verifying correctness of a clause. This is a refinement and an extension of the analyzer proposed in [7]. Then, we describe a procedure analyzer, based on the clause analyzer, for verifying correctness of a whole procedure.

4.1 The Clause Analyzer

The clause analyzer takes as inputs (1) a clause $cl = p(X_1, \ldots, X_n)\colon -L_1, \ldots, L_f$ where $n, f \geq 0$ and $X_1, \ldots, X_n$ are distinct variables, (2) a behaviour for each subgoal in cl (except $= /2$ but including p/n), (3) an element from the $Prepost$ component in the behaviour for p/n of the form $\langle\langle sv_{in}, sv_{out}, frm, \alpha, E\rangle, Se\rangle$, (4) an abstract substitution β on the variables $X_1, \ldots, X_n$ in the head of the clause respecting the precondition $\langle sv_{in}, frm, \alpha\rangle$, i.e., β is smaller than or equal to the abstract substitution $\langle sv_{in}, frm, \alpha\rangle$, according to the partial order defined on $\mathbf{Pat}(\Re)$. It checks the following:

1. for any subcall q/m in the body of cl, let $(q, [X_1, \ldots, X_m], Prepost_q)$ be the behaviour for q/m. The procedure q/m is called with arguments respecting at least one precondition $\langle sv'_{in}, frm', \alpha'\rangle$ in the $Prepost_q$ set;
2. if sol/∞ satisfies the restriction of E to sol, then at most one subcall in the body of cl can produce an infinite number of solutions and none of the preceding literals in this clause produces more than one solution. Otherwise, the execution of cl terminates.

If one of these properties can not be inferred then the clause analyzer fails. Otherwise, it returns an abstract sequence B_{cl} expressing information about types, modes, size relations, number of solutions and termination for the execution of the clause cl.

In order to compute its results, the clause analyzer computes a set of abstract sequences, $B_0, B_1, \ldots, B_f$, on the variables in cl and an abstract sequence B_{out} expressing the same properties as B_f but restricted to the variables $X_1, \ldots, X_n$ in the head of cl. The following main operations are required to analyze a clause.

Initial operation: it extends the abstract substitution β to an abstract sequence B_0 on all the variables in cl.

Derivation operation: it computes the abstract sequence B_i from B_{i-1} and the literal L_i ($1 \leq i \leq f$). In fact, there are two kinds of derivation operations: the *deriv-unif* (for the $=/2$ literals) and the *deriv-normal* (for procedure calls).

Reduction operation: it computes B_{out} from B_f by restricting it to the variables $X_1, \ldots, X_n$.

Let us illustrate them with an example. Consider the second clause of the procedure $LP_3(select/3)$ and the behaviour for $select/3$ described above. Let $\beta = \langle sv, frm, \alpha \rangle$ be an abstract substitution of the form

$$
\begin{array}{lll}
sv\colon X_1 \mapsto 1 & frm\colon 1 \mapsto ? & \alpha : 1/gr \\
X_2 \mapsto 2 & 2 \mapsto ? & 2/any \\
X_3 \mapsto 3 & 3 \mapsto ? & 3/gr
\end{array}
$$

The clause analyzer computes $B_0, B_1, \ldots, B_3, B_{out}$ as follows:

$$
\begin{array}{l}
\beta \\
select(X_1, X_2, X_3) \leftarrow B_0 \; X_2 = [X_4|X_5], \\
\qquad\qquad\qquad\qquad B_1 \; X_3 = [X_4|X_6], \\
\qquad\qquad\qquad\qquad B_2 \; select(X_1, X_5, X_6) \; B_3. \\
B_{out}
\end{array}
$$

Initial Operation. First, the abstract substitution β is extended to an abstract sequence B_0 on all the variables in the clause stating that the new variables are not instantiated and used nowhere else. In the example,

$$
\begin{array}{lllll}
sv_{in}^0\colon X_1 \mapsto 1 & sv^0\colon X_1 \mapsto 1 & frm^0\colon 1 \mapsto ? & \alpha^0 : 1/gr & E^0 : sol = 1 \\
X_2 \mapsto 2 & X_2 \mapsto 2 & 2 \mapsto ? & 2/any & \\
X_3 \mapsto 3 & X_3 \mapsto 3 & 3 \mapsto ? & 3/gr & \\
& X_4 \mapsto 4 & 4 \mapsto ? & 4/var & \\
& X_5 \mapsto 5 & 5 \mapsto ? & 5/var & \\
& X_6 \mapsto 6 & 6 \mapsto ? & 6/var &
\end{array}
$$

Derivation operation. We compute B_1 from B_0 and the literal $X_2 = [X_4|X_5]$. In this case, the *deriv-unif* operation is used. A new term (represented by the index 7) is introduced, representing the result of the unification of X_2 with $[X_4|X_5]$. The sv_{in} component maintain the link with the term denoted by 2 while the actual binding of X_2 after the unification is kept by sv. Since it is not sure that the unification succeeds, the information that a failure may occur is expressed in the multiplicity component. Information on size relations after the unification is expressed by the equation $sz(7) = sz(5) + 1$. Thus, B_1 is

$$sv_{in}^1\colon X_1 \mapsto 1 \quad sv^1\colon X_1 \mapsto 1 \quad frm^1\colon 1 \mapsto? \quad \alpha^1\colon 1/gr \quad E^1\colon 0 \leq sol \leq 1$$
$$\begin{array}{lllll}
X_2 \mapsto 2 & X_2 \mapsto 7 & 2 \mapsto? & 2/any & sz(7) = sz(5) + 1 \\
X_3 \mapsto 3 & X_3 \mapsto 3 & 3 \mapsto? & 3/gr & \\
 & X_4 \mapsto 4 & 4 \mapsto? & 4/any & \\
 & X_5 \mapsto 5 & 5 \mapsto? & 5/any & \\
 & X_6 \mapsto 6 & 6 \mapsto? & 6/var & \\
 & & 7 \mapsto [4|5] & 7/nv &
\end{array}$$

Another derivation operation applies to derive B_2 from B_1 and the literal $X_3 = [X_4|X_6]$. Also in this case, the *deriv-unif* operation is used. Observe that the groundness of the term indexed by 3 propagates to the terms that correspond (through sv) to X_4 and X_6. Moreover, in this case no new term is created, as the term indexed by 3 is ground before the unification step. The abstract sequence B_2 is

$$sv_{in}^2\colon X_1 \mapsto 1 \quad sv^2\colon X_1 \mapsto 1 \quad frm^2\colon 1 \mapsto? \quad \alpha^2\colon 1/gr \quad E^2\colon 0 \leq sol \leq 1$$
$$\begin{array}{lllll}
X_2 \mapsto 2 & X_2 \mapsto 7 & 2 \mapsto? & 2/any & sz(7) = sz(5) + 1 \\
X_3 \mapsto 3 & X_3 \mapsto 3 & 3 \mapsto [4|6] & 3/gr & sz(3) = sz(6) + 1 \\
 & X_4 \mapsto 4 & 4 \mapsto? & 4/gr & \\
 & X_5 \mapsto 5 & 5 \mapsto? & 5/any & \\
 & X_6 \mapsto 6 & 6 \mapsto? & 6/gr & \\
 & & 7 \mapsto [4|5] & 7/nv &
\end{array}$$

The abstract sequence B_3 is obtained through *deriv-normal* by combining B_2 with the behaviour of *select/3*. In particular, we need to find a pair $\langle B, Se \rangle$ in the *Prepost* component of the behaviour that matches with B_2 regarding *directionality* and *termination*. In our example, this is true when considering the prepost component $\langle B^2, X_3 \rangle$ defined at the end of Section 3.
Let $B^2 = \langle sv_{in}, sv_{out}, frm, \alpha, E \rangle$ and let $\tau = \{X_1 \mapsto X_1, X_2 \mapsto X_5, X_3 \mapsto X_6\}$ be the renaming function that is used to restrict B_2 to the clause $select(X_1, X_5, X_6)$.

First, we need to verify directionality: that the abstract substitution obtained by applying τ to $\langle sv^2, frm^2, \alpha^2 \rangle$ is at least as precise (i.e., smaller or equal in the ordering on $\mathbf{Pat}(\Re)$) as $\langle sv_{in}, frm, \alpha \rangle$. In particular, if we look at modes, it is easy to verify that

$$\begin{aligned}
&\mathbf{in}(\alpha^2(sv^2(\tau(X_1))), \alpha^2(sv^2(\tau(X_2))), \alpha^2(sv^2(\tau(X_3)))) = \\
&\mathbf{in}(\alpha^2(sv^2(X_1)), \alpha^2(sv^2(X_5)), \alpha^2(sv^2(X_6))) = \\
&\mathbf{in}(\alpha^2(1), \alpha^2(5), \alpha^2(6)) = \\
&\mathbf{in}(gr, any, gr) = \\
&\mathbf{in}(\alpha(sv(X_1)), \alpha(sv(X_2)), \alpha(sv(X_3))
\end{aligned}$$

Second, since sol/∞ is not a solution in E^2, we have to prove termination: according to the size expression $Se = X_3$ in the *Prepost* component selected, we need to verify that the size of the third term of the new activation call is strictly smaller than the size of the third parameter before the execution. Formally, we need to verify that

$$sz(sv^2(\tau(X_3))) < sz(sv_{in}^2(X_3))$$

Indeed,

$$
\begin{aligned}
sz(sv_{in}^2(X_3)) &= sz(3) && \text{by definition of } sv_{in}^2 \\
&= sz(6) + 1 && \text{by definition of } E^2 \\
&> sz(6) \\
&= sz(sv^2(\tau(X_3))) && \text{by definition of } sv^2 \text{ and } \tau.
\end{aligned}
$$

Thus, both directionality and termination of the application condition are satisfied. Therefore, we can apply the out-conditions of B^2. In particular, we derive that the terms indexed by 5 and 6 are bound to ground lists, and we get the multiplicity equations $0 \leq sol \leq sz(6) + 1$ and $sz(5) = sz(6) + 1$. We obtain the following abstract sequence B_3:

$sv_{in}^3\colon X_1 \mapsto 1$	$sv^3\colon X_1 \mapsto 1$	$frm^3\colon 1 \mapsto ?$	$\alpha^3 : 1/gr$	$E^3 : 0 \leq sol \leq sz(6) + 1$
$X_2 \mapsto 2$	$X_2 \mapsto 7$	$2 \mapsto ?$	$2/any$	$sz(7) = sz(5) + 1$
$X_3 \mapsto 3$	$X_3 \mapsto 3$	$3 \mapsto [4|6]$	$3/grlist$	$sz(3) = sz(6) + 1$
	$X_4 \mapsto 4$	$4 \mapsto ?$	$4/gr$	$sz(5) = sz(6) + 1$
	$X_5 \mapsto 5$	$5 \mapsto ?$	$5/grlist$	
	$X_6 \mapsto 6$	$6 \mapsto ?$	$6/grlist$	
		$7 \mapsto [4|5]$	$7/grlist$	

Reduction operation. The abstract sequence B_{out} is computed by restricting B_3 to the variables X_1, X_2, X_3. It results in

$sv_{in}^o\colon X_1 \mapsto 1$	$sv^o\colon X_1 \mapsto 1$	$frm^o\colon 1 \mapsto ?$	$\alpha^o : 1/gr$	$E^o : 0 \leq sol \leq sz(6) + 1$
$X_2 \mapsto 2$	$X_2 \mapsto 7$	$2 \mapsto ?$	$2/any$	$sz(7) = sz(5) + 1$
$X_3 \mapsto 3$	$X_3 \mapsto 3$	$3 \mapsto [4|6]$	$3/grlist$	$sz(3) = sz(6) + 1$
		$4 \mapsto ?$	$4/gr$	$sz(5) = sz(6) + 1$
		$5 \mapsto ?$	$5/grlist$	
		$6 \mapsto ?$	$6/grlist$	
		$7 \mapsto [4|5]$	$7/grlist$	

4.2 The Procedure Analyzer

The clause analyzer is used to define a procedure analyzer for verifying total correctness of a full procedure. It takes as inputs (1) a Prolog procedure P defining a predicate p/n and consisting of a finite sequence of clauses $cl_1, \ldots, cl_m$, (2) a behaviour for each subprocedure in P. For any abstract substitution respecting at least one precondition in the behaviour for p/n,

1. it checks whether for each clause cl_i of P, the clause analyzer does not fail returning the abstract sequence B_{cl_i};

2. it computes the abstract operation $\mathbf{CONC}(B_{cl_1}, \ldots, B_{cl_n})$ which approximates the sequence of answer substitutions for the whole procedure (taking into account mutual exclusivity between clauses and incompleteness due to an infinite computation) and verifies the postconditions, i.e., types, modes. size relations, multiplicity. This operation can be seen as an extension of the corresponding operation in [15];

3. if the sequence of answer substitutions can be infinite, then at most one clause of P can produce an infinite number of solutions and if this is not the last clause, then the executions of all the following clauses in P are finitely failed.

If one of these properties can not be inferred then the procedure analyzer fails. This simply means that the correctness of the procedure P cannot be proven by the analyzer.

5 Abstract Operations

In this section[9], we formally describe the main operations used by the clause analyzer, namely **INIT**, **REDUCE**, **DERIV_UNIF**, **DERIV_NORMAL**. For each of these operations we provide a specification and an implementation. The specification is given in terms of the concretization function Cc whereas the implementation applies abstract operations on the $\Re$-domain (corresponding to the α component in the abstract substitutions) defined in [5]. We also assume the existence of operations on the multiplicity component E of the abstract sequences. We call them $\Im$-operations. If we restrict to sets of linear equations, then we can always reduce E to the canonical form which is supplied by the so-called *row-echelon form*. In this case, the $\Im$-operations are similar to the abstract operations defined by De Schreye, Verschaetse and Bruynooghe in [10]. Notice also that implementations proposed in this section are only tentative since the actual coding of the analyzer is still underway. Future developments may reveal that better implementations are possible.

5.1 Constrained Mapping

The notion of *constrained mapping* (see [17]) is used in the implementation of the **DERIV_UNIF** and **DERIV_NORMAL** operations. Intuitively, let I and J be two sets of indices denoting arbitrary terms and α_I and α_J be two abstract objects parametrized by the indices in I and J, respectively. Let also $tr : I - J$ be a total function expressing that, for every $i \in I$, the element denoted by i is equal to the element denoted by $tr(i)$. A constrained mapping is a pair $(tr^<, tr^>)$ where $tr^<$ applies to abstract objects parametrized by the indices in J and expresses them in terms of the indices in I, e.g., $tr^<(\alpha_J) = \alpha_I$, while $tr^>$ applies to abstract objects parametrized by the indices in I and expresses them in terms of the indices in J, e.g., $tr^>(\alpha_I) = \alpha_J$.

---

[9] This section is quite technical, and can be skipped at a first reading.

Let f_1 and f_2 be two functions (tuples are functions) with domains D_1 and D_2, respectively, such that $D_1 \cap D_2 = \emptyset$. We denote $f_1 \square f_2$ the function f with domain $D_1 \cup D_2$ such that for all $d \in D_1 : f(d) = f_1(d)$ and for all $d \in D_2 : f(d) = f_2(d)$.

In the following, since sv, frm, ... are functions over finite domains, they are referred as sets of assignments.

5.2 $\Re$-Operations and $\Im$-Operations

Let us recall from [5, 10] the specification of some abstract operations which are used in the implementation of the analyzer, namely, $\Re\_\text{INTR}$, $\Re\_\text{PROJ}$ (on the α component, [5]), $\Im\_\text{PROJ}$ and $\Im\_\text{EXTG}$ (on the size component E), and AI_VAR, AI_FUNC, RESTRG and EXTG (on abstract substitutions, [5]),

$\Re\_\text{INTR}(\alpha, p, k) = \alpha'$. Let α be an element of the domain $\Re$ that gives information on term tuples $\langle t_1, \ldots, t_p \rangle$ and $k \geq 0$. This operation introduces k variables in locations $p+1, \ldots, p+k$.

$$\left. \begin{array}{l} \langle t_1, \ldots, t_p \rangle \in Cc(\alpha) \\ Y_1, \ldots, Y_k \text{ are new distinct variables} \end{array} \right\} \Rightarrow \langle t_1, \ldots, t_p, Y_1, \ldots, Y_k \rangle \in Cc(\alpha').$$

$\Re\_\text{PROJ}(\alpha, \{i_1, \ldots, i_n\}) = \alpha'$. Let α be an element of the domain $\Re$ representing term tuples $\langle t_1, \ldots, t_p \rangle$ such that $i_1, \ldots, i_n \in \{1, \ldots, p\}$ and let $\langle j_1, \ldots, j_q \rangle$ be obtained from $\langle 1, \ldots, p \rangle$ by removing the indices $i_1, \ldots, i_n$.

$$\langle t_1, \ldots, t_p \rangle \in Cc(\alpha) \Rightarrow \langle t_{j_1}, \ldots, t_{j_q} \rangle \in Cc(\alpha').$$

$\Im\_\text{PROJ}(E, \{i_1, \ldots, i_n\}) = E'$. Let E be a set of (in)equations over the set $\text{Exp}_{\{sz(1), \ldots, sz(p)\}, sol}$ and let $\langle j_1, \ldots, j_q \rangle$ be obtained from $\langle 1, \ldots, p \rangle$ by removing the indices $i_1, \ldots, i_n$. Let also $x_1, \ldots, x_p, x_{p+1} \in \mathbb{N}$.

$$\left. \begin{array}{l} \langle sz(1)/x_1, \ldots, sz(p)/x_p, sol/x_{p+1} \rangle \\ \text{is a solution of } E \end{array} \right\} \Rightarrow \begin{array}{l} \langle sz(j_1)/x_{j_1}, \ldots, sz(j_q)/x_{j_q}, sol/x_{p+1} \rangle \\ \text{is a solution of } E'. \end{array}$$

The specification for $\Im\_\text{PROJ}(E, sol) = E'$ is similar.

$\Im\_\text{EXTG}(p(X_{i_1}, \ldots, X_{i_n}), E_1, E_2) = E'$. This operation is used to extend the size relation and the number of solutions information for a clause before a literal $p(X_{i_1}, \ldots, X_{i_n})$ (i.e., E_1) with the size relation and the number of solutions information obtained from the behaviour of p/n. Let E_1 and E_2 be two sets of (in)equations over the sets $\text{Exp}_{\{(sz(j))_{j \in I_1}, sol\}}$ and $\text{Exp}_{\{(sz(h))_{h \in I_2}, sol\}}$, respectively. Let also $\{X_1, \ldots, X_m\}$ be the set of all variables occurring in the clause. E' is a set of (in)equations over $\text{Exp}_{\{(sz(k))_{k \in I'}, sol\}}$ such that

$$\left. \begin{array}{l} (\|t_j\|)_{j \in I_1} \square \{sol \mapsto sol_1\} \text{ is a solution of } E_1 \\ (\|s_h\|)_{h \in I_2} \square \{sol \mapsto sol_2\} \text{ is a solution of } E_2 \\ \theta_1 = \{X_1/t_{j_1}, \ldots, X_m/t_{j_m}\}, \ j_1, \ldots, j_m \in I_1 \\ \theta_2 = \{X_1/s_{h_1}, \ldots, X_m/s_{h_n}\}, \ h_1, \ldots, h_n \in I_2 \\ \exists \sigma : \forall j, 1 \leq j \leq n, \ X_j \theta_2 = X_{i_j} \theta_1 \sigma \end{array} \right\} \Rightarrow \begin{array}{l} (\|u_k\|)_{k \in I'} \square \{sol \mapsto sol_1 \times sol_2\} \\ \text{is a solution of } E' \\ \theta_1 \sigma = \{X_1/u_{k_1}, \ldots, X_m/u_{k_m}\}, \\ \{k_1, \ldots, k_m\} \subseteq I' \end{array}$$

Conditions on domains and codomains of substitutions which prevent renaming variable clashes between θ_1 and θ_2 are also required for allowing more precise implementations of the operation.

AI_VAR$(\beta, X = t) = \beta'$ and **AI_FUNC**$(\beta, X = t) = \beta'$. The **AI_VAR** operation unifies X and t in the abstract substitution β when t is a variable. The **AI_FUNC** operation is analogous in the case that t is a non-variable term.

$$\left. \begin{array}{l} \theta \in Cc(\beta) \\ \sigma \in mgu(X\theta, t\theta) \end{array} \right\} \Rightarrow \theta\sigma \in Cc(\beta').$$

RESTRG$(p(X_{i_1}, \ldots, X_{i_n}), \beta) = \beta'$. The **RESTRG** operation expresses an abstract substitution β on the parameters $X_{i_1}, \ldots, X_{i_n}$ of the call $p(X_{i_1}, \ldots, X_{i_n})$ in terms of the formal parameters $X_1, \ldots, X_n$.

$$\theta \in Cc(\beta) \Rightarrow \{X_1/X_{i_1}\theta, \ldots, X_n/X_{i_n}\theta\} \in Cc(\beta').$$

EXTG$(p(X_{i_1}, \ldots, X_{i_n}), \beta_1, \beta_2) = \beta'$. This operation is used to instantiate abstractly a clause substitution (i.e., β_1) with the result of the execution of a procedure call (i.e., β_2). Let β_1 and β_2 be two abstract substitutions such that $\{X_{i_1}, \ldots, X_{i_n}\} \subseteq \{X_1, \ldots, X_m\} = dom(\beta_1)$ and $\{X_1, \ldots, X_n\} = dom(\beta_2)$.

$$\left. \begin{array}{l} \theta_1 \in Cc(\beta_1) \\ \theta_2 \in Cc(\beta_2) \\ \exists\sigma : \forall j, 1 \leq j \leq n, \; X_j\theta_2 = X_{i_j}\theta_1\sigma \end{array} \right\} \Rightarrow \theta_1\sigma \in Cc(\beta').$$

Again, conditions on domains and codomains of substitutions are required.

5.3 The Initial Operation: INIT$(\beta, m) = B'$

This operation extends the abstract substitution β on the variables $X_1, \ldots, X_n$ $(0 \leq n)$ in the head of a clause cl to an abstract sequence B' on all the variables $X_1, \ldots, X_m$ $(n \leq m)$ in cl.

Specification. Let $\langle Y_1, \ldots, Y_{m-n} \rangle$ denote new free variables. INIT(β, m) produces an abstract sequence B' such that

$$\left. \begin{array}{l} \sigma \in Cc(\beta) \\ \sigma' = \sigma \circ \{X_{n+1}/Y_1, \ldots, X_m/Y_{m-n}\} \end{array} \right\} \Rightarrow (\sigma, \langle \sigma' \rangle) \in Cc(B').$$

Implementation. Let $\beta = \langle sv, frm, \alpha \rangle$ with $dom(frm) = I_p$. The implementation of the `INIT` operation applies the $\Re$-`INTR` operation in order to extend the α component of the abstract substitution. $\text{INIT}(\beta, m) = B'$ where $B' = \langle sv'_{in}, sv', frm', \alpha', E' \rangle$ is defined as follows:

- $sv'_{in} = sv$;
- $sv' = sv \cup \{X_{n+1} \mapsto p+1, \ldots, X_m \mapsto p+m-n\}$;
- $frm' = frm \cup \{p+1 \mapsto ?, \ldots, p+m-n \mapsto ?\}$;
- $\alpha' = \Re\text{-INTR}(\alpha, p, m-n)$;
- $E' = \{sol = 1\}$.

5.4 The Reduction Operation: REDUCE(B, n) = B'

It computes B' from the abstract sequence B on the variables $X_1, \ldots, X_m$ in the clause cl by restricting it to the variables $X_1, \ldots, X_n$ $(n \leq m)$ in the head.

Specification. Let S and S' be (possibly infinite) sequences of substitutions.

$$\left. \begin{array}{l} (\sigma, S) \in Cc(B) \\ S = \langle \sigma_1, \sigma_2, \ldots \rangle \\ S' = \langle \sigma_{1|\{X_1, \ldots, X_n\}}, \sigma_{2|\{X_1, \ldots, X_n\}}, \ldots \rangle \end{array} \right\} \Rightarrow (\sigma, S') \in Cc(B').$$

Implementation. Let $B = \langle sv_{in}, sv, frm, \alpha, E \rangle$, with $dom(frm) = I_p$. The implementation of the `REDUCE` operation uses the $\Re$-`PROJ` operation on the α component of the abstract sequence B and the $\Im$-`PROJ` operation on the equation set E. $\text{REDUCE}(B, n) = B'$ where $B' = \langle sv'_{in}, sv', frm', \alpha', E' \rangle$ is defined as follows:

- $sv'_{in} = sv_{in}$;
- $sv' = \{(X_i \mapsto j) \in sv \mid 0 \leq i \leq n\}$;
- $frm' = \{(i \mapsto frm_i) \in frm \mid i \in (codom(sv'_{in}) \cup codom(sv'))\} \cup \{(j \mapsto frm_j) \in frm \mid \exists i \in (codom(sv'_{in}) \cup codom(sv')) : j \text{ is reachable from } i \text{ by } frm\}$;
- $\alpha' = \Re\text{-PROJ}(\alpha, I_p \setminus dom(frm'))$;
- $E' = \Im\text{-PROJ}(E, I_p \setminus dom(frm'))$.

5.5 The Derivation Operation: DERIV_UNIF($B, X = t$) = B'

This operation computes B' from the abstract sequence B and the literal $X = t$.

Specification. Let S and S' be (possibly infinite) sequences of substitutions.

$$\left. \begin{array}{l} (\sigma, S) \in Cc(B) \\ \langle \sigma_{i_1}, \sigma_{i_2}, \ldots \rangle \text{ is the greatest subsequence of } S \\ \text{s.t. } mgu(X\sigma_{i_j}, t\sigma_{i_j}) \neq \emptyset, j \in J \\ \sigma'_{i_j} \in mgu(X\sigma_{i_j}, t\sigma_{i_j}), j \in J \\ S' = \langle \sigma_{i_1} \circ \sigma'_{i_1}, \sigma_{i_2} \circ \sigma'_{i_2}, \ldots \rangle \end{array} \right\} \Rightarrow (\sigma, S') \in Cc(B').$$

Implementation. Let $B = \langle sv_{in}, sv, frm, \alpha, E \rangle$. The implementation of the DERIV_UNIF operation requires the AI_VAR and AI_FUNC operations for unifying X and t in the abstract substitution $\langle sv, frm, \alpha \rangle$. If variable X occurs in t, the analyzer fails. Otherwise, DERIV_UNIF$(B, X = t) = B'$ where $B' = \langle sv'_{in}, sv', frm', \alpha', E' \rangle$ is defined as follows:

- $sv'_{in} = sv_{in}$;
- $\langle sv', frm', \alpha' \rangle = \begin{cases} \text{AI\_VAR}(\langle sv, frm, \alpha \rangle, X = t) & \text{if } t \text{ is a variable} \\ \text{AI\_FUNC}(\langle sv, frm, \alpha \rangle, X = t) & \text{if } t = f(\ldots); \end{cases}$
- $E' = \begin{cases} (tr\Box\{sol \mapsto sol\})^{>}(E) & \text{if either } X \text{ or } t \text{ are variables in } \alpha \\ convex\_hull((tr\Box\{sol \mapsto sol\})^{>}(E), \{0 \leq sol\}) & \text{otherwise.} \end{cases}$

where $tr : I \rightarrow I'$ and $\langle sv, frm, \alpha \rangle$ and $\langle sv', frm', \alpha' \rangle$ are parametrized by the indices in I and I', respectively.

5.6 The Derivation Operation: DERIV_NORMAL$(B, Beh_p, \tau) = B'$

This operation computes B' from the abstract sequence B, the behaviour Beh_p of the form $(p, [X_1, \ldots, X_n], Prepost)$ for the procedure call $p(X_{i_1}, \ldots, X_{i_n})$ with $i_1, \ldots, i_n \in \{1, \ldots, m\}$ and the renaming function τ assigning each X_j to X_{i_j}, $(1 \leq j \leq n)$. The DERIV_NORMAL operation is defined only if there exists at least one $\langle B_i, Se_i \rangle$ in $Prepost$ such that B satisfies the corresponding preconditions. Formally, we say that $B = \langle sv_{in}, sv, frm, \alpha, E \rangle$ satisfies the preconditions expressed in $B_i = \langle sv^i_{in}, sv^i, frm^i, \alpha^i, E^i \rangle$ iff

- RESTRG$(p(X_{i_1}, \ldots, X_{i_n}), \langle sv, frm, \alpha \rangle) \leq \langle sv^i_{in}, frm^i, \alpha^i \rangle$;
- and, in the case of a recursive call, $E \Rightarrow sz(sv(\tau(Se_i))) < sz(sv_{in}(Se_i))$ (termination criterion).

Specification. Assume that B satisfies the preconditions corresponding to the subset $\langle B_1, Se_1 \rangle, \ldots, \langle B_q, Se_q \rangle$ of $Prepost$. The following holds:

$$\left. \begin{array}{l} (\sigma, S) \in Cc(B) \\ S = \langle \sigma_1, \sigma_2, \ldots \rangle \\ (\sigma^j, S^j) \in Cc(B^j), \ 1 \leq j \leq q \\ S^j = \langle \sigma^j_1, \sigma^j_2, \ldots \rangle, \ 1 \leq j \leq q \\ S' = \langle (\sigma_1 \circ \sigma^1_1 \circ \tau^{-1}), (\sigma_1 \circ \sigma^1_2 \circ \tau^{-1}), ..., (\sigma_2 \circ \sigma^1_1 \circ \tau^{-1}), ..\rangle \end{array} \right\} \Rightarrow (\sigma, S') \in Cc(B').$$

Implementation. For all $i = 1, \ldots, q$, let $(tr^{\leq}_i, tr^{\geq}_i)$ be a constrained mapping with $tr_i : I_i \rightarrow I$ where B_i and B are parametrized by the indices in I_i and I, respectively. The implementation operation uses the greatest lower bound $\sqcap$ operator on abstract substitutions. It is as follows:

- $sv'_{in} = sv_{in}$;
- $\langle sv', frm', \alpha' \rangle = \text{EXTG}(p(X_{i_1}, \ldots, X_{i_n}), \langle sv, frm, \alpha \rangle, \sqcap^q_{j=1} \langle sv^j, frm^j, \alpha^j \rangle)$;
- $E' = \Im\_\text{EXTG}(p(X_{i_1}, \ldots, X_{i_n}), E, \bar{E})$

where $\bar{E} = convex\_hull((tr_1\Box\{sol \mapsto sol\})^{>}(E^1), \ldots, (tr_q\Box\{sol \mapsto sol\})^{>}(E^q))$.

6 Complexity Analysis

The analyzer can be used for performing complexity analysis of Prolog programs in the spirit of [9]. In the context of program development, the complexity analysis is useful to choose the most efficient version of a procedure.

We can estimate the time complexity of a procedure by using the information relative to the size relations and the number of solutions computed by the analyzer at each program point. It depends on the complexity of each literal called in the body of its clauses. Because of nondeterminism, the cost of such a literal depends on the number of solutions generated by the execution of previous literals in the body. Moreover, the cost of a recursive call depends on the depth of the recursion during the computation, which in turn depends on the size of its input arguments. Called predicates are analyzed before the corresponding callers. If two predicates call each other, then they are analyzed together.

The time complexity function for recursive procedures is given in the form of difference equations which are transformed into closed form functions (when possible) using difference equation solving techniques[10].

Let cl be a clause of the form $H \leftarrow L_1, \ldots, L_f$ ($f \geq 0$), $\bar{A}$ represents a (chosen) input size for cl, and $\bar{A}_i$ represents a (chosen) input size for L_i. Time complexity of cl can be expressed as

$$t_{cl}(\bar{A}) = \tau + \sum_{i=1}^{f} Max_i(\bar{A}_i)\, t_i(\bar{A}_i)$$

where τ is the time needed to unify the call with the head H of cl, $Max_i(\bar{A}_i)$ is an upper bound to the number of solutions generated by the literals preceding L_i, and $t_i(\bar{A}_i)$ is the time complexity of L_i.

Several criteria may be adopted to select the arguments that provide the input size for a procedure call. In [9], Debray et al. choose the arguments which are called with ground mode. Our proposal is to use the size expression information in the specification.

There are also different metrics that can be used as unit of time complexity, e.g., the number of resolutions, the number of unifications, or the number of instructions executed. We believe that the number of unification steps is a reasonable choice for estimating the time complexity of a procedure. In this case, since we assume that programs are normalized, i.e., heads are atoms containing distinct variables only, τ is equal to 1. Moreover, the time needed to solve an equality built-in which is called with at least one variable argument is equal to 1. When L is a ground list, and H and T are variables, three unification steps are needed for executing the built-in $L = [H|T]$. For instance, if $L = [a, b]$ then the following steps are performed: (1) replace $[a, b] = [H|T]$ by two equations $H = a$ and $T = [b]$, (2) bind H to a, (3) bind T to $[b]$. Finally, the time complexity for the built-in $list(T)$ is proportional to the size of its argument T. In fact, the execution of such a built-in has to traverse the whole data structure of the term

---

[10] For the automatic resolution of difference equations the reader is referred to [4, 13].

T in order to check whether it is a list. Here, we assume that the time complexity due to the execution of $list(T)$ is equal to the size of T plus 1 (noted $T + 1$).

Example 3. Let us now compute and compare the time complexities for the procedures $LP_2(select/3)$ and $LP_3(select/3)$ assuming they are called with the arguments being ground, variable and ground, respectively (they respect the second directionality in the specification depicted in Figure 1).

Complexity analysis for $LP_2(select/3)$. The time complexity for $LP_2(select/3)$ in terms of the size of the input ground argument L_s, noted $t_{select,2}$, can be estimated as follows. First, we compute the time complexity $t^i_{select,2}(0)$ for each clause called with L_s being the empty list. In the first clause, both head unification and the body literals may succeed, whereas, in the second clause, only head unification and the first body literal may succeed. This leads to

$$t^1_{select,2}(0) = 4 + (1 + T)$$
$$= 5 + L_s \qquad \text{(since, } T = L_s)$$
$$= 5 \qquad \text{(since the size of the empty list is 0)}$$
$$t^2_{select,2}(0) = 2.$$

Then, the time complexity $t^i_{select,2}(L_s)$ for each clause called with a non empty list L_s is estimated. Since L_s is ground, the cost of the built-in $L_s = [H|T_s]$ in the second clause is equal to 3. In this case both the size relation and the multiplicity information computed by the analyzer are used.

$$t^1_{select,2}(L_s) = 5 + T$$
$$= 5 + L_s \qquad \text{(since } T = L_s)$$
$$t^2_{select,2}(L_s) = 5 + t_{select,2}(T_s) + (T_s + 1)(T + 1)$$
$$= 5 + t_{select,2}(L_s - 1) + L_s(T + 1) \qquad \text{(since } T_s = L_s - 1)$$
$$= 5 + t_{select,2}(L_s - 1) + L_s(L_s + 1) \qquad \text{(since } T = L_s).$$

This leads to the system

$$t_{select,2}(0) \; = 7$$
$$t_{select,2}(L_s) = 10 + 2L_s + L_s^2 + t_{select,2}(L_s - 1)$$

which can be solved returning the time complexity

$$t_{select,2} \equiv \lambda x. \, 7 + \Sigma_{i=1}^{x}(10 + 2i + i^2) \qquad \text{(}x \text{ stands for the size of } L_s).$$

Complexity analysis for $LP_3(select/3)$. We compute now the time complexity for $LP_3(select/3)$. As above, when L_s is the empty list, we obtain

$$t^1_{select,3}(0) = 5$$
$$t^2_{select,3}(0) = 2.$$

In the case of a non empty list L_s, we compute

$$t^1_{select,3}(L_s) = 5 + L_s$$

$$t^2_{select,3}(L_s) = 5 + t_{select,3}(T_s)$$
$$= 5 + t_{select,3}(L_s - 1) \quad \text{(since } T_s = L_s - 1\text{)}.$$

We obtain the equation system

$$t_{select,3}(0) = 7$$
$$t_{select,2}(L_s) = 10 + L_s + t_{select,3}(L_s - 1)$$

which returns the time complexity

$$t_{select,3} \equiv \lambda x.\, 7 + \Sigma^x_{i=1}(10 + i) \quad \text{(x stands for the size of L_s)}.$$

Now, it is easy to compare the time complexities $t_{select,2}$ and $t_{select,3}$ that we have estimated for the procedures $LP_2(select/3)$ and $LP_3(select/3)$, respectively, only considering the second directionality in the specification depicted in Figure 1 with the second argument being a variable. The same reasoning can be applied for the other directionality in the specification of $select/3$. In that case, the time complexity can be estimated in terms of the size of the second argument. By combining these results, $LP_3(select/3)$ results to be more efficient than $LP_2(select/3)$.

7 Conclusion and Future Work

In this paper, an analyzer for Prolog procedures has been presented that verifies total correctness with respect to Devilles's formal specification. An automatic complexity analysis based on the information deduced by the analyzer was also proposed. We are conscious that the effective impact of these ideas can be evaluated only after the full implementation of the analyzer, which is in progress, now. The main goal of the implementation, based on the generic abstract interpretation algorithm GAIA [16], is to investigate the practicality of the automatic complexity analysis in the context of a logic procedure synthesizer that derives the most efficient procedure among the set of all correct ones.

References

1. A. Bossi, N. Cocco, and M. Fabris. Norms on Terms and Their Use in Proving Universal Termination of a Logic Program, Theoretical Computer Science, 124:297-328, 1994.
2. C. Braem, B. Le Charlier, S. Modart, and P. Van Hentenryck. Cardinality Analysis of Prolog. In Proc. Int'l Logic Programming Symposium, (ILPS'94), Ithaca, NY. The MIT Press, Cambridge, Mass., 1994.
3. K.L. Clark. Negation as Failure. In H. Gallaire and J. Minker editors, Advances in Data Base Theory, Plenum Press, New York, pp. 293-322, 1978.
4. J. Cohen and J. Katcoff. Symbolic solution of finite-difference equations. ACM Transactions on Mathematical Software, 3(3):261–271, 1977.
5. A. Cortesi, B. Le Charlier and P. van Hentenryck, Conceptual and Software Support for Abstract Domain Design: Generic Structural Domain and Open Product. Technical Report CS-93-13, Brown University, 1993.

6. A. Cortesi, B. Le Charlier and P. van Hentenryck, Combinations of Abstract Domains for Logic Programming, In Proc. 21th Annual ACM SIGPLAN-SIGACT Symposium on Principles of Programming Languages (POPL'94), ACM-Press. New York, pp. 227-239, 1994.

7. P. De Boeck and B. Le Charlier. Static Type Analysis of Prolog Procedures for Ensuring Correctness. In P. Deransart and J. Maluszyński, editors, Proc. Second Int'l Symposium on Programming Language Implementation and Logic Programming, (PLILP'90), LNCS 456, Springer-Verlag, Berlin, 1990.

8. P. De Boeck and B. Le Charlier. Mechanical Transformation of Logic Definitions Augmented with Type Information into Prolog Procedures: Some Experiments. In Proc. Int'l Workshop on Logic Program Synthesis and Transformation. (LOP-STR'93). Springer Verlag, July 1993.

9. S. K. Debray and N. W. Lin. Cost analysis of logic programs. ACM Transactions on Programming Languages and Systems, 15(5):826-875, 1993.

10. D. De Schreye, K. Verschaetse, and M. Bruynooghe. A Framework for analyzing the termination of definite logic programs with respect to call patterns. In H. Tanaka, editor, FGCS'92, 1992.

11. Y. Deville. *Logic Programming: Systematic Program Development.* Addison-Wesley, 1990.

12. J. Henrard and B. Le Charlier. FOLON: An Environment for Declarative Construction of Logic Programs (extended abstract). In M. Bruynooghe and M. Wirsing, editors, Proc. Fourth Int'l Workshop on Programming Language Implementation and Logic Programming (PLILP'92), LNCS 631 Springer-Verlag. pp. 237-231, 1992.

13. J. Ivie. Some MACSYMA programs for solving recurrence relations. ACM Transactions on Mathematical Software, 4(1):24–33, 1978.

14. B. Le Charlier, and S. Rossi. Automatic Derivation of Totally Correct Prolog Procedures from Logic Descriptions. Research Report RP-95-009, University of Namur.

15. B. Le Charlier, S. Rossi, and P. Van Hentenryck. An Abstract Interpretation Framework which Accurately Handles Prolog Search-Rule and the Cut. In Proc. Int. Logic Programming Symposium, (ILPS'94), Ithaca, NY. The MIT Press. Cambridge, Mass., 1994.

16. B. Le Charlier and P. Van Hentenryck. Experimental evaluation of a generic abstract interpretation algorithm for Prolog. ACM Transactions on Programming Languages and Systems, 16(1), pp. 35–101,1994.

17. C. Leclère and B. Le Charlier. Two Dual Abstract Operations to Duplicate. Eliminate, Equalize, Introduce and Rename Place-Holders Occurring Inside Abstract Descriptions. Research Paper N. RP-96-028, University of Namur, Belgium. September 1996.

18. J. W. Lloyd. Foundations of Logic Programming. Springer-Verlag, Berlin. 1987. Second edition.

19. P. van Hentenryck, A. Cortesi, and B. Le Charlier, Evaluation of the Domain Prop. The Journal of Logic Programming 23(3):237-278, 1995.

Logic Program Specialisation:
How to Be More Specific

Michael Leuschel* and Danny De Schreye**

K.U. Leuven, Department of Computer Science
Celestijnenlaan 200A, B-3001 Heverlee, Belgium
e-mail: {michael,dannyd}@cs.kuleuven.ac.be

Abstract. Standard partial deduction suffers from several drawbacks when compared to top-down abstract interpretation schemes. Conjunctive partial deduction, an extension of standard partial deduction, remedies one of those, namely the lack of side-ways information passing. But two other problems remain: the lack of success-propagation as well as the lack of inference of global success-information. We illustrate these drawbacks and show how they can be remedied by combining conjunctive partial deduction with an abstract interpretation technique known as more specific program construction. We present a simple, as well as a more refined integration of these methods. Finally we illustrate the practical relevance of this approach for some advanced applications, where it surpasses the precision of current abstract interpretation techniques.

The full version of this paper can be found in [1].

References

1. M. Leuschel and D. Schreye. Logic program specialisation: How to be more specific. In H. Kuchen and S.D. Swierstra, editors, *Proceedings of the International Symposium on Programming Languages, Implementations, Logics and Programs (PLILP'96)*, LNCS 1140, pages 137–151, Aachen, Germany, September 1996. Springer Verlag. Extended version as Technical Report CW 232, K.U. Leuven. Accessible via http://www.cs.kuleuven.ac.be/~lpai.

---

* Supported by the Belgian GOA "Non-Standard Applications of Abstract Interpretation"
** Senior Research Associate of the Belgian Fund for Scientific Research

Conjunctive Partial Deduction in Practice

Jesper Jørgensen* Michael Leuschel** Bern Martens***

K.U. Leuven, Department of Computer Science
Celestijnenlaan 200A, B-3001 Heverlee, Belgium
e-mail: {jesper,michael,bern}@cs.kuleuven.ac.be

Abstract. Recently, partial deduction of logic programs has been extended to conceptually embed folding. To this end, partial deductions are no longer computed of single atoms, but rather of entire conjunctions; Hence the term "conjunctive partial deduction".

Conjunctive partial deduction aims at achieving unfold/fold-like program transformations such as tupling and deforestation within fully automated partial deduction. However, its merits greatly surpass that limited context: Also other major efficiency gains can be obtained through considerably improved side-ways information propagation.

In this paper, we present a first investigation of conjunctive partial deduction in practice. We describe the concrete options used in the implementation(s), look at abstraction in a practical Prolog context, include and discuss an extensive set of benchmark results. ¿From these, we can conclude that conjunctive partial deduction can indeed pay off in practice, beating its conventional precursor on a number of small to medium size programs. However, controlling it in a perfect way proves far from obvious, and a range of challenging open problems remain as topics for further research.

1 Introduction

Partial deduction [29, 17, 9] is a well-known technique for automatic specialisation of logic programs. It takes as input a program and a (partially instantiated) query and returns as output a program tuned towards answering the given query and any of its instances. The process proceeds by building incomplete SLD(NF)-trees for the goal atoms, assembling specialised clauses from the leaves, and subsequently doing likewise for (new) atoms occurring in these clauses.

An important feature (in fact, a bug, one might say) lies in the fact that specialised clauses are produced for individual, separate atoms. As a consequence, partial deduction is unable to achieve typical transformations involving elimination of redundant variables [35, 36, 37], as exemplified by the query

---

* Partially supported by the HCM Network "Logic Program Synthesis and Transformation", and partially by the Belgian GOA "Non-Standard Applications of Abstract Interpretation".

** Supported by the Belgian GOA "Non-Standard Applications of Abstract Interpretation"

*** Partially supported as a postdoctoral fellow by the K.U.Leuven Research Council, Belgium, and partially by the HCM Network "Logic Program Synthesis and Transformation", contract nr. CHRX-CT-93-00414, University of Padova, Italy.

$\leftarrow da(Xs, Ys, Zs, R)$ and the following program:

$$da(Xs, Ys, Zs, R) \qquad \leftarrow app(Xs, Ys, T), app(T, Zs, R).$$
$$app([\ ], Ys, Ys).$$
$$app([H|Xs], Ys, [H|Zs]) \leftarrow app(Xs, Ys, Zs).$$

The desired, but "classically" unachievable transformed program is:

$$da([\ ], Ys, Zs, R) \qquad \leftarrow app(Ys, Zs, R).$$
$$da([X|Xs], Ys, Zs, [X|Rs]) \leftarrow da(Xs, Ys, Zs, Rs).$$
$$app([\ ], Ys, Ys).$$
$$app([X|Xs], Ys, [X|Zs]) \qquad \leftarrow app(Xs, Ys, Zs).$$

To overcome such limitations, [24, 18] develop *conjunctive partial deduction*. As the name suggests, this extension of convential partial deduction no longer automatically splits up goals into constituting atoms, but attempts to specialise the program with respect to (entire) conjunctions of atoms. Sometimes, splitting a goal into subparts is still necessary to guarantee termination, but, in general, it is avoided when the latter is not the case. The necessary extensions to the basic framework [29] are elaborated in [24], while [18] discusses control aspects and [25] studies the integration with bottom-up abstract interpretation techniques. Finally, [27] develops a supporting transformation to remove remaining useless variables from programs produced by conjunctive partial deduction proper. Some essentials are (mostly) informally recapitulated below; For a formal exposé, we refer to [24, 18, 25, 27].

The resulting technique incorporates part of the unfold/fold technology [8, 41, 32], and bears some relationship to automated methods proposed in [35, 36, 37]. It also approaches more closely techniques for the specialisation and transformation of functional programs, such as deforestation [44], and supercompilation [42, 40]. Especially the latter constituted, together with unfold/fold transformations, a source of inspiration for the conception and design of conjunctive partial deduction.

In the present paper, we endeavour to put conjunctive partial deduction on trial. We use a large set of small and medium size benchmark programs taken from [22]. Together, we claim, they give a good impression of specialisation and transformation obtained by various methods on a declarative subset of Prolog. We will be particularly concerned with the resulting speedups, and also pay attention to the complexity of the transformation process itself. (In order for a method to be practically viable, it is not sufficient that it terminates "in theory"; It should actually do so within reasonable time bounds, i.e. steer clear of combinatorial explosions.) We will endeavour to make this paper as much as possible self-contained, or at least understandable in broad lines without the reader having to consult numerous other papers. However, since experiments and their results are the true subject matter of the current paper, and these experiments have been performed using methods constituted of diverse elements presented in more detail elsewhere, we will occasionally be forced to refer the reader seeking more technical details on the transformations involved to these earlier sources.

In Section 2 then, we do briefly recapitulate core notions from "classical" as well as conjunctive partial deduction. Section 3 brushes up a well-known termination problem connected to Prolog's left-to-right (unfair) computation rule, as well as some other aspects with a slightly pedestrian, "get things going in practice" flavour, not addressed before in conjunctive partial deduction in a general logic programming setting [24, 18]. Next, Sections 4 and 5 constitute the main body of the paper, describing the particular transformation method(s) and benchmarks used, showing the results, and highlighting the most interesting aspects of the latter.

2 Background

We assume the reader to be familiar with the basic concepts of logic programming and ("conventional" or "classical" or "standard") partial deduction, as presented in [28] and [29]. Throughout the paper, we only consider definite programs and goals.

2.1 Controlling Conventional Partial Deduction

In recent years, following the foundational paper by Lloyd and Shepherdson [29], considerable progress has been achieved on the issue of controlling automated partial deduction. In that context, a clear conceptual distinction was introduced between local and global control [17, 31].

The former deals with the construction of (possibly incomplete) SLD-trees for the atoms to be partially deduced. In essence, it consists of an unfolding strategy. Requirements are: termination, good specialisation, avoiding search space explosion as well as work duplication. Approaches have been based on one or more of the following elements:

- determinacy [15, 16]
  Only (except once) select atoms that match a single clause head. The strategy can be refined with a so-called "look-ahead" to detect failure at a deeper level. Methods solely based on this heuristic, apart from not guaranteeing termination, tend not to worsen a program, but are often somewhat too conservative.
- well-founded measures [7, 30]
  Imposing some (essentially) well-founded order on selected atoms guarantees termination, but, on its own, can lead to overly eager unfolding.
- homeomorphic embedding [40, 26]
  Instead of well-founded ones, well-quasi-orders can be used [38, 2]. Homeomorphic embedding on selected atoms has recently gained popularity as the basis for such an order.

At the global control level, closedness [28] is ensured and the degree of polyvariance is decided: For which atoms should partial deductions be produced? Obviously, again, termination is an important issue, as well as obtaining a good overall specialisation. The following ingredients are important in recent approaches:

- characteristic trees [15, 16, 23, 21]

  A characteristic tree is an abstraction of an SLD-tree. It registers which atoms have been selected and which clauses were used for resolution. As such, it provides a good characterisation of the computation and specialisation connected with a certain atom (or goal). Its use in partial deduction lies in the control of polyvariance: Produce one specialised definition per characteristic tree encountered.

- global trees [31, 26]

  Partially deduced atoms (or characteristic atoms, see below) can be registered in a tree structure that is kept well-founded or well-quasi-ordered to ensure (global) termination. In general, doing so, while maintaining closedness, requires abstraction (generalisation).

- characteristic atoms [21, 26]

  Recent work has shown that the best control of polyvariance can be obtained not on the basis of either syntactical structure (atoms) or specialisation behaviour (characteristic trees) separately, but rather through a combination of both. Such pairs consisting of an atom and an associated (imposed) characteristic tree are called *characteristic atoms*.

Finally, subsidiary transformations, applicable in a post-processing phase, have been proposed, e.g. to remove certain superfluous structures [14, 1] or to reduce unnecessary polyvariance [26].

2.2 Conjunctive Partial Deduction

As explained in Section 1, conjunctive partial deduction has been designed with the aim of overcoming some limitations inherent in its conventional relative. The essential aspect lies in the joint treatment of entire conjunctions of atoms, connected through shared variables, at the global level (complemented, of course, with some renaming to deliver program clauses). Basically, this can be seen as a refinement of abstraction with respect to the conventional case. Indeed, in conjunctive partial deduction, a conjunction can be abstracted by either splitting it into subconjunctions, or generalising syntactic structure, or through a combination of both. See also e.g. [36] for a related generalisation operation in the context of an unfold/fold transformation technique. In classical partial deduction, on the other hand, any conjunction is always split (i.e. abstracted) into its constituent atoms before lifting the latter to the global level. Details can be found in [24, 18].

Apart from this aspect, the conventional control notions described above also apply in a conjunctive setting. Notably, the concept of characteristic atoms can be generalised to *characteristic conjunctions*, which are just pairs consisting of a conjunction and an associated characteristic tree.

3 Conjunctive Partial Deduction for Pure Prolog

We will for the remainder of the paper only be concerned with conjunctive partial deduction for pure Prolog. This means, besides disallowing non-pure features, that we suppose a static (unfair) computation rule, e.g. left-to-right, and that we will demand preservation of termination under that computation rule (in the sequel assumed "left-to-right", unless explicitly stated otherwise).

3.1 Unfolding rules

In the given context, determinate unfolding has been proposed as a way to ensure that partial deduction will never actually worsen the behaviour of the program [15, 16]. Indeed, even fairly simple examples suffice to show that non-leftmost, non-determinate unfolding may duplicate (large amounts of) work in the transformation result. Leftmost, non-determinate unfolding, usually allowed to compensate for the all too cautious nature of purely determinate unfolding, avoids the more drastic deterioration pitfalls, but can still lead to multiplying unifications.

3.2 Splitting and Abstraction

A termination problem specific to conjunctive partial deduction lies in the possible appearance of ever growing conjunctions at the global level (see Section 3 of [30] for a comparable phenomenon in the context of local control). To cope with this, abstraction [17, 26, 18] provides for the possibility of *splitting* a conjunction into several parts, thus producing *subconjunctions* of the original one. The details can be found in [18]. Let us present a simple example. Consider the two conjunctions Q_1 and Q_2:

$$Q_1 = p(X, Y) \wedge q(Y, Z)$$

$$Q_2 = p(f(X), Y) \wedge r(Z, R) \wedge q(Y, Z)$$

If specialisation of Q_1 leads to specialisation of Q_2, there is a danger of non-termination. The method proposed in [18] prevents this by first splitting Q_2 into $Q = p(f(X), Y) \wedge q(Y, Z)$ and $r(Z, R)$ and subsequently taking the msg of Q_1 and Q. As a result, only $r(Z, R)$ will be considered for further specialisation.

Now, given a left-to-right computation rule, the above operation alters the sequence in which goals are executed. Indeed, the p- and q-subgoals will henceforth be treated jointly (they will probably be renamed to a single atom). Consequently, there is no way an r-call can be interposed. From a purely declarative point of view, there is of course no reason why goals should not be interchanged, but under a fixed (unfair) computation rule, however, such *non-contiguous* splitting can worsen program performance, and even destroy termination.

In fact, the latter point has already been addressed in the context of unfold/fold transformations (see e.g. [6, 3, 5, 4]). To the best of our knowledge, however, no satisfactory solutions, suitable to be incorporated into a fully automatic system, have yet been proposed. Below, we present an example by way of illustration for the benefit of those readers who are not yet familiar with the phenomenon from the work on unfold/fold transformations.

Consider the following program:

```
flipallint(XT,TT) :- flip(XT,TT),allint(TT).
flip(leaf(X),leaf(X)).
flip(tree(XT,Info,YT),tree(FYT,Info,FXT)) :- flip(XT,FXT), flip(YT,FYT).
allint(leaf(X)) :- int(X).
allint(tree(L,Info,R)) :- int(Info), allint(L), allint(R).
int(0).
int(s(X)) :- int(X).
```

The deforested version, obtained by conjunctive partial deduction using the control of [18], would be:

```
flipallint(leaf(X),leaf(X)) :- int(X).
flipallint(tree(XT,Info,YT),tree(FYT,Info,FXT)) :-
        int(Info), flipallint(XT,FXT), flipallint(YT,FYT).
```

where the transformed version of int is unchanged. Under a left-to-right computation rule, the query flipallint(tree(leaf(Z),0,leaf(a)),Res) terminates with the original, but not with the deforested program.

Contiguous Splitting For this reason, in the benchmarks below, we have in all but two cases *limited splitting to be contiguous*, that is, we split into contiguous subconjunctions only. (This can be compared with the outruling of goal switching in [3].) As a consequence, compared to the basic (declarative) method in [18], on the one hand, some opportunities for fruitful program transformation are left unexploited, but, on the other hand, Prolog programs are significantly less prone to actual deterioration rather than optimisation. There are many variations on how to define contiguous subconjunctions. In [18], a non-contiguous method for splitting was presented, based on *maximal connected subconjunctions*[4]:

Definition 1. (maximal connected subconjunctions) Given a conjunction $Q \equiv A_1 \wedge \ldots \wedge A_n$[5], the collection mcs$(Q) =_r \{Q_1, \ldots, Q_m\}$ of *maximal connected subconjunctions* is defined through the following conditions:

1. $Q =_r Q_1 \wedge \ldots \wedge Q_m$
2. If a variable X occurs in both A_i and A_j where $i < j$, then A_i occurs before A_j in the same Q_k.

We can define the basic notion of maximal contiguous connected subconjunctions in a similar way:

Definition 2. (maximal contiguous connected subconjunctions) For a given conjunction $Q \equiv A_1 \wedge \ldots \wedge A_n$, the collection mccs$(Q) = \{Q_1, \ldots, Q_m\}$ of *maximal contiguous connected subconjunctions* is defined through the following conditions:

---

[4] This notion is closely related to those of "variable-chained sequence" and "block" of atoms used in [35, 36].

[5] In this definition and the remainder of this paper, $=_r$ is modulo reordering and $\equiv$ is not.

1. $Q \equiv Q_1 \wedge \ldots \wedge Q_m$
2. $mcs(Q_i) =_r \{Q_i\}$ for all $i \leq m$
3. $Vars(Q_i) \cap Vars(Q_{i+1}) = \emptyset$ for all $i < m$

The conjunctions $p(X) \wedge p(Y) \wedge q(X, Y)$, $r(Z, T)$ and $p(Y)$ are the maximal contiguous connected subconjunctions (mccs) of $p(X) \wedge p(Y) \wedge q(X, Y) \wedge r(Z, T) \wedge p(Y)$. Other definitions of contiguous subconjunctions could disallow built-ins and/or negative literals in the subconjunctions or allow unconnected atoms inside the subconjunctions, e.g. like $p(S)$ in $p(X) \wedge p(S) \wedge q(X, Y)$.

Static conjunctions Actually, the global control regime used in some of our experiments deviates from the one described by [18] in one further aspect. Even though abstraction (splitting) ensures that the length of conjunctions (the number of its atoms) remains finite, there are (realistic) examples where the length gets very large. This, combined with the use of homeomorphic embeddings (or lexicographical orderings for that matter), leads to very large global trees, large residual programs and a bad transformation time complexity.

Take for example global trees just containing atomic goals with predicates of arity k and having as argument just ground terms $s(s(\ldots s(0)\ldots))$ representing the natural numbers up to a limit n. Then we can construct branches in the global tree having as length $l = (n + 1)^k$. Indeed for $n = 1, k = 2$ we can construct a branch of length $2^2 = 4$: $p(s(0), s(0)), p(s(0), 0), p(0, s(0)), p(0, 0)$ while respecting homeomorphic embedding or lexicographical ordering.[6]

When going to conjunctive partial deduction the number of argument positions k is no longer bounded, meaning that, even when the terms are restricted to some natural depth, the size of the global tree can be arbitrarily large. Such a kind of explosion can actually occur for realistic examples, notably for meta-interpreters manipulating the ground representation and specialised for partially known queries (see the benchmarks, e.g. groundunify.complex and liftsolve.db2).

One way to ensure that this does not happen is to limit the conjunctions that may occur at the global level. For this we have introduced the notion of *static conjunctions*. A static conjunction is any conjunction that can be obtained by *non-recursive* unfolding of the goal to be partially evaluated (or a generalisation thereof). The idea is then, by a static analysis, to compute a set of static conjunctions S from the program and the goal, and then during partial deduction only to allow conjunctions (at the global level) that are abstracted by one of the elements of S. This is ensured by further splitting of the disallowed conjunctions. (A related technique is used in [36].) In our implementation, we use a very simpleminded way of approximating the set of static conjunctions, based on counting the maximum number of occurences of each predicate symbol in a

---

[6] Of course, by not restricting oneself to natural numbers up to a limit n we can construct arbitrarily large branches starting from the same $p(s(0), s(0))$: $p(s(0), s(0)), p(s(s(\ldots s(0)\ldots))), 0), p(s(s(\ldots 0\ldots))), 0), \ldots$

conjunction in the program or in the goal to be partially deduced. Then S approximates all conjunctions where each predicate occurs at most as many times as specified by its associated maximum. In the example above, the maximum for flip and allint is 2, while for the other predicates it is 1.

Another approach, investigated in the experiments, is to avoid using homeomorphic embeddings on conjunctions, but go to a less explosive strategy, e.g. requiring a decrease in the total term size. As we will see later in the benchmarks (e.g. Csc-th-t in Table 4), the combination of these two methods leads to reasonable transformation times and code size while maintaining good specialisation.

4   The System and the Implemented Methods

The partial evaluation system we used is called ECCE and is developed by Leuschel [22]. The system consists of a generic algorithm to which one may add one's own methods for unfolding, partitioning, abstraction, etc. All built-ins handled by the system are supposed to be declarative (e.g. ground is supposed to be delayed until ground,...). Some of the built-ins that are handled are: =, is, $<$, $=<$, $<$, $>=$, nonvar, ground, number, atomic, call, $\setminus==$, $\setminus=$. In the following we will give a short description of the different methods that we used in the experiments.

4.1   The Algorithm

The system implements a variant of the concrete algorithm described in [18]. The algorithm uses a global tree γ with nodes labeled with (characteristic) conjunctions. When a conjunction Q gets unfolded, then the conjunctions in the bodies of the resultants of Q (maybe further split by the abstraction) are added as child nodes (leaves) of Q in the global tree.

Algorithm

Input: a program P and a goal $\leftarrow Q$
Output: a set of conjunctions $\mathcal{Q}$
Initialisation: $i := 0$; $\gamma_0 :=$ the global tree with a single node, labeled Q
repeat

    1. for all leaves L in γ_i labeled with conjunction Q_L and for all bodies B in $U(P, Q_L)$ do:
        (a) $\mathcal{Q} = partition(B)$
        (b) for all Q_i in $\mathcal{Q}$ do:
            i. remove Q_i from $\mathcal{Q}$
            ii. if $whistle(\gamma_i, L, Q_i)$ then $\mathcal{Q} = \mathcal{Q} \cup abstract(\gamma_i, L, Q_i)$
                elseif Q_i is not an instance of a node in γ_i **then** add a child L' to L with label Q_i
    2. $i := i + 1$
until $\gamma_i = \gamma_{i-1}$
output the set of nodes in γ_i

The function U does the local unfolding. It takes a program and a conjunction and produces a set of (generalised) resultants: $Q \leftarrow Q'$. The function *partition* does the initial splitting of the bodies into maximal contiguous connected sub-conjunctions (or mcs's or plain atoms for standard partial deduction). Then for each of the subconjunctions it is checked if there is a risk of non-termination. This is done by the function *whistle*. The whistle will look at the labels (conjunctions) on the branch in the global tree to which the new conjunction Q_i is going to be added as a child and if Q_i is "larger" than one of these, it returns true. Finally, if the "whistle blows" for some subconjunction Q_i, then Q_i is abstracted by using the function *abstract*. After the algorithm terminates the residual program is obtained from the output by unfolding and renaming (details can be found in [24, 18, 27]).

Concrete Settings We have concentrated on four local unfolding rules:

1. safe determinate (t-det.): do determinate unfolding allowing one left-most non-determinate step using homeomorphic embedding with covering ancestors of selected atoms to ensure finiteness.

2. safe determinate indexed unfolding (l-idx). The difference with t-det. is that more than one left-most non-determinate unfolding step is allowed. However only "indexed" unfolding is then allowed, i.e. it is ensured that the unification work that might get duplicated is captured by the Prolog indexing (which may depend on the particular compiler). Again, homeomorphic embeddings are used to ensure finiteness.

3. homeomorphic embedding and reduction of search space (h-rs): non-left-most unfolding is allowed if the search space is reduced by the unfolding. In other words, an atom $p(\bar{t})$ can be selected if it does not match all the clauses defining p. Again, homeomorphic embeddings are used to ensure finiteness. Note that, in contrast to 2 and 3, this method might worsen the backtracking behaviour.

4. "Mixtus"-like unfolding (x): See [38] for further details (we used $max\_rec = 2$, $max\_depth = 2$, $maxfinite = 7$, $maxnondeterm = 10$ and only allowed non-determinate unfolding when no user predicates were to the left of the selected literal).

The measures that we have used in whistles are the following:

1. homeomorphic embedding (homeo.) on the conjunctions
2. termsize on the conjunctions
3. homeomorphic embedding (homeo.) on the conjunctions and homeomorphic embedding on the associated characteristic trees
4. termsize on the conjunctions and homeomorphic embedding on the characteristic trees

Abstraction is always done by possibly splitting conjunctions further and then taking the msg as explained in Subsection 3.2. One method (SE-hh-x) also uses the ecological partial deduction principle [21] to ensure preservation of characteristic trees upon generalisation. (Splitting considerably complicates this issue. Further research is therefore necessary before it can be properly dealt with in a conjunctive partial deduction setting.) The methods we have used for partitioning are based either on splitting into mcs's (non-contiguous) or into maximal contiguous connected subconjunctions. Additionally we may limit the size of conjunctions by using static conjunctions.

All unfolding rules were complemented by a simple more specific transformation in the style of SP [16] and allow the selection of ground negative literals. Post-processing removal of unnecessary polyvariance [26], determinate post-unfolding as well as redundant argument filtering [27] were always enabled.

A further extension wrt [21, 26] relates to built-ins which are also registered in the characteristic tree.

5 Benchmarks and Conclusion

For the experimentation, we have adopted a practical approach and measured what a normal user sees. In particular, we do not count the number of inferences (the cost of which varies a lot) or some other abstract measure, but the actual execution time and size of compiled code (using Prolog by BIM 4.0.12).

The benchmark programs are taken from [22]; Short descriptions are given in Appendix A. Tables showing the results of the experiments, as well as further details, can be found in Appendix B. The results are summarised in Tables 1 and 2. We also compared to the existing systems MIXTUS [38], PADDY [34] and SP [16, 17]. In Table 1, transformation times (TT) of ECCE and MIXTUS also include time to write to file. Time for SP does not and for PADDY we do not know. The ∞ means "real" or abnormal termination (crash or heap overflow) occurred for some examples. > 12h, on the other hand, signifies that the execution had not terminated after 12 hours (see Appendix B for a more precise explanation). The unfolding used by SP does not seem to be simply determinate unfolding (look e.g. at the results for *depth.lam*), hence the "?" in Table 1.

5.1 Analysing the Results

One conclusion of the experiments is that conjunctive partial deduction (using determinate unfolding and contiguous splitting) pays off while guaranteeing no (serious) slowdown. In fact, the cases where there is a slowdown are some of those that were designed to show the effect of deforestation (flip, match-append, maxlength and upto.sum2). Two of these are handled well by the methods using non-contiguous splitting. On the fully unfoldable benchmarks, S-hh-t gave a speedup of 2.57 while Csc-hh-t achieved a speedup of 5.90, illustrating nicely that conjunctive partial deduction diminishes the need for agressive unfolding. Notice that Mixtus and Paddy have very agressive unfolding rules and fare well on the fully unfoldable benchmarks. However, on the non-fully unfoldable ones, even S-hh-t, based on determinate unfolding, is already better. The best standard partial deduction method, for both runtime and (apart from SP) code size, is SE-hh-x. Still, compared to any of the standard partial deduction methods, our

System	Partition			Whistle		Unf	Total Speedup	Total TT (min)
	C/S	S/D	Contig	Conj	Chtree			
Cdc-hh-t	Conj	dyn.	contig	homeo	homeo	t-det	1.93	62.46
Csc-hh-t	Conj	static	contig	homeo	homeo	t-det	1.89	29.72
Csc-th-t	Conj	static	contig	termsize	homeo	t-det	1.92	5.95
Csc-hn-t	Conj	static	contig	homeo	none	t-det	1.89	35.49
Csc-tn-t	Conj	static	contig	termsize	none	t-det	1.76	2.67
Cdc-th-t	Conj	dyn.	contig	termsize	homeo	t-det	1.96	31.18
Csc-th-li	Conj	static	contig	termsize	homeo	l-idx	1.89	$> 12h + 12.95$
Cdm-hh-t	Conj	dyn.	mcs	homeo	homeo	t-det	2.00	$> 12h + 110.49$
Csm-hh-h	Conj	static	mcs	homeo	homeo	h-rs	0.77	$> 12h + 73.55$
S-hh-t	Std	-	-	homeo	homeo	t-det	1.56	3.00
S-hh-li	Std	-	-	homeo	homeo	l-idx	1.65	14.95
SE-hh-x	Std-Eco	-	-	homeo	homeo	mixtus	1.76	2.96
Mixtus	Std	-	-	mixtus	none	mixtus	1.65	$\infty + 2.71$
Paddy	Std	-	-	mixtus	none	mixtus	1.65	$\infty + 0.31$
SP	Std	-	-	pred =	=	det ?	1.34	$3*\infty + 1.99$

Table 1. Overview of all methods

System	Total Speedup	Weighted Speedup	Fully Unfoldable Speedup	Not Fully Unfoldable Speedup	Average Relative Size (orig = 1)
Cdc-hh-t	1.93	2.44	5.90	1.66	2.39
Csc-hh-t	1.89	2.38	5.90	1.62	2.02
Csc-th-t	1.92	2.44	5.90	1.65	1.68
Csc-hn-t	1.89	2.40	5.90	1.62	1.67
Csc-tn-t	1.76	2.18	4.48	1.54	1.53
Cdc-th-t	1.96	<u>2.49</u>	5.90	1.69	2.27
Csc-th-li	1.89	2.38	7.07	1.61	1.79
Cdm-hh-t	<u>2.00</u>	2.39	5.90	<u>1.72</u>	3.17
Csm-hh-h	0.77	0.52	6.16	0.63	3.91
S-hh-t	1.56	1.86	2.57	1.42	1.60
S-hh-li	1.65	2.09	4.88	1.42	1.61
SE-hh-x	1.76	2.24	<u>8.36</u>	1.48	1.46
Mixtus	1.65	2.11	8.13	1.38	1.67
Paddy	1.65	2.00	8.12	1.38	2.49
SP	1.34	1.54	2.08	1.23	<u>1.18</u>

Table 2. Short summary of the results (higher speedup and lower code size is better, the notion "weighted" is explained in Appendix B)

conjunctive methods (except for Csm-hh-h, Csc-tn-t, which are not meant to be competitors anyway) have a better average speedup.

Furthermore, the experiments also show that the process of performing conjunctive partial deduction can be made efficient, especially if one uses determinate unfolding combined with a termsize measure on conjunctions (Csc-th-t, and also Csc-tn-t) in which case the average transformation time is comparable with that of standard partial deduction. Of course only further experiments may show how the transformation times grow whith the size of programs. In fact, the system was not written with efficiency as a first concern and there is a lot of room for improvement on this point.

Next, the experiments demonstrate that using the termsize measure instead of homeomorphic embedding on conjunctions clearly improves the average transformation time without loosing too much specialisation. But they also show that if one uses the termsize measure, then the use of characteristic trees becomes vital (compare Csc-th-t and Csc-tn-t). However, methods with homeomorphic embedding on conjunctions (e.g. Csc-hn-t), do not seem to benefit from adding homeomorphic embedding on characteristic trees as well (e.g. Csc-hh-t). This, at first sight somewhat surprising phenomenon, can be explained by the fact that, for the benchmarks at hand, the homeomorphic embedding on conjunctions, in a global tree setting, is already a very generous whistle, and, in the absence of negation (see the discussions in [26]), a growing of the conjunction will often result in a growing of the characteristic tree as well. Even more surprisingly, on the other hand, nevertheless adding embedding checks on characteristic trees does *not* result in larger overall transformation times. Quite on the contrary: it even reduces them!

Comparing Csc-hh-t and Cdc-hh-t, one can see that using static conjunctions also pays off in terms of faster transformation time without much loss of specialisation. If one looks more closely at the results for both methods, then the speedup and the transformation times are more or less the same for the two methods except for the rather few cases where static conjunctions were really needed: groundunify.complex, liftsolve.db2, regexp.r2, regexp.r3, remove2 and imperative.power. For those cases, the loss of speedup due to the use of static conjunctions was small or insignificant while the improvement in transformation time was considerable.

Comparing Csc-th-li to Csc-th-t, one sees that indexed unfolding does not seem to have a definite effect for conjunctive partial deduction. In some cases, the speedup is better, and in some other cases worse. Only for relative.lam is indexed unfolding much better than determinate, but this corresponds to a case where the program can be completely unfolded. This is of course partially due to the fact that conjunctive partial deduction diminishes the need for aggressive unfolding. For standard partial deduction however, indexed (as well as "Mixtus"-like) unfolding leads to a substantial improvement over determinate unfolding. Note that the "Mixtus"-like unfolding used by SE-hh-x does not seem to pay off for conjunctive partial deduction at all. In a preliminary experiment, the method Csc-th-x only produced a total speedup of 1.69, i.e. only slightly better than MIXTUS or PADDY and worse than SE-hh-x. Still, for some examples, it would be highly beneficial to allow more than "just" determinate unfolding (notably `depth.lam`, `grammar.lam` and `relative.lam` — examples where SE-hh-x performs much better than all the conjunctive methods based on determinate unfolding). In future work, we will examine how more aggressive unfolding rules can be more sucessfully used for conjunctive partial deduction.

For some benchmarks, the best speedup is obtained by the non-safe methods Cdm-hh-t or Csm-hh-h based on non-contiguous mcs splitting. But one can also see that these methods may in some cases lead to a considerable slowdown (`missionaries` and `remove`) and sometimes even to errors (`imperative.power` and `upto.sum1`) because the point at which built-ins are evaluated has been changed. This shows that methods based on non-contiguous splitting can lead to better specialisation due to *tupling* and *deforestation*, but that we need some method to control the splitting and unfolding to ensure that no slowdown, or change in termination can occur.

5.2 Conclusion

It looks like conjunctive partial deduction can be performed with acceptable efficiency and pays off with respect to standard partial deduction, but there are still many unsolved problems. Indeed, the speedups compared to standard partial deduction are significant on average, but less dramatic and less systematic than we initially expected. Apparently, this is partly due to the fact that non-contiguous conjunctive partial deduction on the one hand often leads to serious slowdowns and is not really practical for most applications, while contiguous conjunctive partial deduction on the other hand is in general too weak to deforest or tuple datastructures.

Therefore it is vital, if one wants to more heavily exploit the advantages of conjunctive partial deduction, to add non-contiguous splitting (i.e. reordering) in a safe way which guarantees no serious slowdown. A first step towards a solution is presented in [5], but it remains quite restrictive and considers only ground queries. Another, more pragmatic approach might be based on making use of some mode system to allow reordering of literals as long as the resulting conjunction remains well-moded. This would be very similar to the way in which the compiler for Mercury [39] reorders literals to create different modes for the same predicate. For the semantics of Mercury any well-moded re-ordering of the literals is allowed. Although this approach does not ensure the preservation of termination, it is then simply considered a programming error if one well-moded query terminates while the other does not. So, conjunctive partial deduction, not unlike program transformation in general, may be much more viable in a truly declarative setting. Of course, also in that context, finding a good way to prevent slowdowns remains a pressing open question. A promising direction might be to incorporate more detailed efficiency and cost estimation into the global and local control of conjunctive partial deduction, e.g. based on [12, 13]. Other topics for further work include implementation improvements, research into more sophisticated local control, and methods for improved information passing between the local and global control levels.

Finally, we perceive the extensive experimentation in itself, and the set of benchmarks assembled to that end, as a noteworthy contribution of this paper. Indeed, we feel that if one wants to progress towards more practical or even industrial applications of program transformation, extensive and realistic empirical experiments are called for. Our benchmark suite, containing some difficult benchmarks especially designed to put transformation methods under stress, might form a suitable basis to gauge progress along the difficult path towards practical applicability. The interested reader may consult [22] for further details.

Acknowledgements This work developed out of joint work with Danny De Schreye, André de Waal, Robert Glück and Morten Heine Sørensen on conjunctive partial deduction. The authors would like to thank Annalisa Bossi for enlightening comments on termination issues in the context of unfold/fold transformations. Futhermore, we wish to acknowledge stimulating discussions with Fergus Henderson, Robert Kowalski, Dan Sahlin and Zoltan Somogyi, as well as interesting remarks and challenging criticism by anonymous referees.

References

1. K. Benkerimi and P. M. Hill. Supporting transformations for the partial evaluation of logic programs. *Journal of Logic and Computation*, 3(5):469–486, 1993.
2. R. Bol. Loop checking in partial deduction. *Journal of Logic Programming*, 16:25–46, 1993.
3. A. Bossi and N. Cocco. Preserving Universal Termination through Unfold/Fold. In G. Levi and M. Rodriguez-Artalejo, editors, *Proc. 4th International Conference on Algebraic and Logic Programming*, Lecture Notes in Computer Science 850, pages 269–286, Madrid, Spain, 1994. Springer-Verlag.
4. A. Bossi and N. Cocco. Replacement can Preserve Termination. *In this Volume*.
5. A. Bossi, N. Cocco and S. Etalle. Transformation of Left Terminating Programs: The Reordering Problem. In M. Proietti, editor, Logic Program Synthesis and Transformation. *Proceedings of LOPSTR'95*, Lecture Notes in Computer Science 1048, pages 33–45, Utrecht, Netherlands, September 1995. Springer-Verlag.
6. A. Bossi and S. Etalle. Transforming Acyclic Programs. *Transactions on Programming Languages and Systems*, 16(4):1081–1096,1994.
7. M. Bruynooghe, D. De Schreye, and B. Martens. A general criterion for avoiding infinite unfolding during partial deduction. *New Generation Computing*, 11(1):47–79, 1992.
8. R.M. Burstall and J. Darlington. A transformation system for developing recursive programs. *Journal of the ACM*, 24(1):44–67, 1977.
9. D. De Schreye, M. Leuschel, and B. Martens. Program specialisation for logic programs. Tutorial. Abstract in J. Lloyd, editor, *Proceedings ILPS'95*, pages 615–616, Portland, Oregon, December 1995, MIT Press.
10. D. A. de Waal and J. Gallagher. Specialisation of a Unification Algorithm. In K.-K. Lau and T. Clement, editors, *Proceedings of LOPSTR'91*, pages 205–220, Springer-Verlag, 1993.
11. D. A. de Waal and J. Gallagher. The applicability of logic program analysis and transformation to theorem proving. In A. Bundy, editor, *Proceedings CADE-12*, pages 207–221, Nancy, France, June/July 1994. Springer-Verlag, LNAI 814.

12. S. Debray and N.-W. Lin. Cost analysis of logic programs. *ACM Transactions on Programming Languages and Systems*, 15(5):826–875, November 1993.
13. S. Debray, P. López García, M. Hermenegildo, and N.-W. Lin. Estimating the computational cost of logic programs. In B. Le Charlier, editor, *SAS'94*, LNCS 864, pages 255–265, Namur, Belgium, September 1994. Springer-Verlag.
14. J. Gallagher and M. Bruynooghe. Some low-level source transformations for logic programs. In M. Bruynooghe, editor, *Meta'90*, pages 229–244, Leuven, April 1990.
15. J. Gallagher and M. Bruynooghe. The derivation of an algorithm for program specialisation. *New Generation Computing*, 9(3 & 4):305–333, 1991.
16. J. Gallagher. A system for specialising logic programs. Technical Report TR-91-32, University of Bristol, November 1991.
17. J. Gallagher. Tutorial on specialisation of logic programs. In *Proceedings PEPM'93*, pages 88–98. ACM Press, 1993.
18. R. Glück, J. Jørgensen, B. Martens, and M.H. Sørensen. Controlling conjunctive partial deduction of definite logic programs. In H. Kuchen and S.D. Swierstra, editors, *Proceedings of the International Symposium on Programming Languages: Implementations, Logics and Programs (PLILP'96)*, LNCS 1140, pages 152–166, Aachen, Germany, September 1996. Extended version as Technical Report CW 226, K.U. Leuven. Accessible via http://www.cs.kuleuven.ac.be/~lpai.
19. T. Horváth. Experiments in partial deduction. Master's thesis, Departement Computerwetenschappen, K.U.Leuven, Leuven, Belgium, July 1993.
20. J. Lam and A. Kusalik. A comparative analysis of partial deductors for pure Prolog. Technical report, Department of Computational Science, University of Saskatchewan, Canada, May 1990. Revised April 1991.
21. M. Leuschel. Ecological partial deduction: Preserving characteristic trees without constraints. In M. Proietti, editor, Logic Program Synthesis and Transformation. *Proceedings of LOPSTR'95*, Lecture Notes in Computer Science 1048, pages 1–16, Utrecht, Netherlands, September 1995. Springer-Verlag.
22. M. Leuschel. The ECCE partial deduction system and the DPPD library of benchmarks. Accessible via http://www.cs.kuleuven.ac.be/~lpai.
23. M. Leuschel and D. De Schreye. An almost perfect abstraction operation for partial deduction using characteristic trees. Technical Report CW 215, Departement Computerwetenschappen, K.U. Leuven, Belgium, October 1995. Submitted for Publication. Accessible via http://www.cs.kuleuven.ac.be/~lpai.
24. M. Leuschel, D. De Schreye, and A. de Waal. A conceptual embedding of folding into partial deduction: Towards a maximal integration. In Michael Maher, editor, *Proceedings of the Joint International Conference and Symposium on Logic Programming JICSLP'96*, pages 319–332, Bonn, Germany, September 1996. MIT Press. Extended version as Technical Report CW 225, K.U. Leuven. Accessible via http://www.cs.kuleuven.ac.be/~lpai.
25. M. Leuschel and D. De Schreye. Logic program specialisation: How to be more specific. In H. Kuchen and S.D. Swierstra, editors, *Proceedings of the International Symposium on Programming Languages: Implementations, Logics and Programs (PLILP'96)*, LNCS 1140, pages 137–151, Aachen, Germany, September 1996. Extended version as Technical Report CW 232, K.U. Leuven. Accessible via http://www.cs.kuleuven.ac.be/~lpai.
26. M. Leuschel and B. Martens. Global control for partial deduction through characteristic atoms and global trees. In Olivier Danvy, Robert Glück, and Peter Thiemann, editors, *Proceedings of the 1996 Dagstuhl Seminar on Partial Evaluation*, LNCS 1110, pages 263–283, Schloß Dagstuhl, 1996. Ex-

tended version as Technical Report CW 220, K.U. Leuven. Accessible via http://www.cs.kuleuven.ac.be/~lpai.

27. M. Leuschel and M.H. Sørensen. Redundant argument filtering of logic programs. *In this Volume.*

28. J.W. Lloyd. *Foundations of Logic Programming.* Springer-Verlag, 1987.

29. J. W. Lloyd and J. C. Shepherdson. Partial evaluation in logic programming. *The Journal of Logic Programming*, 11:217–242, 1991.

30. B. Martens and D. De Schreye. Automatic finite unfolding using well-founded measures. *Journal of Logic Programming*, 28:89–146, 1996. Extended version as Technical Report CW180, Departement Computerwetenschappen, K.U.Leuven, October 1993, accessible via http://www.cs.kuleuven.ac.be/~lpai.

31. B. Martens and J. Gallagher. Ensuring global termination of partial deduction while allowing flexible polyvariance. In L. Sterling, editor, *Proceedings ICLP'95*, pages 597–613, Kanagawa, Japan, June 1995. MIT Press. Extended version as Technical Report CSTR-94-16, University of Bristol.

32. A. Pettorossi and M. Proietti. Transformation of logic programs: Foundations and techniques. *Journal of Logic Programming*, 19 & 20:261–320, 1994.

33. D. L. Poole and R. Goebel. Gracefully adding negation and disjunction to Prolog. In E. Shapiro, editor, *Proceedings ICLP'86*, pages 635–641, London, U.K., July 1986. Springer-Verlag, LNCS 225.

34. S. Prestwich. The PADDY partial deduction system. Technical Report ECRC-92-6, ECRC, Munich, Germany, 1992.

35. M. Proietti and A. Pettorossi. Unfolding – definition – folding, in this order for avoiding unnecessary variables in logic programs. In *Proceedings PLILP'91*, pages 347–358. Springer-Verlag, LNCS 528, 1991.

36. M. Proietti and A. Pettorossi. The loop absorption and the generalization strategies for the development of logic programs and partial deduction. *Journal of Logic Programming*, 16:123–161, 1993.

37. M. Proietti and A. Pettorossi. Completeness of some transformation strategies for avoiding unnecessary logical variables. In P. Van Hentenryck, editor, *Proceedings ICLP'94*, pages 714–729, Italy, June 1994. MIT Press.

38. D. Sahlin. Mixtus: An automatic partial evaluator for full Prolog. *New Generation Computing*, 12(1):7–51, 1993.

39. Z. Somogyi, F. Henderson, and T. Conway. The execution algorithm of Mercury: An efficient purely declarative logic programming language. *The Journal of Logic Programming*, 1996. To Appear.

40. M.H. Sørensen and R. Glück. An algorithm of generalization in positive supercompilation. In J. Lloyd, editor, *Proceedings ILPS'95*, pages 465–479, Portland, Oregon, December 1995, MIT Press.

41. H. Tamaki and T. Sato. Unfold/fold transformation of logic programs. In S-Å. Tärnlund, editor, *Proceedings ICLP'84*, pages 127–138, Uppsala, July 1984.

42. V.F. Turchin. The concept of a supercompiler. *ACM Transactions on Programming Languages and Systems*, 8(3):292–325, 1986.

43. V.F. Turchin. The algorithm of generalization in the supercompiler. In D. Bjørner, A.P. Ershov and N.D. Jones, editors, *Partial Evaluation and Mixed Computation*, pages 531–549. North-Holland, 1988.

44. P.L. Wadler. Deforestation: Transforming programs to eliminate intermediate trees. *Theoretical Computer Science*, 73:231–248, 1990.

A   Benchmark Programs

The benchmark programs were carefully selected and/or designed in such a way that they cover a wide range of different application areas, including: pattern matching, databases, expert systems, meta-interpreters (non-ground vanilla, mixed, ground), and more involved particular ones: a model-elimination theorem prover, the missionaries-cannibals problem, a meta-interpreter for a simple imperative language. The benchmarks marked with a star (*) can be fully unfolded. Full descriptions can be found in [22].

Benchmark	Description
advisor*	A very simple expert system - benchmark by Thomas Horváth [19].
applast	The append-last program.
contains.kmp	A benchmark based on the "contains" Lam & Kusalik benchmark [20], but with improved run-time queries.
depth.lam*	A Lam & Kusalik benchmark [20].
doubleapp	The double append example. Tests whether deforestation can be done.
ex_depth	A variation of depth.lam with a more sophisticated object program.
flip	A simple deforestation example from Wadler [44].
grammar.lam	A Lam & Kusalik benchmark [20].
groundunify.complex	A ground unification algorithm calculating explicit substitutions [10].
groundunify.simple*	A ground unification algorithm calculating explicit substitutions.
imperative.power	A solver for a simple imperative language. Specialise a power sub-program for a known power and base but unknown environment.
liftsolve.app	The lifting meta-interpreter for the ground representation with append as object program.
liftsolve.db1*	The lifting meta-interpreter [16] with a simple, fully unfoldable object program.
liftsolve.db2	The lifting meta-interpreter with a partially specified object program.
liftsolve.lmkng	Testing part of lifting meta-interpreter (generates an ∞ number of chtrees).
map.reduce	Specialising the higher-order map/3 (using call and =..) for the higher-order reduce/4 in turn applied to add/3.
map.rev	Specialising the higher-order map for the reverse program.
match-append	A very naive matcher, written using 2 appends. Same queries as match.kmp.
match.kmp	Try to obtain a KMP matcher. A benchmark based on the "match" Lam & Kusalik benchmark [20] but with improved run-time queries.
maxlength	Tests whether tupling can be done.
memo-solve	A variation of ex_depth with a simple loop prevention mechanism based on keeping a call stack.
missionaries	A program for the missionaries and cannibals problem.
model_elim.app	Specialise the Poole & Goebel [33] model elimination prover (also used by de Waal & Gallagher [11]) for the append program.
regexp.r1	A naive regular expression matcher. Regular expression: (a+b)*aab.
regexp.r2	Same program as regexp.r1 for ((a+b)(c+d)(e+f)(g+h))*.
regexp.r3	Same program as regexp.r1 for ((a+b)(a+b)(a+b)(a+b)(a+b)(a+b))*.
relative.lam*	A Lam & Kusalik benchmark [20].
remove	A sophisticated deforestation example.
remove2	Another sophisticated deforestation example. Adapted from Turchin [43].
rev_acc_type	A benchmark generating an ∞ number of different characteristic trees.
rev_acc_type.inffail	A simple benchmark with infinite determinate failure at pe time.
rotateprune	A more sophisticated deforestation example [35].
ssuply.lam*	A Lam & Kusalik benchmark [20].
transpose.lam*	A Lam & Kusalik benchmark [20].
upto.sum1	Calculates the sum of squares for 1 up to n. Adapted from Wadler [44].
upto.sum2	Calculates the square of integers in nodes of a tree and sums these up. Adapted from Wadler [44].

Table 3. Description of the benchmark programs

B Benchmark Results

We benchmarked time and size of compiled code under Prolog by BIM 4.0.12.
The timings were not obtained via a loop with an overhead but via special prolog
files (generated automatically by our partial deduction system). These files call
the original and specialised programs directly (i.e. without overhead) at least
100 times for the respective run-time queries. The timings were obtained via the
time/2 predicate of Prolog by BIM 4.0.12 on a Sparc Classic under Solaris. The
compiled code size was obtained via *statistics*/4 and is expressed in units, where
1 unit = 4.08 bytes (in the current implementation of Prolog by BIM).

All timings were for renamed queries, except for the original and for SP (which
does not rename the top-level query — this puts SP at a disadvantage of about
10% in average). Note that Paddy systematically included the original program
and the specialised part could only be called in a renamed style. We removed the
original program whenever possible and added 1 clause which allows calling the
specialised program in an unrenamed style as well (just like Mixtus and Ecce)
to avoid distortion in the code size (and speedup) figures.

Runtimes (RT) are given relative to the runtimes of the original programs.
In computing averages and totals, time and size of the original program were
taken in case of non-termination or an error occurring during transformation.
The total speedups are obtained by the formula

$$\frac{n}{\sum_{i=1}^{n} \frac{spec_i}{orig_i}}$$

where $n = 36$ is the number of benchmarks and $spec_i$ and $orig_i$ are the absolute execution times of the specialised and original programs respectively. The
weighted total speedups are obtained by using the code size $size_i$ of the original
program as a weight for computing the average:

$$\frac{\sum_{i=1}^{n} size_i}{\sum_{i=1}^{n} size_i \frac{spec_i}{orig_i}}$$

TT is the transformation time in seconds.

Timing in (BIM) Prolog, especially on Sparc machines, can sometimes be
problematic. For instance, for `maxlength`, deforestation does not seem to pay
off. However, with reordering of clauses we go from a relative time of 1.4 (i.e.
a slowdown) to a relative time of 0.9 (i.e. a speedup)! On Sicstus Prolog 3, we
even get a 20 % speedup for this example (without reordering)! The problem is
probably due to the caching behaviour of the Sparc processor.

The following versions of the existing systems have been used: version 0.3.3
of MIXTUS , the version of PADDY delivered with ECLIPSE 3.5.1 and a version of
SP dating from September 25th, 1995. We briefly explain the use of ∞ in the
tables:

- ∞, SP: this means real non-termination
- ∞, MIXTUS: heap overflow after 20 minutes
- ∞, PADDY: thorough system crash after 2 minutes

It seems that the latest version 0.3.6 of MIXTUS does terminate for the missionaries example, but we did not yet have time to redo the experiments. PADDY and SP did not terminate for one other example (memo-solve and imperative.power respectively) when we accidentally used *not* instead of \+ (*not* is not defined in SICStus Prolog; PADDY and SP follow this convention). After changing to \+, both systems terminated.

> 12h means that the specialisation was interrupted after 12 hours (though, theoretically, it should have terminated by itself when granted sufficient time to do so). **bi err** means that an error occured while running the program due to a call of a built-in where the arguments were not sufficiently instantiated.

Finally, a brief remark on the match-append benchmark. The bad figures of most systems seem to be due to a bad choice of the filtering, further work will be needed the avoid this kind of effect. Also, none of the presented methods was able to deforest this particular example. However, if we run for instance Csc-hh-t twice on match-append we get the desired deforestation and a much improved performance (relative time of 0.03 !). It should be possible to get this effect directly by using a more refined control.

Benchmark	Cdc-hh-t (DynamicContig-hh-det)			Csc-hh-t (StaticContig-hh-det)			Csc-th-t (StaticContig-th-det)		
	RT	Size	TT	RT	Size	TT	RT	Size	TT
advisor	0.47	412	0.90	0.47	412	0.86	0.47	412	0.87
applast	0.36	202	0.92	0.36	202	0.80	0.36	202	0.67
contains.kmp	0.11	1039	5.61	0.11	1039	5.41	0.11	1039	5.44
depth.lam	0.15	1837	4.11	0.15	1837	4.01	0.15	1837	3.82
doubleapp	0.80	362	0.85	0.80	362	0.88	0.80	362	0.84
ex_depth	0.26	508	3.30	0.29	407	1.62	0.29	407	1.60
flip	1.33	686	1.41	1.33	686	1.25	1.33	686	1.02
grammar.lam	0.16	309	1.94	0.16	309	1.84	0.16	309	1.82
groundunify.complex	0.40	6247	118.69	0.47	6277	19.47	0.47	6277	19.08
groundunify.simple	0.25	368	0.78	0.25	368	0.80	0.25	368	0.75
imperative.power	0.40	36067	906.60	0.40	3132	71.37	0.40	3293	42.85
liftsolve.app	0.05	1179	5.75	0.05	1179	5.98	0.05	1179	5.74
liftsolve.db1	0.01	1280	22.39	0.01	1280	14.23	0.01	1280	13.33
liftsolve.db2	0.16	17472	2599.03	0.21	21071	1594.90	0.17	5929	198.19
liftsolve.lmkng	1.02	1591	3.09	1.02	1591	2.66	1.02	1591	2.63
map.reduce	0.07	507	0.78	0.07	507	0.85	0.07	507	0.80
map.rev	0.11	427	0.83	0.11	427	0.82	0.11	427	0.80
match-append	1.21	406	1.29	1.21	406	1.14	1.21	406	1.17
match.kmp	0.73	639	1.16	0.73	639	1.15	0.73	639	1.15
maxlength	1.40	620	1.22	1.40	620	1.14	1.40	620	1.17
memo-solve	0.81	1095	5.88	0.81	1095	2.53	0.81	1095	4.54
missionaries	0.69	2960	7.93	0.69	2960	7.59	0.69	2960	7.13
model_elim.app	0.12	451	2.65	0.12	451	2.66	0.12	451	2.58
regexp.r1	0.39	557	1.76	0.39	557	1.36	0.39	557	1.41
regexp.r2	0.41	833	3.57	0.53	692	1.52	0.53	692	1.55
regexp.r3	0.31	1197	6.85	0.44	873	1.82	0.44	873	1.87
relative.lam	0.07	1011	5.80	0.07	1011	5.39	0.07	1011	5.32
remove	0.62	1774	5.34	0.62	1774	4.89	0.62	1774	4.92
remove2	0.87	1056	3.42	0.92	831	2.08	0.92	831	2.13
rev_acc_type	1.00	242	1.01	1.00	242	0.91	1.00	242	0.96
rev_acc_type.inffail	0.63	864	3.21	0.63	864	3.01	0.63	864	3.09
rotateprune	0.71	1165	3.08	0.71	1165	2.80	0.71	1165	2.81
ssuply.lam	0.06	262	1.31	0.06	262	1.17	0.06	262	1.19
transpose.lam	0.17	2312	2.87	0.17	2312	2.45	0.17	2312	2.53
upto.sum1	1.20	848	4.00	1.20	848	3.64	0.88	734	3.03
upto.sum2	1.12	623	1.48	1.12	623	1.46	1.12	623	1.48
Average	0.52	2484	103.91	0.53	1648	49.35	0.52	1228	9.73
Total	18.66	89408	3740.8	19.10	59311	1776.5	18.73	44216	350.3
Total Speedup	**1.93**			**1.89**			**1.92**		
Weighted Speedup	**2.44**			**2.38**			**2.44**		

Table 4. Ecce Determinate Conjunctive Partial Deduction (A)

Benchmark	Csc-hn-t (StaticContig-hn-det)			Csc-tn-t (StaticContig-tn-det)			Cdc-th-t (DyanmicContig-th-det)		
	RT	Size	TT	RT	Size	TT	RT	Size	TT
advisor	0.47	412	0.88	0.47	412	1.20	0.47	412	0.82
applast	0.36	202	0.64	0.36	202	0.73	0.36	202	0.86
contains.kmp	0.11	1039	5.19	0.63	862	1.16	0.11	1039	5.22
depth.lam	0.15	1837	3.95	0.15	1837	4.18	0.15	1837	3.53
doubleapp	0.80	362	0.86	0.80	362	1.13	0.80	362	0.86
ex_depth	0.29	407	1.60	0.29	407	1.75	0.27	508	3.08
flip	1.33	686	1.07	1.33	686	1.14	1.33	686	1.41
grammar.lam	0.16	309	1.77	0.16	309	1.98	0.16	309	1.76
groundunify.complex	0.40	4869	15.03	0.47	5095	18.67	0.40	6247	81.35
groundunify.simple	0.25	368	0.76	0.25	368	0.94	0.25	368	0.73
imperative.power	0.37	2881	49.33	0.37	2881	32.88	0.40	37501	1039.48
liftsolve.app	0.05	1179	5.50	0.05	1179	5.65	0.05	1179	5.43
liftsolve.db1	0.01	1280	13.60	0.01	1280	13.56	0.01	1280	20.39
liftsolve.db2	0.17	10146	1974.50	0.33	3173	19.84	0.17	11152	628.47
liftsolve.lmkng	1.09	1416	1.82	1.07	1416	2.09	1.02	1591	2.89
map.reduce	0.07	507	0.83	0.07	507	1.09	0.07	507	0.77
map.rev	0.11	427	0.79	0.11	427	1.04	0.11	427	0.80
match-append	1.21	406	0.91	1.21	406	1.06	1.21	406	1.18
match.kmp	0.73	639	1.11	0.73	613	1.69	0.73	639	1.22
maxlength	1.40	620	1.20	1.40	620	1.31	1.40	620	1.13
memo-solve	0.81	1095	4.28	1.38	1709	6.73	0.81	1095	10.32
missionaries	0.69	2960	7.06	0.71	3083	6.03	0.69	2960	7.86
model_elim.app	0.12	451	2.63	0.12	451	2.75	0.12	451	2.60
regexp.r1	0.39	557	1.38	0.39	557	1.84	0.39	557	1.76
regexp.r2	0.53	692	1.55	0.53	692	1.66	0.43	833	3.55
regexp.r3	0.44	873	1.81	0.44	873	2.00	0.30	1197	6.01
relative.lam	0.07	1011	5.34	0.45	1252	6.78	0.07	1011	5.74
remove	0.65	1191	2.42	0.65	1191	2.19	0.62	1774	5.39
remove2	0.92	831	2.04	0.92	831	1.89	0.87	1056	3.45
rev_acc_type	1.00	242	0.67	1.00	242	0.84	1.00	242	1.04
rev_acc_type.inffail	0.63	598	0.87	0.63	598	0.98	0.63	864	3.24
rotateprune	0.71	1165	2.79	0.71	1165	2.55	0.71	1165	3.10
ssuply.lam	0.06	262	1.15	0.06	262	1.32	0.06	262	1.32
transpose.lam	0.17	2312	2.46	0.17	2312	2.62	0.17	2312	2.51
upto.sum1	1.20	848	3.77	0.88	734	2.83	0.88	734	3.40
upto.sum2	1.12	623	1.45	1.12	623	1.39	1.12	623	1.49
Average	0.53	1270	58.97	0.57	1100	4.37	0.51	2345	51.78
Total	19.04	45703	2123.01	20.40	39617	157.49	18.35	84408	1864.16
Total Speedup	**1.89**			**1.76**			**1.96**		
Weighted Speedup	**2.40**			**2.18**			**2.49**		

Table 5. Ecce Determinate Conjunctive Partial Deduction (B)

Benchmark	Csc-th-li (StaticContig-th-lidx) (Non-det. unfolding)			Cdm-hh-t (DynamicMcs-hh-det) (Cautious Deforestation)			Csm-hh-h (StaticMcs-hh-hrs) (Aggressive Deforestation)		
	RT	Size	TT	RT	Size	TT	RT	Size	TT
advisor	0.32	809	0.85	0.47	412	0.80	0.46	647	1.00
applast	0.34	145	0.67	0.36	202	0.97	0.36	145	0.85
contains.kmp	0.10	1227	15.73	0.11	1039	5.16	0.10	814	5.77
depth.lam	0.15	1848	12.65	0.15	1837	3.99	0.15	1848	5.91
doubleapp	0.82	277	0.98	0.80	362	0.84	0.82	277	0.83
ex_depth	0.27	659	6.31	0.26	508	3.15	0.34	1240	6.18
flip	0.95	493	1.26	0.75	441	1.11	0.69	267	0.81
grammar.lam	0.14	218	2.15	0.16	309	1.74	0.16	309	2.21
groundunify.complex	0.47	19640	117.12	0.40	6247	137.68	0.47	8113	77.21
groundunify.simple	0.25	368	0.76	0.25	368	0.75	0.25	399	1.27
imperative.power	0.69	3605	155.55	0.37	103855	4548.51	bi err	85460	1617.93
liftsolve.app	0.05	1179	6.04	0.05	1179	5.44	0.06	1210	6.26
liftsolve.db1	0.02	1326	19.94	0.01	1280	20.85	0.02	1311	18.10
liftsolve.db2	-	-	> 12h	0.17	17206	1813.49	-	-	> 12h
liftsolve.lmkng	1.00	1591	4.22	1.02	1591	2.85	1.24	1951	8.89
map.reduce	0.08	348	0.78	0.07	507	0.85	0.08	348	0.84
map.rev	0.13	285	0.79	0.11	427	0.88	0.13	285	0.75
match-append	1.36	362	1.02	1.21	406	1.20	1.36	362	0.98
match.kmp	0.65	543	1.65	0.73	639	1.18	0.65	543	0.94
maxlength	1.30	620	1.22	1.40	620	1.18	1.10	314	1.19
memo-solve	0.95	1015	3.69	1.12	1294	22.69	1.50	3777	34.84
missionaries	0.54	15652	348.68	-	-	> 12h	21.17	43268	2537.39
model_elim.app	0.13	444	3.11	0.12	451	2.77	0.12	451	3.20
regexp.r1	0.20	457	1.04	0.39	557	1.91	0.20	457	1.21
regexp.r2	0.41	831	4.98	0.41	833	3.65	0.57	1954	6.43
regexp.r3	0.31	1041	14.70	0.31	1197	6.84	1.89	9124	31.07
relative.lam	0.00	261	6.19	0.07	1011	5.84	0.01	954	7.31
remove	0.87	1369	7.31	0.62	1774	5.51	6.40	4116	7.69
remove2	0.93	862	3.51	0.87	1056	3.65	0.94	862	2.34
rev_acc_type	1.00	242	1.21	1.00	242	1.08	1.00	242	1.73
rev_acc_type.inffail	0.66	700	2.24	0.63	864	3.26	0.61	786	1.94
rotateprune	0.80	1470	4.62	0.71	1165	4.01	0.17	691	2.33
ssuply.lam	0.06	262	1.41	0.06	262	1.36	0.06	262	1.69
transpose.lam	0.18	2312	2.99	0.17	2312	2.77	0.19	2436	4.34
upto.sum1	0.88	734	2.81	bi err	448	3.43	bi err	479	3.79
upto.sum2	1.00	654	1.48	0.65	394	1.50	0.58	242	1.11
Average	0.53	1824	21.70	0.50	4380	189.23	1.30	5027	125.90
Total	19.03	63849	759.66	18.01	153295	6622.9	46.84	175944	4406.33
Total Speedup	1.89			2.00			0.77		
Weighted Speedup	2.38			2.39			0.52		

Table 6. Ecce Non-Determinate Conjunctive Partial Deduction

| Benchmark | S-hh-t | | | S-hh-li | | | SE-hh-x | | |
| | (StdPD-hh-det) | | | (StdPD-hh-lidx) | | | (StdEcoPD-hh-mixtus) | | |
	RT	Size	TT	RT	Size	TT	RT	Size	TT
advisor	0.47	412	0.87	0.31	809	0.85	0.31	809	0.78
applast	1.05	343	0.71	1.48	314	0.75	1.48	314	0.70
contains.kmp	0.85	1290	2.69	0.55	1294	5.97	0.09	685	4.48
depth.lam	0.94	1955	1.47	0.62	1853	3.76	0.02	2085	1.91
doubleapp	0.95	277	0.65	0.95	216	0.58	0.95	216	0.53
ex_depth	0.76	1614	2.54	0.44	1649	4.26	0.32	350	1.58
flip	1.05	476	0.77	1.03	313	0.65	1.03	313	0.53
grammar.lam	0.16	309	1.91	0.14	218	2.43	0.14	218	1.90
groundunify.complex	0.40	5753	13.47	0.47	8356	50.63	0.53	4800	0.75
groundunify.simple	0.25	368	0.78	0.25	368	0.77	0.25	368	22.03
imperative.power	0.42	2435	75.10	0.58	2254	62.97	0.54	1578	27.42
liftsolve.app	0.05	1179	6.05	0.06	1179	6.40	0.06	1179	6.57
liftsolve.db1	0.01	1280	13.27	0.02	1326	20.82	0.02	1326	7.33
liftsolve.db2	0.18	3574	16.86	0.76	3751	242.86	0.61	4786	34.25
liftsolve.lmkng	1.07	1730	1.80	1.07	1730	2.12	1.02	2385	2.75
map.reduce	0.07	507	0.91	0.08	348	0.82	0.08	348	0.86
map.rev	0.11	427	0.83	0.13	285	0.88	0.11	427	0.89
match-append	1.21	406	0.64	1.36	362	0.75	1.36	362	0.68
match.kmp	0.73	639	1.16	0.65	543	1.77	0.70	669	1.23
maxlength	1.20	715	1.07	1.10	715	1.16	1.10	421	0.95
memo-solve	1.17	2318	4.74	1.20	2238	4.96	1.09	2308	4.31
missionaries	0.81	2294	5.11	0.66	13168	430.99	0.72	2226	9.21
model_elim.app	0.63	2100	2.82	0.13	444	3.18	0.13	532	3.56
regexp.r1	0.50	594	1.28	0.20	457	1.03	0.29	435	0.98
regexp.r2	0.57	629	1.28	0.61	737	4.67	0.51	1159	4.87
regexp.r3	0.50	828	1.74	0.38	961	14.00	0.42	1684	14.92
relative.lam	0.82	1074	1.89	0.00	261	5.88	0.00	261	4.06
remove	0.71	955	1.46	0.68	659	1.02	0.68	659	0.90
remove2	0.74	508	1.15	0.75	453	1.30	0.80	440	1.00
rev_acc_type	1.00	242	0.70	1.00	242	0.92	1.00	242	0.83
rev_acc_type.inffail	0.63	864	1.48	0.80	850	1.25	0.60	527	0.80
rotateprune	0.71	1165	1.77	1.02	779	1.10	1.02	779	0.88
ssuply.lam	0.06	262	1.15	0.06	262	1.51	0.06	262	1.18
transpose.lam	0.17	2312	2.49	0.17	2312	2.99	0.17	2312	1.98
upto.sum1	1.06	581	2.18	1.07	581	1.80	1.20	664	3.11
upto.sum2	1.10	623	1.50	1.05	485	1.38	1.05	485	0.94
Average	0.64	1196	4.90	0.61	1466	24.70	0.57	1073	4.77
Total	23.12	43038	176.29	21.86	52772	889.18	20.47	38614	171.65
Total Speedup	**1.56**			**1.65**			**1.76**		
Weighted Speedup	**1.86**			**2.09**			**2.24**		

Table 7. Ecce Standard Partial Deduction Methods

Benchmark	Mixtus			Paddy			SP		
	RT	Size	TT	RT	Size	TT	RT	Size	TT
advisor	0.31	809	0.85	0.31	809	0.10	0.40	463	0.29
applast	1.27	309	0.28	1.30	309	0.08	0.84	255	0.15
contains.kmp	0.16	533	2.48	0.11	651	0.55	0.75	985	1.13
depth.lam	0.04	1881	4.15	0.02	2085	0.32	0.53	928	0.99
doubleapp	1.00	295	0.30	0.98	191	0.08	1.02	160	0.11
ex_depth	0.40	643	2.40	0.29	1872	0.53	0.27	786	1.35
flip	1.03	495	0.37	1.02	290	0.12	1.02	259	0.13
grammar.lam	0.17	841	2.73	0.43	636	0.22	0.15	280	0.71
groundunify.complex	0.67	5227	11.68	0.60	4420	1.53	0.73	4050	2.46
groundunify.simple	0.25	368	0.45	0.25	368	0.13	0.61	407	0.20
imperative.power	0.56	2842	5.35	0.58	3161	2.18	1.16	1706	6.97
liftsolve.app	0.06	1179	4.78	0.06	1454	0.80	0.23	1577	2.46
liftsolve.db1	0.01	1280	5.36	0.02	1280	1.20	0.82	4022	3.95
liftsolve.db2	0.31	8149	58.19	0.32	4543	1.60	0.82	3586	3.71
liftsolve.lmkng	1.16	2169	4.89	0.98	1967	0.32	1.16	1106	0.37
map.reduce	0.68	897	0.17	0.08	498	0.20	0.09	437	0.23
map.rev	0.11	897	0.16	0.26	2026	0.37	0.13	351	0.20
match-append	0.47	389	0.27	0.98	422	0.12	0.99	265	0.18
match.kmp	1.55	467	4.89	0.69	675	0.28	1.08	527	0.49
maxlength	1.20	594	0.72	0.90	398	0.17	0.90	367	0.31
memo-solve	0.60	1493	12.72	1.48	3716	1.70	1.15	1688	3.65
missionaries	-	-	∞	-	-	∞	0.73	16864	82.59
model_elim.app	0.13	624	5.73	0.10	931	0.90	-	-	∞
regexp.r1	0.20	457	0.73	0.29	417	0.13	0.54	466	0.37
regexp.r2	0.82	1916	2.85	0.67	3605	0.63	1.08	1233	0.67
regexp.r3	0.60	2393	4.49	1.26	10399	1.35	1.03	1646	1.20
relative.lam	0.01	517	7.76	0.00	517	0.42	0.69	917	0.35
remove	0.81	715	0.49	0.71	437	0.12	0.75	561	0.29
remove2	1.01	715	0.84	0.84	756	0.12	0.82	386	0.25
rev_acc_type	1.00	497	0.99	0.99	974	0.33	-	-	∞
rev_acc_type.inffail	0.97	276	0.77	0.94	480	0.28	-	-	∞
rotateprune	1.02	756	0.49	1.01	571	0.12	1.00	725	0.31
ssuply.lam	0.06	262	0.93	0.08	262	0.08	0.06	231	0.52
transpose.lam	0.18	1302	3.89	0.18	1302	0.43	0.26	1267	0.52
upto.sum1	0.96	556	1.80	1.08	734	0.30	1.05	467	0.48
upto.sum2	1.06	462	0.44	1.06	462	0.13	1.01	431	0.21
Average	0.61	1234	4.44	0.61	1532	0.51	0.75	1497	3.57
Total	21.83	43205	155.37	21.87	53618	17.95	26.86	49399	117.80
Total Speedup	**1.65**			**1.65**			**1.34**		
Weighted Speedup	**2.11**			**2.00**			**1.54**		

Table 8. Existing systems

Redundant Argument Filtering
of Logic Programs

Michael Leuschel[1] & Morten Heine Sørensen[2]

[1] Department of Computer Science, Katholieke Universiteit Leuven,
Celestijnenlaan 200A, B-3001, Heverlee, Belgium, michael@cs.kuleuven.ac.be.
[2] Department of Computer Science, University of Copenhagen,
Universitetsparken 1, DK-2100 Copenhagen, Denmark. rambo@diku.dk.

Abstract. This paper is concerned with the problem of removing *redundant arguments* from logic programs. Such arguments can be removed without affecting correctness, in a certain sense. Most program specialisation techniques, even though they filter arguments and remove clauses, fail to remove a substantial number of redundant arguments, yielding in some cases rather inefficient residual programs. We formalise the notion of a redundant argument and show that one cannot effectively remove all redundant arguments. We then give a safe, effective approximation of the notion of a redundant argument and describe several simple and efficient algorithms based on the approximative notion. We conduct extensive experiments with our algorithms on mechanically generated programs illustrating the practical benefits of our approach.

1 Introduction

Automatically generated programs often contain redundant parts. For instance, programs produced by partial deduction [20] often have *useless clauses* and *redundant structures*, see e.g. [7]. This has motivated uses of *regular approximations* to detect useless clauses [9, 6, 5] and the *renaming* (or *filtering*) transformation [8, 2] that removes redundant structures. In this paper we are concerned with yet another notion of redundancy which may remain even after these transformations have been applied, viz. *redundant arguments*. These seem to appear particularly often in programs produced by *conjunctive partial deduction* [17, 11], a recent extension of standard partial deduction that can perform tupling and deforestation.

For example, consider the goal $\leftarrow doubleapp(Xs, Ys, Zs, R)$ and the program:

$$doubleapp(Xs, Ys, Zs, R) \leftarrow app(Xs, Ys, \underline{T}), app(\underline{T}, Zs, R)$$
$$app([\ ], Ys, Ys) \leftarrow$$
$$app([H|Xs], Ys, [H|Zs]) \leftarrow app(Xs, Ys, Zs)$$

Given Xs, Ys, Zs, the goal $\leftarrow doubleapp(Xs, Ys, Zs, R)$ concatenates the three lists Xs, Ys, Zs yielding as result R. This is achieved via two calls to *app* and the local variable T. The first call to *app* constructs from the lists Xs and Ys an intermediate list T, which is then traversed when appending Zs. While the goal *doubleapp*(Xs, Ys, Zs, R) is simple and elegant, it is rather inefficient since construction and traversal of such intermediate data structures is expensive.

Partial deduction within the framework of Lloyd and Shepherdson [20] cannot substantially improve the program since the atoms *app*(Xs, Ys, T), *app*(T, Zs, R) are transformed independently. However, as shown in [17, 11], conjunctive partial deduction of ← *doubleapp*(Xs, Ys, Zs, R) gives the following equivalent program:

$$doubleapp(Xs, Ys, Zs, R) \qquad \leftarrow da(Xs, Ys, \underline{T}, Zs, R)$$
$$da([\ ], Ys, \underline{Ys}, Zs, R) \qquad \leftarrow a(Ys, Zs, R)$$
$$da([H|Xs'], Ys, [H|T'], Zs, [H|R']) \leftarrow da(Xs', Ys, \underline{T'}, Zs, R')$$
$$a([\ ], Ys, Ys) \qquad \leftarrow$$
$$a([H|Xs'], Ys, [H|Zs']) \qquad \leftarrow a(Xs', Ys, Zs')$$

Here the concatenation of the lists Xs and Ys is still stored in T, but is not used to compute the result in R. Instead the elements encountered while traversing Xs and Ys are stored directly in R. Informally, the third argument of *da* is redundant. Thus, although this program represents a step in the right direction, we would rather prefer the following program:

$$doubleapp(Xs, Ys, Zs, R) \quad \leftarrow da'(Xs, Ys, Zs, R)$$
$$da'([\ ], Ys, Zs, R) \qquad \leftarrow a'(Ys, Zs, R)$$
$$da'([H|Xs'], Ys, Zs, [H|R']) \leftarrow da'(Xs', Ys, Zs, R')$$
$$a'([\ ], Ys, Ys) \qquad \leftarrow$$
$$a'([X|Xs], Ys, [X|Zs]) \qquad \leftarrow a'(Xs, Ys, Zs)$$

Automation of the step from *da*/5 to *da'*/4 was left open in [17, 11] (although correctness conditions were given in [17]). The step cannot be obtained by the renaming operation in [8, 2] which only improves programs where some atom in some body contains functors or multiple occurrences of the same variable. In fact, this operation has *already* been employed by conjunctive partial deduction to arrive at the program with *da*/5. The step also cannot be obtained by other transformation techniques, such as partial deduction itself, or the more specific program construction of [22] which calculates more specific versions of programs. Indeed, any method which preserves the least Herbrand model, or the computed answer semantics for all predicates, is incapable of transforming *da*/5 to *da'*/4.

Redundant arguments also appear in a variety of other situations. For instance, they appear in programs generated by standard partial deduction when conservative unfolding rules are used.

As another example, redundant arguments arise when one re-uses general predicates for more specific purposes. For instance, define the *member*/2 predicate by re-using a general *delete*/3 predicate:

$$member(X, L) \qquad \leftarrow delete(X, L, DL)$$
$$delete(X, [X|T], T) \qquad \leftarrow$$
$$delete(X, [Y|T], [Y|DT]) \leftarrow delete(X, T, DT)$$

Here the third argument of *delete* is redundant but cannot be removed by any of the techniques cited above.

In this paper we rigorously define the notion of a redundant argument, and show that the task of removing all redundant arguments is uncomputable. We then present an efficient algorithm which computes a safe approximation of the redundant arguments and removes them. Correctness of the technique is also established. On a range of programs produced by conjunctive partial deduction (with renaming), an implementation of our algorithm reduces code size and execution time by an average of approximately 20%. The algorithm never increases code size nor execution time.

2 Correct Erasures

In the remainder we adopt the terminology and notation from [19]. Moreover, $Pred(P)$ denotes the set of predicates occurring in a logic program P, $arity(p)$ denotes the arity of a predicate p, $Clauses(P)$ denotes the set of clauses in P, $Def(p, P)$ denotes the definitions of p in P, and $vars(U)$ denotes the set of variables occurring in U, where U may be a term, an atom, a conjunction, a goal, or a program. An atom, conjunction, goal, or program, in which every predicate has arity 0 is called *propositional*. In this paper all goals and programs are *definite*, except when explicitly stated otherwise.

In this section we formalise *redundant arguments* in terms of *correct erasures*.

Definition 1. Let P be a program.
1. An *erasure* of P is a set of tuples (p, k) with $p \in Pred(P)$, and $1 \leq k \leq arity(p)$.
2. The *full erasure* for P is $\top_P = \{(p, k) \mid p \in Pred(P) \wedge 1 \leq k \leq arity(p)\}$.

The effect of applying an erasure to a program is to erase a number of arguments in every atom in the program. For simplicity of the presentation we assume that, for every program P and goal G of interest, each predicate symbol occurs only with one particular arity (this will later ensure that there are no unintended name clashes after erasing certain argument positions).

Definition 2. Let G be a goal, P a program, and E an erasure of P.
1. For an atom $A = p(t_1, \ldots, t_n)$ in P, let $1 \leq j_1 < \ldots < j_k \leq n$ be all the indexes such that $(p, j_i) \notin E$. We then define $A|E = p(t_{j_1}, \ldots, t_{j_k})$.
2. $P|E$ and $G|E$ arise by replacing every atom A by $A|E$ in P and G, respectively.

How are the semantics of P and $P|E$ of Def. 2 related? Since the predicates in P may have more arguments than the corresponding predicates in $P|E$, the two programs have incomparable semantics. Nevertheless, the two programs may have the same semantics for some of their arguments.

Example 1. Consider the program P:

$$p(0, 0, 0) \qquad \leftarrow$$
$$p(s(X), f(Y), g(Z)) \leftarrow p(X, Y, Z)$$

The goal $G = \leftarrow p(s(s(0)), B, C)$ has exactly one SLD-refutation, with computed answer $\{B/f(f(0)), C/g(g(0))\}$. Let $E = \{(p, 3)\}$, and hence $P|E$ be:

$$p(0, 0) \qquad \leftarrow$$
$$p(s(X), f(Y)) \leftarrow p(X, Y)$$

Here $G|E = \leftarrow p(s(s(0)), B)$ has exactly one SLD-refutation, with computed answer $\{B/f(f(0))\}$. Thus, although we have erased the third argument of p, the computed answer for the variables in the remaining two arguments is not affected. Taking finite failures into account too, this suggests a notion of equivalence captured in the following definition.

Definition 3. An erasure E is *correct* for a program P and a goal G iff

1. $P \cup \{G\}$ has an SLD-refutation with computed answer θ with $\theta' = \theta \,|_{vars(G|E)}$ iff $P|E \cup \{G|E\}$ has an SLD-refutation with computed answer θ'.
2. $P \cup \{G\}$ has a finitely failed SLD-tree iff $P|E \cup \{G|E\}$ has.

Given a goal G and a program P, we may now say that the i'th argument of a predicate p is *redundant* if there is an erasure E which is correct for P and G and which contains (p, i). However, we will continue to use the terminology with correct erasures, rather than redundant arguments.

Usually there is a certain set of argument positions I which we do not want to erase. For instance, for $G = app([a], [b], R)$ and the append program, the erasure $E = \{(app, 3)\}$ is correct, but applying the erasure will also make the result of the computation invisible. In other words, we wish to retain some arguments because we are interested in their values (see also the examples in Sect. 4). Therefore we only consider subsets of $\top_P \setminus I$ for some I. Not all erasures included in $\top_P \setminus I$ are of course correct, but among the correct ones we will prefer those that remove more arguments. This motivates the following definition.

Definition 4. Let G be a goal, P a program, $\mathcal{E}$ a set of erasures of P, and $E, E' \in \mathcal{E}$.

1. E is *better than* E' iff $E \supseteq E'$.
2. E is *strictly better than* E' iff E is better than E' and $E \neq E'$.
3. E is *best* iff no other $E' \in \mathcal{E}$ is strictly better than E.

Proposition 5. *Let G be a goal, P a program and $\mathcal{E}$ a collection of erasures of P. Among the correct erasures for P and G in $\mathcal{E}$ there is a best one.*

Proof. There are only finitely many erasures in $\mathcal{E}$ that are correct for P and G. Just choose one which is not contained in any other. $\square$

Best correct erasures are not always unique. For $G = \leftarrow p(1, 2)$ and P:

$$p(3, 4) \leftarrow q$$
$$q \qquad \leftarrow$$

both $\{(p,1)\}$ and $\{(p,2)\}$ are best correct erasures, but $\{(p,1),(p,2)\}$ is incorrect.

The remainder of this section is devoted to proving that best correct erasures are uncomputable. The idea is as follows. It is decidable whether $P \cup \{G\}$ has an SLD-refutation for propositional P and G, but not for general P and G. The full erasure of any P and G yields propositional $P|\mathsf{T}_P$ and $G|\mathsf{T}_P$. The erasure is correct iff both or none of $P \cup \{G\}$ and $P|\mathsf{T}_P \cup \{G|\mathsf{T}_P\}$ have an SLD-refutation. Thus a test to decide correctness, together with the test for SLD-refutability of propositional formulae, would give a general SLD-refutability test.

Lemma 6. *There is an effective procedure that decides, for propositional program P and goal G, whether $P \cup \{G\}$ has an SLD-refutation.*
Proof. By a well-known [19, Cor 7.2, Thm. 8.4] result, $P \cup \{G\}$ has an SLD-refutation iff $P \cup \{G\}$ is unsatisfiable. The latter problem is decidable, since P and G are propositional. □

Lemma 7. *Let G be a goal, P a program, and E an erasure of P. If $P \cup \{G\}$ has an SLD-refutation, then so has $P|E \cup \{G|E\}$.*
Proof. By induction on the length of the SLD-derivation of $P \cup \{G\}$. □

Lemma 8. *Let P be a program and G a goal. If $P \cup \{G\}$ has an SLD-refutation, then $P \cup \{G\}$ has no finitely failed SLD-tree.*
Proof. By [19, Thm. 10.3]. □

Proposition 9. *There is no effective procedure that tests, for a program P and goal G, whether T_P is correct for P and G.*
Proof. Suppose such an effective procedure exists. Together with the effective procedure from Lemma 6 this would give an effective procedure to decide whether $P \cup \{G\}$ has an SLD-refutation, which is known to be an undecidable problem:[3]

1. If $P|\mathsf{T}_P \cup \{G|\mathsf{T}_P\}$ has no SLD-refutation, by Lemma 7 neither has $P \cup \{G\}$.
2. If $P|\mathsf{T}_P \cup \{G|\mathsf{T}_P\}$ has an SLD-refutation then:
   (a) If T_P is correct then $P \cup \{G\}$ has an SLD-refutation by Def. 3.
   (b) If T_P is incorrect then $P \cup \{G\}$ has no SLD-refutation. Indeed, if $P \cup \{G\}$ had an SLD-refutation with computed answer θ, then Def. 3(1) would be satisfied with $\theta' = \theta \mid_{vars(G|\mathsf{T}_P)} = \emptyset$. Moreover, by Lemma 8 none of $P \cup \{G\}$ and $P|\mathsf{T}_P \cup \{G|\mathsf{T}_P\}$ would have a finitely failed SLD-tree, so Def. 3(2) would also be satisfied. Thus T_P would be correct, a contradiction. □

Corollary 10. *There is no effective function that maps any program P and goal G to a best, correct erasure for P and G.*
Proof. T_P is the best among all erasures of P, so such a function f would satisfy:

$$f(P,G) = \mathsf{T}_P \quad \Leftrightarrow \quad \mathsf{T}_P \text{ is correct for } P \text{ and } G$$

giving an effective procedure to test correctness of T_P, contradicting Prop. 9. □

---

[3] $G|\mathsf{T}_P$ may contain variables, namely those occurring in atoms with predicate symbols not occurring in P. However, such atoms are equivalent to propositional atoms not occurring in P.

3 Computing Correct Erasures

In this section we present an algorithm which computes correct erasures. Corollary 10 shows that we cannot hope for an algorithm that computes *best* correct erasures. We therefore derive an approximate notion which captures some interesting cases. For this purpose, the following examples illustrate some aspects of correctness.

The first example shows what may happen if we try to erase a variable that occurs several times in the body of a clause.

Example 2. Consider the following program P:

$$p(X) \quad \leftarrow r(X,Y), q(Y)$$
$$r(X,1) \leftarrow$$
$$q(0) \quad \leftarrow$$

If $E = \{(r,2)\}$ then $P|E$ is the program:

$$p(X) \leftarrow r(X), q(Y)$$
$$r(X) \leftarrow$$
$$q(0) \leftarrow$$

In P the goal $G =\leftarrow p(X)$ fails finitely, while in $P|E$ the goal $G|E =\leftarrow p(X)$ succeeds. Thus E is not correct for P and G. The source of the problem is that the existential variable Y links the calls to r and q with each other. By erasing Y in $\leftarrow r(X,Y)$, we also erase the synchronisation between r and q.

Also, if $E = \{(q,1),(r,2)\}$ then $P|E$ is the program:

$$p(X) \leftarrow r(X), q$$
$$r(X) \leftarrow$$
$$q \quad \leftarrow$$

Again, $G|E =\leftarrow p(X)$ succeeds in $P|E$, so the problem arises independently of whether the occurrence of Y in $q(Y)$ is itself erased or not.

In a similar vein, erasing a variable that occurs several times within the same call, but is not linked to other atoms, can also be problematic.

Example 3. If P is the program:

$$p(a,b) \quad \leftarrow$$
$$p(f(X),g(X)) \leftarrow p(Y,Y)$$

and $E = \{(p,2)\}$ then $P|E$ is the program:

$$p(a) \quad \leftarrow$$
$$p(f(X)) \leftarrow p(Y)$$

Here $G =\leftarrow p(f(X),Z)$ fails finitely in P, while $G|E =\leftarrow p(f(X))$ succeeds (with the empty computed answer) in $P|E$.

Note that, for $E = \{(p,1),(p,2)\}$, $P|E$ is the program:

$p.$

$p \leftarrow p.$

Again $G|E =\leftarrow p$ succeeds in $P|E$ and the problem arises independently of whether the second occurrence of Y is erased or not.

Still another problem is illustrated in the next example.

Example 4. Consider the following program P:

$p([],[]) \qquad \leftarrow$

$p([X|Xs],[X|Ys]) \leftarrow p(Xs,[0|Ys])$

If $E = \{(p,2)\}$ then $P|E$ is the program:

$p([]) \qquad \leftarrow$

$p([X|Xs]) \leftarrow p(Xs)$

In P, the goal $G =\leftarrow p([1,1],Y)$ fails finitely, while in $P|E$ the goal $G|E =\leftarrow p([1,1])$ succeeds. This phenomenon can occur when erased arguments of predicate calls contain non-variable terms.

Finally, problems may arise when erasing in the body of a clause a variable which also occurs in a non-erased position of the head of a clause:

Example 5. Let P be the following program:

$p(a,b) \quad \leftarrow$

$p(X,Y) \leftarrow p(Y,X)$

If $E = \{(p,2)\}$ then $P|E$ is the program:

$p(a) \leftarrow$

$p(X) \leftarrow p(Y)$

Here $G =\leftarrow p(c,Y)$ fails (infinitely) in P while $G|E =\leftarrow p(c)$ succeeds in $P|E$. The synchronisation of the alternating arguments X and Y is lost by the erasure.

The above criteria lead to the following sufficient definition, adapted from the definition of correct renamings in [17], in which (1) rules out Example 4, (2) rules out Examples 2 and 3, and (3) rules out Example 5.

Definition 11. Let P be a program and E an erasure of P. E is *safe* for P iff for all $(p,k) \in E$ and all $H \leftarrow C, p(t_1,\ldots,t_n), C' \in Clauses(P)$, it holds that:

1. t_k is a variable X.
2. X occurs only once in $C, p(t_1,\ldots,t_n), C'$.
3. X does not occur in $H|E$.

This in particular applies to goals:

Definition 12. Let P be a program and E an erasure of P. E is *safe* for a goal G iff for all $(p,k) \in E$ where $G =\leftarrow C, p(t_1,\ldots,t_n), C'$ it holds that:

1. t_k is a variable X.
2. X occurs only once in in $C, p(t_1, \ldots, t_n), C'$.

These conditions occur, in a less obvious formulation, among the conditions for Tamaki-Sato folding (see [25]). The method of this paper can be seen as a novel application of Tamaki-Sato folding using a particular control strategy.

Proposition 13. *Let G be a goal, P a program, and E an erasure of P. If E is safe for P and for G then E is correct for P and G.*

Proof. The conditions in Def. 11 and Def. 12 are equivalent to the conditions on correct renamings in [17]. Therefore, Theorem 3.7 from [17] can be invoked as follows (where we extensively use terminology from [17]). Let S be an *independent* set of *maximally general* atoms using the predicate symbols occurring in P, let p be a *partitioning function* such that $p(A_1 \wedge \ldots A_n) = \{A_1, \ldots, A_n\}$ and let the *atomic renaming* σ be such that for $A \in S$: $\alpha(A) = A|E$. Since S is independent there is only one *renaming function* $\rho_{\alpha,p}$ based on α and p. We now have that the *conjunctive partial deduction* $P_{\rho_{\alpha,p}}$, using an *unfolding rule* which just performs one single unfolding step for every $A \in S$, is identical to $P|E$. Note that the thus obtained trees are *non-trivial* wrt p and also that trivially $P_{\rho_{\alpha,p}}$ is *S-closed* wrt p. As already mentioned, safety of E implies that ρ_σ is a *correct renaming* for $P_{\rho_{\alpha,p}} \cup \{G\}$. Theorem 3.7 of [17] then shows that $P|E$ is correct for P and G. $\qquad\square$

The following algorithm constructs a safe erasure for a given program.

Algorithm 1 (RAF)

Input: a program P, an initial erasure E_0.
Output: an erasure E with $E \subseteq E_0$.
Initialisation: $i := 0$;
while there exists a $(p, k) \in E_i$ and a $H \leftarrow C, p(t_1, \ldots, t_n), C' \in \textit{Clauses}(P)$
s.t.:

    1. t_k is not a variable; **or**
    2. t_k is a variable that occurs more than once in $C, p(t_1, \ldots, t_n), C'$; **or**
    3. t_k is a variable that occurs in $H|E_i$
do $E_{i+1} := E_i \setminus \{(p, k)\}$; $i := i + 1$;
return E_i

The above algorithm starts out from an initial erasure E_0, usually contained in $\top_P \setminus I$, where I are positions of interest (i.e. we are interested in the computed answers they yield). Furthermore E_0 should be safe for any goal of interest (see the example in the next section).

Proposition 14. *With input E_0, RAF terminates, and output E is a unique erasure, which is the best safe erasure for P contained in E_0.*

Proof. The proof consists of four parts: *termination* of RAF, *safety* of E for P, *uniqueness* of E, and *optimality* of E. The two first parts are obvious: termination follows from the fact that each iteration of the while loop decreases the size of E_i, and safety is immediate from the definition.

To prove uniqueness, note that the non-determinism in the algorithm is the choice of which (p, k) to erase in the while loop. Given a logic program P, let the *reduction* $E(p, k)F$ denote the fact that E is not safe for P and that an iteration of the while loop may chose to erase (p, k) from E yielding $F = E \backslash \{(p, k)\}$.

Now suppose $E(p, k)F$ and $E(q, j)G$. Then by analysis of all the combinations of reasons that (p, k) and (q, j) could be removed from E it follows that $F(q, j)H$ and $G(p, k)H$ with $H = E \backslash \{(p, k), (q, j)\}$.

This property implies that for any two sequences

$$E(p_1, k_1)F_1 \ldots F_{n-1}(p_n, k_n)F_n \quad \text{and} \quad E(q_1, j_1)G_1 \ldots G_{m-1}(q_m, j_m)G_m$$

there are sequences:

$$F_n(q_1, j_1)G'_1 \ldots G'_{m-1}(q_m, j_m)H \quad \text{and} \quad G_m(p_1, k_1)F'_1 \ldots F'_{n-1}(p_n, k_n)H$$

with $H = F_n \cap G_m$. In particular, if F_n and G_m are safe, so that no reductions apply, it follows that $F_n = G_m$. Hence the output is a unique erasure.

To see that this is the best one among the safe erasures contained in E_0, note that $E(p, k)F$ implies that no safe erasure contained in E contains (p, k). $\quad \square$

4 Applications, Implementation and Benchmarks

We first illustrate the usefulness of the RAF algorithm in the transformation of double-append from Sect. 1. Recall that we want to retain the semantics (and so all the arguments) of *doubleapp*, but want to erase as many arguments in the auxiliary calls to *app* and *da* as possible. Therefore we start RAF with

$$E_0 = \{(da, 1), (da, 2), (da, 3), (da, 4), (da, 5), (a, 1), (a, 2), (a, 3)\}$$

Application of RAF to E_0 yields $E = \{(da, 3)\}$, representing the information that the third argument of *da* can be safely removed, as desired. By construction of E_0, we have that $E \subseteq E_0$ is safe for any goal which is an instance of the goal $\leftarrow doubleapp(Xs, Ys, Zs, R)$. Hence, as long as we consider only such goals, we get the same answers from the program with $da'/4$ as we get from the one with $da/5$.

Let us also treat the member-delete problem from Sect. 1. If we start RAF with

$$E_0 = \{(delete, 1), (delete2), (delete, 3)\}$$

indicating that we are only interested in computed answers to *member/2*, then we obtain $E = \{(delete, 3)\}$ and the following more efficient program $P|E$:

```
member(X, L)    ← delete(X, L)
delete(X, [X|T]) ←
delete(X, [Y|T]) ← delete(X, T)
```

To investigate the effects of Algorithm 1 more generally, we have incorporated it into the ECCE partial deduction system [18]. This system is based on work in [15, 16] and was extended to perform conjunctive partial deduction based on [17, 11, 13]. We ran the system *with* and *without* redundant argument filtering (but always *with* renaming in the style of [8]) on a series of benchmarks of the DPPD library [18] (a brief description can also be found in [13]). An unfolding rule allowing determinate unfolding and leftmost "indexed" non-determinate unfolding (using the homeomorphic embedding relation on covering ancestors to ensure finiteness) was used.[4] For further details, see [13]. The timings were obtained via the *time/2* predicate of Prolog by BIM 4.0.12 (on a Sparc Classic under Solaris) using the "benchmarker" files generated by ECCE. The compiled code size was obtained via *statistics/4* and is expressed in units, were 1 unit corresponds to approximatively 4.08 bytes (in the current implementation of Prolog by BIM).

The results are summarised in Table 1. The weighted speedup is obtained by the formula

$$\frac{n}{\sum_{i=1}^{n} \frac{spec_i}{orig_i}}$$

where $n = 29$ is the number of benchmarks and $spec_i$ and $orig_i$ are the absolute execution times of the specialised and original programs respectively. As can be seen, RAF reduced code size by an average of 21% while at the same time yielding an average additional speedup of 18%. Note that 13 out of the 29 benchmarks benefited from RAF, while the others remained unaffected (i.e. no redundant arguments where detected). Also, none of the programs were deteriorated by RAF. Except on extremely large residual programs, the execution time of the RAF algorithm was insignificant compared to the total partial deduction time. Note that the RAF algorithm was also useful for examples which have nothing to do with deforestation and, when running the same benchmarks with standard partial deduction based on e.g. determinate unfolding, RAF also turned out to be useful, albeit to a lesser extent. In conclusion, RAF yields a practically significant reduction of code size and a practically significant speedup (e.g. reaching a factor of 4.29 for *depth*).

5   Poly-variance, Negation and Further Extensions

In this section we discuss some natural extensions of our technique.

Polyvariant Algorithm

The erasures computed by RAF are *mono-variant*: an argument of some predicate has to be erased in all calls to the predicate or not at all. It is sometimes desirable that the technique be more precise and erase a certain argument only

---

[4] The full system options were: Abs:j, InstCheck:a, Msv:s, NgSlv:g, Part:f, Prun:i, Sel:l, Whistle:d, Poly:y, Dpu: yes, Dce:yes, MsvPost: no.

Benchmark	Code Size		Execution Time			
	w/o RAF	with RAF	Original	w/o RAF	with RAF	Extra Speedup
advisor	809 u	809 u	0.68	0.21	0.21	1.00
applast	188 u	145 u	0.44	0.17	0.10	1.70
contains.kmp	2326 u	1227 u	1.03	0.28	0.10	2.80
contains.lam	2326 u	1227 u	0.53	0.15	0.11	1.36
depth.lam	5307 u	1848 u	0.47	0.30	0.07	4.29
doubleapp	314 u	277 u	0.44	0.42	0.35	1.20
ex_depth	874 u	659 u	1.14	0.37	0.32	1.16
flip	573 u	493 u	0.61	0.66	0.58	1.14
grammar.lam	218 u	218 u	1.28	0.18	0.18	1.00
groundunify.simple	368 u	368 u	0.28	0.07	0.07	1.00
liftsolve.app	1179 u	1179 u	0.81	0.04	0.04	1.00
liftsolve.db1	1326 u	1326 u	1.00	0.01	0.01	1.00
liftsolve.lmkng	2773 u	2228 u	0.45	0.54	0.44	1.23
map.reduce	348 u	348 u	1.35	0.11	0.11	1.00
match.kmp	543 u	543 u	2.28	1.49	1.49	1.00
match.lam	543 u	543 u	1.60	0.95	0.95	1.00
maxlength	1083 u	1023 u	0.10	0.14	0.12	1.17
model_elim.app	444 u	444 u	1.43	0.19	0.19	1.00
regexp.r1	457 u	457 u	1.67	0.33	0.33	1.00
regexp.r2	831 u	799 u	0.51	0.25	0.18	1.39
regexp.r3	1229 u	1163 u	1.03	0.45	0.30	1.50
relative.lam	261 u	261 u	3.56	0.01	0.01	1.00
remove	2778 u	2339 u	4.66	3.83	3.44	1.11
rev_acc_type	242 u	242 u	3.39	3.39	3.39	1.00
rev_acc_type.inffail	1475 u	1475 u	3.39	0.96	0.96	1.00
rotateprune	4088 u	3454 u	5.84	6.07	5.82	1.04
ssuply.lam	262 u	262 u	0.65	0.05	0.05	1.00
transpose.lam	2312 u	2312 u	1.04	0.18	0.18	1.00
Weighted Speedup			1	2.11	2.50	1.18
Average Size	1204.91 u	952.64 u				

Table 1. Code size (in units) and Execution times (in s)

in certain contexts (this might be especially interesting when a predicate also occurs inside a negation, see the next subsection below).

Example 6. Consider the following program P:

$$p(a, b) \leftarrow$$
$$p(b, c) \leftarrow$$
$$p(X, Y) \leftarrow p(X, Z), p(Z, Y)$$

For $E_0 = \{(p, 2)\}$ (i.e. we are only interested in the first argument to p), RAF returns $E = \emptyset$ and hence $P|E = P$. The reason is that the variable Z in the call $p(X, Z)$ in the third clause of P cannot be erased. Therefore no optimisation can occur at all. To remedy this, we need a *poly-variant algorithm* which, in the process of computing a safe erasure, generates duplicate versions of some predicates, thereby allowing the erasure to behave differently on different calls to the same predicate. Such an algorithm might return the following erased program:

$$
\begin{aligned}
p(a) \quad &\leftarrow \\
p(b) \quad &\leftarrow \\
p(X) \quad &\leftarrow p(X, Z), p(Z) \\
p(a, b) \quad &\leftarrow \\
p(b, c) \quad &\leftarrow \\
p(X, Y) &\leftarrow p(X, Z), p(Z, Y)
\end{aligned}
$$

The rest of this subsection is devoted to the development of such a *poly-variant* RAF algorithm.

First, the following, slightly adapted, definition of erasing is needed. The reason is that several erasures might now be applied to the same predicate, and we have to avoid clashes between the different specialised versions for the same predicate.

Definition 15. Let E be an erasure of P. For an atom $A = p(t_1, \ldots, t_n)$, we define $A\|E = p_E(t_{j_1}, \ldots, t_{j_k})$ where $1 \leq j_1 < \ldots < j_k \leq n$ are all the indexes such that $(p, j_i) \notin E$ and where p_E denotes a predicate symbol of arity k such that $\forall p, q, E_1, E_2$ $(p_{E_1} = q_{E_2}$ iff $(p = q \wedge E_1 = E_2))$.

For example we might have that $p(X, Y)\|\{(p, 1)\} = p'(X)$ together with $p(X, Y)\|\{(p, 2)\} = p''(Y)$, thereby avoiding the name clash that occurs when using the old scheme of erasing.

Algorithm 2 (poly-variant RAF)

Input: a program P, an initial erasure E_p for a particular predicate p.
Output: a new program P' which can be called with $\leftarrow p(t_1, \ldots, t_n)\|E_p$ and
   which is correct[5] if E_p is safe for $\leftarrow p(t_1, \ldots, t_n)$.
Initialisation: $New := \{(E_p, p)\}, S := \emptyset, P' = \emptyset;$
while not $New \subseteq S$ **do**
   let $S := S \cup New, S' := New \setminus S$ and $New := \emptyset$
   for every element (E_p, p) of S' **do**
      for every clause $H \leftarrow A_1, \ldots, A_n \in Def(p, P)$
         let $E_{A_i} = \{(q_i, k) \mid A_i = q_i(t_1, \ldots, t_m) \wedge 1 \leq k \leq m \wedge (q_i, k)$ satisfies
            1. t_k is a variable X; **and**
            2. X occurs exactly once in $A_1, \ldots, A_n$; **and**
            3. X does not occur in $H\|E_p$ $\}$
         let $New := New \cup \{(E_{A_i}, q_i) \mid 1 \leq i \leq n\}$
         let $P' := P' \cup \{H\|E_p \leftarrow A_1\|E_{A_1}, \ldots, A_n\|E_{A_n}\}$
return P'

---

[5] In the sense of Def. 3, by simply replacing $P|E$ by P' and $|$ by $\|$.

Note that, in contrast to mono-variant RAF, in the poly-variant RAF algorithm there is no operation that removes a tuple from the erasure E_p. So one may wonder how the poly-variant algorithm is able to produce a correct program. Indeed, if an erasure E_p contains the tuple (p, k) this means that this particular version of p will only be called with the k-th argument being an existential variable. So, it is always correct to erase the position k in the head of a clause C for that particular version of p, because no bindings for the body will be generated by the existential variable and because we are not interested in the computed answer bindings for that variable. However the position k in a call to p somewhere else in the program, e.g. in the body of C, might not be existential. But in contrast to the mono-variant RAF algorithm, we do not have to remove the tuple (p, k): we simply generate another version for p where the k-th argument is not existential.

Example 7. Let us trace Algorithm 2 by applying it to the program P of Example 6 above and with the initial erasure $E_p = \{(p, 2)\}$ for the predicate p. For this example we can suppose that p_{E_p} is the predicate symbol p with arity 1 and $p_\emptyset$ is simply p with arity 2.

1. After the first iteration we obtain $New = \{(\emptyset, p), (\{(p, 2)\}, p)\}$, as well as $S = \{(\{(p, 2)\}, p)\}$ and $P' =$
   $$p(a) \leftarrow$$
   $$p(b) \leftarrow$$
   $$p(X) \leftarrow p(X, Z), p(Z)$$
2. After the second iteration we have $New = \{(\emptyset, p)\}$, $S = \{(\{(p, 2)\}, p), (\emptyset, p)\}$, meaning that we have reached the fixpoint. Furthermore P' is now the desired program of Example 6 above, i.e. the following clauses have been added wrt the previous iteration:
   $$p(a, b) \leftarrow$$
   $$p(b, c) \leftarrow$$
   $$p(X, Y) \leftarrow p(X, Z), p(Z, Y)$$

The erasure E_p is safe for e.g. the goal $G =\leftarrow p(a, X)$, and the specialised program P' constructed for E_p is correct for $G || E_p =\leftarrow p(a)$ (in the sense of Def. 3, by simply replacing $P|E$ by P' and $|$ by $||$). For instance $P \cup \{\leftarrow p(a, X)\}$ has the computed answer $\{X/b\}$ with $\theta' = \{X/b\}|_\emptyset = \emptyset$ and indeed $P' \cup \{\leftarrow p(a)\}$ has the computed answer $\emptyset$.

Termination of the algorithm follows from the fact that there are only finitely many erasures for every predicate. The result of Algorithm 2 is identical to the result of Algorithm 1 applied to a suitably duplicated and renamed version of the original program. Hence correctness follows from correctness of Algorithm 1 and of the duplication/renaming phase.

Handling Normal Programs

When treating *normal* logic programs an extra problem arises: erasing an argument in a negative goal might modify the floundering behaviour wrt SLDNF. In fact, the conditions of safety of Def. 11 or Def. 12 would ensure that the negative call will always flounder! So it does not make sense to remove arguments to negative calls (under the conditions of Def. 11, Def. 12) and in general it would even be incorrect to do so. Take for example the goal $\leftarrow ni$ and program P:

$$
\begin{aligned}
int(0) &\leftarrow \\
int(s(X)) &\leftarrow int(X) \\
ni &\leftarrow \neg int(Z) \\
p(a) &\leftarrow
\end{aligned}
$$

By simply ignoring the negation and applying the RAF Algorithm 1 for $E_0 = \{(int, 1)\}$ we obtain $E = E_0$ and the following program $P|E$ which behaves incorrectly for the query $G =\leftarrow ni$ (i.e. $G|E$ fails and thereby falsely asserts that everything is an integer)[6]:

$$
\begin{aligned}
int &\leftarrow \\
int &\leftarrow int \\
ni &\leftarrow \neg int \\
p(a) &\leftarrow
\end{aligned}
$$

This problem can be solved by adopting the pragmatic but safe approach of keeping all argument positions for predicates occuring inside negative literals. Hence, for the program P above, we would obtain the correct erasure $E = \emptyset$. This technique was actually used for the benchmark programs with negation of the previous section.

Further Improvements

Finally we mention that, in some cases, the conditions of Def. 12 can be relaxed. For instance, the erasure $\{(p, 1), (q, 1)\}$ is safe for the goal $p(X)$ and program:

$$
\begin{aligned}
p(X) &\leftarrow q(f(X)) \\
q(Z) &\leftarrow
\end{aligned}
$$

The reason is that, although the erased argument of $q(f(X))$ is a non-variable, the value is never used. So, whereas the RAF Algorithm 1 detects existential arguments (which might return a computed answer binding), the above is an argument which is non-existential and non-ground but whose value is never used (and for which no computed answer binding will be returned).

Those kind of arguments can be detected by another post-processing phase, executing in a similar fashion as RAF, but using reversed conditions.

---

[6] For instance in the programming language Gödel, the query $\leftarrow ni$ flounders in P while $\leftarrow ni|E =\leftarrow ni$ fails in $P|E$. Note however that in Prolog, with its unsound negation, the query $\leftarrow ni$ fails both in P and $P|E$. So this approach to erasing inside negation is actually sound wrt unsound Prolog.

Algorithm 3 (FAR)
Input: a program P.
Output: a correct erasure E for P (and any G).
Initialisation: $i := 0$; $E_0 = \top_P$;
while there exists a $(p, k) \in E_i$ and a $p(t_1, \ldots, t_n) \leftarrow B \in Clauses(P)$ such
    that
    1. t_k is not a variable; **or**
    2. t_k is a variable that occurs more than once in $p(t_1, \ldots, t_n)$; **or**
    3. t_k is a variable that occurs in $B|E_i$
do $E_{i+1} := E_i \setminus \{(p, k)\}$; $i := i + 1$;
return E_i

The justifications for the points 1–3 in the FAR algorithm are as follows:

1. If t_k is a non-variable term this means that the value of the argument will be unified with t_k. This might lead to failure or to a computed answer binding being returned. So the value of the argument is used after all and might even be instantiated.
2. If t_k is repeated variable in the head of a clause it will be unified with another argument leading to the same problems as in point 1.
3. If t_k is a variable which occurs in non-erased argument in the body of a clause then it is passed as an argument to another call in which the value might be used after all and even be instantiated.

These conditions guarantee that an erased argument is never inspected or instantiated and is only passed as argument to other calls in positions in which it is neither inspected nor instantiated.

Note that this algorithm looks very similar to the RAF Algorithm 1, except that the roles of the head and body of the clauses have been reversed. This has as consequence that, while RAF detects the arguments which are existential (and in a sense propagates unsafe erasures top-down, i.e. from the head to the body of a clause), FAR detects arguments which are never used (and propagates unsafe erasures bottom-up, i.e. from the body to the head of a clause). Also, because the erasures calculated by this algorithm do *not* change the computed answers, we can safely start the algorithm with the complete erasure $E_0 = \top_P$. It can again be seen that the outcome of the algorithm is unique.

Also note that the two algorithms RAF and FAR cannot be put into one algorithm in a straightforward way, because erasures have different meanings in the two algorithms. We can however get an optimal (mono-variant) result by running sequences of FAR and RAF alternately — until a fix-point is reached (this process is well-founded as only finitely many additional argument positions can be erased). Unfortunately, as the following examples show, one application each of RAF and FAR is not sufficient to get the optimal result.

Example 8. Let P be the following program:

$$p \qquad \leftarrow q(a, Z)$$
$$q(X, X) \leftarrow$$

Applying FAR does not give any improvement because of the multiple occurrence of the variable X in the head of the second clause. After RAF we obtain:

$$p \quad \leftarrow q(a)$$
$$q(X) \leftarrow$$

Now applying FAR we get the optimally erased program:

$$p \leftarrow q$$
$$q \leftarrow$$

So in this example the FAR algorithm benefitted from erasure performed by the RAF algorithm. The following example shows that the converse can also hold.

Example 9. Take the following program:

$$p \quad \quad \leftarrow q(X, X)$$
$$q(a, Z) \leftarrow$$

Applying RAF does not give any improvement because of the multiple occurrence of the variable X (but this time inside a call and not as in the Example 8 above inside the head). However applying FAR gives the following:

$$p \quad \leftarrow q(X)$$
$$q(a) \leftarrow$$

And now RAF can give an improvement, leading to the optimal program:

$$p \leftarrow q$$
$$q \leftarrow$$

The reason that each of the algorithms can improve the result of the other is that RAF cannot erase multiply occurring variables in the body while FAR cannot erase multiply occurring variables in the head. So, one can easily extend Examples 8 and 9 so that a sequence of applications of RAF and FAR is required for the optimal result. We have not yet examined whether the RAF and FAR algorithm can be combined in a more refined way, e.g. obtaining the optimal program in one pass and maybe also weakening the respective safety conditions by using information provided by the other algorithm.

Poly-variance for FAR

The RAF algorithm looks at *every call* to a predicate p to decide which arguments can be erased. Therefore, the poly-variant extension was based on producing specialised (but still safe) erasures for *every distinct use* of the predicate p. The FAR algorithm however looks at *every head of a clause* defining p to decide which arguments can be erased. This means that an argument might be erasable wrt one clause while not wrt another. We clearly cannot come up with a poly-variant extension of FAR by generating different erasures for every clause.

But one could imagine detecting for every call the clauses that match this call and then derive different erased versions of the same predicate. In the context of optimising residual programs produced by (conjunctive) partial deduction this does not seem to be very interesting. Indeed, every call will usually match every clause of the specialised predicate (especially for partial deduction methods which preserve characteristic trees like [15, 16]).

Negation and FAR

In contrast to RAF, the erasures obtained by FAR *can* be applied inside negative calls. The conditions of the algorithm ensure that any erased variable never returns any interesting[7] computed binding. Therefore removing such arguments, in other words allowing the selection of negative goals even for the case that this argument is non-ground, is correct wrt the completion semantics by correctness of the weaker safeness conditions for SLDNF (see page 94 of [19]). Take for example the following program P:

$$r(X) \leftarrow \neg p(X)$$
$$p(X) \leftarrow q(f(X))$$
$$q(Z) \leftarrow$$

By ignoring the negation and applying the FAR algorithm, we get the erasure $E = \{(q, 1), (p, 1), (r, 1)\}$ and thus $P|E$:

$$r \leftarrow \neg p$$
$$p \leftarrow q$$
$$q \leftarrow$$

Using $P|E \cup \{G|E\}$ instead of $P \cup \{G\}$ is correct. In addition $P|E \cup \{G|E\}$ will never flounder when using standard SLDNF, while P will flounder for any query $G = \leftarrow r(t)$ for which t is not ground. In other words, the FAR algorithm not only improves the efficiency of a program, but also its "floundering behaviour" under standard SLDNF.

Implementation

The FAR algorithm has also been implemented (by slightly re-writing the RAF algorithm) and incorporated into the ECCE system [18]. Preliminary experiments indicate that, when executed once after RAF, it is able to remove redundant arguments much less often than RAF, although in some cases it can be highly beneficial (e.g. bringing execution time of the final specialised program from 6.3 s down to 4.1 s for the memo-solve example of the DPPD library [18]). Also, it seems that an optimisation similar to FAR has recently been added to the Mercury compiler, where it is e.g. useful to get rid of arguments carrying unused type information.

---

[7] An erased variable V might only return bindings of the form V/F where F is a fresh existential variable.

6 Related Work and Conclusion

It would seem that our algorithm RAF for removal of redundant arguments is related to Proietti and Pettorossi's *Elimination Procedure* (EP) for removal of *unnecessary variables*. However, it would be a mistake to compare RAF and EP directly. RAF is intended as a simple, efficient post-processing phase for program transformers, in particular for conjunctive partial deduction, whereas EP is a less efficient, but far more powerful unfold/fold-based transformation which can remove intermediate data structures from programs. For instance, it can transform the naive double-append program to the version with $da'/4$ directly. Thus one should rather compare EP to the composition of conjunctive partial deduction with RAF.

The work in [17], among other work, helped to bridge the gap between the partial deduction and the unfold/fold areas. Roughly, the proofs in [17] show that, for every conjunctive partial deduction program specialisation, there exists an equivalent transformation sequence consisting of Tamaki-Sato definition steps and unfolding steps, followed by Tamaki-Sato folding steps. There are however some subtle differences between control in conjunctive partial deduction and control in the unfold/fold approach. Indeed, an unfold/fold transformation is usually described as doing the definition steps first (and at that point one knows which arguments are existential because existentiality can be propagated top-down — but one does not yet have the whole specialised program available) while conjunctive partial deduction can be seen as doing the definition introduction and the corresponding folding steps only at the very end (when producing the residual code). Therefore the use of an algorithm like RAF is required for conjunctive partial deduction to detect the existential variables for the respective definitions. But on the other hand this also gives conjunctive partial deduction the possibility to base its choice on the *entire* residual program. For instance one may use a mono-variant algorithm (to limit the code size) or an algorithm like FAR which, due to its bottom-up nature, has to examine the entire residual program.

Another related work is [4], which provides some pragmatics for removing unnecessary variables in the context of optimising binarized Prolog programs.

Yet another related work is that on *slicing* [29], useful in the context of debugging. RAF can also be used to perform a simple form of program slicing; for instance, one can use RAF to find the sub-part of a program which affects a certain argument. However, the slice so obtained is usually less precise than the one obtained by the specific slicing algorithm of [29] which takes Prolog's left-to-right execution strategy into account and performs a data-dependency analysis.

Similar work has also been considered in other settings than logic programming. Conventional compiler optimisations use data-flow analyses to detect and remove *dead code*, i.e. commands that can never be reached and assignments to variables whose values are not subsequently required, see [1]. These two forms of redundancy are similar to useless clauses and redundant variables.

Such techniques have also appeared in functional programming. Chin [3] describes a technique to remove *useless variables*, using an abstract interpretation (forwards analysis). A concrete program is translated into an abstract one working on a two-point domain. The least fix-point of the abstract program is computed, and from this an approximation of the set of useless variables can be derived.

Hughes [12] describes a backwards analysis for *strictness analysis*. Such analyses give for each parameter of a function the information either that the parameter *perhaps is not* used, or that the parameter *definitely is* used. The analysis in [12] can in addition give the information that a parameter *definitely is not* used, in which case it can be erased from the program.

Another technique can be based on Seidl's work [30]. He shows that the corresponding question for higher-level grammars, *parameter-reducedness*, is decidable. The idea then is to approximate a functional program by means of a higher-level grammar, and decide parameter-reducedness on the grammar.

Most work on program slicing has been done on imperative programs [33]. Reps [28] describes program slicing for functional programs as a backwards transformation.

Compared to all these techniques our algorithm is strikingly simple, very efficient, and easy to prove correct. The obvious drawback of our technique is that it is less precise. Nevertheless, the benchmarks show that our algorithm performs well on a range of mechanically generated programs, indicating a good trade-off between complexity and precision.

Acknowledgements. The work reported in this paper grew out of joint work with D. De Schreye, R. Glück, J. Jørgensen, B. Martens, and A. de Waal, to whom we are grateful for discussions. D. De Schreye, J. Jørgensen, B. Martens and anonymous referees provided valuable comments on a draft of the paper. We are also indebted to T. Reps for discussions on slicing, J. Hric and J. Gallagher for comments which led to the FAR algorithm, F. Henderson and Z. Somogyi for discussions on Mercury, as well as A. Pettorossi and M. Proietti for insightful discussions on the relation between this work and the unfold/fold approach.

References

1. A. Aho, R. Sethi, and J.D. Ullman. *Compilers: Principles, Techniques, and Design*. Addison-Wesley, 1986.
2. K. Benkerimi and P. M. Hill. Supporting transformations for the partial evaluation of logic programs. *Journal of Logic and Computation*, 3(5):469–486, October 1993.
3. W.-N. Chin. *Automatic Methods for Program Transformation*. PhD thesis, Imperial College, University of London, 1990.
4. B. Demoen. On the transformation of a Prolog program to a more efficient binary program. In K.-K. Lau and T.P. Clement, editors, *Logic Program Synthesis and Transformation*. Proceedings of LOPSTR'92, pages 242–252. Springer Verlag.
5. D.A. de Waal. Analysis and Transformation of Proof Procedures. PhD Thesis, Department of Computer Science, University of Bristol, 1992.

6. D.A. de Waal and J. Gallagher. The applicability of logic program analysis and transformation to Theorem Proving. In A. Bundy, editor, *Automated Deduction—CADE-12*, pages 207–221, 1994. Springer Verlag.

7. J. Gallagher. Tutorial on specialisation of logic programs. In *Symposium on Partial Evaluation and Semantics-Based Program Manipulation*, pages 88–98. ACM Press, 1993.

8. J. Gallagher and M. Bruynooghe. Some low-level transformations for logic programs. In M. Bruynooghe, editor, *Proceedings of Meta90 Workshop on Meta Programming in Logic*, pages 229–244, Leuven, Belgium, 1990.

9. J. Gallagher and D.A. de Waal. Deletion of redundant unary type predicates from logic programs. In K.-K. Lau and T.P. Clement, editors, *Logic Program Synthesis and Transformation*. Proceedings of LOPSTR'92, pages 151–167. Springer Verlag.

10. R. Glück and M.H. Sørensen. Partial deduction and driving are equivalent. In M. Hermenegildo and J. Penjam, editors, *Programming Language Implementation and Logic Programming. Proceedings, Lecture Notes in Computer Science* 844, pages 165–181, Madrid, Spain, 1994. Springer-Verlag.

11. R. Glück, J. Jørgensen, B. Martens, and M.H. Sørensen. Controlling conjunctive partial deduction of definite logic programs. In H. Kuchen and S.D.. Swierstra, editors, *Programming Language Implementation and Logic Programming. Proceedings, Lecture Notes in Computer Science* 1140, pages 152–166, Aachen, Germany, 1996. Springer-Verlag.

12. J. Hughes. Backwards analysis of functional programs. In D. Bjørner, A.P. Ershov, and N.D. Jones, editors, *Partial Evaluation and Mixed Computation*, pages 187–208, Amsterdam, 1988. North-Holland.

13. J. Jørgensen, M. Leuschel and B. Martens. Conjunctive partial deduction in practice. In J. Gallagher, editor, *Pre-Proceedings of LOPSTR'96*, pages 46–62, Stockholm, Sweden, August 1996. Extended version as Technical Report CW 242, Katholieke Universiteit Leuven, 1996.

14. J. Komorowski. Partial evaluation as a means for inferencing data structures in an applicative language: A theory and implementation in the case of Prolog. In *9th ACM Symposium on Principles of Programming Languages*, pages 255–167. ACM Press, 1982.

15. M. Leuschel. Ecological partial deduction: Preserving characteristic trees without constraints. In M. Proietti, editor, *Proceedings of LOPSTR'95, Lecture Notes in Computer Science* 1048, pages 1–16, 1996. Springer-Verlag.

16. M. Leuschel and B. Martens. Global control for partial deduction through characteristic atoms and global trees. In O. Danvy, R. Glück, and P. Thiemann, editors, *Proceedings Dagstuhl Seminar on Partial Evaluation, Lecture Notes in Computer Science* 1110, pages 263–283, Schloss Dagstuhl, Germany, February 1996. Springer-Verlag.

17. M. Leuschel, D. De Schreye, and A. de Waal. A Conceptual Embedding of Folding into Partial Deduction: Towards a Maximal Integration. In M. Maher, editor, *Proceedings of the Joint International Conference and Symposium on Logic Programming, JICSLP'96*, pages 319–332, Bonn, Germany, September 1996. MIT Press.

18. M. Leuschel. The ECCE partial deduction system and the DPPD library of benchmarks. Accessible via http://www.cs.kuleuven.ac.be/~lpai.

19. J.W. Lloyd. *Foundations of Logic Programming*, North-Holland, New York, 1987.

20. J.W. Lloyd and J.C. Shepherdson. Partial evaluation in logic programming. *Journal of Logic Programming*, 11(3-4):217–242, 1991.

21. J.W. Lloyd, editor. *Logic Programming: Proceedings of the 1995 International Symposium.* MIT Press, 1995.

22. K. Marriott, L. Naish, and J.-L. Lassez. Most specific logic programs. In *Proceedings of the Joint International Conference and Symposium on Logic Programming*, Seattle, 1988. IEEE, MIT Press.

23. B. Martens. *On the Semantics of Meta-Programming and the Control of Partial Deduction in Logic programming.* PhD thesis, Katholieke Universiteit Leuven, 1994.

24. B. Martens and J. Gallagher. Ensuring global termination of partial deduction while allowing flexible polyvariance. In L. Sterling, editor, *Proceedings ICLP'95*, pages 597–611, Shonan Village Center, Kanagawa, Japan, June 1995. MIT Press.

25. A. Pettorossi and M. Proietti. Transformation of logic programs: Foundations and techniques. *Journal of Logic Programming*, 19 & 20:261–320, 1994.

26. M. Proietti and A. Pettorossi. Unfolding – definition – folding, in this order for avoiding unnecessary variables in logic programs. In *Programming Language Implementation and Logic Programming, Lecture Notes in Computer Science 528*, pages 347–358. Springer-Verlag, 1991.

27. M. Proietti and A. Pettorossi. The loop absorption and the generalization strategies for the development of logic programs and partial deduction. *Journal of Logic Programming*, 16:123–161, 1993.

28. T. Reps. Program specialization via program slicing. In O. Danvy, R. Glück, and P. Thiemann, editors, *Proceedings Dagstuhl Seminar on Partial Evaluation*, pages 409–429, Schloss Dagstuhl, Germany, 1996. Springer-Verlag.

29. S. Schoenig and M. Ducassé. A hybrid backward slicing algorithm producing executable slices for Prolog. In *Proceedings of the 7th Workshop on Logic Programming Environments*, pages 41–48, Portland, USA, December 1995.

30. H. Seidl. Parameter-reduction of higher-level grammars. *Theoretical Computer Science*, 55:47–85, 1987.

31. M.H. Sørensen and R. Glück. An algorithm of generalization in positive supercompilation. In [21], pages 465–479.

32. M.H. Sørensen, R. Glück, and N.D. Jones. Towards unifying deforestation, supercompilation, partial evaluation, and generalized partial computation. In D. Sannella, editor, *Programming Languages and Systems, Lecture Notes in Computer Science 788*, pages 485–500. Springer-Verlag, 1994.

33. F. Tip. A survey of program slicing techniques. *Journal of Programming Languages* 3:121–181, 1995.

34. V.F. Turchin. The algorithm of generalization in the supercompiler. In D. Bjørner, A.P. Ershov, and N.D. Jones, editors, *Partial Evaluation and Mixed Computation*, pages 531–549. North-Holland, 1988.

35. P.L. Wadler. Deforestation: Transforming programs to eliminate intermediate trees. *Theoretical Computer Science*, 73:231–248, 1990. Preliminary version in ESOP'88, LNCS vol. 300.

Replacement Can Preserve Termination

Annalisa Bossi, Nicoletta Cocco

Dip. di Matematica Appl. e Informatica
Università di Venezia-Ca' Foscari
Via Torino, 155, Mestre-Venezia, Italy
bossi@dsi.unive.it, cocco@dsi.unive.it

Abstract. We consider the replacement transformation operation, a very general and powerful transformation, and study under which conditions it preserves universal termination besides computed answer substitutions. With this *safe replacement* we can significantly extend the safe unfold/fold transformation sequence presented in [11]. By exploiting typing information, more useful conditions can be defined and we may deal with some special cases of replacement very common in practice, namely switching two atoms in the body of a clause and the associativity of a predicate. This is a first step in the direction of exploiting a Pre/Post specification on the intended use of the program to be transformed. Such specification can restrict the instances of queries and clauses to be considered and then relax the applicability conditions on the transformation operations.

Keywords and Phrases: program transformations, universal termination, replacement, typing.

1 Introduction

When transforming programs it is necessary to take into consideration also their operational behaviour, such as their termination properties. For logic programs this makes everything more complicated: the semantics is no more declarative, the order of atoms in the clause bodies becomes relevant, the applicability of basic transformation operations must be restricted in order to ensure that also termination is preserved.

In [11] we studied which restrictions are necessary for having a safe transformation sequence able to preserve both computed answer substitutions and universal termination for any query in the original program. Such safe sequence uses few basic operations, namely the introduction of a new definition, unfold and fold of contiguous ordered atoms. This severely limits the number of transformations: we need at least to be able to reorder the atoms before folding. In this paper we substantially extend the safe sequence by adding the possibility to apply also a replacement operation. Replacement is a powerful transformation which can perform also the reordering of atoms in the bodies. We define general conditions under which the replacement preserves both computed answer substitutions and universal termination. Such conditions are very strict but by using typing and moding information we can weaken them. This is not surprising since these are the information used to prove also termination. With such an *extended safe sequence* many more transformations can be performed, for example the accumulator strategy used to linearize predicates. In fact such strategy makes use of replacement both for exploiting associativity of some predicate and for reordering the atoms before folding.

Section 2 contains some notation and very briefly recalls the definitions in [11]. Section 3 discusses general applicability conditions for replacement. and shows how to use typing information in order to weaken such conditions. In Section 4 a well-known example of accumulator strategy is obtained through the extended safe sequence. Some conclusive remarks are in Section 5. Two Appendices follow where proofs are given.

2 Preliminaries

Given a substitution η, we denote by $Dom(\eta)$ its domain, by $Ran(\eta)$ the set of variables that appear in the terms of the range of η and $Var(\eta) = Dom(\eta) \cup Ran(\eta)$. Given a substitution η and a set of variables X, we denote by $\eta_{|X}$ the substitution obtained from η by restricting its domain to X. Given an expression (term, atom, query,...) E, we denote the set of variables occurring in it by $Var(E)$. We often write $\eta_{|E}$ to denote $\eta_{|Var(E)}$. A *renaming* is a substitution which is a permutation of its domain. We write $E \sim E'$ to denote that E and E' are *variant expressions*, that is there exists a renaming ρ such that $E = E'\rho$.

We consider definite logic programs executed by means of the *LD-resolution*, which consists of the usual *SLD*-resolution combined with the leftmost selection rule. Throughout the paper we use queries instead of goals. A *query* is a sequence of atoms. □ stands for the *empty query* and **fail** for a failing query. An *LD-derivation* ending with □ is a *successful LD-derivation*, one ending with **fail** is a *failing one*.

We denote sequences by bold characters and we use an identifier, l, to label clauses and derivations. Then $l : \mathbf{Q} \xmapsto{\sigma}_P \mathbf{R}$ stands for "there exists a (partial) *LD*-derivation, l, of the query $\mathbf{Q}$ in P ending in the query $\mathbf{R}$ and σ is the composition of the *mgu's* applied during the derivation". Similarly $\mathbf{Q} \xmapsto{\sigma}_P$ □ denotes a successful *LD*-derivation of $\mathbf{Q}$ in P with *computed answer substitution (c.a.s.)* $\sigma_{|\mathbf{Q}}$. The *length* of an *LD*-derivation l is denoted by $|l|$.

The rest of the notation is more or less standard and essentially follows [1, 24].

2.1 Safe unfold/fold transformation sequence

We now recall the main definitions we gave in [11] for representing both the outcomes of successful computations and the existence of a non-terminating computation.

Definition 1 [11]. Given a program P and a query $\mathbf{Q}$ we define

$$\mathcal{M}[P](\mathbf{Q}) = \{\sigma \mid \text{there is a successful } LD\text{-derivation of } \mathbf{Q} \text{ in } P \text{ with c.a.s. } \sigma\}$$
$$\cup \{\bot \mid \text{there is an infinite } LD\text{-derivation of } \mathbf{Q} \text{ in } P\}.$$

A *query* $\mathbf{Q}$ *is universally terminating in* P iff all *LD*-derivations for $\mathbf{Q}$ in P are finite, that is $\bot \notin \mathcal{M}[P](\mathbf{Q})$.

Let P_1, P_2 be programs and $\mathbf{Q}$ a query. We say that $\mathbf{Q}$ is *equivalent in P_1 and P_2*, and write

$$\mathbf{Q} \text{ in } P_1 \simeq \mathbf{Q} \text{ in } P_2,$$

iff $\mathcal{M}[P_1](\mathbf{Q}) = \mathcal{M}[P_2](\mathbf{Q})$. □

In [11] we consider the two inclusions of Definition 1 separately and introduce two corresponding requirements on transformations. They correspond, with our semantics, to the usual requirements of completeness and correctness.

Definition 2 [11]. Let P' be obtained by transforming a program P and let $\mathbf{Q}$ be a query.
We say that *the transformation of P into P' is complete wrt $\mathbf{Q}$* iff:

$$if\ \mathbf{Q} \vdash\!\!\!-\!\!{}^{\theta}_{P}\ \square, \text{ then there exists } \mathbf{Q} \vdash\!\!\!-\!\!{}^{\theta'}_{P'}\ \square \text{ and } \mathbf{Q}\theta = \mathbf{Q}\theta'.$$

We say that *the transformation of P into P' is complete* when it is complete wrt any query. □

A *transformation of a program P into P' is complete* iff for any query its successful *LD*-derivations are preserved. Complete transformations do not lose c.a.s, but they could lose or add infinite derivations.

Definition 3 [11]. We say that *the transformation of P into P' is non-increasing wrt $\mathbf{Q}$* iff the following condition holds:

- for any partial *LD*-derivation of $\mathbf{Q}$ in P': $l' : \mathbf{Q} \vdash\!\!\!-\!\!{}^{\delta'}_{P'}\ \mathbf{R}'$, there exists a partial *LD*-derivation of $\mathbf{Q}$ in P, $l : \mathbf{Q} \vdash\!\!\!-\!\!{}^{\delta}_{P}\ \mathbf{R}$, of length greater or equal to the one in P', $\mid l \mid \geq \mid l' \mid$ and if $\mathbf{R}' = \square$ (i.e. we are considering a successful *LD*-derivation of $\mathbf{Q}$ in P') then $\mathbf{R} = \square$ and $\mathbf{Q}\delta \sim \mathbf{Q}\delta'$ (*correctness*).

We say that *the transformation of P into P' is non-increasing* when it is non-increasing wrt any query.

□

A non-increasing transformation cannot add c.a.s. and it preserves termination. Non-increasingness is a very strong requirement, it basically ensures that the depth of the *LD*-tree associated to a universally terminating query $\mathbf{Q}$ cannot be increased by the transformation.

Theorem 4 [11]. *Let P' be obtained from P through a transformation which is complete and non-increasing wrt $\mathbf{Q}$. Then if $\mathbf{Q}$ is universally terminating in P,*

$$\mathbf{Q} \text{ in } P \simeq \mathbf{Q} \text{ in } P'.$$

□

In [11] we considered basic transformation operations, such as new definition introduction, unfold and fold, which are required in standard transformation sequences [32, 36, 37].

It is a common technique in program transformation to group the predicates one wants to manipulate under a new name. It corresponds to extend the program with a new definition clause which abstracts such predicates.

Definition 5. Let P be a program, $N = new(\mathbf{t})$ be an atom where *new* is a new predicate symbol not occurring in P, $\mathbf{B}$ a sequence of atoms defined in P such that $Var(N) \subseteq Var(\mathbf{B})$ and $def : N \leftarrow \mathbf{B}.$ a new clause. Then the program $P' = P \cup \{def\}$ is an extension of P and def is *a new definition in P'.* □

Theorem 6 [11]. *Let P' be obtained as an extension of P with a new definition $def : N \leftarrow \mathbf{B}$.*
Then for any substitution θ such that $Var(\theta) \cap Var(def) \subseteq Var(N)$,

$$\mathcal{M}[P](\mathbf{B}\theta)_{|N_\theta} = \mathcal{M}[P'](N\theta)$$

and for any query $\mathbf{Q}$ in P

$$\mathbf{Q} \text{ in } P \simeq \mathbf{Q} \text{ in } P'.$$

□

Unfolding an atom in the body of a clause corresponds to performing one partial evaluation step of all *LD*-derivations which may apply that clause. Unfolding in logic programs was originally considered by Komorowski [23] and formally studied by Sato and Tamaki [37] and others.

Definition 7. Let $c : H \leftarrow \mathbf{A}, B, \mathbf{C}.$ be a clause of P. Suppose that $d_1, \ldots, d_n$ are all the clauses of P whose head unifies with B and for $i \in [1, n]$, $d_i' : H_i \leftarrow \mathbf{B_i}.$ is a variant of d_i with no common variables with c. Let, for $i \in [1, n]$, $\theta_i = mgu(B, H_i)$ and $c_i : (H \leftarrow \mathbf{A}, \mathbf{B_i}, \mathbf{C})\theta_i$. Then we define

$$unfold(P, B, c) = (P \setminus \{c\}) \cup \{c_1, \ldots, c_n\},$$

and say that $unfold(P, B, c)$ is the result of *unfolding B in c in P*, briefly it is *an unfolding of P.*
The clauses $\{c_1, \ldots, c_n\}$ are called unfoldings of c. □

Unfolding is a complete transformation for all queries. The result is due to the independence of the selection rule and the fact that unfolding preserves the computed answer substitution semantics [10, 22]. In [11] we proved that it is also non-increasing. Hence no restrictive condition is necessary in order to preserve universal termination and c.a.s. when using unfolding alone.
The stronger property of being strictly decreasing becomes useful when composing unfolding with folding.

Definition 8 [11]. *Let P be a program and P' be obtained from P by unfolding an atom B in a clause c in P and let $\mathbf{G}$ be a class of queries. Unfolding B in c in P is decreasing (wrt $\mathbf{G}$)* iff for any query $\mathbf{Q} \in \mathbf{G}$ and for any partial LD-derivation, which at some point uses an unfolding of c as input clause, $l' : \mathbf{Q} \stackrel{\theta'}{\longmapsto}_{P'} \mathbf{R}'$, there exists an LD-derivation $l : \mathbf{Q} \stackrel{\theta}{\longmapsto}_P \mathbf{R}$ in P such that $| l' | < | l |$.
□

Lemma 9. *Let $c : N \leftarrow \mathbf{A}, B, \mathbf{C}.$ be the only clause in P defining the predicate symbol of N. Let α be a substitution such that $\mathbf{A}\alpha$ has no failing derivation in P. Then, unfolding B in c in P is decreasing wrt $\mathbf{G} = \{N\alpha\}$.* □

This is a generalization of Corollary 15 in [11] which states that unfolding the leftmost atom in the body of the definition c is decreasing wrt $\{N\alpha\}$ for all substitutions α. This more general statement is a consequence of case 1 in the proof of Theorem 3.4 in [11]. In our safe transformation sequence we require that unfolding B in c in P is decreasing for any substitution α produced by using c as an input clause in an LD-derivation in P, namely for any α such that $Var(\alpha) \cap Var(c) \subseteq Var(N)$.

Example 1. Let us consider the program P which is meant to generate all the non-empty lists consisting of at most three elements and which are prefixes of a set of predefined lists.

```
c: prefix3(Ys) ← ourlists(Xs), prefix(Xs, Ys), length(Ys, N),
      lesseq3(N).
   ourlists([1, 2, 3, 4, 5]).
   ourlists([1, 1, 1, 1]).
   ourlists([a, b, c, d, e, f]).
   prefix(Xs, []).
   prefix([X |Xs], [X |Ys]) ← prefix(Xs, Ys).
   length([], 0).
   length([X |Xs], s(N)) ← length(Xs, N).
   lesseq3(s(0)).
   lesseq3(s(s(0))).
   lesseq3(s(s(s(0)))).
```

Unfolding $prefix(Xs,Ys)$ in c in P is decreasing wrt $\{prefix3(Ys)\alpha\}$ for all substitutions α produced by using c as an input clause in an LD-derivation in P, since the corresponding instance $ourlists(Xs)\alpha$ is never failing. □

Note that in order to apply the sufficient condition for a decreasing unfold given by Lemma 9, we need to be able to characterize when a query has no failing derivation, which is not a trivial task in general.

Folding a predicate in the body of a clause replaces a conjunction of atoms with an equivalent atom, which are in general instances respectively of the body and the head of a definition clause. Fold is generally performed as a final transformation step in order first to pack back unfolded predicates in a definition and to introduce recursion, *recursive folding*, then to bypass the body predicates which are in clauses not related with the definition itself, *propagation folding*. The definition of fold we gave in [11] is completely general and valid both for recursive and propagation folding. It does not specify any restrictive condition apart from the obvious ones preventing from incorrect instantiations of variables.

Definition 10. Let P be a program, $def : N \leftarrow \mathbf{B}$. a new definition in P and $Y = Var(\mathbf{B}) \setminus Var(N)$. Let P_1 be obtained by transforming P and $c : H \leftarrow \mathbf{A}, \mathbf{B}\tau, \mathbf{C}$. a clause in P_1. If

- τ restricted to $(Dom(\tau) \setminus Var(N))$ is a renaming;
- $Var(Y\tau) \cap Var(H, \mathbf{A}, \mathbf{C}, N\tau) = \emptyset$;

then we define
$$fold(P_1, c, \mathbf{B}\tau, def) = (P_1 \setminus \{c\}) \cup \{c'\}$$

where $c' : H \leftarrow \mathbf{A}, N\tau, \mathbf{C}.$ and we say that $fold(P_1, c, \mathbf{B}\tau, def)$ is the result of *folding* c *with def in* P_1. □

Note that if the condition for folding holds, then we also have:
$$Var(H, \mathbf{A}, \mathbf{C}) \cap Var(\mathbf{B}\tau) = Var(H, \mathbf{A}, \mathbf{C}) \cap Var(N\tau).$$

By combining new definition, unfold and fold operations, in [11] we get a transformation schema which is similar to the one defined by Tamaki and Sato in [37] but more restrictive. Since we are considering LD-derivations, the order of the atoms in the clause bodies is taken into account, namely we can fold only consecutive atoms. Furthermore our transformation schema requires the operations to be performed in a fixed order: in particular it requires an initial decreasing unfolding step to be applied to a new definition clause and does not allow a *propagation folding* to take place before *recursive foldings*. We believe that in practice this restriction does not bother so much, since it corresponds to the natural procedure that one follows in transforming a program.

Definition 11 [11]. Let P be a program, and

(i) P_0 be an extension of P with *a new definition, def* $: N \leftarrow \mathbf{B}.$:
$$P_0 = P \cup \{def\};$$

(ii) P_1 be obtained from P_0 by a *decreasing unfolding of def wrt* $\{N\alpha\}$ for any substitution α:
$$P_1 = P \cup Q_1,$$

where Q_1 is obtained by unfolding def;

(iii) P_2, be obtained from P_1 by a *non-increasing and complete transformation* applied to clauses which are not in P:
$$P_2 = P \cup Q_2,$$

where Q_2 is obtained by the transformation of Q_1;

(iv) P_3, be obtained from P_2 by *recursive folding with def* in Q_2:
$$P_3 = P \cup Q_3,$$

where Q_3 is obtained by recursive folding in Q_2;

(v) P_4, be obtained from P_3 by *propagation folding with def* to clauses in P:
$$P_4 = P_{fold} \cup Q_3,$$

where P_{fold} is obtained by propagation folding in P

then P_4 *is obtained from a program* P *and a new definition clause def by a safe transformation sequence.* □

In [11] we proved that *a safe transformation sequence is both complete and non-increasing* and then *it is semantics preserving for all universally terminating queries.* The restrictions we impose on the sequence are meant to preserve the decreasing property introduced at step (ii) in order to prevent recursive folding from introducing loops.

Example 2. Let us consider the following trivial transformation sequence:

i)

P_0: q ← q, r.
d: t ← r, q̲.

Note that t fails.

ii)   unfold q in d:

P_0:q ← q, r.
Q_1:t ← r̲,̲ q̲, r.

iv)   recursive fold with d in Q_1:

P_0:q ← q, r.
Q_3:t ← t, r.

Now t diverges. The problem is due to the fact that step (ii) does not correspond to a decreasing unfolding.

□

Examples of using a safe unfold/fold transformation sequence can be easily found among the transformations which start from a generate-and-test program or in general which eliminate intermediate data structures.

On the other hand, many common transformations cannot fit into a safe unfold/fold sequence unless we introduce some further basic operation. In fact the restriction of considering relevant the order of atoms in the bodies could be a serious limitation since it requires that the atoms to be folded are next to each other in exactly the same sequence as in the body of the folding clause. This can be solved as we proposed in [14], namely by introducing a further basic transformation operation, the *switch* one (called also clause rearrangement in [29, 30]), which allows for atoms reordering. Other interesting transformations, which cannot be captured with the previous basic operations alone, deal with linearization of recursion by introducing an accumulator. They make use of the associative property of some predicate, for example the append predicate for lists. In order to extend the safe unfold/fold sequence for capturing these cases, in the next section we consider a more general and powerful basic operation: the replacement of a sequence of atoms in a body with another sequence.

3 Replacement

3.1 Safe Replacement

In point (iii) of Definition 11 we allowed *any complete and non-increasing transformation* to be applied to clauses not in P, namely in Q_1. In order to enrich our transformation strategy we single out conditions under which a replacement is complete and non-increasing, namely when we can replace a sequence of atoms by another sequence without losing universal termination. Replacement has been already studied with respect to various declarative semantics (see [12, 13, 21, 26, 29, 30, 35, 37]). We give here a very general definition.

Definition 12. Let $\mathbf{B}'$ be a sequence of atoms defined in P, $c : H \leftarrow \mathbf{A}, \mathbf{B}, \mathbf{C}$. be a clause in P and let $c' : H \leftarrow \mathbf{A}, \mathbf{B}', \mathbf{C}$.
Let X be the set of *common variables* and Y be the set of *private variables in* $\mathbf{B}$ *and* $\mathbf{B}'$, namely $X = Var(\mathbf{B}) \cap Var(\mathbf{B}')$ and $Y = Var(\mathbf{B}, \mathbf{B}') \setminus X$.
If *the variables in* Y *are local wrt* c *and* c', that is $Var(H, \mathbf{A}, \mathbf{C}) \cap Y = \emptyset$, then we define

$$replace(P, c, \mathbf{B}, \mathbf{B}') = (P \setminus \{c\}) \cup \{c'\}$$

and say that $replace(P, c, \mathbf{B}, \mathbf{B}')$ is the result of *a replacement of* $\mathbf{B}$ *with* $\mathbf{B}'$ *in* c *in* P. □

Note that a replacement must be syntactically correct, namely private variables Y must not produce different bindings of $\mathbf{B}$ and $\mathbf{B}'$ with their contexts c and c'.
Definition 12 specifies only such a syntactic condition on variables, hence in general such transformation does not produce an equivalent program. A further requirement to impose is the equivalence of $\mathbf{B}$ and $\mathbf{B}'$ wrt common variables in our semantics. But this is not enough as the following simple examples show.

Example 3. 1)   Let us consider the well-known program *app*, for appending two lists and let c be
$p(X1, X2, X3, Ys) \leftarrow app(X1, X2, Ts), app(Ts, X3, Ys)$.
and $\mathbf{B} = app(X1, X2, Ts), app(Ts, X3, Ys)$,
while $\mathbf{B}' = app(Ts, X3, Ys), app(X1, X2, Ts)$.
Then the common variables are $X = \{X1, X2, X3, Ys, Ts\}$ and there is no private one, $Y = \emptyset$.
This is a particular case of replacement, a *switch* operation, permuting two adjacent atoms.
$\mathbf{B}$ is equivalent to $\mathbf{B}'$ wrt our semantics and both $\mathcal{M}[P](\mathbf{B})_{|X}$ and $\mathcal{M}[P](\mathbf{B}')_{|X}$ contain $\{\perp\}$.
But let us consider now the substitution $\theta = \{X1 = [a], X2 = [b]\}$.
$Dom(\theta) \subseteq X$ with $Var(\theta) \cap Y = \emptyset$, then
$\mathcal{M}[P](\mathbf{B}\theta)_{|X\theta} = \{\{Ts = [a, b], Ys = [a, b \mid X3]\}\}$,
while
$\mathcal{M}[P](\mathbf{B}'\theta)_{|X\theta} = \{\{Ts = [a, b], Ys = [a, b \mid X3]\}, \perp\}$.
Hence *even if* $\mathbf{B}$ *is equivalent to* $\mathbf{B}'$ *wrt* X *in our semantics, this is not sufficient to guarantee that* c *and* c' *will produce the same result when used as input clauses in an LD-derivation.* We have to take into account their instances.

2)   Let us consider:

c: p ← s, r.
    r.

where p finitely fails with the LD-derivation: $p \longmapsto_P s, r \longmapsto_P$ **fail**.
Let $\mathbf{B} = s, r$ and $\mathbf{B}' = r, s$, then X and Y are empty. $\mathbf{B}$ and $\mathbf{B}'$ are equivalent wrt
our semantics:

$\mathcal{M}[P](\mathbf{B})_{|X} = \mathcal{M}[P](\mathbf{B}')_{|X} = \emptyset$.

By replacement we obtain:

c': p ← r, s.
    r.

p is still finitely failing but through a longer LD-derivation: $p \mid \longrightarrow_P r, s \mid \longrightarrow_P$
$s \longmapsto_P$ **fail**.
In this example the semantics is preserved but *the transformation is not non-increasing*. □

Definition 13. Let $\mathbf{B}$ and $\mathbf{B}'$ be sequences of atoms, $c : H \leftarrow \mathbf{A}, \mathbf{B}, \mathbf{C}$. a clause in
a program P. Let X be the set of *common variables* and Y be the set of *private
variables* in $\mathbf{B}$ and $\mathbf{B}'$. Let $c' : H \leftarrow \mathbf{A}, \mathbf{B}', \mathbf{C}$.
Replacing $\mathbf{B}$ with $\mathbf{B}'$ in c is safe wrt P iff

– *the variables in Y are local wrt c and c':*

$$Var(H, \mathbf{A}, \mathbf{C}) \cap Y = \emptyset;$$

for all substitutions θ such that $Var(\theta) \cap Var(c) \subseteq Var(H, \mathbf{A})$, $Var(\theta) \cap Y = \emptyset$,

– $\mathbf{B}$ *and* $\mathbf{B}'$ *are equivalent in c wrt P:*

$$\mathcal{M}[P](\mathbf{B}\theta)_{|X\theta} = \mathcal{M}[P](\mathbf{B}'\theta)_{|X\theta};$$

– $\mathbf{B}'$ *is non-increasing in c wrt $\mathbf{B}$ in P:*
  for any partial LD-derivation $l' : \mathbf{B}'\theta \mid \overset{\delta'}{\longrightarrow}_P \mathbf{R}'$, there exists a partial LD-
  derivation $l : \mathbf{B}\theta \mid\longrightarrow^{\delta}_P \mathbf{R}$, of length greater or equal to the one of $\mathbf{B}'\theta$, $\mid l \mid \geq \mid l' \mid$
  and if $\mathbf{R}' = \square$ (i.e. we are considering a successful LD-derivation of $\mathbf{B}'\theta$ in P)
  then $\mathbf{R} = \square$ and $X\theta\delta' \sim X\theta\delta$. □

Intuitively, a replacement of $\mathbf{B}$ by $\mathbf{B}'$ in c is safe wrt P if, for all the instances of $\mathbf{B}$
produced by c as input clause, the computational behaviour of all the corresponding
instances of $\mathbf{B}'$ in P is the same and the LD-derivations are not longer.
Note that safety is a property not computable in general, but often verifiable in P.

Lemma 14. *Let P be a program and $\mathbf{B}, \mathbf{B}'$ be sequences of atoms whose relations
are defined in P. Assume that P' is obtained from P by replacing $\mathbf{B}$ with $\mathbf{B}'$ in a
clause of P, with a safe replacement wrt P. Then the transformation of P into P'
is complete and non-increasing.* □

The proof is given in Appendix A.

Corollary 15. *Let P be a program and* **B**, **B**′ *be sequences of atoms whose relations are defined in P. Assume that P′ is obtained from P by replacing* **B** *with* **B**′ *in a clause of P, with a safe replacement wrt P. Then for any query* **Q**, *universally terminating in P:*

$$\textbf{Q} \text{ in } P \simeq \textbf{Q} \text{ in } P'.$$

□

Corollary 15 follows from Theorem 4

We give a few simple examples of replacements which are safe and then universal termination preserving.

Example 4. 1)   Let us consider the program *P*:

```
c: p ← q, r.
   r.
   s ← q.
```

Let **B** = q, r and **B**′ = q. Clearly replacing **B** with **B**′ in *c* is safe wrt *P* since it is trivially syntactically correct and both **B** and **B**′ are finitely failing with *LD*-derivations of equal length.
The resulting program is *P*′:

```
c: p ← q.
   r.
   s ← q.
```

This transformation is an example of *eliminating all the atoms which follow a failing one in a clause body.*

2)   Let *P* be the program:

```
c: p(X) ← s(a), r(Y), q(X).
   r(X) ← q(X).
   q(a).
   q(b).
   s(X).
```

Let **B** = $s(a), r(Y)$ and **B**′ = $r(Y), s(a)$. This is a safe replacement in *c* since it satisfies the first syntactic condition and it satisfies also the two further conditions because of the equivalence of **B** and **B**′ in *c* and non-increasingness of **B**′ in *c* wrt **B** in *P* in definition 13.
This is an example of *switching two independent, universally terminating and not finitely failing atoms* which is a simple case of safe replacement.

3)   Let *P* be the program:

```
c: p(Z) ← app(l₁, l₂, Y1), app(Y1, l₃, Z).
```

where app is the usual append predicate and l_1, l_2, l_3 are lists of fixed length.
Let $\mathbf{B} = app(l_1, l_2, Y1), app(Y1, l_3, Z)$ and $\mathbf{B}' = app(l_2, l_3, Y2), app(l_1, Y2, Z)$. This replacement in c satisfies the syntactic condition and it satisfies the two further conditions for safety because of the equivalence of $\mathbf{B}$ and $\mathbf{B}'$ in c and non-increasingness of $\mathbf{B}'$ in c wrt $\mathbf{B}$ in P. In fact an instantiation θ of Z will determine in both $\mathbf{B}$ and $\mathbf{B}'$ either success or failure. In any case $\mathbf{B}'\theta$ will have a shorter derivation wrt the corresponding one of $\mathbf{B}\theta$.

This is a replacement which corresponds to an algebraic property: the *associative property* of app. □

The conditions for a safe replacement are very restrictive since they require both equivalence and non-increasingness properties for all θ-instances of $\mathbf{B}$ and $\mathbf{B}'$, where θ is such that $Var(\theta) \cap Var(c) \subseteq Var(H, \mathbf{A})$, $Var(\theta) \cap Y = \emptyset$. This corresponds to requiring equivalence and non-increasingness properties for all instances of $\mathbf{B}$ and $\mathbf{B}'$ produced in an LD-derivation by the input clause c. This is a very strong requirement and very difficult to verify in general. The ideal situation would be to require equivalence and non-increasingness only for those instances of $\mathbf{B}$ and $\mathbf{B}'$ which we use, namely the ones which can appear in the resolvents of LD-derivations of our queries.

In order to relax our requirements, typing information can be very useful. It is very reasonable to assume typing information for a program we want to transform, since typing information is relevant for termination. Given a program P, termination properties can be stated only for specific queries. For example the query $app([X1, X2, X3], Ys, Zs)$, where app stands for the usual program for appending lists, has only one LD-derivation which terminates with c.a.s. $\{(Zs = [X1, X2, X3 |Ys])\}$, while for the query $app(Xs, [], Zs)$ we also have a non-terminating LD-derivation. What is actually relevant for termination is the instantiation of the predicates in the query. This instantiation will make some terms "sufficiently structured" to ensure termination. Typing information concerns precisely terms instantiation and structure.

Example 5. 1)   Let us consider the program P:

```
sacc([], Acc, Acc).
c: sacc([X |Xs], Tot, Acc) ← sumlist(Xs, S), sum(X, Acc, T),
       sum(S, T, Tot).
```

It corresponds to an intermediate step in a transformation which is meant to linearize the predicate $sumlist(Xs, S)$ which is not tail-recursive.
The typing is:
sacc has the first and the last terms in input, respectively a list of natural numbers and a natural number, while the second term is a natural number in output;
sumlist has the first term in input, a list of naturals, while the second term is a natural in output;
sum has the first two terms which are naturals in input and the third one in output.
Now let $\mathbf{B} = sumlist(Xs, S), sum(X, Acc, T)$ and $\mathbf{B}' = sum(X, Acc, T), sumlist(Xs, S)$.
Intuitively when c is instantiated "correctly wrt the typing", then both $\mathbf{B}$ and $\mathbf{B}'$

are also "correct", they terminate and are equivalent in c. Moreover they have LD-derivations of the same length. Hence *such a switching of atoms is both complete and non-increasing.*

Note that *this is not a safe replacement*, since the equivalence and the non-increasing properties are not satisfied for all θ instantiations. For example with $\theta = \{X = 0, Acc = s(0), Xs = a\}$, $c\theta$ is not "correct" wrt the typing and $\mathbf{B'}\theta$ is not non-increasing in c wrt $\mathbf{B}\theta$ since it has a longer failing derivation.

2)   Let P be the program:

```
   racc([], Ys, Acc) ← app([], Acc, Ys).
c: racc([X |Xs], Ys, Acc) ← reverse(Xs, Rs'), app(Rs', [X], Rs),
       app(Rs, Acc, Ys).
```

This is also an intermediate step of a transformation, shown in Section 4, which introduces an accumulator to linearize the naive $reverse(Xs, Ys)$ predicate.

racc has the first and the last terms which are lists in input, while the second term is a list in output;

reverse has the first term which is a list in input and the second one a list in output;

app has the first two terms which are lists in input and the third one in output.

Now let $\mathbf{B} = app(Rs', [X], Rs), app(Rs, Acc, Ys)$ and $\mathbf{B}' = app([X], Acc, Ts), app(Rs', Ts, Ys)$.

Intuitively when c is instantiated "correctly wrt the typing", then both $\mathbf{B}$ and $\mathbf{B}'$ are also "correct", they terminate and are equivalent in c. Moreover any LD-derivation of $\mathbf{B}$ is longer than the corresponding one of $\mathbf{B}'$. Hence *wrt to this typing, the replacement of $\mathbf{B}$ with $\mathbf{B}'$ in c is both complete and non-increasing.*

Also this one is not a safe replacement. Let us consider the substitution $\theta = \{Rs' = a\}$, then $c\theta$ is not "correctly" typed and $\mathbf{B}'\theta$ is not non-increasing in c wrt $\mathbf{B}\theta$ in P. In fact $\mathbf{B}\theta$ fails by a shorter derivation.

$\square$

3.2   Replacement with Typing Information

In this section we make use of one of the possible specifications of modes and types for weakening the conditions required on replacement in order to be safe and then preserve our semantics. We only briefly recall the main definitions and properties of such types. A complete treatment can be found in [2, 3] and [20].

Definition 16 [3]. A *type* is a decidable set of terms closed under substitution. $\square$

Certain types are of special interest since they are used very frequently in our programs:

   $List$ — the set of lists,
   Nat — the set of natural numbers,
   $ListNat$ — the set of lists of natural numbers,
   $Ground$ — the set of ground terms,
   $GroundList$ — the set of lists of ground terms,
   Any — the set of all terms.

Definition 17 [3].

- A *type judgement* is a statement of the form

$$s : S \Rightarrow t : T. \tag{1}$$

- A *type judgement (1) is true*

$$\models s : S \Rightarrow t : T,$$

iff for all substitutions θ, $s\theta \in S$ implies $t\theta \in T$. □

For example, the type judgement $s(s(x)) : Nat, \; l : ListNat \Rightarrow [x \mid l] : ListNat$ is true. Obviously in order to prove that a type judgement is true we need a type theory.

Definition 18 [3]. Consider an n-ary predicate symbol p.
A *type for p* is a function t_p from $[1, n]$ to the set of types.
A *mode for p* is a function m_p from $[1, n]$ to the set $\{+, -\}$.
If $m_p(i) = $ '$+$', we call m_i an *input position of p* and if $m_p(i) = $ '$-$', we call i an *output position of p* (both wrt m_p).
A predicate symbol with a mode and a type is a *typed predicate*. □

This definition assumes one mode per predicate in a program. Multiple modes may be obtained by simply renaming the predicates.
We consider a combination of modes and types and adopt the following

Assumption *Every considered predicate has a fixed mode and a fixed type associated with it, namely it is typed.* □

An n-ary predicate p with a mode m_p and type t_p will be denoted by

$$p(m_p(1) : t_p(1), \ldots, m_p(n) : t_p(n)).$$

For example, $app(+ : List, \; + : List, \; - : List)$ denotes a ternary predicate app with the first two positions moded as input and typed as $List$, and the third position moded as output and typed as $List$.
To simplify the notation, when writing an atom as $p(\mathbf{u} : \mathbf{S}, \mathbf{v} : \mathbf{T})$ we assume that $\mathbf{u} : \mathbf{S}$ is a sequence of typed terms filling in the input positions of p and $\mathbf{v} : \mathbf{T}$ is a sequence of typed terms filling in the output positions of p. We call a construct of the form $p(\mathbf{u} : \mathbf{S}, \mathbf{v} : \mathbf{T})$ a *typed atom*. We say that a typed atom $p(s_1 : S_1, \ldots, s_n : S_n)$ is *correctly typed in position i* if $s_i \in S_i$ and simply *correctly typed* if it is so in all its positions.

Definition 19 [3].

- A query $p_1(\mathbf{i_1} : \mathbf{I_1}, \mathbf{o_1} : \mathbf{O_1}), \ldots, p_n(\mathbf{i_n} : \mathbf{I_n}, \mathbf{o_n} : \mathbf{O_n})$ is *well-typed* iff for $j \in [1, n]$

$$\models \mathbf{o_1} : \mathbf{O_1}, \ldots, \mathbf{o_{j-1}} : \mathbf{O_{j-1}} \Rightarrow \mathbf{i_j} : \mathbf{I_j}.$$

- A clause $p_0(\mathbf{o_0} : \mathbf{O_0}, \mathbf{i_{n+1}} : \mathbf{I_{n+1}}) \leftarrow p_1(\mathbf{i_1} : \mathbf{I_1}, \mathbf{o_1} : \mathbf{O_1}), \ldots, p_n(\mathbf{i_n} : \mathbf{I_n}, \mathbf{o_n} : \mathbf{O_n})$. is *well-typed* iff for $j \in [1, n+1]$

$$\models \mathbf{o_0} : \mathbf{O_0}, \ldots, \mathbf{o_{j-1}} : \mathbf{O_{j-1}} \Rightarrow \mathbf{i_j} : \mathbf{I_j}.$$

– A program is *well-typed* iff every clause of it is. □

Note that a query with only one atom is well-typed iff this atom is correctly typed in its input positions.

The following Lemma and Corollary, stated in [3, 20], are extremely important for our purposes since they show the persistence of the notion of being well-typed through *LD*-derivations.

Lemma 20 [3, 20]. *An LD-resolvent of a well-typed query and a well-typed clause is well-typed.*
An instance of a well-typed query (resp. clause) is well-typed. □

Corollary 21 [3, 20]. *Let P and Q be well-typed and let l be an LD-derivation of Q in P. All atoms selected in l are correctly typed in their input positions.* □

Example 6. Let us consider the usual program for appending two lists:

```
app([], Ys, Ys).
app([X |Xs] , Ys, [X |Zs]) ← app(Xs, Ys, Zs).
```

We may easily prove that the *app* program (namely, both its clauses) is well-typed wrt each of the following types:
$$app(+ : List, + : List, - : List), app(+ : List, + : List, + : List),$$
$$app(+ : List, - : Any, - : Any), app(- : List, - : List, + : List),$$
$$app(+ : List, - : List, + : List), app(- : List, + : List, + : List).$$
The former three typings correspond to using *app* for concatenating lists, the latter ones correspond to using *app* for splitting a list.

Let us consider the first of these typings, $app(+ : List, + : List, - : List)$. The query $app([], a, a)$ is not well-typed wrt it, but it has a successful *LD*-derivation with empty c.a.s.

On the other hand the query $app([1], [2], a)$ is well-typed wrt the same typing, but it is not correctly typed in all its positions and it fails.

The query $app([1], [2], [3])$ is correctly typed, but this query also fails. □

Termination of *LD*-derivations is related to well-typing and in the termination proofs we can make use of typing information. The typical situation is as follows. We have a program P and a query Q which are well-typed wrt a given typing. The typing specifies the structure of input terms. By associating some measure to input terms (a norm in [15], a level mapping in [5]) we may prove that Q universally terminates in P. But also a termination by failure is possible, in fact the previous examples show that the well-typing of a query and a program does not imply the absence of failures. Also the correct typing of the query does not imply the absence of failures. Hence there is no easy way to relate well-typing and successful *LD*-derivations. On the other hand, by adopting a more informative Pre/Post typing specification, it is possible to characterize only successful finite derivations. In the previous examples the specification $Pre(app(x, y, z)) = \{x \in List, y \in List, z \in Var\}$, $Post(app(x, y, z)) = \{x \in List, y \in List, z \in List\}$, when satisfied, can be proved to ensure successful termination of a query. We have just added to the typing the further information that, before the computation of the *app* predicate, the output term can only be a variable. Clearly the queries $app([1], [2], a)$ and $app([1], [2], [3])$ are no longer correct wrt this specification and any query correct wrt it cannot fail and still terminates. In [3] relations among well-typing and correctness wrt Pre/Post specifications are examined. See also [9, 17, 19] for verification techniques of correctness wrt Pre/Post specifications. In this paper we consider only the well-typing properties for simplicity, but other properties such as being simply moded [6] could be useful in a stronger Pre/Post specification approach.

Because of the Corollary 21 we can restrict the equivalence and non-increasingness conditions to well-typed instances of $\mathbf{B}$ and $\mathbf{B}'$. Note that in the previous examples only well-typed instances of $\mathbf{B}$ and $\mathbf{B}'$ are actually interesting for replacement.

Definition 22. Let $\mathbf{B}$ and $\mathbf{B}'$ be sequences of atoms, P a well-typed program and $c : H \leftarrow \mathbf{A}, \mathbf{B}, \mathbf{C}.$ a clause in P. Let X be the set of *common variables* and Y the set of *private variables* in $\mathbf{B}$ and $\mathbf{B}'$. Let $c' : H \leftarrow \mathbf{A}, \mathbf{B}', \mathbf{C}.$
Replacing $\mathbf{B}$ with $\mathbf{B}'$ in c is safe wrt P and its typing iff

– *the variables in Y are local wrt c and c':*

$$Var(H, \mathbf{A}, \mathbf{C}) \cap Y = \emptyset;$$

for all substitutions θ such that $Var(\theta) \cap Var(c) \subseteq Var(H, \mathbf{A})$, $Var(\theta) \cap Y = \emptyset$ and $c\theta$ is well-typed,

– $c'\theta$ *is also well-typed;*
– $\mathbf{B}$ *and $\mathbf{B}'$ are equivalent in c wrt P:*

$$\mathcal{M}[P](\mathbf{B}\theta)_{|X\theta} = \mathcal{M}[P](\mathbf{B}'\theta)_{|X\theta};$$

– $\mathbf{B}'$ *is non-increasing in c wrt $\mathbf{B}$ in P:*

for any partial LD-derivation $l' : \mathbf{B}'\theta \overset{\delta'}{\longmapsto}_P \mathbf{R}'$, there exists a partial LD-derivation $l : \mathbf{B}\theta \overset{\delta}{\longmapsto}_P \mathbf{R}$, of length greater or equal to the one of $\mathbf{B}'\theta$, $| l | \geq | l' |$ and if $\mathbf{R}' = \square$ (i.e. we are considering a successful LD-derivation of $\mathbf{B}'\theta$ in P) then $\mathbf{R} = \square$ and $X\theta\delta' \sim X\theta\delta$. $\qquad\square$

Lemma 23. *Let P be a well-typed program and $\mathbf{B}$, $\mathbf{B}'$ be sequences of atoms whose relations are defined in P. Assume that P' is obtained from P by replacing $\mathbf{B}$ with $\mathbf{B}'$ in a clause of P, with a safe replacement wrt P and its typing. Then the transformation of P into P' is complete and non-increasing wrt well-typed queries.* $\qquad\square$

The proof is analogous to the one of Lemma 14 since when considering both well-typed programs and queries, all the resolvents in partial LD-derivations are also well-typed. Then, by Corollary 21 all the instances of $\mathbf{B}$ and $\mathbf{B}'$ mentioned in the proof of 14 are well-typed ones.

Corollary 24. *Let P be a well-typed program and $\mathbf{B}$, $\mathbf{B}'$ be sequences of atoms whose relations are defined in P. Assume that P' is obtained from P by replacing $\mathbf{B}$ with $\mathbf{B}'$ in a clause of P, with a safe replacement wrt P and its typing. Then for all well-typed queries $\mathbf{Q}$, universally terminating in P:*

$$\mathbf{Q} \text{ in } P \simeq \mathbf{Q} \text{ in } P'.$$

$\qquad\square$

Since we introduce the well-typing conditions, we want to analyze if well-typing is preserved through transformations.

We know, see [2, 3], that the unfold operation preserves well-typing. A safe replacement wrt P and its typing guarantees the preservation of well-typing by definition. Hence it is sufficient to require that also new definitions are well-typed. This can be guaranteed by an appropriate definition of the typing of the new predicate and of the order of the atoms in the body of the definition clause.

Example 7. Let us consider the well-known program *reverse*:

```
reverse([], []).
reverse([X |Xs], Ys) ← reverse(Xs, Rs), app(Rs, [X], Ys).
```

with the obvious typing $reverse(+ : List, - : List)$ and $app(+ : List, + : List, - : List)$.

We want to introduce the new definition:

```
racc(Xs, Ys, Acc) ← reverse(Xs, Rs), app(Rs, Acc, Ys).
```

for obtaining a *reverse* with accumulator.

By choosing the typing:

$racc(+ : List, - : List, + : List)$.

the new definition is well-typed wrt the given typing. □

Note that by imposing this condition on new definitions we ensure that also folding with such definitions preserves well-typing.

With this assumption on new definitions, well-typing is preserved through each step of the safe transformation sequence. We can then use the well-typing also for weakening the condition for the decreasing unfold in step (ii) of 11. Namely the substitutions α in Lemma 9 and in Definition 11, step (ii), have to be such that $N\alpha$ is still well-typed.

4   Example

Let us consider the naive *reverse* definition:

```
reverse([], []).
reverse([X |Xs], Ys) ← reverse(Xs, Rs), app(Rs, [X], Ys).
```

With typing $reverse(+ : List, - : List)$ and $app(+ : List, + : List, - : List)$, any well-typed query $reverse(x, y)$, namely with $x \in List$, universally terminates. This may be proved by means of any technique for proving universal termination such as [5, 15, 31, 39, 38].

By applying our safe transformation sequence, extended by the safe replacement, we obtain a new well-typed program which is equivalent to the original one wrt that query, but more efficient. This is a well-known example of optimization by introduction of an accumulator [8, 16, 27, 34, 29, 40].

Let us apply the safe transformation sequence.

i)   We introduce the new definition:

d: racc(Xs, Ys, Acc) ← <u>reverse(Xs, Rs)</u>, app(Rs, Acc, Ys).

with typing $racc(+ : List, - : List, + : List)$. Wrt this typing the new clause is well-typed and a well-typed query $racc(x, y, z)$ universally terminates.

In order to optimize the new predicate $racc$ we apply:

ii)   unfold $reverse$ in d (decreasing unfold)

```
racc([], Ys, Acc) ← app([], Ys, Acc).
racc([X |Xs], Ys, Acc) ← reverse(Xs, Rs'), app(Rs', [X], Rs),
    app(Rs, Acc, Ys).
```

iii)   unfold app in the first clause and apply the associative property of append to the second one. Note that the replacement of $\mathbf{B} = app(Rs', [X], Rs), app(Rs, Acc, Ys)$ with $\mathbf{B}' = app([X], Acc, Ts), app(Rs', Ts, Ys)$ is safe wrt its typing. In fact the replacement satisfies the first syntactic condition and it preserves well-typing. Moreover, since θ in Definition 22 cannot modify $\{Rs, Ts\}$, $\mathbf{B}$ and $\mathbf{B}'$ are equivalent in the second clause wrt the program and this can be proved by transformation as in [34, 29]. By analyzing both successful and failing LD-derivations we can prove also that $\mathbf{B}'$ is non-increasing in the clause wrt $\mathbf{B}$. The proofs are given in Appendix B.

```
racc([], Ys, Ys).
racc([X |Xs], Ys, Acc) ← reverse(Xs, Rs'), app([X], Acc, Ts),
    app(Rs', Ts, Ys).
```

We unfold $app([X], Acc, Ts)$ twice in the second clause:

racc([X |Xs], Ys, Acc) ← <u>reverse(Xs, Rs')</u>, <u>app(Rs', [X |Acc], Ys)</u>.

iv)   Fold (recursive) with d in this last clause, thus obtaining:

```
racc([], Ys, Ys).
racc([X |Xs], Ys, Acc) ← racc(Xs, Ys, [X |Acc]).
```

v)   We can now apply a propagation folding with d in the original $reverse$ definition thus obtaining the final program:

```
reverse([], []).
reverse([X |Xs], Ys) ← racc(Xs, Ys, [X]).
racc([], Ys, Ys).
racc([X |Xs], Ys, Acc) ← racc(Xs, Ys, [X |Acc]).
```

The new definition of $reverse$ thus obtained is optimized wrt the initial one in d. In fact its complexity is now linear wrt the size of the first list.

5   Conclusion

In this paper we singled out general conditions under which the powerful replacement operation is safe, namely it is complete and non-increasing and then it preserves both c.a.s. and universal termination.

If typing information are available, which is a very reasonable assumption, the conditions can be weakened, thus allowing us to deal with some special cases of replacement interesting in practical transformations: associativity of predicates and switching of adjacent atoms for reordering clause bodies.

By extending our safe transformation sequence in [11] with typing information and safe replacements, we can capture rather complex transformations. For example we can linearize a predicate by introducing an accumulator.

In [14] we give a sufficient condition for switching two atoms in a body while preserving left-termination [4]. But when dealing with general replacement, and then more sophisticated transformations, typing becomes essential.

Other approaches to program transformations which are meant to preserve termination are [33] and [18]. Pettorossi and Proietti in [33] were the first ones to propose a transformation system preserving the "sequence of answer substitutions semantics" (a semantics for Prolog programs defined in [7, 28]). Their system is rather restricted, unfolding is possible only for leftmost or deterministic atoms and no reordering of atoms is allowed.

Cook and Gallagher in [18] defined a transformation system based on unfolding and replacement where the preservation of termination is verified a posteriori. Clearly our operations have more complicated applicability conditions since they have to incrementally ensure termination.

In order to use our general framework, we need to develop techniques for verifying the conditions for special cases of safe replacement very common in practice. For example for the associativity of append or for switching two adjacent atoms with no variable in common.

By exploiting more powerful typing specifications, such as Pre/Post ones, we could also characterize not finitely failing atoms, namely atoms which have no failing derivation. This could be used to further simplify the conditions in Definition 22.

Acknowledgements

We want thank to Alberto Pettorossi, John Gallagher and the anonymous referees for their useful comments.

This work was supported partly by the HCM Network "Logic Programs Synthesis and Transformations" (CEE CHRX-CT-93-00414) and partly by the Italian MURST with the National Research Project on "Modelli della Computazione e dei Linguaggi di programmazione" (40% funding).

References

1. K. R. Apt. Introduction to Logic Programming. In J. van Leeuwen, editor, *Handbook of Theoretical Computer Science*, volume B: Formal Models and Semantics. Elsevier, Amsterdam and The MIT Press, Cambridge, 1990.
2. K. R. Apt. Declarative programming in Prolog. In D. Miller, editor, *Proceedings of the 1993 International Symposium on Logic Programming*, pages 12–35. The MIT Press, 1993.
3. K. R. Apt and E. Marchiori. Reasoning about Prolog programs: from modes through types to assertions. *Formal Aspects of Computing*, 6(6A):743–765, 1994.

4. K. R. Apt and D. Pedreschi. Studies in Pure Prolog: termination. In J.W. Lloyd, editor, *Proceedings of the Simposium in Computational Logic*, pages 150–176, Berlin, 1990. Springer-Verlag.

5. K. R. Apt and D. Pedreschi. Proving termination of general Prolog programs. In T. Ito and A. Meyer, editors, *Proceedings of the International Conference on Theoretical Aspects of Computer Software*, Lecture Notes in Computer Science 526, pages 265–289, Berlin, 1991. Springer-Verlag.

6. K. R. Apt and Pellegrini. On the occur-check free Prolog programs. Technical Report TRCS-R9238, CWI, Amsterdam, The Netherlands, 1992.

7. M. Baudinet. *Logic Programming Semantics: Techniques and Applications*. PhD thesis, Stanford University, Stanford, California, 1989.

8. R.S. Bird. The Promotion and Accumulation Strategies in Transformational Programming. *TOPLAS ACM*, 6(4):487–504, 1984.

9. A. Bossi and N. Cocco. Verifying correctness of logic programs. In J. Diaz and F. Orejas, editors, *TAPSOFT '89, Barcelona, Spain, March 1989, (Lecture Notes in Computer Science, vol. 352)*, pages 96–110. Springer-Verlag, 1989.

10. A. Bossi and N. Cocco. Basic Transformation Operations which preserve Computed Answer Substitutions of Logic Programs. *Journal of Logic Programming*, 16:47–87, 1993.

11. A. Bossi and N. Cocco. Preserving universal termination through unfold/fold. In G. Levi and M Rodriguez-Artalejo, editors, *Proceedings ALP'94, Madrid, Spain*, September 1994.

12. A. Bossi, N. Cocco, and S. Etalle. Transforming Normal Programs by Replacement. In A. Pettorossi, editor, *Meta Programming in Logic - Proceedings META '92*, volume 649 of *Lecture Notes in Computer Science*, pages 265–279. Springer-Verlag, Berlin, 1992.

13. A. Bossi, N. Cocco, and S. Etalle. Simultaneous Replacement in Normal Programs. *Journal of Logic and Computation*, 6(1):79–120, 1996.

14. A. Bossi, N. Cocco, and S. Etalle. Transformation of Left Terminating Programs: The Reordering Problem. In M. Proietti, editor, *Proceedings LOPSTR'95*, volume 1048 of *Lecture Notes in Computer Science*, pages 33–45. Springer-Verlag, Berlin, 1996.

15. A. Bossi, N. Cocco, and M. Fabris. Norms on terms and their use in proving universal termination of a logic program. *Theoretical Computer Science*, 124:297–328, 1994.

16. D.R. Brough and C.J. Hogger. Compiling Associativity into Logic Programs. *Journal of Logic Programming*, 4:345–359, 1987.

17. L. Colussi and E. Marchiori. Proving correctness of logic programs using axiomatic semantics. In *Proceedings ICLP'91*, pages 629–644. MIT Press, 1991.

18. J. Cook and J.P. Gallagher. A transformation system for definite programs based on termination analysis. In G. Levi and M. Rodriguez-Artalejo, editors, *LOPSTR'94*. Springer-Verlag, 1994.

19. W. Drabent and J. Maluszynski. Inductive assertion method for logic programs. *Theoretical Computer Science*, 59:133–155, 1988.

20. U. S. Reddy F. Bronsard, T. K. Lakshman. A framework of directionalities for proving termination of logic programs. In K. R. Apt, editor, *Proceedings of the Joint International Conference and Symposium on Logic Programming*, pages 321–335. The MIT Press, 1992.

21. P.A. Gardner and J.C. Shepherdson. Unfold/fold transformations of logic programs. In J-L Lassez and editor G. Plotkin, editors, *Computational Logic: Essays in Honor of Alan Robinson*. MIT Press, 1991.

22. T. Kawamura and T. Kanamori. Preservation of Stronger Equivalence in Unfold/Fold Logic Programming Transformation. In *Proc. Int'l Conf. on Fifth Generation Computer Systems*, pages 413–422. Institute for New Generation Computer Technology, Tokyo, 1988.

23. H. Komorowski. Partial evaluation as a means for inferencing data structures in an applicative language: A theory and implementation in the case of Prolog. In Ninth ACM Symposium on Principles of Programming Languages, Albuquerque, New Mexico, pages 255–267. ACM, 1982.

24. J. W. Lloyd. *Foundations of Logic Programming*. Springer-Verlag, Berlin, 1987. Second edition.

25. J. W. Lloyd and J. C. Shepherdson. Partial Evaluation in Logic Programming. *Journal of Logic Programming*, 11:217–242, 1991.

26. M.J. Maher. Correctness of a logic program transformation system. IBM Research Report RC13496, T.J. Watson Research Center, 1987.

27. K. Marriot and H. Sondergaard. Difference-list Transformation for Prolog. *New Generation Computing*, 11:125–177, 1993.

28. N.Jones and A. Mycroft. Stepwise development of operational and denotational semantics for Prolog. In *International Symposium on Logic Programming, Atlantic City, NJ, (U.S.A.)*, pages 289–298, 1984.

29. A. Pettorossi and M. Proietti. Transformation of Logic Programs: Foundations and Techniques. *Journal of Logic Programming*, 19(20):261–320, 1994.

30. A. Pettorossi and M. Proietti. Transformation of Logic Programs. In J.A. Robinson editors D.M. Gabbay, C.J. Hogger, editor, *Handbook of Logic and Artificial Intelligence*. Oxford University Press, 1995.

31. L. Pluemer. *Termination proofs for logic programs*, volume 446 of *Lecture Notes in Artificial Intelligence*. Springer-Verlag, Berlin, 1990.

32. M. Proietti and A. Pettorossi. The synthesis of eureka predicates for developing logic programs. In N. Jones, editor, *ESOP'90, (Lecture Notes in Computer Science, Vol. 432)*, pages 306–325. Springer-Verlag, 1990.

33. M. Proietti and A. Pettorossi. Unfolding, definition, folding, in this order for avoiding unnesessary variables in logic programs. In Maluszynski and M. Wirsing, editors, *PLILP 91, Passau, Germany (Lecture Notes in Computer Science, Vol.528)*, pages 347–358. Springer-Verlag, 1991.

34. M. Proietti and A. Pettorossi. Synthesis of Programs from Unfold/Fold Proofs. In Y. Deville, editor, *LOPSTR'93*, pages 141–158, 1994.

35. T. Sato. An equivalence preserving first order unfold/fold transformation system. In *Second Int. Conference on Algebraic and Logic Programming, Nancy, France, October 1990, (Lecture Notes in Computer Science, Vol. 463)*, pages 175–188. Springer-Verlag, 1990.

36. H. Seki. Unfold/fold transformation of stratified programs. *Journal of Theoretical Computer Science*, 86:107–139, 1991.

37. H. Tamaki and T. Sato. Unfold/Fold Transformations of Logic Programs. In Sten-Åke Tärnlund, editor, *Proc. Second Int'l Conf. on Logic Programming*, pages 127–139, 1984.

38. K. Verschaetse. *Static termination analysis for definite Horn clause programs*. PhD thesis, Dept. Computer Science, K. U. Leuven, 1992.

39. K. Verschaetse and D. De Schreye. Deriving termination proofs for logic programs, using abstract procedures. In *Proc. Eighth Int'l Conf. on Logic Programming*, pages 301–315, 1991.

40. J. Zhang and P. W. Grant. An Automatic Difference-list Transformation Algorithm for Prolog. In *Proceedings of the European Conference on Artificial Intelligence, ECAI'88*, pages 320–325. Pitman, 1988.

6 Appendix A

We add here some definitions used in the proofs.

We consider only *well-formed derivations*, namely all the mgu's employed are idempotent and every input clause (variant of the clause applied at each step) is standardized apart wrt both the initial query and all the input clauses used in the previous steps.

From [25] we say that *two LD-derivations are similar* iff their initial queries are variants of each other, they have the same length and for every *LD*-derivation step, the input clauses employed are variants of each other. For two similar *LD*-derivations of the same query we know that at each level the resultants are variants of each other and then also c.a.s. are variants of each other.

Now let us come to the main proof of the paper.

Lemma 14 *Let P be a program and $\mathbf{B}$, $\mathbf{B}'$ be sequences of atoms whose relations are defined in P. Assume that P' is obtained from P by replacing $\mathbf{B}$ with $\mathbf{B}'$ in a clause of P, with a safe replacement wrt P. Then*

1. *the transformation of P into P' is non-increasing.*
2. *the transformation of P into P' is complete.*

Proof.
Point 1.   We have to prove that for any query $\mathbf{Q}$ and for any partial *LD*-derivation of $\mathbf{Q}$ in P': $l' : \mathbf{Q} \mid\!\!\xmapsto{\delta'}_{P'} \mathbf{R}'$, there exists a partial *LD*-derivation of $\mathbf{Q}$ in P, $l : \mathbf{Q} \mid\!\!\xmapsto{\delta}_P \mathbf{R}$, with $| l | \geq | l' |$. Moreover if $\mathbf{R}' = \square$, then $\mathbf{R} = \square$ and $\mathbf{Q}\delta \sim \mathbf{Q}\delta'$.
The proof proceeds by induction on $| l' |$.
The base case, $| l' | = 0$, is trivial.
For the inductive case let us consider a partial LD-derivation of $\mathbf{Q}$ in P':

$l' : \mathbf{Q} \mid\!\!\xmapsto{\delta'}_{P'} \mathbf{R}'$, with $| l' | > 0$.

Let c and c' be respectively $H \leftarrow \mathbf{A}, \mathbf{B}, \mathbf{C}$. and $H \leftarrow \mathbf{A}, \mathbf{B}', \mathbf{C}$. The Lemma trivially holds if the clause c' is not used in the derivation l'. It is also immediate if the clause c' is not the first clause used in the derivation (straightforward application of the inductive hypothesis). The interesting case is when c' is the first clause used in the derivation, that is:

$l' : \mathbf{Q} \mid\!\!\xmapsto{\xi}_{P'} (\mathbf{A}, \mathbf{B}', \mathbf{C}, \mathbf{D})\xi \mid\!\!\xmapsto{\gamma'}_{P'} \mathbf{R}'$, where $\delta' = \xi\gamma'$, $\mathbf{Q} = (G, \mathbf{D})$ and $\xi = mgu(H, G)$.
For the sake of simplicity we assume that both c and c' are standardized apart wrt $\mathbf{Q}$ and that the first step of l' is performed by applying exactly c' as input clause.
We distinguish three cases according to the form of l'.

Case 1. The derivation stops inside $\mathbf{A}\xi$:

$l' : \mathbf{Q} \mid\!\!\xmapsto{\xi}_{P'} (\mathbf{A}, \mathbf{B}', \mathbf{C}, \mathbf{D})\xi \mid\!\!\xmapsto{\gamma'}_{P'} \mathbf{E}', (\mathbf{B}', \mathbf{C}, \mathbf{D})\xi\gamma'$, with $\mathbf{R}' = \mathbf{E}', (\mathbf{B}', \mathbf{C}, \mathbf{D})\xi\gamma'$,
and there is a derivation $\mathbf{A}\xi \mid\!\!\xmapsto{\gamma'}_{P'} \mathbf{E}'$, of length $| l' | - 1$. By inductive hypothesis there also exists $l_A : \mathbf{A}\xi \mid\!\!\xmapsto{\gamma}_P \mathbf{E_1}$, with $| l_A | \geq (| l' | - 1)$. Hence in P there exists a

derivation which applies c as the first input clause and then a derivation $\mathbf{A}\xi \overset{\vec{\gamma}}{\longmapsto}_P \mathbf{E}$ similar to l_A:

$l : \mathbf{Q} \overset{\xi}{\longmapsto}_P (\mathbf{A},\mathbf{B},\mathbf{C},\mathbf{D})\xi \overset{\vec{\gamma}}{\longmapsto}_P \mathbf{E}, (\mathbf{B},\mathbf{C},\mathbf{D})\xi\gamma$, with $|l| = |l_A| + 1 \geq |l'|$.

Case 2. The derivation stops inside $\mathbf{B}'\xi$:

$l' : \mathbf{Q} \overset{\xi}{\longmapsto}_{P'} (\mathbf{A},\mathbf{B}',\mathbf{C},\mathbf{D})\xi \overset{\vec{\eta}'}{\longmapsto}_{P'} (\mathbf{B}',\mathbf{C},\mathbf{D})\xi\eta' \overset{\vec{\beta}'}{\longmapsto}_{P'} \mathbf{E}', (\mathbf{C},\mathbf{D})\xi\eta'\beta'$,

with $\mathbf{R}' = \mathbf{E}', (\mathbf{C},\mathbf{D})\xi\eta'\beta'$ and $\delta' = \xi\eta'\beta'$.

Then there are the derivations $l_1' : \mathbf{A}\xi \overset{\vec{\eta}'}{\longmapsto}_{P'} \square$, $l_2' : \mathbf{B}'\xi\eta' \overset{\vec{\beta}'}{\longmapsto}_{P'} \mathbf{E}'$ and $|l'| = 1 + |l_1'| + |l_2'|$. As in the previous case we can apply the inductive hypothesis to $\mathbf{A}\xi$, then there exists

$l_1 : \mathbf{A}\xi \overset{\vec{\eta}}{\longmapsto}_P \square$, with $|l_1| \geq |l_1'|$ and $\mathbf{A}\xi\eta_1 \sim \mathbf{A}\xi\eta'$.

In P, by using c at the first step and then a derivation similar to l_1, we can construct:

$der : \mathbf{Q} \overset{\xi}{\longmapsto}_P (\mathbf{A},\mathbf{B},\mathbf{C},\mathbf{D})\xi \overset{\vec{\eta}}{\longmapsto}_P (\mathbf{B},\mathbf{C},\mathbf{D})\xi\eta$.

Now since $Dom(\eta) \cap Var((\mathbf{A},\mathbf{B},\mathbf{C},\mathbf{D})\xi) \subseteq Var(\mathbf{A}\xi)$, $Dom(\eta') \cap Var((\mathbf{A},\mathbf{B}',\mathbf{C},\mathbf{D})\xi) \subseteq Var(\mathbf{A}\xi)$ and $\mathbf{A}\xi\eta \sim \mathbf{A}\xi\eta_1 \sim \mathbf{A}\xi\eta'$, we have that $\mathbf{B}\xi\eta \sim \mathbf{B}\xi\eta'$.

Moreover let $X = Var(\mathbf{B}) \cap Var(\mathbf{B}')$ and $Y = Var(\mathbf{B},\mathbf{B}') \setminus X$; since Y are local wrt c and c', $Var(H, \mathbf{A}, \mathbf{C}) \cap Y = \emptyset$, then, $(Var(\xi\eta') \cap Var(\mathbf{B})) = (Var(\xi\eta') \cap Var(\mathbf{B}')) \subseteq Var(H, \mathbf{A})$ and $Dom(\xi\eta'_{|Var(\mathbf{B},\mathbf{B}')}) \subseteq X$, $Var(\xi\eta'_{|Var(\mathbf{B},\mathbf{B}')}) \cap Y = \emptyset$.

We can apply the inductive hypothesis to l_2' and there also exists

$l_2 : \mathbf{B}'\xi\eta' \overset{\vec{\beta}_1}{\longmapsto}_P \mathbf{E}_1$, with $|l_2| \geq |l_2'|$.

Then, by the non-increasing hypothesis and since $\mathbf{B}\xi\eta' \sim \mathbf{B}\xi\eta$, there exists a derivation

$d_2 : \mathbf{B}\xi\eta \overset{\vec{\beta}_*}{\longmapsto}_P \mathbf{E}_*$,

such that $|d_2| \geq |l_2| \geq |l_2'|$.

By considering an appropriate derivation similar to d_2, together with der we have:

$l : \mathbf{Q} \overset{\xi}{\longmapsto}_P (\mathbf{A},\mathbf{B},\mathbf{C},\mathbf{D})\xi \overset{\vec{\eta}}{\longmapsto}_P (\mathbf{B},\mathbf{C},\mathbf{D})\xi\eta \overset{\vec{\beta}}{\longmapsto}_P \mathbf{E}, (\mathbf{C},\mathbf{D})\xi\eta\beta$,

with $|l| \geq |l'|$.

Case 3. The derivation passes $\mathbf{B}'\xi$:

$l' : \mathbf{Q} \overset{\xi}{\longmapsto}_{P'} (\mathbf{A},\mathbf{B}',\mathbf{C},\mathbf{D})\xi \overset{\vec{\eta}'}{\longmapsto}_{P'} (\mathbf{B}',\mathbf{C},\mathbf{D})\xi\eta' \overset{\vec{\beta}'}{\longmapsto}_{P'} (\mathbf{C},\mathbf{D})\xi\eta'\beta' \overset{\vec{\alpha}'}{\longmapsto}_{P'} \mathbf{R}'$,

where $\delta' = \xi\eta'\beta'\alpha'$.

Then there are the derivations

$l_1' : \mathbf{A}\xi \overset{\vec{\eta}'}{\longmapsto}_{P'} \square$,

$l_2' : \mathbf{B}'\xi\eta' \overset{\vec{\beta}'}{\longmapsto}_{P'} \square$,

and

$l_3' : (\mathbf{C},\mathbf{D})\xi\eta'\beta' \overset{\vec{\alpha}'}{\longmapsto}_{P'} \mathbf{R}'$,

and $|l'| = 1 + |l_1'| + |l_2'| + |l_3'|$.

By inductive hypothesis, there exists

$l_1 : \mathbf{A}\xi \overset{\vec{\eta}_1}{\longmapsto}_P \square$, with $|l_1| \geq |l_1'|$ and $\mathbf{A}\xi\eta_1 \sim \mathbf{A}\xi\eta'$.

As in case 2:

- by using c at the first step and then an appropriate derivation similar to l_1, we can construct the derivation:

    $der : \mathbf{Q} \overset{\xi}{\longmapsto}_P (\mathbf{A},\mathbf{B},\mathbf{C},\mathbf{D})\xi \overset{\vec{\eta}}{\longmapsto}_P (\mathbf{B},\mathbf{C},\mathbf{D})\xi\eta$;

- $\mathbf{B}\xi\eta \sim \mathbf{B}\xi\eta'$;
- let $X = Var(\mathbf{B}) \cap Var(\mathbf{B}')$ and $Y = Var(\mathbf{B}, \mathbf{B}') \setminus X$, since we assumed that the replacement is safe then $Var(\xi\eta') \cap Var(\mathbf{B})) = Var(\xi\eta') \cap Var(\mathbf{B}') \subseteq Var(H, \mathbf{A})$ and $Dom(\xi\eta'_{|(\mathbf{B},\mathbf{B}')}) \subseteq X$ and $Var(\xi\eta'_{|(\mathbf{B},\mathbf{B}')}) \cap Y = \emptyset$;
- by applying the inductive hypothesis to l_2' we have

  $l_2 : \mathbf{B}'\xi\eta' \overset{\beta_1}{\longmapsto}_P \square$ with $|l_2| \geq |l_2'|$, $\mathbf{B}'\xi\eta'\beta_1 \sim \mathbf{B}'\xi\eta'\beta'$;
- by the hypothesis that $\mathbf{B}'$ is non-increasing wrt $\mathbf{B}$ in P and since $\mathbf{B}\xi\eta \sim \mathbf{B}\xi\eta'$

  $d_2 : \mathbf{B}\xi\eta \overset{\beta*}{\longmapsto}_P \square$, with $|d_2| \geq |l_2| \geq |l_2'|$ and $X\xi\eta\beta* \sim X\xi\eta'\beta_1 \sim X\xi\eta'\beta'$.

Hence we may compose *der* with an appropriate derivation similar to d_2:

$\quad der' : \mathbf{Q} \overset{\xi}{\longmapsto}_P (\mathbf{A}, \mathbf{B}, \mathbf{C}, \mathbf{D})\xi \overset{\eta}{\longmapsto}_P (\mathbf{B}, \mathbf{C}, \mathbf{D})\xi\eta \overset{\beta}{\longmapsto}_P (\mathbf{C}, \mathbf{D})\xi\eta\beta.$

By the hypothesis of syntactic correctness, $(\mathbf{C}, \mathbf{D})\xi\eta\beta \sim (\mathbf{C}, \mathbf{D})\xi\eta'\beta'$.
Hence by applying the inductive hypothesis to l_3', there exists

$\quad l_3 : (\mathbf{C}, \mathbf{D})\xi\eta'\beta' \overset{\alpha_1}{\longmapsto}_P \mathbf{R}_1$, with $|l_3| \geq |l_3'|$

and if $\mathbf{R}' = \square$, then also $\mathbf{R}_1 = \square$ and $(\mathbf{C}, \mathbf{D})\xi\eta'\beta'\alpha_1 \sim (\mathbf{C}, \mathbf{D})\xi\eta'\beta'\alpha'$.
Then there also exists

$\quad d_3 : (\mathbf{C}, \mathbf{D})\xi\eta\beta \overset{\alpha*}{\longmapsto}_P \mathbf{R}*$, with $|d_3| \geq |l_3'|$

and if $\mathbf{R}' = \square$, then also $\mathbf{R}* = \square$ and $(\mathbf{C}, \mathbf{D})\xi\eta\beta\alpha* \sim (\mathbf{C}, \mathbf{D})\xi\eta'\beta'\alpha'$.
Therefore, by choosing an appropriate derivation similar to d_3, there is the derivation

$\quad l : \mathbf{Q} \overset{\xi}{\longmapsto}_P (\mathbf{A}, \mathbf{B}, \mathbf{C}, \mathbf{D})\xi \overset{\eta}{\longmapsto}_P (\mathbf{B}, \mathbf{C}, \mathbf{D})\xi\eta \overset{\beta}{\longmapsto}_P (\mathbf{C}, \mathbf{D})\xi\eta\beta \overset{\alpha}{\longmapsto}_P \mathbf{R}$, with

$|l| \geq |l'|$
and if $\mathbf{R}' = \square$, then also $\mathbf{R} = \square$ and $\mathbf{Q}\xi\eta\beta\alpha \sim \mathbf{Q}\xi\eta'\beta'\alpha'$.

Point 2. We have to prove, for all queries $\mathbf{Q}$, that if $\mathbf{Q} \overset{\theta}{\longmapsto}_P \square$, then $\mathbf{Q} \overset{\theta'}{\longmapsto}_{P'} \square$ and $\mathbf{Q}\theta \sim \mathbf{Q}\theta'$.

It can be proved by induction on the length of $l : \mathbf{Q} \overset{\theta}{\longmapsto}_P \square$. As in the previous proof, the base case $|l| = 1$ is trivial since $\mathbf{Q}$ must be an atom and there must exist a fact F in $P \cap P'$ such that $F\theta = \mathbf{Q}\theta$.
For the inductive step the only interesting case is when c is the first clause used in the derivation.
Let

$\quad l : \mathbf{Q} \overset{\xi}{\longmapsto}_P (\mathbf{A}, \mathbf{B}, \mathbf{C}, \mathbf{D})\xi \overset{\eta}{\longmapsto}_P (\mathbf{B}, \mathbf{C}, \mathbf{D})\xi\eta \overset{\beta}{\longmapsto}_P (\mathbf{C}, \mathbf{D})\xi\eta\beta \overset{\alpha}{\longmapsto}_P \square,$

where $\theta = \xi\eta\beta\alpha$.
Then there are the derivations

$\quad l_1 : \mathbf{A}\xi \overset{\eta}{\longmapsto}_P \square,$

$\quad l_2 : \mathbf{B}\xi\eta \overset{\beta}{\longmapsto}_P \square,$

$\quad l_3 : (\mathbf{C}, \mathbf{D})\xi\eta\beta \overset{\alpha}{\longmapsto}_P \square.$

By inductive hypothesis, there exists

$\quad l_1' : \mathbf{A}\xi \overset{\eta_1}{\longmapsto}_{P'} \square$, with $\mathbf{A}\xi\eta_1 \sim \mathbf{A}\xi\eta$.

By using c' at the first step and then an appropriate derivation similar to l_1', we can construct the derivation

$\quad der : \mathbf{Q} \overset{\xi}{\longmapsto}_{P'} (\mathbf{A}, \mathbf{B}', \mathbf{C}, \mathbf{D})\xi \overset{\eta'}{\longmapsto}_{P'} (\mathbf{B}', \mathbf{C}, \mathbf{D})\xi\eta',$

with $\mathbf{A}\xi\eta_1 \sim \mathbf{A}\xi\eta'$.
Let $X = Var(\mathbf{B}') \cap Var(\mathbf{B})$,

- by the hypothesis of syntactic correctness

  $\mathbf{B}'\xi\eta \sim \mathbf{B}'\xi\eta'$;

- by syntactic correctness and by equivalence hypotheses there exists

  $l_2' : \mathbf{B}'\xi\eta \overset{\beta_1}{\longmapsto}_P \square$ and $X\xi\eta\beta_1 \sim X\xi\eta\beta$;

- by inductive hypothesis

  $d_2 : \mathbf{B}'\xi\eta \overset{\beta*}{\longmapsto}_{P'} \square$, with $X\xi\eta\beta* \sim X\xi\eta\beta_1$.

Hence we may compose *der* with an appropriate derivation similar to d_2, thus obtaining:

$$der' : \mathbf{Q} \overset{\xi}{\longmapsto}_{P'} (\mathbf{A}, \mathbf{B}', \mathbf{C}, \mathbf{D})\xi \overset{\eta'}{\longmapsto}_{P'} (\mathbf{B}', \mathbf{C}, \mathbf{D})\xi\eta' \overset{\beta'}{\longmapsto}_{P'} (\mathbf{C}, \mathbf{D})\xi\eta'\beta'.$$

By the hypothesis of syntactic correctness, $(\mathbf{C}, \mathbf{D})\xi\eta\beta \sim (\mathbf{C}, \mathbf{D})\xi\eta'\beta'$, hence there exists

$l_3' : (\mathbf{C}, \mathbf{D})\xi\eta'\beta' \overset{\alpha_1}{\longmapsto}_P \square$,

and $(\mathbf{C}, \mathbf{D})\xi\eta'\beta'\alpha_1 \sim (\mathbf{C}, \mathbf{D})\xi\eta\beta\alpha$.

Then, by inductive hypothesis, also

$d_3 : (\mathbf{C}, \mathbf{D})\xi\eta'\beta' \overset{\alpha*}{\longmapsto}_{P'} \square$,

with $(\mathbf{C}, \mathbf{D})\xi\eta'\beta'\alpha* \sim (\mathbf{C}, \mathbf{D})\xi\eta\beta\alpha$.

Therefore, by choosing an appropriate derivation similar to d_3, we can complete *der'*

$$l' : \mathbf{Q} \overset{\xi}{\longmapsto}_{P'} (\mathbf{A}, \mathbf{B}', \mathbf{C}, \mathbf{D})\xi \overset{\eta'}{\longmapsto}_{P'} (\mathbf{B}', \mathbf{C}, \mathbf{D})\xi\eta' \overset{\beta'}{\longmapsto}_{P'} (\mathbf{C}, \mathbf{D})\xi\eta'\beta' \overset{\alpha*}{\longmapsto}_{P'} \square,$$

with $\mathbf{Q}\xi\eta\beta\alpha \sim \mathbf{Q}\xi\eta'\beta'\alpha'$. $\square$

7 Appendix B

Let us consider the clause:

```
c: racc([X|Xs], Ys, Acc) ← reverse(Xs, Rs'), app(Rs', [X], Rs),
       app(Rs, Acc, Ys).
```

with typing $racc(+ : List, - : List, + : List), app(+ : List, + : List, - : List)$.
We want to prove that the replacement of $\mathbf{B} = app(Rs', [X], Rs), app(Rs, Acc, Ys)$
with $\mathbf{B}' = app([X], Acc, Ts), app(Rs', Ts, Ys)$ is safe wrt its typing.
θ in Definition 22 cannot modify $\{Rs, Ts\}$, hence $\mathbf{B}$ and $\mathbf{B}'$ are equivalent wrt the program. This can be proved by transformation as in [34, 29].
Let us apply to $\mathbf{B}$ our safe transformation sequence.
i)   We define

```
d: p1(Rs', [X], Acc, Ys) ← app(Rs', [X], Rs), app(Rs, Acc, Ys).
```

with typing $p1(+ : List, + : List, + : List, - : List)$ d is well-typed and the well-typed instances of d exactly correspond to the instances $\mathbf{B}\theta$ of Definition 22.
ii)   We unfold the first atom in d. It is a decreasing unfold.

```
1: p1([], [X], Acc, Ys) ← app([X], Acc, Ys).
2: p1([X'|Xs'], [X], Acc, Ys) ← app(Xs', [X], Ts),
       app([X'|Ts], Acc, Ys).
```

iii) We unfold twice 1 and once the second atom in 2.

```
3: p1([], [X], Acc, [X| Acc]).
4: p1([X'| Xs'], [X], Acc, [X'|Ys']) ← app(Xs', [X], Ts),
      app(Ts, Acc, Ys').
```

iv)   We apply (recursive) fold to 4, thus obtaining the final program:

```
3: p1([], [X], Acc, [X| Acc]).
5: p1([X'| Xs'], [X], Acc, [X'|Ys']) ← p1(Xs', [X], Acc, Ys').
```

We now apply the safe transformation sequence to $\mathbf{B'}$.
i)   We define

```
d: p2(Rs', [X], Acc, Ys) ← app([X], Acc, Ts), app(Rs', Ts, Ys).
```

with typing $p2(+ : List, + : List, + : List, - : List)$ d is well-typed and the well-typed instances of d exactly correspond to the instances $\mathbf{B'}\theta$ of Definition 22.
ii)   We unfold the second atom in d.
By Lemma 9 it is a decreasing unfold wrt $\mathbf{G} = \{p2(Rs',[X],Acc,Ys)\alpha\}$ for all α which can be applied in an LD-derivation to d, when used as input clause. In fact for all substitutions α such that $Var(\alpha) \cap Var(d) \subseteq \{Rs',X,Acc,Ys\}$ and $d\alpha$ well-typed, we have that $Ts\alpha = Ts$ and then $app([X],Acc,Ts)\alpha$ cannot fail.

```
1: p2([], [X], Acc, Ts) ← app([X], Acc, Ts).
2: p2([X'| Xs'], [X], Acc, [X|Ys']) ← app([X], Acc, Ts),
      app(Xs', Ts, Ys').
```

iii)   We unfold twice the first atom in 1.

```
3: p2([], [X], Acc, [X| Acc]).
2: p2([X'| Xs'], [X], Acc, [X'|Ys']) ← app([X], Acc, Ts),
      app(Xs', Ts, Ys').
```

iv)   We apply (recursive) fold to 2, thus obtaining the final program:

```
3: p2([], [X], Acc, [X| Acc]).
4: p2([X'| Xs'], [X], Acc, [X'|Ys']) ← p2(Xs', [X], Acc, Ys').
```

The two programs obtained by $\mathbf{B}$ and $\mathbf{B'}$ through a safe transformation sequence are identical modulo predicate renaming. In this way we proved that $\mathbf{B}\theta$ and $\mathbf{B'}\theta$ are equivalent wrt our semantics and wrt their common variables for all instances θ as in Definition 22.

Now we have to prove that $\mathbf{B'}$ is non-increasing in c wrt $\mathbf{B}$ in P.
Since we already proved the equivalence of $\mathbf{B}$ and $\mathbf{B'}$ in c, in order to prove that $\mathbf{B'}$ is non-increasing in c wrt $\mathbf{B}$ in P, it is sufficient to prove:

for any finite LD-derivation $l' : \mathbf{B'}\theta \vdash\!\!\!\overset{\delta'}{\longrightarrow}_P \mathbf{R}$, where either $\mathbf{R} = \square$ or $\mathbf{R} = \mathbf{fail}$, there exists a corresponding finite LD-derivation $l : \mathbf{B}\theta \vdash\!\!\!\overset{\delta}{\longrightarrow}_P \mathbf{R}$, with $X\theta\delta' \sim X\theta\delta$, which is not shorter: $|l| \geq |l'|$.

This, together with the equivalence condition, clearly imply the non-increasing condition in Definition 22.

Let $l \in List$ then $|l|$ denotes the length of the list.
Let $app(+ : List, + : List, - : List)$ be the typing for app.
First of all we state the following two properties.

a)   *Successful derivations of a well-typed query $app(Xs, Ys, Zs)\theta$ have length*
   $|Xs\theta| + 1$.
This can be easily proved by induction on $|Xs\theta|$.

b)   *Finitely failing derivations of a well-typed query $app(Xs, Ys, Zs)\theta$ have length*
$min(|Xs\theta|, n)$, *where n is the position of the leftmost failing element in $Zs\theta$.*
The failure may be due only to an "incorrect" instantiation of the output term Zs.
This can be revealed in the LD-derivation by unification either while traversing the
term $Xs\theta$ or, immediately, when the base case in the definition of app is reached.

Let us come back to our problem.
Successful derivations of $\mathbf{B'}\theta$, because of property (a), have length
   $|X\theta| + 1 + |Rs'\theta| + 1 = |Rs'\theta| + 3$.
Successful derivations of $\mathbf{B}\theta$, because of property (a), have length
   $|Rs'\theta| + 1 + (|Rs'\theta| + 1) + 1 = 2|Rs'\theta| + 3$.
Hence the non-increasing property of Definition 22 is satisfied for successful deriva-
tions.
Finitely failing derivations of $\mathbf{B'}\theta$, because of property (b) and because $Ts\theta = Ts$,
can fail only in the second atom. Let n be the position of the leftmost failing element
in $Ys\theta$. Hence failing derivations have length
   $|X\theta| + 1 + min(|Rs'\theta| + 1, n) = 2 + min(|Rs'\theta|, n)$.
Finitely failing derivations of $\mathbf{B}\theta$, because of property (b) and because $Rs\theta = Rs$,
can also fail only in the second atom. Hence they have length
   $|Rs'\theta| + 1 + min(|Rs'\theta| + 1, n)$.
Then the non-increasing property of Definition 22 is satisfied for finitely failing
derivations.

A Transformation Tool for Pure Prolog Programs

Jacob Brunekreef

Programming Research Group, University of Amsterdam
Kruislaan 403, 1098 SJ Amsterdam, The Netherlands
e-mail: jacob@wins.uva.nl

Abstract. This paper describes an interactive tool for transforming pure Prolog programs. The choice of (pure) Prolog semantics induces a number of conditions that have to be satisfied before a particular transformation step can be applied. The transformation tool has been developed using a programming environment based on algebraic specification. The paper describes the tool and reports on the design decisions, the implemented transformation steps, and the user interface.

1 Introduction

Program transformation is an important software methodology. Its theoretical backgrounds have been (and are still) extensively studied. In the field of logic programming a recent overview can be found in [14]. Considerably less effort seems to have been devoted to concrete implementations of transformation systems.

In this paper we present TransLog: an interactive tool for transforming (pure) Prolog programs. The tool supports a set of well-known transformation steps, such as unfolding and folding. It can, for example, be applied in the stepwise derivation of an efficient program from a less efficient initial program. TransLog is easy to use: a program in a transformation sequence is displayed in a separate window, a transformation step is executed by selecting (a part of) a program and clicking a button besides the program window.

The paper is organized as follows. First, a list of design decisions is presented and discussed in Sect. 2. This list has served as the starting point for the specification of the transformation tool. In Sect. 3 the set of transformations supported by the tool is introduced. In this section also the implications of the choice of pure Prolog semantics are discussed. Section 4 gives an impression of what the TransLog tool looks like. In Sect. 5 we describe our experiences with the development and the application of the tool. Section 6 contains a short overview of related work. We discuss future work in Sect. 7.

TransLog has been developed with the ASF+SDF Meta-environment of Klint ([11]), a programming environment based on algebraic specification. In an appendix to the paper we briefly discuss this formalism.

2 Design Decisions

A number of design issues had to be considered while specifying the TransLog tool. In this section we list the most important ones and motivate the decisions that have been made.

1. Select the Prolog syntax for the logic program language.

   The choice of the Prolog syntax is motivated by the context: we want a concrete transformation tool to take an executable program as 'input' and to produce an executable program as 'output'. A sufficient subset of the Prolog syntax is supported, including various list-notations, integers, infix notation, etc.

2. Implement the most important transformation steps.

   In the TransLog tool six transformation steps have been implemented: unfolding, folding, goal definition, argument permutation (an instance of goal replacement), goal switching and definition elimination. With these transformation steps a relevant subset of examples from the literature could be dealt with. The six transformation steps are presented in more detail in Sect. 3.

3. Preservation of semantics.

   A transformation step is correct (with respect to a given semantics) only if the resulting program has the same semantics as the original one. To achieve correctness most transformation steps require appropriate applicability conditions which –in general– depend on the chosen semantics. Since we have the Prolog syntax, we focus on the Prolog semantics given by the 'sequence of answer substitutions' semantics, a semantics for Prolog programs, defined in [3, 9]. The applicability conditions for the transformation steps will be mostly taken from [17]. However, as we will see in Sect. 3, not all transformation steps listed above preserve pure Prolog semantics. The choice of the six transformation steps is the result of a trade-off between, on the one hand, the strictness of the tool and, on the other hand, its application range: in various examples in the literature these steps are applied.

4. Navigation options.

   The TransLog tool is equipped with two navigation options. These options allow the user to switch from the current program P_i to the previous program P_{i-1} or the next program P_{i+1} (if present) in a transformation sequence $P_0 \ldots P_{i-1}, P_i, P_{i+1}, \ldots P_n$. From a program P_j $(0 \leq j \leq n)$ a new transformation step may be selected. After execution of this step, the old sequence $P_{j+1} \ldots P_n$ is deleted.

5. Develop the tool with the ASF+SDF Meta-environment.

   Most work with respect to the implementation of transformation systems for logic programs is based on Prolog. The advantages of Prolog-based systems are clear: the language is well-suited for the symbolic manipulations that are required, furthermore one gets for instance unification for free. The TransLog tool has been developed with the ASF+SDF Meta-environment, which is based on algebraic specification. This environment, with its built-in parser, conditional equations, list matching properties and generic user interface primitives, constitutes a powerful programming environment for the specification of program transformations. We do not hold the opinion that one approach is definitely better than the other one.

6. A transformation step is performed by 'select-and-click'.

The execution of a transformation step includes the selection of an expression (program, clause, goal), followed by clicking on a button that represents a transformation step. An expression is selected by placing the 'focus' (a rectangle) around it. The folding and goal definition transformation steps require some additional editing.

3 Six Transformation Steps

The TransLog tool offers six transformation steps for Prolog programs. The formal definitions of these transformations, as well as examples in which they are applied, can be found in many places, see e.g. [14]. We will do with short and informal definitions.

- *Unfold*: a goal in the body of a clause is replaced by its 'definition'.
- *Fold*: a sequence of goals in the body of a clause is replaced by its 'defining goal'. This transformation can be viewed as an inverse unfold transformation.
- *Define*: a new predicate is defined in a clause; the clause is added to the program.
- *AssocPerm*: a permutation of arguments for associative predicates is performed. This transformation is an instance of the more general *goal replacement* transformation.
- *Switch*: two adjacent goals in the body of a clause are switched.
- *CleanUp*: clauses (predicate definitions) that are no longer needed are removed.

In a transformation sequence $P_0 \ldots P_n$, the transformation of a program P_i to a program P_{i+1} ($0 \leq i < n$) is supposed to preserve as much as possible the semantic properties of P_i. For our transformation tool we have chosen to adhere to the 'sequence of answer substitutions' semantics, mentioned earlier. This means that the order and multiplicity of answers which are produced by a query have to be taken into account. Furthermore, due to the left-to-right selection of body goals, in the evaluation of a query some answers may not be found. So, within the context of the chosen semantics, most transformation steps will only be allowed under strict conditions. The remainder of this section deals with the conditions that have to be satisfied. Most conditions are based on the PEPM '91 paper of Pettorossi and Proietti [17], extended in their survey paper [14]. We will pay attention to the question whether or not a condition is (efficiently) computable. For the unfold and fold transformation steps we will informally describe how these steps have been implemented in the TransLog tool.

Preliminaries. We suppose a program P_i to be a *definite* Prolog program (without negative literals). A program P_i can be split in two parts, one part defining *new* predicates, the other part defining *old* predicates. New predicates appear in the head of exactly one clause of P_i, not in the body of any clause. Predicates that are not new are called old.

3.1 Unfold

Within the context of our Prolog semantics two particular unfold transformation steps are totally correct:

1. *Leftmost unfolding.* The unfold transformation is applied to the leftmost goal in the body of the unfolded clause.
2. *Deterministic non-left-propagating unfolding.* There exists one unfolding clause. No undesirable variable substitutions propagate to the head of the unfolded clause or the goal(s) left of the unfolded goal in the body of the clause.

Unfolding the leftmost goal of a body is always allowed. In case of non-leftmost unfolding, determinism (the presence of at most one unfolding clause) is needed in order to maintain the order of the computed answers. Left-propagation of variable substitutions in body goals is forbidden, because the termination properties of a program may have been changed. For example, let P_0 be the following program:

```
p(X):-q(X),r(X).     q(a):-q(a).     r(b).
```

Unfolding r(X) in the first clause results in the program P_1:

```
p(b):-q(b).     q(a):-q(a).     r(b).
```

The query "?- p(X)" is non-terminating for P_0, for P_1 the same query immediately fails.

The conditions concerning determinism and non-left propagation of substitutions are computable. They have been implemented in the TransLog tool. The second condition is 'expensive', because the whole program has to be searched for the (non-)presence of a second unfolding clause[1].

In the TransLog tool the unfold transformation step has been implemented as follows.

Let $C = H :\!\!- B^*, B, B^{*\prime}$. be the unfolded clause. Let B be the body goal to-be-unfolded. B^* and $B^{*\prime}$ denote (possibly empty) sequences of body goals. Let P_i be the current program.

The result of the unfold step is computed by inspecting the clauses of P_i, starting with the first clause. In case of leftmost unfolding (B^* is empty), all clauses are inspected. The new clauses that result from the unfold step are accumulated in a sequence C_u. In the case of non-leftmost-unfolding, the conditions concerning determinism and non-left propagation are checked. The result will be either a

---

[1] Although common practice in Prolog programs, we do not require that the clauses defining a particular predicate are grouped together.

sequence of at most one clause, or the detection of a violation of one of the applicability conditions. In the latter case the unfold step results in an 'error report', otherwise the clause C is replaced by the sequence C_u: $P_{i+1} = P_i \backslash \{C\} \cup \{C_u\}$.

For each unfolding clause C' the unfold step leads to the construction of a resolvent of C:

$$C'' = (H \text{ :- } B^*, \text{body of } C', B^{*\prime}.)\theta.$$

The substitution θ is derived from the most general unifier (mgu) of the unfolded body goal B and the head of the clause C'.

3.2 Fold

The conditions for a semantics preserving fold transformation step are very complex. Several sets of conditions, for various semantics, have been proposed by, e.g., Tamaki and Sato [20] and Seki [19]. In [14], Pettorossi and Proietti take the Tamaki & Sato folding (T&S-folding) as a starting point. In order to be (partially) correct within the context of Prolog semantics, they require this folding either to be *reversible*, or to satisfy two other conditions. A folding step is reversible if the folding clause is in the same program P_i as the folded clause and these clauses do not coincide. (So, an unfold step in the resulting program P_{i+1} may result in the program P_i again.) For the case that the intended T&S folding is not an instance of reversible folding, the following conditions have to be satisfied (we will refer to them as the T&S conditions):

1. No folding step is applied after a definition elimination step.
2. Either the head of the folded clause holds an old predicate, or the leftmost goal of the body of the folded clause is *fold-allowing*.

The first condition guarantees that the definition of the predicate in the head of the folding clause has not been removed from the current program. It seems that this condition can be relaxed, by requiring that the particular predicate is still defined in the current program. According to the second condition, body goals are labeled *fold-allowing* or *not-fold-allowing*[2]. Initially, only the body goals of the P_{old} part of P_0 are labeled fold-allowing. A transformation step may change the label of a body goal. See [14] for details.

In the TransLog tool the fold transformation step has been implemented as follows.

Let $C = H \text{ :- } B^*, B^+, B^{*\prime}.$ be the folded clause. Let B^+ be the sequence of body goals to-be-folded. B^* and $B^{*\prime}$ denote (possibly empty) sequences of body goals. Let P_i be the current program, let P_{new} be the program consisting of new defined clauses.

---

[2] These labels correspond to the labels *not-inherited* and *inherited*, introduced by Seki([19]).

First, a reversible folding step is tried, taking the T&S conditions into account. If this step is not possible, then P_{new} is searched for a folding clause, taking into account both the T&S conditions and the applicability conditions, mentioned above. If the conditions fail, the result is an error report. Otherwise, the fold step leads to the replacement of the clause C by a clause $C' = H :\!\!- B^*, (\text{head}(D))\theta, B^{*\prime}.$, with θ the mgu of B^+ and the body of the folding clause D. This results in the program $P_{i+1} = P_i \backslash \{C\} \cup \{C'\}$

The T&S conditions imply the following tests:

1. θ restricted to the set vars(body(D)) - vars(head(D)) is a variable renaming whose image has an empty intersection with the set vars($H, B^*, \text{head}(D)\theta, B^{*\prime}$).
2. The predicate symbol of head(D) occurs only once in P_i or P_{new}. Thus, D is not recursive.

The fold conditions have a large impact on the implementation of the TransLog tool. Body goals have to be labeled *fold-allowing* or *not-fold-allowing* from the start of a transformation sequence (the initial program P_0). After a transformation step labels have to be updated. Labeling of body goals requires an 'internal' program representation that is different from the program that is displayed to the user. The computation of the conditions listed above is rather 'expensive': several programs (P_i, P_{new}) have to be traversed, possibly more than once.

3.3 Define

In a definition introduction step a new predicate is defined. This predicate may not occur in the sequence of transformed programs that has been constructed so far. Following Tamaki and Sato, we require that the body of a new clause only contains old predicates. (Otherwise, a new clause cannot be used as a folding clause.) In the TransLog tool this condition is checked. Furthermore, the tool considers the initial program P_0 to contain old predicates only. Each newly defined clause is added to P_{new}: a sequence of clauses that may be used for folding purposes later on. Initially, this sequence is empty.

3.4 AssocPerm

Some predicates, e.g. the append/3 predicate, represent an operation that is associative. This suggests that a goal sequence

```
append(L1,L2,Z),append(Z,L3,L)
```

may be replaced by the goal sequence

```
append(L2,L3,ZZ),append(L1,ZZ,L)
```

corresponding with a permutation of the arguments of the append goals. This transformation step is an instance of a *goal replacement* step. In general the validity of a goal replacement step is undecidable. As indicated by Pettorossi and

Proietti ([15]), the permutation of arguments representing associative properties of e.g. the append predicate is not (totally) correct with respect to Prolog semantics. The transformation of

P_0: `p(A,B,C,D):-append(A,B,E),append(E,C,D).` to
P_1: `p(A,B,C,D):-append(B,C,F),append(A,F,D).`

does not preserve termination properties. With the usual definition of the append predicate, the query "`?- p(A,[H],D,[])`" is non-terminating using P_0, but finitely failing using P_1.

The transformation step stated above may be considered as 'a step forward in a computation'[3]. It is easy to see that, applying the usual definition of the append predicate with recursion on the first argument, the number of recursive calls of the append predicate is decreased. The reverse replacement increases the number of recursive calls. This observation can be generalized to any associative predicate `p(X,Y,Z)` that is defined with recursion on its first argument. We have decided to add the replacement of the goal sequence '`p(A,B,E),p(E,C,D)`' by the sequence '`p(B,C,F),p(A,F,D)`' (with p an arbitrary predicate) to our tool. The user has to be aware of the fact that this transformation step is not semantics preserving in all cases.

In the TransLog tool one syntactic condition is checked: in the particular clause the 'moving variable' (`E/F` in the example above) has to be local to the two goals involved in this transformation step.

3.5 Switch

In our Prolog semantics the body of a clause is a sequence of goals and not a multi-set. So, a *rearrangement* of two goals in a body may lead to a change in the semantics of a clause (a program). Therefore, goal switching is not allowed in [17, 14]. In a recent work of Bossi, Cocco and Etalle [5] it is investigated when this transformation step preserves left-termination properties. The implementation of goal switching in the TransLog tool is motivated by its appearance in a number of examples. In many cases a switch of two adjacent goals is needed for rearranging the body goals in order to make a folding step possible.

3.6 CleanUp

It is obvious that the elimination of a clause (a predicate definition) will lead to a change in the semantics of a program. Within the context of our Prolog semantics, even the removal of a duplicate clause leads to a change. When we consider a transformation sequence to be meant for 'improving efficiency by introducing new predicates', at the end of a sequence some old predicates will be of no interest any more. The clauses defining these predicates may be removed from the current program without changing the semantic properties for the queries of interest.

---

[3] In [4] such a replacement step is called *non-increasing*.

In the TransLog tool the CleanUp transformation step has been implemented as semantics preserving *with respect to a particular selected predicate*. The clause(s) defining this predicate, as well as the clauses defining the predicates that can be 'reached' from these defining clauses, are not removed from the program by a CleanUp transformation step. All other clauses are removed.

4   The TransLog Tool

In this section we give an impression of the appearance and functionality of TransLog. A transformation session starts with the opening of a TransLog window that contains the initial program. This program can be loaded from a file. In Fig. 1 a TransLog window is showed with the initial program of a simple transformation sequence.

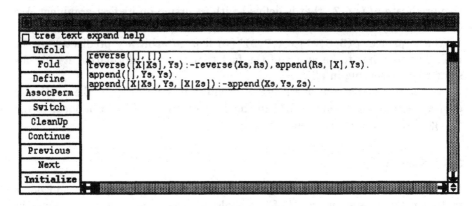

Fig. 1. An initial TransLog window

A rectangle, called the *focus*, has been placed around the whole program. At the left side of the window ten buttons are present. Each button is related to a specific action on (a part of) the contents of the window. The upper six buttons are related to the six transformation steps that have been implemented. The Continue button is used in a dialogue. Dialogues are part of the Fold step and the Define step. The Previous and Next buttons represent the navigation options in a sequence of (transformed) programs. The Initialize button takes care of the initialization of the navigation structure. A button can be disabled (dimmed) or enabled (highlighted). At startup-time only the Initialize button is enabled.

The definition of the reverse predicate displayed in Fig. 1 implies two list traversals: one for the recursive definition of the reverse predicate, one for the append predicate. In a sequence of (user-directed) transformation steps the initial $\mathcal{O}(N^2)$ program is transformed to a more efficient $\mathcal{O}(N)$ program.

The second window (Fig. 2) shows the dialogue concerning the definition of a new predicate. The revacc predicate defines a list reversal with an accumulator.

The body of the clause contains the 'old' predicates reverse and append. The definition of the new predicate has been typed in, the focus has been placed around this clause. The Continue button is the only button that is enabled.

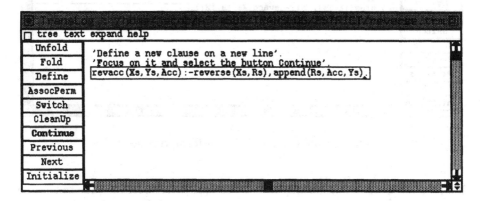

Fig. 2. A dialog related with the definition of a new predicate

The third window (Fig. 3) shows the initial program with the new clause included. The focus is placed around the first body goal of the revacc clause, the body goal that will be unfolded in the next transformation step of this sequence. Several buttons (including the Unfold button) are enabled.

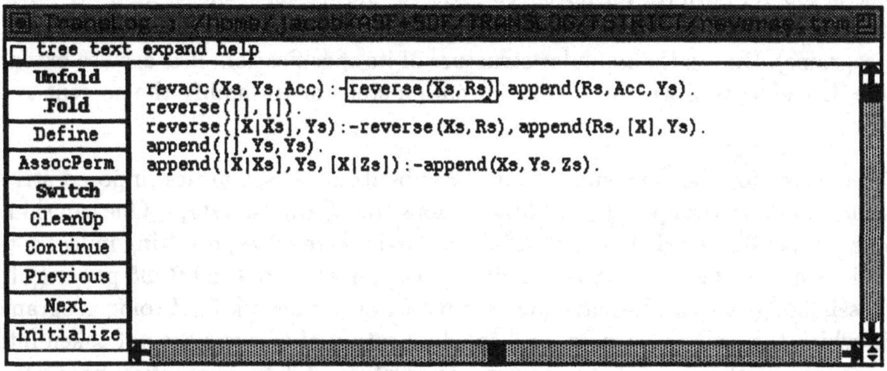

Fig. 3. A body goal has been selected for unfolding

The last window (Fig. 4) shows the final result of the transformation sequence. The revacc predicate is recursively defined. The reverse predicate is defined in terms of the revacc predicate. In the definition of this predicate a list is traversed only once. The append predicate is not needed any more and has been removed from the program.

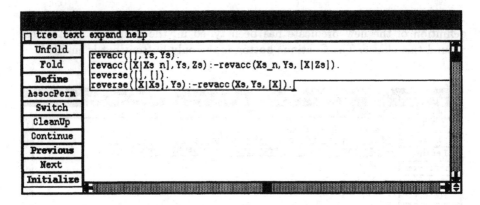

Fig. 4. The final result of a transformation sequence

If a required transformation step from P_i to P_{i+1} is not possible (due to e.g. the absence of a folding clause or the failure of an applicability condition), an error message is displayed in the TransLog window, instead of the new program. After clicking on the Previous button the program P_i is displayed again.

5 Experiences

The transformation tool TransLog, described in this paper, has been constructed within a few man–months. The ASF+SDF Meta-environment showed to be a useful tool for both the formal specification of the syntax of the language (Prolog) and the specification of transformation steps on terms of this language (Prolog programs). Due to the modular structure of its specification, it is easy to extend the TransLog tool with new transformation steps or to modify the current system.

The choice for the 'sequence of answer substitutions' semantics imposed strict conditions on the applicability of the various transformation steps. One can think of an approach that is based on a less restrictive semantics, resulting in less conditions and/or less restrictive conditions. E.g., in their LOPSTR '95 paper ([5]), Bossi, Cocco and Etalle introduce a semantical framework for Prolog programs in which the order of answers and the duplication of answers are not taken into account. Furthermore, they require preservation of *left-termination* properties instead of universal termination properties. We have not followed this approach, because we wanted to investigate to what extent a strict set of conditions can be implemented in a concrete tool. Furthermore, the central property of left-termination is not computable, so left-termination of the initial program has to be guaranteed by the user.

Several examples of transformation sequences from the literature have been used as input for testing the TransLog tool. We used 'accumulator' examples, leading to a more efficient version of, for instance, the reverse predicate (see Sect. 4) and the quicksort predicate (see below). We also used 'tupling' examples, leading to a more efficient version of, for instance, the mintree predicate ([14]) and the median predicate ([7]). Most examples could be executed without any problem. However, some examples failed, due to two reasons: left propagation of unwanted variable substitutions in combination with an unfold step on a non-leftmost body goal, and a failure of the final re-definition step in a transformation sequence. Below we will elaborate on the latter issue.

The purpose of many unfold-fold based transformation sequences is: given an inefficient definition of a predicate p, obtain a more efficient definition of this predicate. A basic schema for this kind of transformation sequences is:

1. Define a new (eureka) predicate in terms of the old predicates.
2. Find a more efficient definition of this predicate by unfolding, folding, goal switching, etc.
3. Re-define the predicate p in terms of the new predicate.
4. Remove obsolete predicate definitions from the program.

In a number of examples the re-definition step appears to be a folding step, with the original definition of the eureka predicate (in P_{new}) as a folding clause. However, in some examples the re-definition step cannot be mimicked by a well-defined transformation step, and the TransLog tool is unable to execute this step. We illustrate this point with an example.

The following program represents the well-known quicksort algorithm. The definition of the partition predicate is omitted. Clauses have been numbered for reference purposes.

```
(1)  qsort([],[]).
(2)  qsort([X|Xs],Ys):-partition(Xs,X,L,B),qsort(L,Ls),
                        qsort(B,Bs),append(Ls,[X|Bs],Ys).
(3)  append([],Ys,Ys).
(4)  append([X|Xs],Ys,[X|Zs]):-append(Xs,Ys,Zs).
```

In order to get rid of the append goal in the recursive qsort clause, we define the new predicate qacc (quicksort-with-accumulator) in the following clause:

```
(5)  qacc(Xs,Ys,Acc):-qsort(Xs,Zs),append(Zs,Acc,Ys).
```

In a number of transformation steps this definition is transformed to

```
(6)  qacc([],Ys,Ys).
(7)  qacc([X|Xs_n],Ys,Acc):-partition(Xs_n,X,L,B),
                            qacc(B,Zs_n,Acc),qacc(L,Ys,[X|Zs_n]).
```

These clauses do not include any call of the append predicate. Now, we would like to re-define the qsort predicate in terms of the qacc predicate, and obtain a clause like

```
     qsort(Xs,Ys):-qacc(Xs,Ys,[]).
```

This cannot be achieved by folding or any other well-defined transformation step. So, the correctness of the re-definition step has to be proved separately. The proof is usually absent in the examples in the literature. We give the proof for the qsort predicate. The transformation steps in the proof are performed by the TransLog tool. Take clause (7), with an empty accumulator:

```
(8)  qacc([X|Xs_n],Ys,[]):-partition(Xs_n,X,L,B),qacc(B,Zs_n,[]),
                           qacc(L,Ys,[X|Zs_n]).
```

Unfold both qacc goals in the body of this clause, taking the original definition of the qacc predicate (clause (5)) as unfolding clause. We obtain:

```
(9)  qacc([X|Xs_n],Ys,[]):-partition(Xs_n,X,L,B),qsort(B,Zs_n),
                           append(Zs_n,[],Zs),qsort(L,Zs_n_n),
                           append(Zs_n_n,[X|Zs],Ys).
```

The first append-goal only succeeds if Zs_n and Zs are equal. This cannot be derived from the definition of the append predicate. A simple inductive proof –outside the scope of the TransLog tool– is needed. We omit this proof. We remove the append goal and make Zs_n equal to Zs:

```
(10) qacc([X|Xs_n],Ys,[]):-partition(Xs_n,X,L,B),qsort(B,Zs),
                           qsort(L,Zs_n_n),
                           append(Zs_n_n,[X|Zs],Ys).
```

The body of this clause is –modulo goal switching and variable renamings– equal to the body of the original qsort clause (clause (2)), which means that we can derive the desired result by folding clause (2) with clause (10) as folding clause. We get

```
(11) qsort([X|Xs],Ys):-qacc([X|Xs],Ys,[]).
```

Together with the clauses for the partition predicate, the clauses (1), (11), (6) and (7) define the required efficient implementation of the quicksort algorithm.

In a slightly different basic transformation schema, also present in the literature, step 3 (the re-definition step) is replaced by the definition of a new predicate p', defined in terms of the eureka predicate. Then, the equivalence of the original predicate p and the predicate p' has to be proved by transformation. This leads to proofs like the one given above.

6 Related Work

As mentioned in the introduction, there seems to exist a limited amount of publications considering the *implementation* of unfold/fold transformation systems. We are aware of the following work.

- *Spes*, implemented by Alexandre et al. ([2]), is an interactive transformation system for logic programs (Horn clauses). It supports unfolding, folding and definition introduction. For definite programs these transformation steps preserve the least Herbrand model. Some strategies using unfolding and folding have been implemented. Furthermore, algorithms that infer automatically static information about predicates (i.e. types and modes) have been included. The transformation history is stored in a 'development tree'.

  Spes has been implemented in the functional language CAML and comprises about ten thousand lines of code.

- *Transformer*, implemented by Aioni ([1]), transforms a positive logic program P in a positive logic program P'. The system supports unfolding, folding, goal definition, goal deletion and goal replacement. The transformation steps are supposed to preserve the least Herbrand model. The Tamaki & Sato conditions concerning a folding step (see Sect. 3.2) are checked automatically. The system can be used in two modes: an interactive mode in which a transformation sequence is constructed in a step-by-step user-directed way, and an automatic mode in which the application of the transformation rules is controlled by a transformation strategy. These strategies are separately defined. As with the Spes system, the transformation history is stored in a tree.

  Transformer has been implemented in Prolog.

- O'Keefe and Naish have implemented a logic program transformation system, operating on NU-Prolog programs. This system requires the user to direct each step of a transformation sequence. It has been extended by Traill with 'higher level commands' in order to include some strategies for generic classes of programs. One strategy is directed to the reduction of the built-in predicates *call/N* and *not/N*, the other strategy aims at the reduction of the use of the *append/3* predicate. See [21].

  The system has been implemented in NU-Prolog.

With respect to basic transformation steps there is no big difference in functionality between TransLog and the systems mentioned above. TransLog applies a very restrictive set of applicability conditions. We recall from Sect. 2 that the preservation of semantics has been one of the main issues while developing the tool. Our tool lacks the inclusion of any kind of automatic transformation strategy. This is a subject of future research.

In this section we also briefly mention work that has been done in the related field of the implementation of *partial deduction* systems. These systems aim at optimizing a logic program with respect to a (partially instantiated) query. Unfolding, folding, goal definition, etc. are also applied, but in a slightly different context. We refer to the work of Gallagher ([8]), the PAL system of Komorowski (mentioned in e.g. [12]), Mixtus of Sahlin ([18]), Logimix of Mogensen and Bondorf ([13]), PADDY of Prestwitch ([16]), and the ECCE system of Leuschel (referred to in [10]).

7 Future Work

There are many directions for future work on the TransLog tool. We mention a few.

- Investigate the incorporation of 'transformation strategies': well-defined sequences of transformation steps that can automatically be applied to a certain class of programs.
- Add a 'modular approach' to the system. In this approach a program consists of several modules. In each module export predicates ('visible predicates') are defined, as well as a number of local predicates. In this approach program transformation can be applied in order to obtain a more efficient definition (implementation) of an exported predicate.
- Investigate other semantical frameworks. As indicated in this paper, in a less restrictive semantical setting more transformations will preserve the semantics of the original program.
- Pay more attention to efficient specifications. Until now, we focussed more on correctness than on efficient specifications. Probably, a redesign with respect to this topic will reduce the response times. At this moment, a single transformation step requires a few seconds on a powerful machine.

Acknowledgements Krzysztof Apt (CWI and University of Amsterdam) is acknowledged for his initiating and stimulating role with respect to the work described in this paper. Thanks to Sandro Etalle (University of Genova) for his comments on a previous version of this paper. The anonymous referees are acknowledged for their helpful comments.

References

1. O. Aioni. A System for the Automatic Transformation of Logic programs. Technical Report Report R 0195, Electronics Department, University of Roma Tor Vergata, 1995.
2. F. Alexandre, K. Bsaïes, J.P. Finance, and A. Quéré. Spes: A System for Logic Program Transformation. In *Proceedings of the International Conference on Logic Programming and Automated reasoning (LPAR '92)*, LNCS 624, pages 445–447. Springer-Verlag, 1992.
3. M. Baudinet. *Logic Programming Semantics: Techniques and Applications*. PhD thesis, Stanford University, Stanford, California, 1989.
4. A. Bossi and N. Cocco. Replacement Can Preserve Termination. In this volume.
5. A. Bossi, N. Cocco, and S. Etalle. Transformation of Left Terminating Programs: the Reordering Problem. In *LOPSTR '95 – Fifth International Workshop on Logic Program Synthesis and Transformation*, number 1048 in LNCS, pages 33–45. Springer-Verlag, 1995.
6. J.J. Brunekreef. A Transformation Tool for Pure Prolog Programs –The Algebraic Specification–. Technical Report P9607, Programming Research Group, University of Amsterdam, 1996.
7. S. Etalle. *Transformation and Analysis of (Constraint) Logic Programs*. PhD thesis, University of Amsterdam, 1995.

8. J. Gallagher. A system for specialising logic programs. Technical Report TR-91-32, University of Bristol, 1991.

9. N. Jones and A. Mycroft. Stepwise Development of Operational and Denotational Semantics for Prolog. In *Proceedings of the 1984 International Symposium on Logic Programming*, pages 281–288. IEEE, 1984.

10. J. Jørgensen, M. Leuschel, and B. Martens. Conjunctive Partial Deduction in Practice. In this volume.

11. P. Klint. A meta–environment for generating programming environments. *ACM Transactions on Software Engineering and Methodology*, 2(2):176–201, 1993.

12. J. Komorowski. A Prolegomenon to Partial Deduction. *Fundamenta Informaticae*, 18(1):41–64, 1993.

13. T.Æ. Mogensen and A. Bondorf. Logimix: A Self-Applicable Partial Evaluator for Prolog. In *LOPSTR '92 – Proceedings of the second international workshop on Logic Program Synthesis and Transformation*, Workshops in Computing, pages 214–227. Springer–Verlag, 1992.

14. A. Pettorossi and M. Proietti. Transformation of Logic Programs: Foundations and Techniques. *Journal of Logic Programming*, 19, 20:261–320, 1994.

15. A. Pettorossi and M. Proietti. Private communication, 1996.

16. S. Prestwitch. Online Partial Deduction of Large Programs. In *ACM SIGPLAN Symposium on Partial Evaluation and Semantics-Based Program Manipulation (PEPM '93)*, pages 111–118. ACM press, 1993.

17. M. Proietti and A. Pettorossi. Semantics Preserving Transformation Rules for Prolog. In *ACM SIGPLAN Symposium on Partial Evaluation and Semantics-Based Program Manipulation (PEPM '91)*. ACM press, 1991.

18. D. Sahlin. The Mixtus Approach to Automatic Partial Evaluation of Full Prolog. In S. Debray and M. Hermenegildo, editors, *Proc. of the North American Conf. on Logic Programming*, pages 377–398, 1990.

19. H. Seki. Unfold/fold transformation of stratified programs. *Theoretical Computer Science*, 86:107–139, 1991.

20. H. Tamaki and T. Sato. Unfold/Fold Transformation of Logic Programs. In S.-Å. Tärnlund, editor, *Proceedings of the 2nd International Conference on Logic Programming*, pages 127–138, Uppsala, Sweden, 1984.

21. T. Traill. Transformation of Logic Programs. Honours Thesis, Dept. of Computer Science, University of Melbourne, 1994.

Appendix: the ASF+SDF Meta-environment

The ASF+SDF Meta-environment of Klint ([11]) is an interactive development environment for the generation of interactive systems for manipulating programs, specifications, or other texts written in a formal language. The generation process is controlled by a definition of the language, which may include features such as syntax definition and checking, type checking, prettyprinting and execution of programs.

SDF is a shorthand for Syntax Definition Formalism. In SDF both the lexical syntax and the context-free syntax of a language can be defined in an algebraic style. ASF is a shorthand for Algebraic Specification Formalism. In ASF any function may be defined on terms, constructed according to the syntax defined in an SDF specification. In our case a term will be a program, a clause, a goal. Functions define transformations on these terms.

ASF+SDF specifications have a modular structure. Different parts of a specification can be written down in separate modules. A module can be imported by another module.

The ASF+SDF Meta-environment offers the possibility of syntax-directed editing of ASF+SDF specifications. Each individual module can be created and edited by invoking a *module editor* for it. After each editing operation the implementation of a module is updated immediately. A lexical scanner, a parser, a prettyprinter and a term rewriting system (the implementation of the set of equations) are derived from the module automatically.

A module is divided in two parts. In the first part the signature (sorts and lexical syntax/context-free syntax) of terms is specified. The second part contains the equations defining the operations on the terms. For each module one or more *term editors* may be invoked in order to edit and evaluate terms defined by the particular module. A term editor uses the syntax defined in the module for parsing the textual representation of terms. The equations of the module are used to reduce a term to its normal form. A term editor can be customized by adding buttons or pull-down menu's to the editor window. In this way the user interface of a particular application can be designed. The windows of Sect. 4 are examples of a customized term editor.

The ASF+SDF Meta-environment runs on Unix platforms. The current version is based on Inria's LeLisp. This means that, before running the Meta-environment, one also has to acquire a copy of LeLisp. This makes the current system not really portable. This aspect will be improved in a future version of the system.

The specification of the TransLog tool contains twenty-three modules, which can be grouped in five different subsets: *basic modules* with some elementary specification of layout characters and basic data types, *syntax modules* with the definition of the lexical and context-free Prolog syntax, *unification modules*, related with unification and substitutions on Prolog terms, *transformation modules* specifying the various transformation steps and *user interface modules*, related with the TransLog user interface. The modules contain about 325 (conditional) equations, ranging from very simple to rather complex. In [6] the complete annotated algebraic specification of the TransLog tool is given.

Enhancing Partial Deduction
via Unfold/Fold Rules

Alberto Pettorossi [1]   Maurizio Proietti [2]   Sophie Renault [1]

1 Department of Informatics, University of Roma Tor Vergata,
Via della Ricerca Scientifica, 00133 Roma, Italy. {adp,renault}@iasi.rm.cnr.it
2 IASI-CNR, Viale Manzoni 30, 00185 Roma, Italy. proietti@iasi.rm.cnr.it

Abstract. We show that sometimes partial deduction produces poor program specializations because of its limited ability in (i) dealing with conjunctions of recursively defined predicates, (ii) combining partial evaluations of alternative computations, and (iii) taking into account unification failures. We propose to extend the standard partial deduction technique by using versions of the definition rule and the folding rule which allow us to specialize predicates defined by disjunctions of conjunctions of goals. We also consider a case split rule to take into account unification failures. Moreover, in order to perform program specialization via partial deduction in an automatic way, we propose a transformation strategy which takes as parameters suitable substrategies for directing the application of every transformation rule.
Finally, we show through two examples that our partial deduction technique is superior to standard partial deduction. The first example refers to the automatic derivation of the Knuth-Morris-Pratt string matching algorithm, and the second example refers to the construction of a parser for a given regular expression. In both examples, the specialized programs are derived starting from naive, non-deterministic initial programs, whereas standard partial deduction can derive similar specialized programs only when complex, deterministic initial programs are provided.

1   Introduction

Partial deduction is a powerful tool for program specialization and it has been successfully applied for the derivation of very efficient specialized programs. In practice, however, some efficiency improvements in the specialized programs cannot be realized, because partial deduction, as formalized by Lloyd and Shepherdson [13], here also called standard partial deduction, is not capable to perform specializations w.r.t. a conjunction of two or more atoms at the same time. Moreover, standard partial deduction cannot combine together the evaluation of several alternative computations, nor it takes into account the negative information which is generated by unification failures. In this paper we study the problem of how to overcome these limitations, and the solution we propose is based on the enhancement of the basic rules used for performing partial deduction. We also propose a strategy for applying these enhanced rules. This strategy allows us to achieve high levels of efficiency by specializing *disjunctions of conjunctions of goals*. For this reason the novel technique we propose is called *disjunctive partial deduction*. The specialized programs we derive avoid the use of intermediate data structures and unnecessary nondeterministic predicates.

In Section 2 we first illustrate the power of the standard partial deduction technique by recalling the derivation of the programs corresponding to the finite automata generated by the Knuth-Morris-Pratt string matching algorithm. Then we illustrate the limitations of standard partial deduction by showing that the same efficient matching algorithms can only be derived by starting from initial programs which already specify some suitable details on the matching process itself. In Section 3 we indicate how within the framework of program transformation, an improved version of the partial deduction technique can be obtained by providing some enhanced transformation rules and a related strategy for their application. In Section 4 we present two examples which illustrate the use of those rules and strategy. Finally, in Section 5 we briefly compare our techniques with related proposals reported in the literature.

2   Partial Deduction and Unfold/Fold Transformations

We recall first how to recast in the unfold/fold transformation framework [2, 15, 25] the standard techniques for partial deduction of definite programs, as they have been formalized by Lloyd and Shepherdson [6, 13].

2.1   Transformation Rules and Strategy for Standard Partial Deduction

It is well known that partial deduction can be seen as a particular instance of the unfold/fold transformation methodology where the following three rules are available (see, for instance, [17, 20]) for transforming a given program P into a new one.

- **Atomic Definition.** It consists in adding to P a clause, called a *definition clause*, of the form $newp(X_1, \ldots, X_m) \leftarrow A$, where $newp$ is a new predicate symbol, A is an atom, and $X_1, \ldots, X_m$ are the variables occurring in A.
- **Unfolding** of a clause C in P w.r.t. an atom A of its body. It consists in replacing C by all clauses obtained by applying SLD-resolution to C and every clause in P whose head is unifiable with A. In particular, the unfolding of a clause w.r.t. an atom which is not unifiable with any head in P, amounts to the deletion of that clause.
- **Atomic Folding** of an atom A in the body of a clause C using a definition clause D. It consists in replacing A, if it is an instance of the body of D, by the corresponding instance of the head of D. Atomic folding of an atom in the body of a definition clause is not allowed.

These rules are instances of Tamaki and Sato's transformation rules and in the case of definite programs, they preserve the success set and the finite failure set semantics [22, 25].

In order to perform partial deduction of a given program whereby getting a specialized program, these three rules have to be applied according to a suitable strategy. We now present one such strategy, which we call *standard strategy*, or simply S. This strategy, depicted in Figure 1, is very similar to the one illustrated by Gallagher in [6]. In Section 3.1 we will propose an enhanced version of this strategy for performing disjunctive partial deduction.

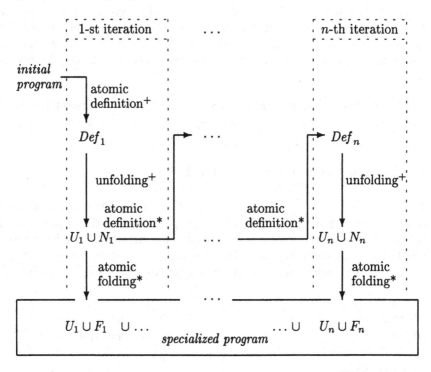

Fig. 1. The strategy S for standard partial deduction. r^+ denotes one or more applications of the rule r, and r^* denotes zero or more applications of r.

Standard Strategy S for Partial Deduction. Given a definite program P and a goal G w.r.t. which we want to specialize P, we start off by introducing a set Def_1 consisting of a definition clause of the form $newp(X_1, \ldots, X_m) \leftarrow A$ for each atom A in G, where $X_1, \ldots, X_m$ are the variables occurring in A. Then, from the program $P \cup Def_1$ we construct a sequence of programs of the form: $P \cup Def_i \cup Q_i$, for $i \geq 1$, with $Q_1 = \{\}$. We construct the program $P \cup Def_{i+1} \cup Q_{i+1}$ from the program $P \cup Def_i \cup Q_i$, during the i-th iteration of the strategy, as follows.

We unfold once or more times each clause in Def_i and we derive a new program $P \cup U_i \cup N_i \cup Q_i$, where U_i and N_i are the unit and non-unit clauses, respectively, derived by unfolding the clauses of Def_i. We then introduce a new set Def_{i+1} of definitions whose bodies are *generalizations* of the atoms occurring in the bodies of the clauses in N_i which cannot be folded using already introduced definition clauses. We fold all these atoms using the clauses in $Def_1 \cup \ldots \cup Def_{i+1}$, thereby obtaining the set F_i of clauses and the new program $P \cup Def_{i+1} \cup Q_{i+1}$, where Q_{i+1} is $U_i \cup F_i \cup Q_i$.

Partial deduction terminates for $i = n$ iff all atoms occurring in the bodies of the clauses of N_n can be folded using the definitions occurring in $Def_1 \cup \ldots \cup Def_n$, that is, Def_{n+1} is empty because no new definition is needed for folding the atoms in the bodies of N_n. The final program is $P \cup Q_{n+1}$, and P can be dropped if we are interested only in goals relative to predicates defined by Def_1, which are the goals w.r.t. which P has been specialized, because during the evaluation of these goals, only calls of predicates in Q_{n+1} may be generated. □

This strategy is parametric in the sense that it takes as parameters subsidiary strategies for directing the unfolding steps and the atomic definition steps.

2.2 Partial Deduction and the KMP Test

The success w.r.t. the so called KMP test [24] is regarded as a significant achievement of partial deduction, and indeed it is possible to derive a program which behaves like the deterministic finite automaton generated by the Knuth-Morris-Pratt string matching algorithm by applying the standard strategy for partial deduction to a general string matching program like the one of Figure 2(A) [5, 6].

Initial matching program for the KMP test

Specialized program w.r.t. $match([a, a, b], S)$

$$
\begin{array}{l}
match(P, S) \leftarrow \\
\quad match1(P, S, P, S) \\
match1([\,], X, Y, Z) \leftarrow \\
match1([A|Ps], [A|Ss], P, S) \leftarrow \\
\quad match1(Ps, Ss, P, S) \\
match1([A|Ps], [B|Ss], P, [C|S]) \leftarrow \\
\quad A \neq B, \ match1(P, S, P, S)
\end{array}
$$

by standard partial deduction $\longrightarrow$

$$
\begin{array}{l}
pd\_match(S) \leftarrow m1(S) \\
m1([a|S]) \leftarrow m2(S) \\
m1([X|S]) \leftarrow a \neq X, \ m1(S) \\
m2([a|S]) \leftarrow m3(S) \\
m2([X|S]) \leftarrow a \neq X, \ m1(S) \\
m3([b|S]) \leftarrow \\
m3([X|S]) \leftarrow b \neq X, \ m2([X|S])
\end{array}
$$

(A) (B)

Fig. 2. (A) Initial string matching program for the KMP test. (B) Specialized program derived by standard partial deduction, where $pd\_match(S)$ is defined by the clause $pd\_match(S) \leftarrow match([a, a, b], S)$. It behaves like the deterministic finite automaton generated by the KMP string matching algorithm.

The aim of partial deduction in the KMP test is to specialize the program of Figure 2(A) w.r.t. a particular goal. If we choose the goal $match([a, a, b], S)$, that is, we want to derive a program which tells us whether or not the pattern $[a, a, b]$ occurs in string S, we introduce the definition clause:

$$pd\_match(S) \leftarrow match([a, a, b], S)$$

Then by using the standard strategy for partial deduction we get the program given in Figure 2(B) which performs the desired task and corresponds to the deterministic finite automaton generated by the KMP string matching algorithm accepting the language $\Sigma^* aab\Sigma^*$ [6]. In this sense we say that standard partial deduction passes the KMP test.

2.3 Some Limitations of Standard Partial Deduction

This ability of standard partial deduction to pass the KMP test is related to the initial string matching program which has been considered. In particular, let us consider the case, call it *strong* KMP *test*, where instead of the program of Figure 2(A), the initial program is the naive string matching program depicted in Figure 3(A).

Initial matching program
for the strong KMP test

Specialized program
w.r.t. $naive\_match([a, a, b], S)$

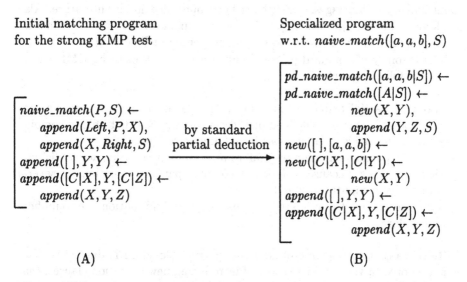

(A)   (B)

Fig. 3. (A) Initial string matching program for the strong KMP test. (B) Specialized program derived by standard partial deduction, where $pd\_naive\_match(S)$ is defined by the clause $pd\_naive\_match(S) \leftarrow naive\_match([a, a, b], S)$. It does *not* behave like the deterministic finite automaton generated by the KMP string matching algorithm.

This program checks whether or not the pattern P occurs in the string S by looking for two strings *Left* and *Right* such that S is the concatenation of *Left*,

P, and *Right*. In this case, in order to derive the specialized program w.r.t. the goal *naive_match*([*a, a, b*], *S*), we start off from the definition clause:

1. *pd_naive_match*(*S*) ← *naive_match*([*a, a, b*], *S*)

Then by using the standard partial deduction strategy *S*, we get the specialized program given in Figure 3(B). The particular subsidiary unfolding strategy which we have used, consists in (i) unfolding the leftmost atom in the body and then (ii) unfolding as long as possible the resulting clauses w.r.t. any atom which unifies with exactly one clause head. Unfortunately, the program of Figure 3(B) does *not* behave like the deterministic finite automaton generated by the KMP string matching algorithm. Indeed, when a mismatch occurs, the search for the pattern *P* within the string *S* is always restarted after a shift of exactly one character from where the pattern was assumed to occur.

Moreover, no sequence of applications of the atomic definition, unfolding, and atomic folding rules can produce from clause 1 and the clauses in Figure 3(A) a program which behaves like the deterministic finite automaton generated by the KMP algorithm.

Thus, we say that standard partial deduction does *not* pass the strong KMP test. This limitation also applies to the automatic derivations based on partial evaluation techniques [9] of specialized KMP matching programs both in functional and logic languages, which have been published in the literature. Also Glück and Klimov in [8], who apply the supercompilation technique, consider an initial program which is similar to the one presented in Figure 2(A).

The inability of standard partial deduction to pass the strong KMP test is due to the following facts:

- standard partial deduction may fail to propagate information across conjunctions of recursively defined predicates, because it is not able to combine separate recursive computations into a unique computation;
- standard partial deduction may fail to propagate information across disjunctions of atoms, because it does not combine partial evaluations of several alternative computations; and
- standard partial deduction may not use negative information due to unification failures.

Technically, the weakness of standard partial deduction is due to the fact that it enforces a very restricted way of introducing new definition clauses, that is, a new predicate may be defined only by introducing exactly one clause which has exactly one atom in its body. This restriction also affects the folding rule, because folding steps are applied by using definition clauses of that form only. The expert reader may realize that these limitations indeed correspond to the fact that partial evaluation à la Lloyd-Shepherdson is performed w.r.t. atomic goals only.

Moreover, standard partial deduction does not provide any support for reasoning by cases, and there is no way of introducing inequalities to take into account unification failures. Consequently, it is impossible to obtain the program of Figure 2(B) if inequalities are not already present in the initial program, as it is the case for the program of Figure 2(A).

In the next section, we show that these limitations on the power of standard partial deduction can be overcome by some transformation techniques based on the use of unfolding/folding rules which are more powerful than the three rules presented in Section 2.1.

3 Disjunctive Partial Deduction via Enhanced Unfold/Fold Rules

Now we introduce our enhanced transformation rules for making the partial deduction technique more powerful, and we present a new strategy for applying these rules. We will then briefly discuss the issue of the mechanization of this new strategy and also the issue of which semantics are preserved while applying the enhanced rules.

3.1 Transformation Rules and Strategy for Disjunctive Partial Deduction

The main improvement to the partial deduction techniques we propose, relies on the enhancement of both the definition rule and the folding rule. For the definition rule we allow new predicates to be defined by means of *one or more* non-recursive clauses which contain *one or more* atoms in their bodies. When combined with folding, this rule allows us to specialize a program w.r.t. a *disjunction of conjunctions of atoms*. For the folding rule we allow to fold *several* clauses at a time, and thus, our extension is similar to the one proposed in [7]. We also use the standard unfolding rule which we have presented in Section 2.1. In addition to the definition, unfolding, and folding rules, we use a subsumption rule, and a case split rule. The subsumption rule is used to eliminate clauses which are implied by other clauses in the program. By the case split rule we replace a clause by two new clauses corresponding to mutually exclusive and exhaustive instantiations of its head. The aim of case split is to increase determinism of programs, as we will indicate below.

Now we formally present our enhanced rules for transforming a given program P into a new one.

- **Definition.** It consists in adding to P the following n clauses, called *definition clauses*, of the form:
  $newp(X_1, \ldots, X_m) \leftarrow Body_1, \ldots, newp(X_1, \ldots, X_m) \leftarrow Body_n,$
  where $newp$ is a new predicate symbol, $Body_1, \ldots, Body_n$ contain only predicates occurring in P, and $X_1, \ldots, X_m$ are variables occurring in $Body_1, \ldots, Body_n$.
- **Unfolding** of a clause C in P w.r.t. an atom A of its body. It consists in replacing C by all clauses obtained by applying SLD-resolution to C and every clause in P whose head is unifiable with A. In particular, the unfolding

of a clause w.r.t. an atom which is not unifiable with any head in P, amounts to the deletion of that clause.

- **Folding** of goals $B_1, \ldots, B_n$ in the bodies of clauses $C_1, \ldots, C_n$, respectively, using definition clauses $D_1, \ldots, D_n$. Suppose that:
  1. $C_1, \ldots, C_n$ are clauses in P of the form: $H \leftarrow F, B_1, G, \ldots, H \leftarrow F, B_n, G$,
  2. $D_1, \ldots, D_n$ are definition clauses of the form:
     $newp(X_1, \ldots, X_m) \leftarrow Body_1, \ldots, newp(X_1, \ldots, X_m) \leftarrow Body_n$
     and let these clauses be exactly those which have been introduced for the predicate $newp$ by an application of the definition rule,
  3. $B_1 = Body_1\theta, \ldots, B_n = Body_n\theta$, for some substitution θ, and
  4. for $i = 1, \ldots, n$, for every variable X in D_i and not in $\{X_1, \ldots, X_m\}$ we have that:
     - $X\theta$ is a variable which does not occur in (H, F, G) and
     - the variable $X\theta$ does not occur in the term $Y\theta$, for each variable Y occurring in $Body_i$ and different from X.

  Folding consists in replacing clauses $C_1, \ldots, C_n$ by the single clause $H \leftarrow F, newp(X_1, \ldots, X_m)\theta, G$.
- **Subsumption**. It consists in the deletion of a clause of P subsumed by another clause in P. (Recall that the clause $(H \leftarrow Body, A)\theta$ is subsumed by $H \leftarrow Body$.)
- **Case Split** of a clause C w.r.t. a substitution $\{X/u\}$. It consists in replacing a clause C of the form $H \leftarrow Body$, by the two mutually exclusive clauses: $(H \leftarrow Body) \{X/u\}$ and $H \leftarrow X \neq u, Body$, where X is a variable occurring in H.

Notice also that the set of clauses for $newp$ in the definition and folding rules is equivalent to the following formula: $newp(X_1, \ldots, X_m) \leftarrow Body_1 \vee \ldots \vee Body_n$ and in this sense we say that our rules allow us to specialize a program w.r.t. a disjunction of conjunctions of atoms. The following example clarifies how the folding rule works.

Example 1. Let us consider the two clauses C_1: $p(X) \leftarrow q(X), r(Y)$ and C_2: $p(X) \leftarrow q(X), s(X)$. They can be folded using the clauses D_1: $new(X, Y) \leftarrow r(Y)$ and D_2: $new(X, Y) \leftarrow s(X)$, thereby deriving clause C: $p(X) \leftarrow q(X), new(X, Y)$. Notice that by unfolding clause C using D_1 and D_2, we get again clauses C_1 and C_2. □

Now we propose a strategy for disjunctive partial deduction which directs the application of those enhanced transformation rules. This strategy, called $\mathcal{D}$, is depicted in Figure 4. It is an enhancement of the strategy $\mathcal{S}$ for standard partial deduction depicted in Figure 1.

In the strategy $\mathcal{D}$ we will allow ourselves to simplify inequalities in bodies of clauses. Every simplification consists in replacing conjunctions of inequalities by equivalent (w.r.t. Clark's equality theory) conjunctions of inequalities. Thus, for instance, (i) $X \neq a, X \neq a$ is replaced by $X \neq a$, (ii) $[\,] \neq [a|X]$ is replaced by

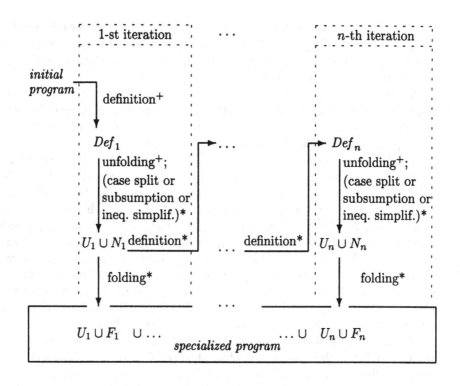

Fig. 4. The strategy $\mathcal{D}$ for disjunctive partial deduction.

true, and (iii) $a \neq a$ is replaced by *false*. Clauses with occurrences of *false* in the body are deleted.

In the strategy $\mathcal{D}$ we will also make use of the following concept of *packet* of clauses for a given predicate. The set of packets of clauses for a predicate, say *newp*, is a partition of the clauses for that predicate such that the following property holds: for any two clauses C_1 and C_2 for *newp* of the form $H_1 \leftarrow Ineqs_1, B_1$ and $H_2 \leftarrow Ineqs_2, B_2$, respectively, where $Ineqs_1$ and $Ineqs_2$ are the conjunctions of all inequalities in their bodies, we have that C_1 and C_2 belong to the same packet iff $H_1 \leftarrow Ineq_1$ and $H_2 \leftarrow Ineq_2$ are equal, modulo variable renaming. We also say that two packets are *mutually exclusive* iff given a clause $H_1 \leftarrow Ineqs_1, B_1$ in the first packet and a clause $H_2 \leftarrow Ineqs_2, B_2$ in the second packet, we have that H_1 and H_2 are *either* not unifiable *or* unifiable via an mgu θ and at least one inequality in $(Ineqs_1\theta, Ineqs_2\theta)$ fails.

Strategy $\mathcal{D}$ for Disjunctive Partial Deduction. Given a program P and a goal G w.r.t. which we want to specialize P, we start off by introducing a set Def_1 consisting of a definition clause of the form $newp(X_1, \ldots, X_m) \leftarrow G$, where $X_1, \ldots, X_m$ are the variables occurring in G. Then, from the program $P \cup Def_1$ we construct a sequence of programs of the form $P \cup Def_i \cup Q_i$, for $i \geq 1$, with $Q_1 = \{\}$. We construct the program $P \cup Def_{i+1} \cup Q_{i+1}$ from the program $P \cup Def_i \cup Q_i$, during the i-th iteration of the strategy, as follows.

We unfold once or more times each clause in Def_i and then for each predicate *newp* occurring in the heads of the clauses derived by unfolding, we apply zero or more times the case split rule so to obtain a new set of clauses which can be partitioned into *mutually exclusive* packets for *newp*.

These applications of the case split rule are interleaved with applications of the subsumption rule and also with steps of simplification of inequalities, whenever possible. Notice that after the applications of the case split and subsumption rules, packets containing unit clauses are singletons.

Let U_i be the set of unit clauses and N_i be the set of packets each of them containing non-unit clauses only, derived from Def_i by the steps of unfolding, case split, subsumption, and simplification we have described. We then introduce a (possibly empty) set Def_{i+1} of new definition clauses such that each packet of clauses in N_i can be folded using clauses in $Def_1 \cup \ldots \cup Def_{i+1}$ producing exactly one clause which has no occurrences of predicates in common with P, with the possible exception of '$\neq$'. Each new predicate is defined by one or more clauses with one or more atoms in their bodies, because we use our enhanced definition rule. We fold the clauses in N_i using the definition clauses belonging to $Def_1 \cup \ldots \cup Def_{i+1}$ and we derive a set F_i of mutually exclusive clauses and a new program $P \cup Def_{i+1} \cup Q_{i+1}$, where Q_{i+1} is $U_i \cup F_i \cup Q_i$.

Analogously to the strategy S, disjunctive partial deduction terminates at the end of the n-th iteration for which it is possible to fold all clauses in N_n using the definition clauses belonging to $Def_1 \cup \ldots \cup Def_n$. Thus, we have that Def_{n+1} is empty, because no new definition is needed for folding the goals in the bodies of N_n. The final specialized program is $P \cup Q_{n+1}$, and P can be dropped if we are interested only in goals relative to predicates defined by Def_1. □

Notice that, in the above strategy D we apply the case split and the subsumption rules so to derive clauses which have mutually exclusive heads. This requirement may be somewhat restrictive when we have to deal with predicates with several arguments. However, our strategy can easily be extended so that one may derive clauses which are mutually exclusive w.r.t. a chosen *subset* of the arguments of their heads.

Like the strategy S also the strategy D is parametric in the sense that it takes as parameters subsidiary strategies for directing the application of each enhanced transformation rule. In Section 4.1 we will see some examples of these subsidiary strategies.

As it will be clear also from the examples given in Section 4 our enhanced definition and folding rules allow us to achieve the effects of other transformation strategies, such as *conjunctive partial deduction* [10] for combining recursive computations, *argument filtering* [12] for eliminating unnecessary arguments, and *renaming* [6] for structure specialization.

Moreover, the combination of the case split rule which realizes a form of reasoning by cases, and the folding rule which allows us to fold several clauses at a time and in particular all clauses belonging to every packet, has the effect of producing specialized programs which are deterministic, from possibly non-deterministic initial programs. The concept of determinism we use, is related to the operational semantics and it corresponds to the fact that at runtime, there exists at most one clause whose head unifies with the current goal and whose body does not fail because of an unsatisfiable inequality.

3.2 Mechanization of the Strategy for Disjunctive Partial Deduction

In order to fully mechanize our strategy for disjunctive partial deduction, we need subsidiary strategies for directing the application of every transformation rule.

In particular, we need a strategy to select the clauses and the atoms w.r.t. which the unfolding rule has to be applied, and since that rule may, in general, be applied infinitely often, that strategy should also indicate when to stop unfolding. For instance, one may use the unfolding strategies which have been proposed for standard partial deduction [6] or for more general transformation techniques [15].

For the definition rule, we need a suitable strategy for suggesting the introduction of generalized definition clauses, because in order to fold the clauses derived by unfolding and case split, some subsets of the bodies of these clauses should be instances of the bodies of the new definition clauses to be introduced. Similarly to the standard partial deduction strategy S, the termination of the disjunctive partial deduction strategy D strongly depends on the chosen generalized definition clauses one introduces. We will not investigate further this issue, which moreover, is not relevant in the examples we will give in Section 4.

3.3 On the Semantics Preserved During Partial Deduction

Without further restrictions, our rules are only *partially correct* w.r.t. the least Herbrand model semantics, that is, if program P_1 is transformed into program P_2 and the set D of new definition clauses is introduced during this transformation, then $M(P_2) \subseteq M(P_1 \cup D)$. Here we assume that the least Herbrand model of the $\neq$ predicate is the set $\{t_1 \neq t_2 \mid t_1 \text{ and } t_2 \text{ are different ground terms}\}$. However, it can easily be shown that, if the rules are applied according to our strategy for standard and disjunctive partial deduction, then they are *totally correct* w.r.t. the least Herbrand model semantics, that is, $M(P_2) = M(P_1 \cup D)$, because each clause is unfolded at least once before folding (see [7] for a similar condition).

As a consequence of the total correctness w.r.t. the least Herbrand model semantics, the success set semantics is preserved when we transform programs according to our strategy for disjunctive partial deduction. We assume here that the success set is computed using SLDNF-resolution where a possibly non-ground inequality succeeds iff the corresponding equality fails.

However, our transformation rules may affect the finite failure set semantics. In particular, the subsumption rule may eliminate infinite failures and folding may turn finite failures into infinite failures. While the elimination of infinite failures can be considered useful in many circumstances, conditions to prevent the introduction of infinite computations should be provided. To this purpose we may extend the conditions given in [22], where the preservation of the finite failure set is proved for a version of the definition and folding rules less general than ours. The preservation of other termination properties, such as left termination, when we use the enhanced rules we have introduced, is left for future studies. However, we believe that one can provide versions of our rules which preserve such properties, by extending the approaches proposed for Tamaki and Sato's rules in [1, 3, 18].

Finally, notice that for an efficient evaluation of the specialized programs, one may remove during a post-processing phase the inequalities which have been introduced by the application of the case split rule. This can be done by replacing inequalities in favour of cuts as specified by the following rule:

Cut Introduction [4]. It consists in replacing the two clauses:
$(H \leftarrow Body_1) \{X/u\}$ and $H \leftarrow X \neq u, Body_2$ by the new clauses:
$(H \leftarrow !, Body_1) \{X/u\}$ and $H \leftarrow Body_2$

where obviously, the resulting program requires a Prolog evaluator. In the above cut introduction rule we assume that the two clauses occur in the program in the order specified by the rule, but not necessarily in consecutive positions. We also assume that any duplicate consecutive occurrence of a cut can be deleted. The correctness of the cut introduction rule w.r.t. the success set semantics, computed by SLDNF-resolution with Prolog strategy, is straightforward if all calls of predicates are ground at runtime, because all clauses of the specialized program are mutually exclusive. This groundness condition which may be checked by standard abstract interpretation techniques, can be relaxed by considering groundness only w.r.t. to a subset of the arguments of each predicate.

4   Examples of Application of the Strategy for Disjunctive Partial Deduction

Now we present two examples of application of our strategy $\mathcal{D}$ for disjunctive partial deduction by which we show that one may overcome the limitations of standard partial deduction which we have mentioned in Section 2.3. In the first example it is shown that our strategy $\mathcal{D}$ is capable to pass the strong KMP test which is not passed by the standard strategy $\mathcal{S}$. In the second example an efficient parser for a given regular expression is automatically derived by partial deduction.

4.1   Strong KMP Test Example

Given the initial program depicted in Figure 5(A), in order to derive a specialized program w.r.t. the goal $naive\_match([a, a, b], S)$, we introduce by the definition rule the following clause:

1. $new1(S) \leftarrow naive\_match([a, a, b], S)$

We then apply in a fully automatic way the strategy $\mathcal{D}$ for disjunctive partial deduction by using the following *subsidiary strategies* for directing the application of every rule. In introducing these strategies we refer to the i-th iteration of

Initial matching program for the strong KMP test	Specialized program w.r.t. $naive\_match([a, a, b], S)$

$$
\left[
\begin{array}{l}
naive\_match(P, S) \leftarrow \\
\quad append(Left, P, X), \\
\quad append(X, Right, S) \\
append([\,], Y, Y) \leftarrow \\
append([C|X], Y, [C|Z]) \leftarrow \\
\quad append(X, Y, Z)
\end{array}
\right.
$$

by disjunctive partial deduction $\longrightarrow$

$$
\left[
\begin{array}{l}
4.\ new1(S) \leftarrow new2(S) \\
9.\ new2([a|S]) \leftarrow new3(S) \\
10.\ new2([C|S]) \leftarrow C \neq a, new2(S) \\
17.\ new3([a|S]) \leftarrow new4(S) \\
18.\ new3([C|S]) \leftarrow C \neq a, new2(S) \\
26.\ new4([b|S]) \leftarrow new5(S) \\
27.\ new4([a|S]) \leftarrow new4(S) \\
28.\ new4([C|S]) \leftarrow C \neq b, C \neq a, new2(S) \\
29.\ new5(S) \leftarrow
\end{array}
\right.
$$

(A)   (B)

Fig. 5. (A) Initial string matching program for the strong KMP test. (B) Specialized program derived by disjunctive partial deduction, where $new1(S)$ is defined by the clause $new1(S) \leftarrow naive\_match([a, a, b], S)$. It behaves like the deterministic finite automaton generated by the KMP string matching algorithm.

the strategy $\mathcal{D}$ and by 'the current program' we mean $P \cup Def_i \cup Q_i$, where P is the initial program. We also assume that at the i-th iteration Def_{i+1} is initially empty.

Unfolding strategy: for every clause in Def_i which has been introduced by the definition rule we unfold it once w.r.t. the leftmost atom in its body, whereby deriving the set V of clauses. Then starting from this set V, we apply as long as possible the following transformation which produces a new set of clauses from an old set of clauses:

"let C be a clause in the set at hand, and B be the leftmost atom, if any, in the body of C such that B unifies with the head of exactly one clause in the current program,

if there exists an atom in the body of C which does not unify with the head of any clause in the current program *then* we delete C *else if* B exists and the argument of the head of C is a variable *then* we replace C by the clauses obtained by unfolding C w.r.t. B".

This strategy is basically the 'determinate unfolding' considered in [6] with the condition that a determinate unfolding step is not performed if the argument of the head of the clause to be unfolded is not a variable.

Notice that this unfolding strategy might not terminate, and in order to avoid infinite loops, the stopping criterium must be strengthened. One may use, for instance, some available techniques for loop-checking (see [6] for a discussion on this issue).

Case split strategy: we apply case split as long as there exist two clauses whose heads H_1 and H_2 are not equal, also considering the inequalities in their bodies, and they are unifiable via an mgu which is not a variable renaming. Without loss of generality, we may assume that there exists a binding $\{X/u\}$ in the mgu of H_1 and H_2 such that $H_1\{X/u\}$ is not a variant of H_1. Then we apply the case split rule to the clause whose head is H_1 w.r.t. $\{X/u\}$ by considering the two cases: $X = u$ and $X \neq u$.

Definition and folding strategy: we consider every packet with non-unit clauses and we fold all clauses in the packet by using the set of definition clauses of a predicate in $Def_1 \cup \ldots \cup Def_i$, such that their bodies are exactly the bodies of the clauses in the packet without the inequalities. If such a predicate does not exist then we introduce it and we add its definition clauses to Def_{i+1}. Thus, no generalization is required in our case during an application of the definition rule.

For the subsumption rule we do not give any particular strategy because we will apply it whenever possible.

We now present the various iterations of the strategy $\mathcal{D}$ for the strong KMP test example. During the first few steps we also provide some comments on the derivation we have performed.

First iteration. By definition we introduce the clause:

1. $new1(S) \leftarrow naive\_match([a, a, b], S)$

Thus, $Def_1 = \{1\}$ and $Q_1 = \{\}$. By unfolding clause 1 we get:

2. $new1(S) \leftarrow append(Left, [a, a, b], X), append(X, Right, S)$

Clause 2 has not been further unfolded because each atom in its body unifies with more than one head in the current program (indeed, the predicate *append* has two clauses). For folding clause 2 we introduce the following definition clause:

3. $new2(S) \leftarrow append(Left, [a, a, b], X), append(X, Right, S)$

By folding clause 2 using clause 3 we get:

4. $new1(S) \leftarrow new2(S)$

Clause 4 is a clause of the specialized program to be derived. We have that $U_1 = \{\}$, $N_1 = \{2\}$, $F_1 = \{4\}$, $Def_2 = \{3\}$ and $Q_2 = \{4\}$. In the following iteration we deal with the new definition clause 3.

Second iteration. By unfolding clause 3 we get:

5. $new2([a|S]) \leftarrow append([a, b], Right, S)$
6. $new2([C|S]) \leftarrow append(Left, [a, a, b], X), append(X, Right, S)$

Clause 5 has not been further unfolded because $[a|S]$ is not a variable, and clause 6 has not been further unfolded because each atom in its body unifies with more than one head in the current program. Now the heads of clauses 5 and 6 are unifiable by the substitution $\{C/a\}$. Thus, by case split of clause 6 w.r.t. $\{C/a\}$ we get:

6.1 $new2([a|S]) \leftarrow append(Left, [a, a, b], X), append(X, Right, S)$
6.2 $new2([C|S]) \leftarrow C \neq a, append(Left, [a, a, b], X), append(X, Right, S)$

For folding clauses (5, 6.1) which belong to the same packet because they have equal heads, we introduce the following definition clauses:

7. $new3(S) \leftarrow append([a, b], Right, S)$
8. $new3(S) \leftarrow append(Left, [a, a, b], X), \; append(X, Right, S)$

By folding clauses (5, 6.1) using clauses (7, 8), and by folding clause 6.2 using clause 3, we get:

9. $new2([a|S]) \leftarrow new3(S)$
10. $new2([C|S]) \leftarrow C \neq a, \; new2(S)$

Clauses 9 and 10 are clauses of the specialized program to be derived. We have that $U_2 = \{\}$, $N_2 = \{5, 6.1, 6.2\}$, $F_2 = \{9, 10\}$, and $Def_3 = \{7, 8\}$, and $Q_3 = Q_2 \cup \{9, 10\}$. In the following iteration we deal with the new definition clauses 7 and 8.

Third iteration. By unfolding clauses 7 and 8 we get:

11. $new3([a|S]) \leftarrow append([b], Right, S)$
12. $new3([a|S]) \leftarrow append([a, b], Right, S)$
13. $new3([C|S]) \leftarrow append(Left, [a, a, b], X), \; append(X, Right, S)$

By case split of clause 13 w.r.t. the substitution $\{C/a\}$ we get:

13.1 $new3([a|S]) \leftarrow append(Left, [a, a, b], X), \; append(X, Right, S)$
13.2 $new3([C|S]) \leftarrow C \neq a, \; append(Left, [a, a, b], X), \; append(X, Right, S)$

For folding clauses (11, 12, 13.1) which belong to the same packet because they have equal heads, we introduce the following definition clauses:

14. $new4(S) \leftarrow append([b], Right, S)$
15. $new4(S) \leftarrow append([a, b], Right, S)$
16. $new4(S) \leftarrow append(Left, [a, a, b], X), \; append(X, Right, S)$

By folding clauses (11, 12, 13.1) using clauses (14, 15, 16), and by folding clause 13.2 using clause 3, we get:

17. $new3([a|S]) \leftarrow new4(S)$
18. $new3([C|S]) \leftarrow C \neq a, \; new2(S)$

Clauses 17 and 18 are clauses of the specialized program to be derived. We have that $U_3 = \{\}$, $N_3 = \{11, 12, 13.1, 13.2\}$, $F_3 = \{17, 18\}$, $Def_4 = \{14, 15, 16\}$, and $Q_4 = Q_3 \cup \{17, 18\}$. In the following iteration we deal with the new definition clauses 14, 15, and 16.

Fourth iteration. By unfolding clauses 14, 15, and 16 we get:

19. $new4([b|S]) \leftarrow append([\,], Right, S)$
20. $new4([a|S]) \leftarrow append([b], Right, S)$
21. $new4([a|S]) \leftarrow append([a, b], Right, S)$
22. $new4([C|S]) \leftarrow append(Left, [a, a, b], X), \; append(X, Right, S)$

By a case split step of clause 22 w.r.t. $\{C/b\}$ and then by a second case split step w.r.t. $\{C/a\}$ we get:

22.1 $new4([b|S]) \leftarrow append(Left, [a, a, b], X), \; append(X, Right, S)$
22.2 $new4([a|S]) \leftarrow b \neq a, \; append(Left, [a, a, b], X), \; append(X, Right, S)$

22.3 $new4([C|S]) \leftarrow C \neq a, C \neq b, append(Left, [a, a, b], X), append(X, Right, S)$

By simplification in the body of (22.2) we get:

23. $new4([a|S]) \leftarrow append(Left, [a, a, b], X), append(X, Right, S)$

For folding clauses (19, 22.1) we introduce the following definition clauses:

24. $new5(S) \leftarrow append([\,], Right, S)$
25. $new5(S) \leftarrow append(Left, [a, a, b], X), append(X, Right, S)$

By folding clauses (19, 22.1) using clauses (24, 25), by folding clauses (20, 21, 23) using clauses (14, 15, 16), and by folding clause 22.3 using clause 3, we get:

26. $new4([b|S]) \leftarrow new5(S)$
27. $new4([a|S]) \leftarrow new4(S)$
28. $new4([C|S]) \leftarrow C \neq b, C \neq a, new2(S)$

Clauses 26, 27, and 28 are clauses of the specialized program to be derived. We have that $U_4 = \{\}$, $N_4 = \{19, 20, 21, 22.1, 23, 22.3\}$, $F_4 = \{26, 27, 28\}$, $Def_5 = \{24, 25\}$, and $Q_5 = Q_4 \cup \{26, 27, 28\}$. In the following iteration we deal with the new definition clauses 24 and 25.

Fifth iteration. By unfolding clauses 24 and 25 we get:

29. $new5(S) \leftarrow$
30. $new5([a|S]) \leftarrow append([a, b], Right, S)$
31. $new5([C|S]) \leftarrow append(Left, [a, a, b], X), append(X, Right, S)$

We discard clauses 30 and 31 because they are subsumed by clause 29. We also have that $U_5 = \{29\}$, $N_5 = \{\}$, $F_5 = \{\}$, $Def_6 = \{\}$, and $Q_6 = Q_5 \cup \{29\}$.

After this fifth iteration we end the application of our strategy $\mathcal{D}$ for disjunctive partial deduction, because we did not introduce any extra definition clause for performing folding steps. The final program is depicted in Figure 5(B). It corresponds to a finite automaton which is deterministic, and in fact, clauses 9, 10, 17, 18, 26, 27, 28, and 29 correspond to the minimal finite automaton. However, in general, our strategy does not ensure the minimality of the derived finite automaton. We leave this problem for future research.

If in the final program we get rid of inequalities by using the cut introduction rule, we get:

$new1(S) \leftarrow new2(S)$
$new2([a|S]) \leftarrow !, new3(S)$
$new2([C|S]) \leftarrow new2(S)$
$new3([a|S]) \leftarrow !, new4(S)$
$new3([C|S]) \leftarrow new2(S)$
$new4([b|S]) \leftarrow !, new5(S)$
$new4([a|S]) \leftarrow !, new4(S)$
$new4([C|S]) \leftarrow new2(S)$
$new5(S) \leftarrow$

4.2 A Parsing Example

In this example we show the derivation of an efficient parser for a given regular expression from a general parser by using the disjunctive partial deduction technique. The initial program, which is a general parser for regular expressions over the alphabet $\{a, b\}$, is the one given in Figure 6(A), where $accepts(E, X, Y)$ holds iff the word represented by the difference list $X \setminus Y$ is in the language denoted by the regular expression E. In particular, $accepts(E, X, [\,])$ means that E accepts X.

Initial program
for parsing regular expressions

$$
\left[
\begin{array}{l}
accepts(a, [a|X], X) \leftarrow \\
accepts(b, [b|X], X) \leftarrow \\
accepts(E1 \cdot E2, S, X) \leftarrow \\
\quad accepts(E1, S, X1), \\
\quad accepts(E2, X1, X) \\
accepts(E1 + E2, S, X) \leftarrow \\
\quad accepts(E1, S, X) \\
accepts(E1 + E2, S, X) \leftarrow \\
\quad accepts(E2, S, X) \\
accepts(E^*, S, S) \leftarrow \\
accepts(E^*, S, X) \leftarrow \\
\quad accepts(E \cdot E^*, S, X)
\end{array}
\right.
$$

(A)

Specialized program
w.r.t. $accepts(a \cdot a^* \cdot b + a \cdot a^*, X, [\,])$

by
disjunctive
partial
deduction

$$
\left[
\begin{array}{l}
6.\ new1([a|X]) \leftarrow new2(X) \\
8.\ new2([\,]) \leftarrow \\
14.\ new2([a|X]) \leftarrow new3(X) \\
15.\ new2(X) \leftarrow X \neq [a|Y], X \neq [\,], new4(X) \\
16.\ new3([\,]) \leftarrow \\
22.\ new3([a|X]) \leftarrow new3(X) \\
23.\ new3(X) \leftarrow X \neq [a|Y], X \neq [\,], new4(X) \\
19.\ new4([b]) \leftarrow \\
24.\ new4([a|X]) \leftarrow new4(X)
\end{array}
\right.
$$

(B)

Fig. 6. (A) General parser for regular expressions. (B) Specialized program derived by disjunctive partial deduction, where $new1(X)$ is defined by the clause $new1(X) \leftarrow accepts(a \cdot a^* \cdot b + a \cdot a^*, X, [\,])$.

We use our strategy $\mathcal{D}$ to derive a deterministic program which tests whether or not a word X is in the language denoted by the regular expression $a \cdot a^* \cdot b + a \cdot a^*$. Thus, we begin by introducing the new definition clause:

1. $new1(X) \leftarrow accepts(a \cdot a^* \cdot b + a \cdot a^*, X, [\,])$

We use the same subsidiary strategies for unfolding, case split, definition, and folding which we have used in the example of the strong KMP test. The various iterations of the strategy $\mathcal{D}$ are given below.

First iteration. By definition we introduce the clause:

1. $new1(X) \leftarrow accepts(a \cdot a^* \cdot b + a \cdot a^*, X, [\,])$

Thus, $Def_1 = \{1\}$ and $Q_1 = \{\}$. By unfolding clause 1 we get:

2. $new1([a|X]) \leftarrow accepts(a^* \cdot b, X, [\,])$

3. $new1([a|X]) \leftarrow accepts(a^*, X, [\,])$

For folding clauses (2, 3) we introduce the following definition clauses:

4. $new2(X) \leftarrow accepts(a^* \cdot b, X, [\,])$
5. $new2(X) \leftarrow accepts(a^*, X, [\,])$

By folding clauses (2, 3) using clauses (4, 5) we get:

6. $new1([a|X]) \leftarrow new2(X)$

Clause 6 is a clause of the specialized program to be derived. We have that $U_1 = \{\}$, $N_1 = \{2, 3\}$, $F_1 = \{6\}$, $Def_2 = \{4, 5\}$, and $Q_2 = \{6\}$. In the following iteration we deal with the new definition clauses 4 and 5.

Second iteration. By unfolding clauses 4 and 5 we get:

7. $new2(X) \leftarrow accepts(a^*, X, [b])$
8. $new2([\,]) \leftarrow$
9. $new2([a|X]) \leftarrow accepts(a^*, X, [\,])$

By a case split step of clause 7 w.r.t. $\{X/[\,]\}$ and then by a second case split step w.r.t. $\{X/[a|Y]\}$ we get:

7.1 $new2([\,]) \leftarrow accepts(a^*, [\,], [b])$
7.2 $new2([a|X]) \leftarrow [a|X] \neq [\,],\ accepts(a^*, [a|X], [b])$
7.3 $new2(X) \leftarrow X \neq [a|Y],\ X \neq [\,],\ accepts(a^*, X, [b])$

We delete clause 7.1 because it is subsumed by clause 8. Then, by simplification in the body of clause 7.2, we get:

10. $new2([a|X]) \leftarrow accepts(a^*, [a|X], [b])$

For folding clauses (9, 10) and clause (7.3) we introduce the following definition clauses:

11. $new3(X) \leftarrow accepts(a^*, X, [\,])$
12. $new3(X) \leftarrow accepts(a^*, [a|X], [b])$
13. $new4(X) \leftarrow accepts(a^*, X, [b])$

By folding clauses (9, 10) using clauses (11, 12) and by folding clause 7.3 using clause 13, we get:

14. $new2([a|X]) \leftarrow new3(X)$
15. $new2(X) \leftarrow X \neq [a|Y],\ X \neq [\,],\ new4(X)$

Clauses 14 and 15 are clauses of the specialized program to be derived. We have that $U_2 = \{8\}$, $N_2 = \{7.3, 9, 10\}$, $F_2 = \{14, 15\}$, $Def_3 = \{11, 12, 13\}$, and $Q_3 = Q_2 \cup \{8, 14, 15\}$. In the following iteration we deal with the new definition clauses 11, 12, and 13.

Third iteration. By unfolding clauses 11, 12, and 13 we get:

16. $new3([\,]) \leftarrow$
17. $new3([a|X]) \leftarrow accepts(a^*, X, [\,])$
18. $new3(X) \leftarrow accepts(a^*, X, [b])$

19. $new4([b]) \leftarrow$
20. $new4([a|X]) \leftarrow accepts(a^*, X, [b])$

By a case split step of clause 18 w.r.t. $\{X/[\,]\}$ and then by a second case split step w.r.t. $\{X/[a|Y]\}$ we get:

18.1 $new3([\,]) \leftarrow accepts(a^*, [\,], [b])$
18.2 $new3([a|X]) \leftarrow [a|X] \neq [\,], \ accepts(a^*, [a|X], [b])$
18.3 $new3(X) \leftarrow X \neq [a|Y], \ X \neq [\,], \ accepts(a^*, X, [b])$

We delete clause 18.1 because it is subsumed by clause 16. Then, by simplification in the body of clause 18.2, we get:

21. $new3([a|X]) \leftarrow accepts(a^*, [a|X], [b])$

By folding clauses (17, 21) using clauses (11, 12), by folding clause 18.3 using clause 13, and by folding clause 20 using clause 13, we get:

22. $new3([a|X]) \leftarrow new3(X)$
23. $new3(X) \leftarrow X \neq [a|Y], \ X \neq [\,], \ new4(X)$
24. $new4([a|X]) \leftarrow new4(X)$

Since no new definition clause has been introduced, the partial deduction process is ended. We have that $U_3 = \{16, 19\}$, $N_3 = \{17, 18.3, 20, 21\}$, $F_3 = \{22, 23, 24\}$, $Def_4 = \{\}$, and $Q_4 = Q_3 \cup \{16, 19, 22, 23, 24\}$. The specialized final program is depicted in Figure 6(B). Also in this final program we could replace the inequalities in favour of cuts. We leave this task to the reader.

Notice that if one uses the strategy for standard partial deduction, instead of the one for the disjunctive partial deduction, it is impossible to derive a final program which is deterministic, because by the atomic folding rule one cannot generate a single clause by folding two different clauses.

5 Discussion and Related Work

We have identified some transformation rules which allow us to derive very efficient specialized programs when in order to propagate some given information about the input data, it is necessary to: (i) deal with conjunctions of recursively defined predicates, (ii) combine alternative computations, and (iii) take into account unification failures. Although these rules are similar to the transformation rules already considered in the literature (see [15] for a survey), their usefulness for the specialization of logic programs has not been yet fully investigated in previous work.

We have proposed a way for combining our transformation rules into a strategy (see Figure 4) for disjunctive partial deduction which is parametric w.r.t. the subsidiary strategies to be used for applying the various transformation rules. Thus, in particular, any unfolding strategy and any strategy for the definition rule, also called the generalization strategy, already developed for program specialization (see, for instance, [6, 11, 20]) may be adapted to our strategy.

The particular unfolding strategy we apply is different from the one in [16] and it works both for the derivation of a program which behaves like the deterministic finite automaton generated by the KMP string matching algorithm, and for the derivation of regular expression parsers. These two program derivations which are fully presented here do not appear in [16]. With respect to that paper, here (i) in Sections 2.1 and 2.2 we have presented a detailed description of standard partial deduction in terms of unfold/fold rules and strategies; (ii) we have explained in Section 2.3 the reasons why standard partial deduction fails to produce a program which behaves like the finite automaton generated by the KMP matching algorithm; and also (iii) we have introduced in Section 3 the cut introduction rule. This rule is used for replacing negative equality tests and deriving very efficient residual programs.

The strategy we presented here is an extension of the one proposed for partial deduction in [6] (see Figure 1). It may also be used for deriving deterministic programs from nondeterministic ones and for avoiding intermediate data structures through the elimination of unnecessary variables [19].

A proposal for integrating partial deduction and the elimination of unnecessary variables has been presented in [10]. Indeed, that work which introduces the conjunctive partial deduction technique, recasts in the style of Lloyd and Shepherdson's approach [6, 13] some known ideas for the elimination of intermediate data structures based on unfolding/folding rules. However, by conjunctive partial deduction it is impossible to combine partial evaluations of alternative branches of SLD-trees, and it is also impossible to introduce inequalities and to simulate the application of the case split rule.

Some issues concerning the program transformation technique we have described here, are further developed in [16] where we introduce *modes* to be used for (i) ensuring that the derived programs are *semi-deterministic*, in the sense that if one considers also the inequalities in the bodies of clauses, at runtime at most one non-unit clause is unifiable with the current goal; (ii) guiding the applications of the case split rule so that case analysis is performed w.r.t. the so called *input arguments* only (they, in general, are a subset of all arguments); (iii) providing an unfolding strategy according to a *producer-consumer* model (only calls with instantiated input arguments are unfolded); and (iv) guiding the generation of the new eureka definitions required for folding.

In [16] we also prove that the transformation rules preserve the given mode information, so that no mode analysis is needed during the transformation process itself. We also use an extra transformation rule, called *head generalization*, whereby terms in the head of a clause are replaced by variables and the corresponding equalities are added to the body. Moreover, in [16] there is an example where it is shown that exponential improvements are possible and there is a fully automatic derivation of a specialized version of a multi-pattern matching program.

A transformation technique which is closely related to ours is supercompilation [8, 26]. Also by this technique it is possible to achieve program specialization and the elimination of intermediate data structures. One major difference with our work is that supercompilation basically deals with functional programs which are deterministic.

Now we want to make some final remarks about the examples of program specialization we have presented. As already mentioned, the known derivations of specialized the KMP matching programs by automatic methods based on partial deduction, are in a sense, less powerful than ours because we use an initial program which is very simple (see clause 1 in Section 4.1), instead of the initial program of Figure 2(A). A relevant exception is the one presented in [21]. In that paper the authors use the unfolding and folding rules together with a case split rule based on type information, in the sense that they assume that the arguments of the predicate *match* are lists. We do not use any type information at all. Moreover, the derivation in [21] is not guided by an automatic strategy. Very simple initial programs are considered also in [23], but in that paper the derivation requires a preliminary transformation into the so called 'failure continuation passing style'.

Similarly to the KMP example, also the published derivations by partial deduction of specialized parsers from general parsers, use rather clever deterministic initial programs (see, for instance, [14]).

Acknowledgments

We would like to thank D. De Schreye, J. Gallagher, R. Glück, M. Leuschel, B. Martens, M. H. Sørensen for stimulating discussions about logic program specialization. Experiments done using the SP specializer by J. Gallagher, were extremely useful to test the ability of the currently used techniques for partial deduction. We also thanks the referees for their useful suggestions and comments.

This work has been partly supported by the EC under the Human Capital and Mobility Project 'Logic Program Synthesis and Transformation', and also by the INTAS Project 93-1702, Murst 40% (Italy), and the Progetto Coordinato 'Programmazione Logica' of the CNR (Italy).

References

1. A. Bossi and N. Cocco. Preserving universal termination through unfold/fold. In *Proceedings ALP '94*, Lecture Notes in Computer Science 850, pages 269–286. Springer-Verlag, 1994.
2. R. M. Burstall and J. Darlington. A transformation system for developing recursive programs. *Journal of the ACM*, 24(1):44–67, January 1977.
3. J. Cook and J. P. Gallagher. A transformation system for definite programs based on termination analysis. In L. Fribourg and F. Turini, editors, *Proceedings of LOP-STR'94 and META'94, Pisa, Italy*, Lecture Notes in Computer Science 883, pages 51–68. Springer-Verlag, 1994.
4. Y. Deville. *Logic Programming: Systematic Program Development*. Addison-Wesley, 1990.
5. H. Fujita. An algorithm for partial evaluation with constraints. Technical Memorandum TM-0367, ICOT, Tokyo, Japan, 1987.

6. J. P. Gallagher. Tutorial on specialization of logic programs. In *Proceedings of ACM SIGPLAN Symposium on Partial Evaluation and Semantics Based Program Manipulation, PEPM '93, Copenhagen, Denmark*, pages 88–98. ACM Press, 1993.

7. M. Gergatsoulis and M. Katzouraki. Unfold/fold transformations for definite clause programs. In M. Hermenegildo and J. Penjam, editors, *Proceedings Sixth International Symposium on Programming Language Implementation and Logic Programming (PLILP '94)*, Lecture Notes in Computer Science 844, pages 340–354. Springer-Verlag, 1994.

8. R. Glück and A.V. Klimov. Occam's razor in metacomputation: the notion of a perfect process tree. In P. Cousot, M. Falaschi, G. Filé, and A. Rauzy, editors, *3rd International Workshop on Static Analysis, Padova, Italy, September 1993*, Lecture Notes in Computer Science 724, pages 112–123. Springer-Verlag, 1993.

9. N. D. Jones, C. K. Gomard, and P. Sestoft. *Partial Evaluation and Automatic Program Generation.* Prentice Hall, 1993.

10. M. Leuschel, D. De Schreye, and A. de Waal. A conceptual embedding of folding into partial deduction: Towards a maximal integration. In M. Maher, editor, *Proceedings of the Joint International Conference and Symposium on Logic Programming, Bonn, Germany*, pages 319–332. MIT Press, 1996.

11. M. Leuschel and B. Martens. Global control for partial deduction through characteristic atoms and global trees. Report CW 220, K.U. Leuven, Belgium, 1995.

12. M. Leuschel and M. H. Sørensen. Redundant argument filtering of logic programs. In J. Gallagher, editor, *Logic Program Synthesis and Transformation, Proceedings LOPSTR '96, Stockholm, Sweden. Report no. 96-020 Stockholm University.*, pages 63–77. Springer-Verlag, 1996. (To appear).

13. J. W. Lloyd and J. C. Shepherdson. Partial evaluation in logic programming. *Journal of Logic Programming*, 11:217–242, 1991.

14. T. Mogensen and A. Bondorf. Logimix: A self-applicable partial evaluator for Prolog. In K.-K. Lau and T. Clement, editors, *Logic Program Synthesis and Transformation, Proceedings LOPSTR '92, Manchester, U.K.*, Workshops in Computing, pages 214–227. Springer-Verlag, 1993.

15. A. Pettorossi and M. Proietti. Transformation of logic programs: Foundations and techniques. *Journal of Logic Programming*, 19,20:261–320, 1994.

16. A. Pettorossi, M. Proietti, and S. Renault. Reducing nondeterminism while specializing logic program. In *Proc. 24-th ACM Symposium on Principles of Programming Languages, Paris, France.* ACM Press, 1997. (To appear).

17. S. Prestwich. Online partial deduction of large programs. In *Proceedings ACM Sigplan Symposium on Partial Evaluation and Semantics-Based Program Manipulation, PEPM '93, Copenhagen, Denmark*, pages 111–118. ACM Press, 1993.

18. M. Proietti and A. Pettorossi. Semantics preserving transformation rules for Prolog. In *ACM Symposium on Partial Evaluation and Semantics Based Program Manipulation, PEPM '91, Yale University, New Haven, Connecticut, USA*, pages 274–284. ACM Press, 1991.

19. M. Proietti and A. Pettorossi. Unfolding-definition-folding, in this order, for avoiding unnecessary variables in logic programs. *Theoretical Computer Science*, 142(1):89–124, 1995.

20. D. Sahlin. Mixtus: An automatic partial evaluator for full Prolog. *New Generation Computing*, 12:7–51, 1993.

21. T. Sato and H. Tamaki. Examples of logic program transformation and synthesis. Case studies of transformation and synthesis of logic programs done up to Feb. 85, 1985.

22. H. Seki. Unfold/fold transformation of stratified programs. *Theoretical Computer Science*, 86:107–139, 1991.

23. D. A. Smith. Partial evaluation of pattern matching in constraint logic programming languages. In *Proceedings ACM Symposium on Partial Evaluation and Semantics Based Program Manipulation, PEPM '91, New Haven, CT, USA*, SIGPLAN Notices, 26, 9, pages 62–71. ACM Press, 1991.

24. M. H. Sørensen, R. Glück, and N. D. Jones. Towards unifying partial evaluation, deforestation, supercompilation, and GPC. In D. Sannella, editor, *Fifth European Symposium on Programming Languages and Systems, ESOP '94*, Lecture Notes in Computer Science 788, pages 485–500. Springer-Verlag, 1994.

25. H. Tamaki and T. Sato. Unfold/fold transformation of logic programs. In S.-Å. Tärnlund, editor, *Proceedings of the Second International Conference on Logic Programming, Uppsala, Sweden*, pages 127–138. Uppsala University, 1984.

26. V. F. Turchin. The concept of a supercompiler. *ACM TOPLAS*, 8(3):292–325, 1986.

Abstract Specialization and Its Application to Program Parallelization

Germán Puebla and *Manuel Hermenegildo*

{german,herme}@fi.upm.es
Department of Computer Science
Technical University of Madrid (UPM)

Abstract. Program specialization optimizes programs for known values of the input. It is often the case that the set of possible input values is unknown, or this set is infinite. However, a form of specialization can still be performed in such cases by means of abstract interpretation, specialization then being with respect to abstract values (substitutions), rather than concrete ones. This paper reports on the application of abstract multiple specialization to automatic program parallelization in the &-Prolog compiler. Abstract executability, the main concept underlying abstract specialization, is formalized, the design of the specialization system presented, and a non-trivial example of specialization in automatic parallelization is given.

1 Introduction

A good number of compiler optimizations can be seen as special cases of partial evaluation [CD93, JGS93]. The main objective of partial evaluation is to automatically overcome losses in performance which are due to general purpose algorithms by specializing the program for known values of the inputs. Much work has been done in partial evaluation (deduction) and specialization of logic programs (see e.g. [LS91, Kom92, GB90, GCS88, JLW90]). It is often the case that the set of possible input values is unknown, or this set is infinite. However, a form of specialization can still be performed in such cases by means of abstract interpretation [CC77], specialization then being with respect to abstract values (substitutions), rather than concrete ones.

A procedure may have different uses within a program, i.e. it is called from different places in the program with different (abstract) input values. In principle, optimizations are then allowable only if the optimization is applicable to all uses of the predicate. However, it is possible that in several different uses the input values allow different and incompatible optimizations and then none of them can take place. This can be overcome by means of program *multiple specialization* [JLW90, GH91, Bru91, Win92] (the counterpart of polyvariant specialization [Bul84]), where a different version of a predicate is generated for each use, so that each one of them is optimized for the particular subset of input values with which each version is to be used.

In [PH95] we presented a framework for abstract multiple specialization. In order to reduce the size of the resulting program as much as possible, the framework incorporates a minimization algorithm that associates a set of optimizations to each of the multiple versions of a procedure generated during multi-variant abstract interpretation. This framework achieves the same results as those of Winsborough's [Win92] but with only a slight modification of a standard abstract interpreter. We argue that the experimental results given in [PH95] showed that multiple specialization is indeed practical and useful in automatic parallelization, and also that such results shed some light on its possible practicality in other applications. However, due to space limitations, the nature of the optimizations, the procedure used to detect them, and the actual source to source transformations by which optimizations are materialized, were not presented. This work tries to fill this gap by describing the application of abstract multiple specialization to automatic program parallelization in the &-Prolog compiler. *Abstract executability*, the main concept underlying abstract specialization, is formalized, the design of the specialization system presented, and a non-trivial example of specialization in automatic parallelization is given.

The structure of the paper is as follows. Section 2 briefly recalls abstract interpretation. In Section 3 the notion of abstract executability is formalized. Then Section 4 presents a particular application of abstract specialization. Section 5 shows the design of the abstract specializer and an example of specialized program. Finally, Section 6 concludes.

2 Abstract Interpretation of Logic Programs

Abstract interpretation [CC77] is a useful technique for performing global analysis of a program in order to compute at compile-time characteristics of the terms to which the variables in that program will be bound at run-time. The interesting aspect of abstract interpretation vs. classical types of compile-time analyses is that it offers a well founded framework which can be instantiated to produce a rich variety of types of analysis with guaranteed correctness with respect to a particular semantics.

In abstract interpretation a program is executed using *abstract substitutions* (λ) instead of actual substitutions (θ). An abstract substitution is a finite representation of a, possibly infinite, set of actual substitutions in the concrete domain (D). The set of all possible terms that a variable can be bound to in an abstract substitution represents an *abstract domain* (D_α) which is usually a complete lattice or cpo which is ascending chain finite.

Abstract substitutions and sets of concrete substitutions are related via a pair of functions referred to as the *abstraction* (α) and *concretization* (γ) functions. The usual definition for partial order ($\sqsubseteq$) over abstract domains, is $\forall \lambda, \lambda' \in D_\alpha$ $\lambda \sqsubseteq \lambda'$ iff $\gamma(\lambda) \subseteq \gamma(\lambda')$. In addition, each primitive operation u of the language (unification being a notable example) is abstracted to an operation u' over the abstract domain. Soundness of the analysis requires that each concrete operation u be related to its corresponding abstract operation u' as follows: for every x in the concrete computational domain, $u(x) \subseteq \gamma(u'(\alpha(x)))$.

We now introduce some notation. A *program* is a sequence of *clauses*. Clauses are of the form $h \leftarrow b$, where h is an atom and b is a possibly empty conjunction of literals. Clauses in the program are written with a unique subscript attached to the head atom (the clause number), and dual subscript (clause number, body position) attached to each literal in the body atom e.g. $H_k \leftarrow B_{k,1}, \ldots, B_{k,n_k}$ where $B_{k,i}$ is a subscripted literal. The clause may also be referred to as clause k, the subscript of the head atom, and each literal in the program is uniquely identified by its subscript k, i.

The goal of the abstract interpreter is, for a given abstract domain, to annotate the program with information about the current environment (i.e. the values of variables), at each program point. Correctness of the analysis requires that annotations be valid for any call (program execution). Different names distinguish abstract substitutions depending on the point in a clause to which they correspond. In particular, we will be interested in the *abstract call substitution* $\lambda_{k,i}$ for each literal $L_{k,i}$ which is the abstract substitution just before calling the literal $L_{k,i}$.

If the analysis is goal oriented, then the abstract interpreter receives as input, in addition to the program, a set of *calling patterns* which are descriptions of the calling modes into the program. In its minimal form (least burden on the programmer) the calling patterns may simply be the names of the predicates which can appear in user queries. In order to increase the precision of the analysis, it is often possible to include a description of the set of abstract (or concrete) substitutions allowable for each predicate by means of *entry* declarations [BCHP96]. Information inferred by goal oriented analysis may be more accurate as each $\lambda_{k,i}$ "only" has to be valid when executing calls described by the calling patterns.

3 Abstract Execution

The concept of *abstract executability* was, to our knowledge, first introduced informally in [GH91]. It allows reducing at compile-time certain literals in a program to the value *true* or *false* using information obtained with abstract interpretation. That work also introduced some simple semantics-preserving program transformations and showed the potential of the technique, including elimination of invariants in loops. We introduce in the following an improved formalization of abstract executability. The set of variables in a literal L is represented as $var(L)$. The restriction of the substitution θ to the variables in L is denoted $\theta|_L$.

Operationally, each literal L in a program P can be viewed as a procedure call. Each run-time invocation of the procedure call L will have a local *environment* e, which stores the particular values of each variable in $var(L)$ for that invocation. We will write $\theta \in e(L)$ if θ is a substitution such that the value of each variable in $var(L)$ is the same in the environment e and the substitution θ.

Definition 1 Run-time Substitution Set. Given a literal L from a program P we define the *run-time substitution set* of L in P as

$$RT(L, P) = \{\theta|_L : e \text{ is a run-time environment for } L \text{ and } \theta \in e(L)\}$$

$RT(L, P)$ is not computable in general. The set of run-time environments for a literal is not known at compile-time. However, it is sometimes possible to find a set of bindings which will appear in *any* environment for L. These "invariants" can be synthesized in a substitution θ_s such that $\forall \theta \in RT(L, P) \, \exists \theta_d :$ $L\theta = L\theta_s\theta_d$. Note that it is always possible to find a trivial $\theta_s = \epsilon$, the empty substitution, which corresponds to having no static knowledge of the run-time environment. In this case, we can simply take $\theta_d = \theta$ for any θ.

The substitutions θ_s and θ_d correspond to the so-called *static* and *dynamic* values respectively in partial evaluation [JGS93]. As a result, we can specialize L for the statically known data θ_s. Specialization is then usually performed by *unfolding* $L\theta_s$. If all the leaves in the SLD tree for $L\theta_s$ are failing nodes and $L\theta_s$ is pure (i.e., its execution does not produce side-effects), then the literal L can be replaced by *false*. If all the leaves are failing nodes except for one which is a success node and $L\theta_s$ is pure then L can be replaced by a set of unifications on $var(L\theta_s)$ which have the same effect as actually executing $L\theta_s\theta_d$ in P. If such set of unifications is empty, L can be replaced by *true*.

The goal of abstract specialization is also to replace a literal by *false*, *true* or a set of unifications, but rather than starting from $RT(L, P)$ it will use information on $RT(L, P)$ provided by abstract interpretation, i.e., the abstract call substitution for L. For simplicity, we will restrict our discussion to replacing L with *false* or *true*.

Definition 2 Trivial Success Set. Given a literal L from a program P we define the *trivial success set* of L in P as

$$TS(L, P) = \begin{cases} \left\{ \begin{array}{l} \theta|_L : L\theta \text{ succeeds exactly once in } P \\ \text{with empty answer substitution } (\epsilon) \end{array} \right\} & \text{if L is pure} \\ \emptyset & \text{otherwise} \end{cases}$$

Definition 3 Finite Failure Set. Given a literal L from a program P we define the *finite failure set* of L in P as

$$FF(L, P) = \begin{cases} \{\theta|_L : L\theta \text{ fails finitely in } P\} & \text{if L is pure} \\ \emptyset & \text{otherwise} \end{cases}$$

Note that if two distinct literals $L_{k,i}$ and $L_{l,j}$ are equal up to renaming then the sets $TS(L_{k,i}, P)$ (resp. $FF(L_{k,i}, P)$) and $TS(L_{l,j}, P)$ (resp. $FF(L_{l,j}, P)$) will also be equal up to renaming. However, there is no a priori relation between $RT(L_{k,i}, P)$ and $RT(L_{l,j}, P)$.

Definition 4 Elementary Literal Replacement. *Elementary Literal Replacement* (ER) of a literal L in a program P is defined as:

$$ER(L, P) = \begin{cases} true & \text{if } RT(L, P) \subseteq TS(L, P) \\ false & \text{if } RT(L, P) \subseteq FF(L, P) \\ L & \text{otherwise} \end{cases}$$

Note that given the definitions of $TS(L,P)$ and $FF(L,P)$, any literal L which is not dead code and produces some side-effect (i.e., L is not pure) will not be affected by elementary literal replacement, i.e., $ER(L,P) = L$.

Theorem 5 Elementary Replacement. *Let P_{ER} be the program obtained by replacing each literal $L_{k,i}$ in P by $ER(L_{k,i},P)$. P and P_{ER} produce the same computed answers and side-effects.*

The idea is to optimize a program by replacing the execution of $L\theta$ with the execution of either the builtin predicate *true* or *fail*, which can be executed in zero or constant time. Even though the above optimization may seem not very widely applicable, for many builtin predicates such as those that check basic types or meta-logical predicates that inspect the instantiation state of terms, this optimization is indeed very relevant. However, elementary replacement is not directly applicable because $RT(L,P), TS(L,P)$, and $FF(L,P)$ are generally not known at specialization time.

Definition 6 Abstract Trivial Success Set. Given an abstract domain D_α we define the *abstract trivial success set* of L in P as

$$TS_\alpha(L,P,D_\alpha) = \{\lambda \in D_\alpha : \gamma(\lambda) \subseteq TS(L,P)\}$$

Definition 7 Abstract Finite Failure Set. Given an abstract domain D_α we define the *abstract finite failure set* of L in P as

$$FF_\alpha(L,P,D_\alpha) = \{\lambda \in D_\alpha : \gamma(\lambda) \subseteq FF(L,P)\}$$

Note that by using the least upper bound operator ($\sqcup$) of the abstract domain D_α, $TS_\alpha(L,P,D_\alpha)$ and $FF_\alpha(L,P,D_\alpha)$ could be represented by a single abstract substitution (rather than a set of them), say $\lambda_{TS_\alpha(L,P,D_\alpha)} = \sqcup_{TS_\alpha(L,P,D_\alpha)}\lambda$ and $\lambda_{FF_\alpha(L,P,D_\alpha)} = \sqcup_{FF_\alpha(L,P,D_\alpha)}\lambda$. However, this alternative approximation of the actual sets $TS(L,P)$ and $FF(L,P)$ can introduce an important loss of accuracy for some abstract domains because $\gamma(\lambda_{TS_\alpha(L,P,D_\alpha)}) \supseteq \bigcup_{TS_\alpha(L,P,D_\alpha)}\gamma(\lambda)$, thus reducing the optimizations achievable by abstract executability .

Definition 8 Abstract Execution. *Abstract Execution* (AE) of L in P with abstract call substitution $\lambda \in D_\alpha$ is defined as:

$$AE(L,P,D_\alpha,\lambda) = \begin{cases} true & \text{if } \lambda \in TS_\alpha(L,P,D_\alpha) \\ false & \text{if } \lambda \in FF_\alpha(L,P,D_\alpha) \\ L & \text{otherwise} \end{cases}$$

If $AE(L,P,D_\alpha,\lambda) = true$ (resp. *false*) we will say that L is abstractly executable to *true* (resp. *false*). If $AE(L,P,D_\alpha,\lambda) = L$ then L is not abstractly executable.

Theorem 9 Abstract Executability. *Let let P_{AE} be the program obtained by replacing each literal $L_{k,i}$ in P by $AE(L_{k,i},P,D_\alpha,\lambda_{k,i})$. P and P_{AE} produce the same computed answers and side-effects.*

The advantage of abstract executability as given in Definition 8 over elementary replacement is that instead of using $RT(L, P)$ which is not computable in general, such sets are approximated by abstract substitutions which for appropriate abstract domains (and widening mechanisms) will be computable in finite time.

Definition 10 Optimal TS$_\alpha$. An abstract trivial success set $TS_\alpha(L, P, D_\alpha)$ is *optimal* iff

$$(\bigcup_{\lambda \in TS_\alpha(L,P,D_\alpha)} \gamma(\lambda)) = TS(L, P)$$

Optimal abstract finite failure sets are defined similarly. One first possible disadvantage of abstract execution with respect to elementary replacement is due to the loss of information associated to using an abstract domain instead of the concrete domain. This is related to the expressive power of the abstract domain, i.e. what kind of information it provides. If $TS_\alpha(L, P, D_\alpha)$ and/or $FF_\alpha(L, P, D_\alpha)$ are not optimal then there may exist literals in the program such that $RT(L, P) \subseteq TS(L, P)$ or $RT(L, P) \subseteq FF(L, P)$ and thus elementary replacement could in principle be applied but abstract execution cannot. In general, domains will be optimal for *some* predicates but not all.

Another possible disadvantage is that even if the abstract domain is expressive enough and both $TS_\alpha(L, P, D_\alpha)$ and $FF_\alpha(L, P, D_\alpha)$ are optimal, the computed abstract substitutions may not be accurate enough to allow abstract execution. Therefore, the choice of the domain should be first guided by the predicates whose optimization is of interest so that $TS_\alpha(L, P, D_\alpha)$ and $FF_\alpha(L, P, D_\alpha)$ are as adequate as possible for them, and second by the accuracy of the abstract substitutions it provides and its computational cost.

Definition 11 Maximal Subset. Let S be a set and let $\sqsubseteq$ be a partial order over the elements of S. We define the *maximal subset* of S with respect to $\sqsubseteq$ as

$$M_\sqsubseteq(S) = \{s \in S : \nexists s' \in S \ (s \neq s' \wedge s \sqsubseteq s')\}^1$$

Abstract execution as given in Definition 8 is not applicable in general because even though each $\lambda_{k,i}$ is computable by means of abstract interpretation, TS_α and FF_α are not computable in general. Additionally, if D_α is infinite, TS_α and FF_α may also be infinite. However, based on the observation that if $\lambda \in TS_\alpha$ then $\forall \lambda' \sqsubseteq \lambda \ \ \lambda' \in TS_\alpha$, the conditions $\lambda \in TS_\alpha(L, P, D_\alpha)$ and $\lambda \in FF_\alpha(L, P, D_\alpha)$ are equivalent to $\exists \lambda' \in M_\sqsubseteq(TS_\alpha(L, P, D_\alpha)) : \lambda \sqsubseteq \lambda'$ and $\exists \lambda' \in M_\sqsubseteq(FF_\alpha(L, P, D_\alpha)) : \lambda \sqsubseteq \lambda'$ respectively and thus can be replaced in Definition 8. Unlike TS_α and FF_α, $M_\sqsubseteq(TS_\alpha(L, P, D_\alpha))$ and $M_\sqsubseteq(FF_\alpha(L, P, D_\alpha))$ are finite for any D_α with finite width. Additionally, they usually have one or just a few elements for most practical domains.

Definition 12 Base Form. The *Base Form* of a literal L which calls predicate *Pred* of arity n (represented as $\overline{L}$) is the literal $Pred(X_1, \ldots, X_n)$ where $X_1, \ldots, X_n$ are distinct free variables.

---

[1] $s \neq s' \wedge s \sqsubseteq s'$ may also be written as $s \sqsubset s'$.

As the number of literals in a program that call a given predicate is not bounded and in order to reduce the number of TS_α and FF_α sets that need to be computed to optimize a program, in what follows we will only consider one TS_α and FF_α per predicate which refers to its base form.

The function named *call_to_entry*, which is normally defined for each domain in most abstract interpretation frameworks, will be used to relate an abstract substitution over the variables of an arbitrary literal with the base form of the literal. The format of this function is $call\_to\_entry(L1, L2, D_\alpha, \lambda)$. Given a literal $L1$ and an abstract substitution $\lambda \in D_\alpha$ over the variables in $L1$, this function computes an abstract substitution over the variables in $L2$ which is the result of unifying $L1$ and $L2$ both with respect to concrete and abstract substitutions.

Using the base form and *call_to_entry* the conditions $\lambda \in TS_\alpha(L, P, D_\alpha)$ and $\lambda \in FF_\alpha(L, P, D_\alpha)$ in Definition 8 can be replaced by $call\_to\_entry(L, \overline{L}, D_\alpha, \lambda) \in TS_\alpha(\overline{L}, P, D_\alpha)$ and $call\_to\_entry(L, \overline{L}, D_\alpha, \lambda) \in FF_\alpha(\overline{L}, P, D_\alpha)$ respectively. The transformed conditions are not equivalent, but are sufficient. This means that correctness is guaranteed, but possibly some optimizations will be lost.

3.1 Optimization of Calls to Builtin Predicates.

Even though abstract executability is applicable to any predicate, in what follows we will concentrate on builtin predicates. This is because the semantics of builtin predicates does not depend on the particular program in which they appear, i.e., $\forall P, P'$ $TS_\alpha(\overline{B}, P, D_\alpha) = TS_\alpha(\overline{B}, P', D_\alpha) = TS_\alpha(\overline{B}, D_\alpha)$. As a result, we can compute $TS_\alpha(\overline{B}, D_\alpha)$ and $FF_\alpha(\overline{B}, D_\alpha)$ once and for all for each builtin predicate B and they will be applicable to all literals that call the builtin predicate in any program.

Definition 13 Operational Abstract Execution of Builtins. *Operational abstract execution* (OAEB) of a literal L with abstract call substitution λ that calls a builtin predicate B is defined as:

$$OAEB(L, D_\alpha, \lambda) = \begin{cases} true & \text{if } \exists \lambda' \in A_{TS}(\overline{B}, D_\alpha) : \\ & \quad call\_to\_entry(L, \overline{B}, D_\alpha, \lambda) \sqcup \lambda' = \lambda' \\ false & \text{if } \exists \lambda' \in A_{FF}(\overline{B}, D_\alpha) : \\ & \quad call\_to\_entry(L, \overline{B}, D_\alpha, \lambda) \sqcup \lambda' = \lambda' \\ L & \text{otherwise} \end{cases}$$

$A_{TS}(\overline{B}, D_\alpha)$ and $A_{FF}(\overline{B}, D_\alpha)$ are approximations of $M_\sqsubseteq(TS_\alpha(\overline{B}, D_\alpha))$ and $M_\sqsubseteq(FF_\alpha(\overline{B}, D_\alpha))$ respectively. This is because there is no automated method that we are aware of to compute $M_\sqsubseteq(TS_\alpha(\overline{B}, D_\alpha))$ and $M_\sqsubseteq(FF_\alpha(\overline{B}, D_\alpha))$ for each builtin predicate $\overline{B}$. For soundness it is required that both $A_{TS}(\overline{B}, D_\alpha) \subseteq TS_\alpha(\overline{B}, D_\alpha)$ and $A_{FF}(\overline{B}, D_\alpha) \subseteq FF_\alpha(\overline{B}, D_\alpha)$. We believe that a good knowledge of D_α allows finding safe approximations, and that in many cases it is easy to find the best possible approximations $A_{TS}(\overline{B}, D_\alpha) = M_\sqsubseteq(TS_\alpha(\overline{B}, D_\alpha))$ and $A_{FF}(\overline{B}, D_\alpha) = M_\sqsubseteq(FF_\alpha(\overline{B}, D_\alpha))$.

Additionally, the condition $call\_to\_entry(L, \overline{B}, D_\alpha, \lambda) \sqsubseteq \lambda'$ has been replaced by the equivalent one $call\_to\_entry(L, \overline{B}, D_\alpha, \lambda) \sqcup \lambda' = \lambda'$, where $\sqcup$ stands for the *least upper bound*, which can be computed effectively.

Theorem 14 Operational Abstract Executability of Builtins. *Let P be a program and let P_{OAEB} be the program obtained by replacing each literal $L_{k,i}$ in P by $OAEB(L_{k,i}, \lambda_{k,i})$ where $\lambda_{k,i}$ is the abstract call substitution for $L_{k,i}$. If $\forall B \; A_{TS}(\overline{B}, D_\alpha) \subseteq TS_\alpha(\overline{B}, D_\alpha) \wedge A_{FF}(\overline{B}, D_\alpha) \subseteq FF_\alpha(\overline{B}, D_\alpha)$ then P_{OAEB} is computable in finite time, and both P and P_{OAEB} produce the same computed answers and side-effects.*

Example 1 Consider an abstract domain D_α consisting of the five elements $\{bottom, int, float, free, top\}$. These elements respectively correspond to the empty set of terms, the set of all integers, the set of floating point numbers, the set of all unbound variables, and the set of all terms. Suppose we are interested in optimizing calls to the builtin predicate *ground/1* by reducing them to the value true. Then, $TS(ground(X_1)) = \{\{X_1/g\}$ where g is any term without variables$\}$ and its abstract version $TS_\alpha(ground(X_1), D_\alpha) = \{int, float, bottom\}$, which is clearly not optimal (there are many ground terms which are neither integers nor floating numbers). We can take $A_{TS}(ground(X_1), D_\alpha) = \{int, float\} = M_{\sqsubseteq}(\{int, float, bottom\})$. Consider the following clause containing the literal *ground(X)*:
$$p(X, Y) \leftarrow q(Y), ground(X), r(X, Y).$$
Assume now that analysis has inferred the abstract substitution just before the literal *ground(X)* to be $\{Y/free, X/int\}$. Then $OAEB(ground(X), D_\alpha, X/int) = true$ (the literal can be replaced by *true*) because $call\_to\_entry(ground(X), ground(X_1), D_\alpha, \{X/int\}) = \{X_1/int\}$, and $X_1/int \sqcup X_1/int = X_1/int$.

If we were also interested in reducing literals that call *ground/1* to false, the most accurate $A_{FF}(ground(X_1), D_\alpha) = \{free\} = M_{\sqsubseteq}(FF_\alpha(ground(X_1), D_\alpha))$ which again is not optimal.

4 The Application: Compile-time Parallelization

The final aim of parallelism is to achieve the maximum speed (effectiveness) while computing the same solution (correctness) as the sequential execution. The two main types of parallelism which can be exploited in logic programs are well known [Con83, CC94]: or-parallelism and and–parallelism. And-parallelism refers to the parallel execution of the goals in the body of a clause (or, more precisely, of the goals in a resolvent). Several models have been proposed to take advantage of such opportunities (see, for example, [CC94] and it references).

Guaranteeing correctness and efficiency in and–parallelism is complicated by the fact that dependencies may exist among the goals to be executed in parallel, due to the presence of shared variables at run–time. It turns out that when these dependencies are present, arbitrary exploitation of and–parallelism does not guarantee efficiency. Furthermore, if certain impure predicates that are relatively common in Prolog programs are used, even correctness cannot be guaranteed.

However, if only *independent goals* are executed in parallel, both correctness and efficiency can be ensured [Con83, HR95]. Thus, the dependencies among

```
:-module(mmatrix,[mmultiply/3]).

mmultiply([],_,[]).
mmultiply([VO|Rest], V1, [Result|Others]):-
        multiply(V1,VO,Result), mmultiply(Rest, V1, Others).

multiply([],_,[]).
multiply([VO|Rest], V1, [Result|Others]):-
        vmul(VO,V1,Result), multiply(Rest, V1, Others).

vmul([],[],0).
vmul([H1|T1], [H2|T2], Result):-
        Product is H1*H2, vmul(T1,T2, Newresult),
        Result is Product+Newresult.
```

Fig. 1. mmatrix.pl

the different goals must be determined, and there is a related parallelization overhead involved. It is vital that such overhead remain reasonable. Herein we follow the approach proposed initially by R. Warren et al [WHD88, HWD92] (see their references for alternative approaches) which combines local analysis and run–time checking with a data-flow analysis based on abstract interpretation [CC77]. This combination of techniques has been shown to be quite useful in practice [WHD88, MJMB89, RD90, Tay90, dMSC93].

4.1 The Annotation Process and Run-time Tests

In the &-Prolog system, the automatic parallelization process is performed as follows [BGH94a]. Firstly, if required by the user, the Prolog program is analyzed using one or more global analyzers, aimed at inferring useful information for detecting independence. Secondly, since side–effects cannot be allowed to execute freely in parallel, the original program is analyzed using the global analyzer described in [MH89] which propagates the side–effect characteristics of builtins determining the scope of side–effects. In the current implementation, side-effecting literals are not parallelized. Finally, the *annotators* perform a source–to–source transformation of the program in which each clause is annotated with parallel expressions and conditions which encode the notion of independence used. In doing this they use the information provided by the global analyzers mentioned before.

The annotation process is divided into three subtasks. The first one is concerned with identifying the dependencies between each two literals in a clause and generating the conditions which ensure their independence. The second task aims at simplifying such conditions by means of the information inferred by the

```
mmultiply([],_,[]).
mmultiply([V0|Rest],V1,[Result|Others]) :-
        (ground(V1),
         indep([[V0,Rest],[V0,Others],[Rest,Result],[Result,Others]]) ->
            multiply(V1,V0,Result) & mmultiply(Rest,V1,Others)
        ;   multiply(V1,V0,Result), mmultiply(Rest,V1,Others)).

multiply([],_,[]).
multiply([V0|Rest],V1,[Result|Others]) :-
        (ground(V1),
         indep([[V0,Rest],[V0,Others],[Rest,Result],[Result,Others]]) ->
            vmul(V0,V1,Result) & multiply(Rest,V1,Others)
        ;   vmul(V0,V1,Result), multiply(Rest,V1,Others)).
```

Fig. 2. Parallel mmatrix

local or global analyzers. In other words, transforming the conditions into the minimum number of tests which, when evaluated at run–time, ensure the independence of the goals involved. Finally, the third task is concerned with the core of the annotation process [BGH94a], namely the application of a particular strategy to obtain an optimal (under such a strategy) parallel expression among all the possibilities detected in the previous step.

4.2 An Example: Matrix Multiplication

We illustrate the process of automatic program parallelization with an example. Figure 1 shows the code of a Prolog program for matrix multiplication. The declaration :-module(mmatrix,[mmultiply/3]). is used by the (goal-oriented) analyzer to determine that the only predicate which may appear in top-level queries is *mmatrix/3*. No information is given about the arguments in calls to the predicate *mmatrix/3*. As mentioned before, this could be done using one or more *entry* declarations [BCHP96]. If for example we want to specialize the program for the case in which the first two arguments of *mmatrix/3* are ground values and we inform the analyzer about this, the program would be parallelized without the need for any run-time tests.

Figure 2 contains the source program after automatic parallelization. if-then-else's, like in Prolog, are written (cond -> then ; else). Even though programs as defined in Section 2 do not have if-then-else's in the body of clauses, this construct poses no additional theoretical difficulties. The same effect (modulo some run-time overhead) can be achieved using conjunctions of literals and the cut. The & signs between goals indicate that they can be executed in parallel. As can be seen, a lot of run-time tests have been introduced. They are used to determine independence at run-time. If the tests hold the parallel code is executed. Otherwise the original sequential code is executed. As usual, ground(X) succeeds if X contains no variables. indep(X,Y) succeeds if X and Y have no variables in common. For conciseness and efficiency, a series of tests indep(X1,X2), ..., indep(Xn-1,Xn) is written as indep([[X1,X2], ..., [Xn-1,Xn]]).

Obviously, the tests will cause considerable overhead in run-time performance, to the point of not even knowing at first sight if the parallelized program will run faster than the sequential one. The predicate *vmul/3* does not appear in Figure 2 because automatic parallelization has not detected any profitable parallelism in it (due to granularity control) and its code remains the same as in the original program.

5 Abstract Specialization in the &-Prolog Compiler

As stated in Section 4.1, analysis information is used in the &-Prolog system to introduce as few run-time tests as possible in the process of automatic program parallelization. However, analysis information allows more powerful program optimizations than the ones performed during program annotation. First, analysis information can be used to perform abstract specialization to all program points, instead of just those ones in which run-time tests are going to be introduced. Second, the abstract interpretation framework used in &-Prolog (PLAI [MH91, MH92, BGH94b]) is multi-variant. This allows, in principle, the introduction of multiple specialization based on abstract interpretation. To this end, the analysis framework has been augmented in order to distinguish abstract substitutions for the different variants and additional structure information has been added to recover the analysis and-or graph (the *ancestors information* of [PH95]).

Analysis information is not directly available at all program points after automatic parallelization because the process modifies certain parts of the program originally analyzed. However, the &-Prolog system uses incremental analysis techniques to efficiently obtain updated analysis information from the one generated for the original program [HMPS95, PH96]. This updated analysis information is then used by the abstract specializer to optimize the program as much as possible.

5.1 Design of the Abstract Multiple Specializer

Conceptually, the process of abstract multiple specialization is composed of five steps, which are shown in Figure 3 (picture on the right), together with the role of abstract specialization in the &-Prolog system (picture on the left).

In the first step (*simplify*) the program optimizations based on abstract execution are performed whenever possible. This saves having to optimize the different versions of a predicate when the optimization is applicable to all versions. Any optimization that is common to all versions of a predicate is performed at this stage. The output is an abstractly specialized program. This is also the final program if multiple specialization is not performed. The remaining four steps are related to *multiple* specialization.

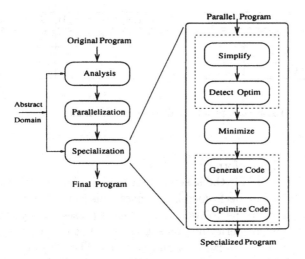

Fig. 3. Program Annotation and Abstract Multiple Specialization

In the second step (*detect optimizations*) information from the multi-variant abstract interpretation is used to detect (but not to perform) the optimizations allowed in each of the (possibly) multiple versions generated for each predicate during analysis. Note that the source for the multiply specialized program has not been generated yet (this will be done in the fourth step, *generate code*) but rather the code generated in the first step is used, considering several abstract substitutions for each program point instead of their lowest upper bound, as is done in the first step. The output of this step is the set of literals that become abstractly executable (and their value) in each version of a predicate due to multiple specialization. Note that these literals are not abstractly executable without multiple specialization, otherwise the optimization would have already been performed in the first step.

The third step (*minimize*) is concerned with reducing the size of the multiply specialized program as much as possible, while maintaining all possible optimizations without the need of introducing run-time tests to select among different versions of a predicate. A detailed presentation of the algorithm used in this step and its evaluation is the subject of [PH95].

In the fourth step (*generate code*) the source code of the minimal multiply specialized program is generated. The result of the minimization algorithm in the previous step indicates the number of implementations needed for each predicate. Each of them receives a unique name. Also, literals must also be renamed appropriately for a predicate with several implementations.

In the fifth step (*optimize code*), the particular optimizations associated with each implementation of a predicate are performed. Other simple program optimizations like eliminating literals in a clause to the right of a literal abstractly executable to false, eliminating a literal which is abstractly executable to true from the clause it belongs instead of introducing the builtin true/1, dead code

Domain	$TS_\alpha(ground(X_1))$	$FF_\alpha(ground(X_1))$	$TS_\alpha(indep(X_1))$	$FF_\alpha(indep(X_1))$
sharing	O	N	O	N
sh+fr	O	S	O	S
asub	O	N	O	N

Table 1. Optimality of Different Domains

elimination, etc. are also performed in this step.

In the implementation, for the sake of efficiency, the first and second steps, and the fourth and fifth are performed in one pass (this is marked in Figure 3 by dashed squares), thus reducing to two the number of passes through the source code. The third step is not performed on source code but rather on a synthetic representation of sets of optimizations and versions. The core of the multiple specialization technique (steps *minimize* and *generate code*) are independent from the actual optimizations being performed.

5.2 Abstract Domains

The abstract specializer is parametric with respect to the abstract domain used. Currently, the specializer can work with all the abstract domains implemented in the analyzer in the &-Prolog system. In order to augment the specializer to use the information provided by a new abstract domain (D_α), correct $A_{TS}(\overline{B}, D_\alpha)$ and $A_{FF}(\overline{B}, D_\alpha)$ sets must be provided to the analyzer for each builtin predicate B whose optimization is of interest. Alternatively, and for efficiency issues, the specializer allows replacing the conditions in Definition 13 with specialized ones because in $\exists \lambda' \in A_{TS}(\overline{B}, D_\alpha) : call\_to\_entry(L, \overline{B}, D_\alpha, \lambda) \sqcup \lambda' = \lambda'$ all values are known before specialization time except for λ which will be computed by analysis. I.e., conditions can be partially evaluated with respect to D_α, $\overline{B}$ and a set of λ', as they are known in advance.

5.3 Example

As seen before, in the context of automatic parallelization in the &-Prolog system abstract interpretation is mostly used to eliminate run-time tests necessary to determine independence. These tests are of two types: ground/1 and indep/1. As these builtin predicates are the main target of optimization, the abstract domains used in analysis should be able to provide useful TS_α and FF_α for them. For the three domains these sets are computable and we can take $A_{TS} = M_\sqsubseteq(TS_\alpha(\overline{B}, D_\alpha))$ and $A_{FF} = M_\sqsubseteq(FF_\alpha(\overline{B}, D_\alpha))$.

Table 1 shows the accuracy of a number of abstract domains (*sharing* [JL92, MH92], *sharing+freeness* (sh+fr) [MH91], and *asub* [Son86, CDY91]) present in the &-Prolog system with respect to the run-time tests. O stands for optimal, S stands for approximate, and N stands for none, i.e. $FF_\alpha(\overline{B}, D_\alpha) = \{\bot\}$. The

```
mmultiply([],_,[]).
mmultiply([V0|Rest],V1,[Result|Others]) :-
        (ground(V1),
         indep([[V0,Rest],[V0,Others],[Rest,Result],[Result,Others]]) ->
             multiply1(V1,V0,Result) & mmultiply1(Rest,V1,Others)
        ;    multiply2(V1,V0,Result), mmultiply(Rest,V1,Others)).
mmultiply1([],_,[]).
mmultiply1([V0|Rest],V1,[Result|Others]) :-
        (indep([[V0,Rest],[V0,Others],[Rest,Result],[Result,Others]]) ->
             multiply1(V1,V0,Result) & mmultiply1(Rest,V1,Others)
        ;    multiply1(V1,V0,Result), mmultiply1(Rest,V1,Others)).

multiply1([],_,[]).
multiply1([V0|Rest],V1,[Result|Others]) :-
        (ground(V1), indep([[Result,Others]]) ->
             vmul(V0,V1,Result) & multiply3(Rest,V1,Others)
        ;    vmul(V0,V1,Result), multiply1(Rest,V1,Others)).
multiply2([],_,[]).
multiply2([V0|Rest],V1,[Result|Others]) :-
        (ground(V1),
         indep([[V0,Rest],[V0,Others],[Rest,Result],[Result,Others]]) ->
             vmul(V0,V1,Result) & multiply4(Rest,V1,Others)
        ;    vmul(V0,V1,Result), multiply2(Rest,V1,Others)).
multiply3([],_,[]).
multiply3([V0|Rest],V1,[Result|Others]) :-
        (indep([[Result,Others]]) ->
             vmul(V0,V1,Result) & multiply3(Rest,V1,Others)
        ;    vmul(V0,V1,Result), multiply3(Rest,V1,Others)).
multiply4([],_,[]).
multiply4([V0|Rest],V1,[Result|Others]) :-
        (indep([[V0,Rest],[V0,Others],[Rest,Result],[Result,Others]]) ->
             vmul(V0,V1,Result) & multiply4(Rest,V1,Others)
        ;    vmul(V0,V1,Result), multiply4(Rest,V1,Others)).
```

Fig. 4. Specialized mmatrix

three of them are optimal for abstractly executing both types of tests to true. However, only sharing+freeness (sh+fr) allows abstractly executing these tests to false, even though not in an optimal way.

The resulting program after abstract multiple specialization is performed is shown in Figure 4. Two versions have been generated for the predicate *mmultiply/3* and four for the predicate *multiply/3*. They all have unique names and literals have been renamed appropriately to avoid run-time tests. As in Figure 2, the predicate *vmul/3* is not presented in the figure because its code is identical

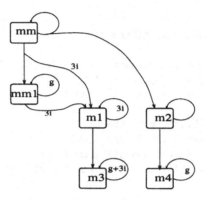

Fig. 5. Call Graph of the Specialized Program

to the one in the original program (and the parallelized program). Only one version has been generated for this predicate even though multi-variant abstract interpretation generated eight different variants for it. As no further optimization is possible by implementing several versions of *vmul/3*, the minimization algorithm has collapsed all the different versions of this predicate into one.

It is important to mention that abstract multiple specialization is able to automatically detect and extract some invariants in recursive loops: once a certain run-time test has succeeded it does not need to be checked in the following recursive calls [GH91]. Figure 5 shows the call graph of the specialized program. mm stands for mmultiply and m for multiply. Edges are labeled with the number of tests which are avoided in each call to the corresponding version with respect to the non specialized program. For example, g+3i means that each execution of this specialized version avoids a groundness and three independence tests. It can be seen in the figure that once the groundness test in any of mm, m1, or m2 succeeds, it is detected as an invariant, and the more optimized versions mm1, m3, and m4 respectively will be used in all remaining iterations.

The specialized version of matrix multiplication obtains speed-ups ranging from 2.75 for one processor to 2.24 with 9 processors with respect to the non-specialized parallel program. The speed-up with respect to the original sequential program is 5.31 for nine processors. The parallelized program without specialization obtains a speed-up of (only) 2.37 with nine processors. Detailed experimental results, including specialization times and size of the resulting specialized programs can be found in [PH95].

6   Conclusions and Future Work

In this paper we have presented the use of abstract (multiple) specialization in the context of a parallelizing compiler and formalized the concept of abstract executability. By means of an example, we have shown the ability of abstract specialization to perform non-trivial optimizations, such as loop-invariant detection, on the parallel code generated.

It remains as future work to improve the abstract specialization system presented in several directions. One of them would be the extension of the abstract specialization framework in order to perform other kinds of optimizations, including those based on concrete (as opposed to abstract) values, as in traditional partial evaluation. Obviously, the specialization system should be augmented in order to be able to detect and materialize the new optimizations.

Another direction would be to devise and experiment with different minimization criteria: even though the programs generated by the specializer are minimal to allow *all* possible optimizations, it would sometimes be useful to obtain smaller programs even if some of the optimizations are lost.

Acknowledgments

This work was funded in part by ESPRIT project 6707 "*ParForCE*" and by CICYT project TIC93-0737-C02-01. Germán Puebla is also funded in part by project C.A.M. AE00157/95. The authors would also like to thank Will Winsborough, Saumya Debray, and John Gallagher for useful discussions on multiple specialization, and Francisco Bueno and María García de la Banda for their help during the implementation and experimentation with the tools herein presented.

References

[BCHP96] F. Bueno, D. Cabeza, M. Hermenegildo, and G. Puebla. Data–flow Analysis of Standard Prolog Programs. In *European Symposium on Programming*, Sweden, April 1996.

[BGH94a] F. Bueno, M. García de la Banda, and M. Hermenegildo. A Comparative Study of Methods for Automatic Compile-time Parallelization of Logic Programs. In *Parallel Symbolic Computation*, pages 63–73. World Scientific Publishing Company, September 1994.

[BGH94b] F. Bueno, M. García de la Banda, and M. Hermenegildo. Effectiveness of Global Analysis in Strict Independence-Based Automatic Program Parallelization. In *International Symposium on Logic Programming*, pages 320–336. MIT Press, November 1994.

[Bru91] M. Bruynooghe. A Practical Framework for the Abstract Interpretation of Logic Programs. *Journal of Logic Programming*, 10:91–124, 1991.

[Bul84] M.A. Bulyonkov. Polivariant Mixed Computation for Analyzer Programs. *Acta Informatica*, 21:473–484, 1984.

[CC77] P. Cousot and R. Cousot. Abstract Interpretation: a Unified Lattice Model for Static Analysis of Programs by Construction or Approximation of Fixpoints. In *Fourth ACM Symposium on Principles of Programming Languages*, pages 238–252, 1977.

[CC94] J. Chassin and P. Codognet. Parallel Logic Programming Systems. *Computing Surveys*, 26(3):295–336, September 1994.

[CD93]   C. Consel and O. Danvy. Tutorial Notes on Partial Evaluation. In *ACM SIGPLAN-SIGACT Symposium on Principles of Programming Languages POPL'93*, pages 493–501, Charleston, South Carolina, 1993. ACM.

[CDY91]   M. Codish, D. Dams, and E. Yardeni. Derivation and Safety of an Abstract Unification Algorithm for Groundness and Aliasing Analysis. In *Eighth International Conference on Logic Programming*, pages 79–96, Paris, France, June 1991. MIT Press.

[Con83]   J. S. Conery. *The And/Or Process Model for Parallel Interpretation of Logic Programs*. PhD thesis, The University of California At Irvine, 1983. Technical Report 204.

[dMSC93]   Vítor Manuel de Morais Santos Costa. *Compile-Time Analysis for the Parallel Execution of Logic Programs in Andorra-I*. PhD thesis, University of Bristol, August 1993.

[GB90]   J. Gallagher and M. Bruynooghe. The Derivation of an Algorithm for Program Specialization. In *1990 International Conference on Logic Programming*, pages 732–746. MIT Press, June 1990.

[GCS88]   J. Gallagher, M. Codish, and E. Shapiro. Specialisation of Prolog and FCP Programs Using Abstract Interpretation. *New Generation Computing*, 6:159–186, 1988.

[GH91]   F. Giannotti and M. Hermenegildo. A Technique for Recursive Invariance Detection and Selective Program Specialization. In *Proc. 3rd. Int'l Symposium on Programming Language Implementation and Logic Programming*, pages 323–335. Springer-Verlag, 1991.

[HMPS95]   M. Hermenegildo, G. Puebla, K. Marriott, and P. Stuckey. Incremental Analysis of Logic Programs. In *International Conference on Logic Programming*, pages 797–811. MIT Press, June 1995.

[HR95]   M. Hermenegildo and F. Rossi. Strict and Non-Strict Independent And-Parallelism in Logic Programs: Correctness, Efficiency, and Compile-Time Conditions. *Journal of Logic Programming*, 22(1):1–45, 1995.

[HWD92]   M. Hermenegildo, R. Warren, and S. Debray. Global Flow Analysis as a Practical Compilation Tool. *Journal of Logic Programming*, 13(4):349–367, August 1992.

[JGS93]   N.D. Jones, C.K. Gomard, and P. Sestoft. *Partial Evaluation and Automatic Program Generation*. Prenctice Hall, New York, 1993.

[JL92]   D. Jacobs and A. Langen. Static Analysis of Logic Programs for Independent And-Parallelism. *Journal of Logic Programming*, 13(2 and 3):291–314, July 1992.

[JLW90]   D. Jacobs, A. Langen, and W. Winsborough. Multiple specialization of logic programs with run-time tests. In *1990 International Conference on Logic Programming*, pages 718–731. MIT Press, June 1990.

[Kom92]   J. Komorovski. An Introduction to Partial Deduction. In A. Pettorossi, editor, *Meta Programming in Logic, Proceedings of META'92*, volume 649 of *LNCS*, pages 49–69. Springer-Verlag, 1992.

[LS91]   J.W. Lloyd and J.C. Shepherdson. Partial Evaluation in Logic Programming. *Journal of Logic Programming*, 11(3–4):217–242, 1991.

[MH89]   K. Muthukumar and M. Hermenegildo. Complete and Efficient Methods for Supporting Side Effects in Independent/Restricted And-parallelism. In *1989 International Conference on Logic Programming*, pages 80–101. MIT Press, June 1989.

[MH91]   K. Muthukumar and M. Hermenegildo. Combined Determination of Sharing and Freeness of Program Variables Through Abstract Interpretation. In *1991 International Conference on Logic Programming*, pages 49–63. MIT Press, June 1991.

[MH92]   K. Muthukumar and M. Hermenegildo. Compile-time Derivation of Variable Dependency Using Abstract Interpretation. *Journal of Logic Programming*, 13(2 and 3):315–347, July 1992.

[MJMB89] A. Marien, G. Janssens, A. Mulkers, and M. Bruynooghe. The Impact of Abstract Interpretation: an Experiment in Code Generation. In *International Conference on Logic Programming*. MIT Press, June 1989.

[PH95]   G. Puebla and M. Hermenegildo. Implementation of Multiple Specialization in Logic Programs. In *Proc. ACM SIGPLAN Symposium on Partial Evaluation and Semantics Based Program Manipulation*. ACM, June 1995.

[PH96]   G. Puebla and M. Hermenegildo. Optimized Algorithms for the Incremental Analysis of Logic Programs. In *International Static Analysis Symposium*, LNCS 1145, pages 270–284. Springer-Verlag, September 1996.

[RD90]   P. Van Roy and A. M. Despain. The Benefits of Global Dataflow Analysis for an Optimizing Prolog Compiler. In *North American Conference on Logic Programming*, pages 501–515. MIT Press, October 1990.

[Son86]   H. Sondergaard. An application of abstract interpretation of logic programs: occur check reduction. In *European Symposium on Programming*, *LNCS 123*, pages 327–338. Springer-Verlag, 1986.

[Tay90]   A. Taylor. LIPS on a MIPS: Results from a prolog compiler for a RISC. In *1990 International Conference on Logic Programming*, pages 174–189. MIT Press, June 1990.

[WHD88]   R. Warren, M. Hermenegildo, and S. Debray. On the Practicality of Global Flow Analysis of Logic Programs. In *Fifth International Conference and Symposium on Logic Programming*, pages 684–699, Seattle, Washington, August 1988. MIT Press.

[Win92]   W. Winsborough. Multiple Specialization using Minimal-Function Graph Semantics. *Journal of Logic Programming*, 13(2 and 3):259–290, July 1992.

Reductions of Petri Nets and Unfolding of Propositional Logic Programs

Laurent Fribourg | Hans Olsén

Ecole Normale Supérieure & CNRS
45 rue d'Ulm, 75005 Paris - France
fribourg@dmi.ens.fr

IDA, Linköping University
S-58183 Linköping - Sweden
hanol@ida.liu.se

Abstract. We present in this paper a new method for computing the reachability set associated with a Petri net. The method proceeds, first, by coding the reachability problem into a predicate defined by a logic program with arithmetic constraints, then by transforming the encoding program. Each transition of the Petri net is encoded as a clause. The guards appearing in the clauses correspond to the enabling conditions of the corresponding transitions. In order to characterize arithmetically the least model of the transformed program, we define a system of two reduction rules which apply iteratively to the program. When the process of reduction terminates with success, it generates a formula of Presburger arithmetic, which contains the components of the initial marking as parameters. In the particular case of a BPP-net (i.e., a Petri net where every transition has exactly one input place), the process is guaranteed to succeed, thus providing us with an exact and generic characterization of the reachability set. We show finally how unfolding of propositional logic programs can be viewed as transformation of BPP-nets.

1 Introduction

The reachability set of a Petri net is the set of all the markings that are reachable from a given initial marking via the firing of enabled transitions. The problem of characterizing reachable sets as arithmetic formulas has been solved for certain classes of Petri nets when the initial marking is assumed to be fully instantiated [5]. When the initial marking is fully generic (i.e., when the numbers of tokens initially assigned to places are parameters), one may use some approximation techniques of linear algebra in order to generate some relations over the markings that are let invariant by the firing of any transition (see, e.g., [3]). These techniques disregard completely the enabling conditions and simply exploit the matrix of incidence (whose (i, j) coordinate represents the change in the number of tokens of place i induced by the firing of transition j). Here, we use a matrix called "incrementation matrix", which is similar to the the transposed form of the *incidence matrix* [3], but keeps track additionally of the enabling conditions of the transitions. When our method succeeds, it generates a Presburger formula having the initial marking components as parameters, which gives a characterization of the reachability set. The method is guaranteed to succeed when applied to BPP nets [4] (i.e., Petri nets with exactly one enabling condition per transition). We also show how unfolding of propositional logic programs can be simulated by transformation of BPP-nets.

2 Preliminaries

Our aim in this paper is to express the least model, of a certain class of constraint logic programs, as a closed form logical formula over the domain $\mathcal{Z}$ [7][8]. We consider programs of the form:

$$
\begin{aligned}
p(\overline{x}) &\leftarrow B(\overline{x}).\\
r_1: \quad p(\overline{x} + \overline{t}_{r_1}) &\leftarrow \overline{x} > \overline{a}_{r_1},\ p(\overline{x}).\\
&\vdots\\
r_m: \quad p(\overline{x} + \overline{t}_{r_m}) &\leftarrow \overline{x} > \overline{a}_{r_m},\ p(\overline{x}).
\end{aligned}
$$

where $\overline{x}$ is a vector of variables ranging over $\mathcal{Z}^n$, for some n, $B(\overline{x})$ a linear integer relation (relation defined by a Presburger formula), $\overline{t}_{r_i} \in \mathcal{Z}^n$ is a vector of constants, and $\overline{a}_{r_i}$ is a vector of constants belonging to $(\mathcal{Z} \cup \{-\infty\})^n$. As usual, $z > -\infty$, $z \neq -\infty$ and $-\infty \pm z = z \pm (-\infty) = -\infty$ for any integer $z \in \mathcal{Z}$, and $-\infty \geq -\infty$. For any vectors $\overline{x}_1$ and $\overline{x}_2$, we define $\overline{x}_1 > \overline{x}_2$ (resp. $\overline{x}_1 \geq \overline{x}_2$) to hold, if and only if the inequalities hold componentwise. $\max(\overline{x}_1, \overline{x}_2)$ is the vector obtained by taking the maximum of $\overline{x}_1$ and $\overline{x}_2$ componentwise. (thus, $\max(\overline{x}_1, \overline{x}_2)$ is the least upper bound in the $\langle (\mathcal{Z} \cup \{-\infty\})^n, \geq \rangle$-lattice. The vector with all components $-\infty$ is the bottom element.). Since $z > -\infty$ holds for any $z \in \mathcal{Z}$, any constraint of the form $x > -\infty$, is simply considered as *true*.

We want to express the least fixed-point as a linear integer arithmetic expression (a Presburger formula).

One can see these programs as classical programs with counters expressed under a logic programming or Datalog form. These programs have thus the power of expressivity of Turing machines. In the following we will refer to this class of programs as *(Datalog) programs with $\mathcal{Z}$-counters*.

We introduce a convenient description of the execution, in a bottom-up manner, of programs of the general form above:

A *clause*, r, is a pair $\langle \overline{t}_r, \overline{a}_r \rangle$, where $\overline{t}_r \in \mathcal{Z}^n$ and $\overline{a}_r \in (\mathcal{Z} \cup \{-\infty\})^n$, and and we say that r is *applicable* at a point $\overline{x} \in \mathcal{Z}^n$ iff $\overline{x} > \overline{a}_r$ holds. The result of applying the rule r at a point $\overline{x}$ is $\overline{x}r = \overline{x} + \overline{t}_r$. More generally, let $\Sigma = \{r_1, \ldots, r_m\}$. A sequence $w \in \Sigma^*$ is called a *path*, and is interpreted as a sequence of forward applications of the clauses (in a bottom-up manner). Given some point $\overline{x}$, the point reached by applying the path w is denoted $\overline{x}w$. Formally: $\overline{x}w = \overline{x} + \overline{t}_w$, where $\overline{t}_w$ is defined by:

$$
\begin{aligned}
\overline{t}_\varepsilon &= \overline{0}\\
\overline{t}_{rw} &= \overline{t}_r + \overline{t}_w
\end{aligned}
$$

Note that the expression $\bar{x}w$ does not take into account the constraints in the bodies of the clauses. We say that a *path* w *is applicable* at a point $\bar{x}$, if all constraints along the path are satisfied, and we write $\bar{x} > \bar{a}_w$, where:

$$\bar{a}_\varepsilon = \overline{-\infty}$$
$$\bar{a}_{rw} = max(\bar{a}_r, \bar{a}_w - \bar{t}_r)$$

The expression $\bar{x} > \bar{a}_w$ is said to be the *constraint* associated to path w at point $\bar{x}$. The definition of $\bar{a}_w$ is based on the observation that $\bar{x} > max(\bar{a}_r, \bar{a}_w - \bar{t}_r)$ iff $\bar{x} > \bar{a}_r \wedge \bar{x} + \bar{t}_r > \bar{a}_w$, which means that $\bar{x} > \bar{a}_{rw}$ holds iff $\bar{x}_i > \bar{a}_{r_i}$ holds for every point $\bar{x}_i$ along the path rw. That is, the constraints associated with the clauses are satisfied at every point along the path.

It is immediately seen that, for programs with $\mathcal{Z}$-counters, the constraint associated with a path, is of the same form as that of a clause of the original program. In general, with every path w, there is associated a clause $\langle w \rangle = (\bar{t}_w, \bar{a}_w)$.
A point $\bar{x}'$ is *reachable* from a point $\bar{x}$ by a path w if $\bar{x}w = \bar{x}'$ and w is applicable at $\bar{x}$:

$$\bar{x} \xrightarrow{w} \bar{x}' \iff \bar{x}w = \bar{x}' \wedge \bar{x} > \bar{a}_w$$

A point $\bar{x}'$ is reachable from a point $\bar{x}$ by a language $L \subseteq \Sigma^*$ if there exists a path $w \in L$ such that $\bar{x}'$ is reachable from $\bar{x}$ by w:

$$\bar{x} \xrightarrow{L} \bar{x}' \iff \exists w \in L : \bar{x} \xrightarrow{w} \bar{x}'$$

We usually write $\bar{x} \xrightarrow{L_1} \bar{x}'' \xrightarrow{L_2} \bar{x}'$, instead of $\bar{x} \xrightarrow{L_1} \bar{x}'' \wedge \bar{x}'' \xrightarrow{L_2} \bar{x}'$. From the definitions above, we immediately get:

Proposition 1. *For any path $w \in \Sigma^*$ and any languages $L_1, L_2 \subseteq \Sigma^*$. We have:*

1. $\bar{x} \xrightarrow{L_1 + L_2} \bar{x}' \iff \bar{x} \xrightarrow{L_1} \bar{x}' \vee \bar{x} \xrightarrow{L_2} \bar{x}'$
2. $\bar{x} \xrightarrow{L_1 L_2} \bar{x}' \iff \exists \bar{x}'' : \bar{x} \xrightarrow{L_1} \bar{x}'' \xrightarrow{L_2} \bar{x}'$
3. $\bar{x} \xrightarrow{w^*} \bar{x}' \iff \exists n \geq 0 : \bar{x}' = \bar{x} + n \cdot \bar{t}_w \wedge \forall 0 \leq n' < n : \bar{x} + n' \cdot \bar{t}_w > \bar{a}_w$

Our method is based on these three equivalences. Note, in the last equivalence, that if $n = 0$, then $\bar{x} = \bar{x}'$ and $\forall 0 \leq n' < n : \bar{x} + n' \cdot \bar{t}_w > \bar{a}_w$ is vacuously true. It is easy to see that, for $n > 0$, the universally quantified subexpression is equivalent to $\bar{x} + (n-1) \cdot \bar{t}_w^- > \bar{a}_w$ where $\bar{t}_w^-$ is the vector obtained from $\bar{t}_w$ by letting all nonnegative components be set to zero. Therefore, the whole equivalence becomes:

3'. $\bar{x} \xrightarrow{w^*} \bar{x}' \iff \bar{x}' = \bar{x} \vee \exists n > 0 : \bar{x}' = \bar{x} + n \cdot \bar{t}_w \wedge \bar{x} + n \cdot \bar{t}_w^- > \bar{a}_w + \bar{t}_w^-$

As a consequence, given a finite sequence of transitions w, the relation $\bar{x} \xrightarrow{w^*} \bar{x}'$ is actually an *existentially* quantified formula of Presburger arithmetic having $\bar{x}$ and $\bar{x}'$ as free variables. More generally, define a *flat* language as:

1. Any finite language is flat.
2. w^* is flat for any $w \in \Sigma^*$.

3. $L_1 + L_2$ and $L_1 L_2$ are flat if L_1 and L_2 are flat.

We call such a language L "flat" because the Kleene's star operator '*' applies only to sequences w of Σ^*. By proposition 1, it follows that the relation $\bar{x} \xrightarrow{L} \bar{x}'$ for a flat language L, can be expressed as an existentially quantified formula of Presburger arithmetic, having $\bar{x}$ and $\bar{x}'$ as free variables. More precisely, the reachability is expressed as a disjunction of a number of matrix expressions of the form:

$$\exists \bar{n}_i : \bar{x}' = \bar{x} + K_i \bar{n}_i \wedge \bar{x} + C_i \bar{n}_i > \bar{a}_i$$

where K_i and C_i are matrices, and $\bar{a}_i$ some vector of constants.

Given a program with $B(\bar{x})$ as a base case and recursive clauses Σ, the least fixed-point of its immediate consequence operator (see [7][8]), which is also the least Z-model, may be expressed as:

$$\text{lfp} = \{\ \bar{x}' \mid \exists \bar{x} : B(\bar{x}) \wedge \bar{x} \xrightarrow{\Sigma^*} \bar{x}'\ \}$$

Our aim is to characterize the membership relation $\bar{y} \in \text{lfp}$ as a closed formula having $\bar{y}$ as a free variable. For solving this problem, it suffices actually to characterize the relation $\bar{x} \xrightarrow{\Sigma^*} \bar{x}'$ as a closed formula having $\bar{x}$ and $\bar{x}'$ as free variables. We may therefore express the least fixpoint on a parametric form:

$$\text{lfp}(\bar{x}) = \{\ \bar{x}' \mid \bar{x} \xrightarrow{\Sigma^*} \bar{x}'\ \}$$

in which case the set lfp above is given by:

$$\text{lfp} = \bigcup_{B(\bar{x})} \text{lfp}(\bar{x})$$

In order to achieve this, our approach here is to find a flat language $L \subseteq \Sigma^*$, such that the following equivalence holds: $\bar{x} \xrightarrow{\Sigma^*} \bar{x}' \Leftrightarrow \bar{x} \xrightarrow{L} \bar{x}'$. This gives us an arithmetic characterization of the least fixed-point. The language L is constructed by making use of decomposition rules on paths. Such rules state that, if a path v links a point $\bar{x}$ to a point $\bar{x}'$ via Σ^*, then v can be replaced by (usually reordered into) a path w of the form $w = w_1 w_2 \cdots w_s$ such that $w_1, w_2, \cdots, w_s$ belong to some restricted languages.

3 Coding of the reachability problem of Petri Nets

Consider a Petri net with n places and m transitions. In this section, we show how to encode the reachability problem via an n-ary predicate p defined by a logic program with arithmetic constraints. Each place of the Petri net will be encoded as an arithmetic variable x_j $(1 \leq j \leq n)$. A marking corresponds to a tuple $(v_1, ..., v_n)$ of n non-negative integers. (The value v_j represents the number of tokens contained in place x_j.) Each transition will be encoded as a recursive clause r_i $(1 \leq i \leq m)$. An atom of the form $p(v_1, ..., v_n)$ means that a marking $(v_1, ..., v_n)$ is reachable from the initial marking. The predicate p is defined as follows:

- The base clause r_0 is of the form:

$p(x_1, ..., x_n) \leftarrow x_1 = v_1^0, ..., x_n = v_n^0.$

where $\bar{v}^0 = \langle v_1^0, ..., v_n^0 \rangle$ denotes the initial marking.

- The clause r_i $(1 \leq i \leq m)$, coding for the i-th transition, is of the form:

$p(x_1 + t_{i,1}, ..., x_n + t_{i,n}) \leftarrow \phi_i(x_1, ..., x_n), p(x_1, ..., x_n).$

where $t_{i,j}$ is the sum of the weights of the output arrows from transition i to place j, minus the sum of the weights of the input arrows from place j to transition i. $\phi_i(x_1, ..., x_n)$ is: $x_{j_1} > a_{j_1} \wedge ... \wedge x_{j_{c_i}} > a_{j_{c_i}} \wedge x_{k_1} = 0 \wedge ... \wedge x_{k_{d_i}} = 0$, when $x_{j_1}, ..., x_{j_{c_i}}$ are the input places, and $x_{k_1}, ..., x_{k_{d_i}}$ the inhibitors places. (The condition ϕ_i expresses that the i-th transition is enabled.)

Note that such a program does not belong to the class we consider due to the constraints of the form $x_{k_{d_i}} = 0$.

The program will be represented under the form of an "incrementation matrix", T as follows: Each clause is associated with a row, and each argument place in the head of the clause is associated with a column of the matrix. The element in the j:th row and k:th column is the coefficient $t_{j,k}$. The j:th row of the matrix will be denoted T_j, and the constraints and the name of the corresponding clause are written to the right row (see example 2).

Example 1. We consider here a Petri net implementing a simple readers-writers protocol. (This is inspired from [1], p.17.) This Petri net has six places encoded by the variables $x_2, x_3, x_4, x_5, x_6, x_7$ and six transitions encoded by the recursive clauses r_1, r_2, r_3, r_4, r_5, r_6. (It will be clear later on why the enumeration of places x_i starts with $i = 2$, and not $i = 1$.) Place x_5 represents the number of idle processes. Place x_6 (resp. x_7) the number of candidates for reading (resp. writing). Place x_4 (resp. x_3) represents the number of current readers (resp. writers). Place x_2 is a semaphore for guaranteeing mutual exclusion of readers and writers. Only two places are initially marked: x_2 and x_5. The latter contains a parametric number of tokens, defined by the parameter q, while the former contains one token (see figure 1). The program P encoding the reachability problem for this Petri Net is the following:

$r_0:$ $p(x_2, x_3, x_4, x_5, x_6, x_7) \leftarrow x_2 = 1, x_3 = 0, x_4 = 0, x_5 = q, x_6 = 0, x_7 = 0.$

$r_1:$ $p(x_2 - 1, x_3 + 1, x_4, x_5, x_6, x_7 - 1) \leftarrow x_2 > 0, x_7 > 0, x_4 = 0,$
$$p(x_2, x_3, x_4, x_5, x_6, x_7).$$

$r_2:$ $p(x_2, x_3, x_4 + 1, x_5, x_6 - 1, x_7) \leftarrow x_2 > 0, x_6 > 0, \quad p(x_2, x_3, x_4, x_5, x_6, x_7).$

$r_3:$ $p(x_2 + 1, x_3 - 1, x_4, x_5 + 1, x_6, x_7) \leftarrow x_3 > 0, \quad\quad\quad p(x_2, x_3, x_4, x_5, x_6, x_7).$

$r_4:$ $p(x_2, x_3, x_4 - 1, x_5 + 1, x_6, x_7) \leftarrow x_4 > 0, \quad\quad\quad p(x_2, x_3, x_4, x_5, x_6, x_7).$

$r_5:$ $p(x_2, x_3, x_4, x_5 - 1, x_6 + 1, x_7) \leftarrow x_5 > 0, \quad\quad\quad p(x_2, x_3, x_4, x_5, x_6, x_7).$

$r_6:$ $p(x_2, x_3, x_4, x_5 - 1, x_6, x_7 + 1) \leftarrow x_5 > 0, \quad\quad\quad p(x_2, x_3, x_4, x_5, x_6, x_7).$

We would like to prove that, for this program, the number of writers x_3 is always 0 or 1. We would like also to prove that there is no reading and writing at the same time, i.e.: $x_3 = 0 \vee x_4 = 0$. Formally, we want to prove the two implications:

$p(x_2, x_3, x_4, x_5, x_6, x_7) \rightarrow (x_3 = 0 \vee x_3 = 1).$

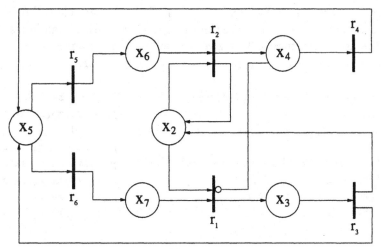

Figure 1

$p(x_2, x_3, x_4, x_5, x_6, x_7) \rightarrow (x_3 = 0 \vee x_4 = 0)$.

The classical methods of verification of Petri nets are able to prove the first implication. By analysing the transitions without taking into account the guards, they generate a set of invariants among which is the formula $x_2 + x_3 = 1$. Since initially $x_2 + x_3 = v_2^0 + v_3^0 = 1 + 0 = 1$, and since the variables x_2 and x_3 take only positive or null values, it follows immediately that x_3 must be 0 or 1. The first property is thus easily proved. The second property of "mutual exclusion" ($x_3 = 0 \vee x_4 = 0$) is more difficult to establish. In the sequel of the examples, we will show how our method allows to solve this problem: we will transform the above program, which defines atom $p(x_2, x_3, x_4, x_5, x_6, x_7)$, into a program defining an atom $p'(x_1, x_2, x_3, x_4, x_5, x_6, x_7)$ such that $p(x_2, x_3, x_4, x_5, x_6, x_7) \Leftrightarrow \exists x_1 \; p'(x_1, x_2, x_3, x_4, x_5, x_6, x_7)$. We will then construct an arithmetic characterization of $p'(x_1, x_2, x_3, x_4, x_5, x_6, x_7)$, from which $x_3 = 0 \vee x_4 = 0$ will easily follow.

4 Replacements of 0-tests

We are now going to transform the encoding program in order to put it into a form that will make the reduction rules possible to apply.

The first transformation rule consists in replacing any guard (within a recursive clause) of the form $x_j = 0$ with $x_j' > 0$, where x_j' is a new variable introduced as a new argument into p, satisfying $x_j' = 1 - x_j$ in the least model of the new program. Its initial value is equal to $1 - v_j^0$ (that is the opposite of the initial value of x_j plus 1). Within each recursive clause of the program, the new argument x_j' is incremented by the opposite of the value the variable x_j is incremented by.

Example 2. We apply the transformation to the program P of example 1, in order to replace the guard $x_4 = 0$ of the first recursive clause. We introduce a new variable, which is to be equal to $1 - x_4$. This new variable will be denoted x_1 (rather than x_4') and introduced in the first place (rather than in last place) inside the list of arguments. This gives the following program P':

$r_0:$ $p'(x_1, x_2, x_3, x_4, x_5, x_6, x_7) \leftarrow x_1 = 1, x_2 = 1, x_3 = 0, x_4 = 0,$
$$x_5 = q, x_6 = 0, x_7 = 0.$$

$r_1:$ $p'(x_1, x_2 - 1, x_3 + 1, x_4, x_5, x_6, x_7 - 1) \leftarrow x_1 > 0, x_2 > 0, x_7 > 0,$
$$p'(x_1, x_2, x_3, x_4, x_5, x_6, x_7).$$

$r_2:$ $p'(x_1 - 1, x_2, x_3, x_4 + 1, x_5, x_6 - 1, x_7) \leftarrow x_2 > 0, x_6 > 0,$
$$p'(x_1, x_2, x_3, x_4, x_5, x_6, x_7).$$

$r_3:$ $p'(x_1, x_2 + 1, x_3 - 1, x_4, x_5 + 1, x_6, x_7) \leftarrow x_3 > 0, p'(x_1, x_2, x_3, x_4, x_5, x_6, x_7).$

$r_4:$ $p'(x_1 + 1, x_2, x_3, x_4 - 1, x_5 + 1, x_6, x_7) \leftarrow x_4 > 0, p'(x_1, x_2, x_3, x_4, x_5, x_6, x_7).$

$r_5:$ $p'(x_1, x_2, x_3, x_4, x_5 - 1, x_6 + 1, x_7) \leftarrow x_5 > 0, \quad p'(x_1, x_2, x_3, x_4, x_5, x_6, x_7).$

$r_6:$ $p'(x_1, x_2, x_3, x_4, x_5 - 1, x_6, x_7 + 1) \leftarrow x_5 > 0, \quad p'(x_1, x_2, x_3, x_4, x_5, x_6, x_7).$

The incrementation matrix T writes:

$$
\begin{array}{ccccccc}
0 & -1 & 1 & 0 & 0 & 0 & -1 \\
-1 & 0 & 0 & 1 & 0 & 0 & 0 \\
0 & 1 & -1 & 0 & 1 & 0 & 0 \\
1 & 0 & 0 & -1 & 1 & 0 & 0 \\
0 & 0 & 0 & 0 & -1 & 1 & 0 \\
0 & 0 & 0 & 0 & -1 & 0 & 1 \\
\end{array}
\qquad
\begin{array}{ll}
x_1 > 0, x_2 > 0, x_7 > 0 : r_1 \\
x_2 > 0, x_6 > 0 \qquad\quad : r_2 \\
x_3 > 0 \qquad\qquad\qquad : r_3 \\
x_4 > 0 \qquad\qquad\qquad : r_4 \\
x_5 > 0 \qquad\qquad\qquad : r_5 \\
x_5 > 0 \qquad\qquad\qquad : r_6 \\
\end{array}
$$
$$x_1 \quad x_2 \quad x_3 \quad x_4 \quad x_5 \quad x_6 \quad x_7$$

5 Construction of Least Fixpoints

5.1 Reachability-equivalence

We are now going to characterize the least fixpoint associated with a program P given under standard form, that is:

$$\text{lfp}(\overline{x}) = \{\overline{x}' \mid \overline{x} \xrightarrow{(r_1 + \ldots + r_m)^*} \overline{x}' \}$$

(We will denote $\{r_1, \ldots, r_m\}$ by Σ_P and the incrementation matrix by T.) To that goal, we will construct a sequence $\{L_i\}_i$ of subsets of $(r_1 + \ldots + r_m)^*$ which are "reachably-equivalent" to $(r_1 + \ldots + r_m)^*$ in the sense that, for any $\overline{x}$ and $\overline{x}'$:

$$\overline{x} \xrightarrow{(r_1 + \ldots + r_m)^*} \overline{x}' \iff \overline{x} \xrightarrow{L_i} \overline{x}'$$

It follows immediately that, for any set L reachably-equivalent to $(r_1 + \ldots + r_m)^*$, the least fixpoint $\text{lfp}(\overline{x})$ of the program can be written as $\{\overline{x}' \mid \overline{x} \xrightarrow{L} \overline{x}' \}$. The latter formulation is interesting because, when L is a flat language, it is easy to translate the expression $\overline{x} \xrightarrow{L} \overline{x}'$, into an arithmetic formula. The goal is to construct a sequence of reachably equivalent languages such that the last language in the sequence is flat.

5.2 Reductions Preserving Reachability-Equivalence

We are going to construct a flat language $L \subseteq (r_1 + \dots + r_m)^*$ by applying repeatedly two reduction rules. Schematically, each reduction rule, when applied to Σ_P^*, transforms it into a reachably-equivalent set of the form $\Sigma_{P_1}^* \Sigma_{P_2}^* \dots \Sigma_{P_c}^*$, where P_i $(1 \leq i \leq c)$ denotes a program of lower dimension than P.

Formally, we define the *dimension* of a program with $\mathcal{Z}$-counters as a pair (m, n) where m is the number of clauses of the program, and n is the number of *non-invariant* variables of the program (i.e. the number of *nonnull* columns in the corresponding incrementation matrix). We also define an order on these dimensions as follows: The dimension (m_1, n_1) is lower than (m_2, n_2) iff $n_1 < n_2$, or $n_1 = n_2$ and $m_1 < m_2$. Each transformation rule thus decomposes the original language Σ^* into either finite languages (for which the reachability problem is solvable in the existential fragment) or into languages associated with programs of lower dimension. There are two kinds of "elementary" programs with a *basic* dimension. The first kind consists in programs of dimension $(m, 1)$, i.e. programs made of m clauses, $r_1, \dots, r_m$ with all but one column being null. As will be seen below, the reachability problem for such programs can be easily solved and expressed in the existential fragment of Presburger arithmetic. The second kind of elementary programs are programs of dimension $(1, n)$, i.e., programs made of a single clause, say r_1. In this case the expression $\bar{x} \xrightarrow{\Sigma^*} \bar{x}'$ reduces to $\bar{x} \xrightarrow{r_1^*} \bar{x}'$, which can be also expressed in the existential fragment of Presburger arithmetic by proposition 1. Therefore the decomposition process must eventually terminate either successfully, thus leading to a characterization of the reachability relation in Presburger arithmetic, or it terminates because no decomposition rule can be applied.

Henceforth we will reason on the incrementation matrices rather than on the programs themselves.

first reduction rule The first reduction rule applies to a matrix T which contains one row T_k whose coefficients are all non-negative (or all negative or null). Let us suppose that all the coefficients are positive or null (the negative or null case is analogous). The fact that coefficients $t_{k,i}$ are positive (for all i) means that an application of clause r_k, will not decrease the value of any variable, so any clause whose guard is satisfied before r_k, will remain applicable after. This is in particular true for r_k itself, so once r_k becomes applicable for the first time, it can be applied any number of times.

From this it follows that any sequence of clauses w of Σ can be reordered so that all the applications of r_k be gathered together. Formally, we have the property:

$$\forall \bar{x}, \bar{x}' : \bar{x} \xrightarrow{\Sigma^*} \bar{x}' \iff \bar{x} \xrightarrow{(\Sigma - \{r_k\})^* r_k^* (\Sigma - \{r_k\})^*} \bar{x}'$$

Clearly, if the program is of dimension $(m, 1)$, every row of the incrementation matrix is either nonnegative or nonpositive, so after applying this reduction $m-1$ times, one is left with languages of dimension $(1, 1)$ only.

second reduction rule The second reduction rule applies to a matrix T whose last l rows (possibly after reordering of rules), T_{l+1} to T_n (for some $0 \leq l \leq n$) satisfies:

- the k-th coefficient $t_{j,k}$ of T_j is equal to -1 for $l+1 \leq j \leq n$.
- the line T_{l+j} is made of coefficients all positive or null, besides the k-th one.
- the constraints of the clauses corresponding to lines $l+1$ to n are all of the form $x_k > 0$.
- the k-th column of T is made of positive or null coefficients, for the rows 1 to l.
- x_k does not occur in any constraint of the clauses corresponding to lines 1 to l.

The matrix T is thus of the following form:

$$
\begin{array}{llll}
\bullet \ldots \bullet + \bullet \ldots \bullet & \cdots & : r_1 \\
\quad\vdots \\
\bullet \ldots \bullet + \bullet \ldots \bullet & \cdots & : r_l \\
+ \ldots + -1 + \ldots + & x_k > 0 & : r_{l+1} \\
\quad\vdots \\
+ \ldots + -1 + \ldots + & x_k > 0 & : r_n \\
\qquad\quad x_k
\end{array}
$$

We will abbreviate as b_i (where $1 \leq i \leq n$) the values of the coefficients $t_{i,k}$ of column k. ($b_1, \ldots, b_l$ are positive or null, and $b_{l+1}, \ldots, b_n$ is -1.) Here again, the fact that $t_{j,i}$, $l+1 \leq j \leq n$, are positive (for all i except k) means that an application of a clause r_j, will not decrease the value of any variable other than x_k, so any clause, $r_{j'}$, $1 \leq j' \leq l$, whose guard is satisfied before r_j, will remain applicable after. Thus, r_j may be applied as soon as its guard becomes satisfied. But now, a clause r_j does not indefinitely apply immediately after its first application: the application of a clause r_j ceases when the k-th coordinate of the current tuple $\overline{x}$ becomes null. Then another clause r_i (for some $1 \leq i \leq l$) must be applied. The k-th coordinate of the newly generated tuple is then equal to b_i. If b_i is strictly positive, then one of the clauses r_j, $(l+1 \leq j \leq n)$ can be applied again a number of times equal to b_i until x_k becomes null again. This shows that any sequence w of Σ can be reordered into a sequence whose core is made of repeated "patterns" of the form $(r_i(r_{l+1} + \ldots + r_n)^{b_i})$, Note also that these "patterns" let x_k invariant, and are applied when $x_k = 0$. Such patterns are also called "cyclic sequences" in the field of Petri nets. Formally, we have the following property:

$$
\forall \overline{x}, \overline{x}' : \overline{x} \xrightarrow{\Sigma^*} \overline{x}' \iff \overline{x} \xrightarrow{(r_1+\ldots+r_l)^*(r_{l+1}+\ldots+r_n)^* exp(r_1+\ldots+r_l)^*} \overline{x}'
$$

where exp is: $(\mu_1 + \ldots + \mu_l)^* \mu'$.
Here μ_i $(1 \leq i \leq l)$ stands for a set of clauses equal to:

- r_i if $b_i = 0$, or

$$- r_i(r_{l+1} + \ldots + r_n)^{b_i}, \text{ if } b_i > 0.$$

The expression μ' denotes a set of "subpatterns". That is, an expression of the form:

$$- \{\varepsilon\} \cup \bigcup_{1 \leq i \leq l} \bigcup_{0 < c < b_i} r_i(r_{l+1} + \ldots + r_n)^c$$

Example 3. Consider the matrix in example 2, representing the program for the protocol. Let us choose $l = 4$ and consider $x_k = x_5$. We see that this matrix conforms to the case discussed above. We have, $b_1 = 0$, $b_2 = 0$, $b_3 = 1$ and $b_4 = 1$. Thus, $\mu_1 = r_1(r_5 + r_6)^0 = r_1$, $\mu_2 = r_2(r_5 + r_6)^0 = r_2$, $\mu_3 = r_3(r_5 + r_6)^1 = r_3 r_5 + r_3 r_6$ and $\mu_4 = r_4(r_5 + r_6)^1 = r_4 r_5 + r_4 r_6$. Furthermore, $\mu' = \varepsilon$. We have:

$$\bar{x} \xrightarrow{(r_1 + r_2 + r_3 + r_4 + r_5 + r_6)^*} \bar{x}' \Leftrightarrow$$

$$\bar{x} \xrightarrow{(r_1 + r_2 + r_3 + r_4)^* (r_5 + r_6)^* (r_1 + r_2 + r_3 r_5 + r_3 r_6 + r_4 r_5 + r_4 r_6)^* (r_1 + r_2 + r_3 + r_4)^*} \bar{x}'$$

and all the paths in $(r_1 + r_2 + r_3 r_5 + r_3 r_6 + r_4 r_5 + r_4 r_6)^*$ keep $x_5 = 0$ invariant. The incrementation matrix T' of the program corresponding to the set of clauses $\{r_1, r_2, r_3, r_3 r_5, r_3 r_6, r_4 r_5, r_4 r_6\}$ is shown below:

x_1	x_2	x_3	x_4	x_5	x_6	x_7		
0	-1	1	0	0	0	-1	$x_2 > 0, x_7 > 0, x_1 > 0 :$	r_1
-1	0	0	1	0	-1	0	$x_2 > 0, x_6 > 0$	$: r_2$
0	1	-1	0	0	1	0	$x_3 > 0, x_5 > -1$	$: r_3 r_5$
0	1	-1	0	0	0	1	$x_3 > 0, x_5 > -1$	$: r_3 r_6$
1	0	0	-1	0	1	0	$x_4 > 0, x_5 > -1$	$: r_4 r_5$
1	0	0	-1	0	0	1	$x_4 > 0, x_5 > -1$	$: r_4 r_6$

Thus, $(r_1 + r_2 + r_3 + r_4)^*$ and $(r_5 + r_6)^*$ involves fewer clauses than the original program, while $(r_1 + r_2 + r_3 r_5 + r_3 r_6 + r_4 r_5 + r_4 r_6)^*$ involves the same number of clauses but lets one more variable, viz. x_5, invariant. (The corresponding column in the incrementation matrix is null.) Note that, in the matrix T' corresponding to the set of cyclic sequences, the constraint $x_5 > -1$ is systematically satisfied since it is applied, to a point of coordinate $x_5 = 0$ and x_5 is let invariant. So for the treatment of the matrix, one may simply ignore the null column as well as the guard $x_5 > -1$. In terms of Petri nets, this corresponds to remove the place x_5 and to perform the "fusion" of transitions r_2, r_3, r_4, which have x_5 as an output place, and transitions r_5, r_6, which have x_5 as an input place. (This term of "fusion" is borrowed from [2]. Our second reduction rule can be seen as a variant of the post-fusion rule of Berthelot, see section 6 in this paper and [10]). By iterating this process on the matrices corresponding to $(r_1 + r_2 + r_3 + r_4)^*$, $(r_5 + r_6)^*$ and $(r_1 + r_2 + r_3 r_5 + r_3 r_6 + r_4 r_5 + r_4 r_6)^*$, it is possible to express arithmetically $\bar{x} \xrightarrow{(r_1 + r_2 + r_3 + r_4 + r_5 + r_6)^*} \bar{x}'$ as a formula of Presburger arithmetic. When the initial tuple $\bar{v}^0$ is $\langle 1, 1, 0, 0, q \rangle$, for any $q \geq 0$, one can simplify it (through a tedious but mechanical process of quantifier elimination) so that $\overline{x}' \in lfp(\overline{v}^0)$ iff:

$$x_1' = 1 - x_4' \wedge$$
$$((x_2' = 1 \wedge x_3' = 0 \wedge x_4' \geq 0) \vee (x_2' = 0 \wedge x_3' = 1 \wedge x_4' = 0)) \wedge$$
$$x_5' \geq 0 \wedge x_6' \geq 0 \wedge x_7' \geq 0 \wedge$$
$$x_3' + x_4' + x_5' + x_6' + x_7' = q$$

From this latter formula, it immediately follows: $x_3' = 0 \vee x_4' = 0$.
Therefore we have: $p'(x_1, x_2, x_3, x_4, x_5, x_6, x_7) \Rightarrow x_3 = 0 \vee x_4 = 0$.

5.3 Particular case of BPP Petri nets

A Petri net is a BPP-net if every transition has exactly one input place. (BPP stands for Basic Parallel Process: this is a class of CCS process defined by Christensen [4].) In case the initial marking is fully instantiated, the reachability set is a finite union of linear sets (i.e., sets of the form $\{u + \Sigma_{i=1}^p \lambda_i v_i \mid \lambda_i \in N\}$ where $u, v_1, .., v_p$ belong to N^n) [6]. When one encodes the reachability problem for BPP-nets, using the method of section 2, the coefficients of the associated incrementation matrix are -1 or 0 on the "diagonal", and are positive or null elsewhere. Therefore, our second reduction rule is applicable. It is easy to see that the new matrices generated have themselves all their lines with positive or null coefficients, except perhaps the "diagonal" coefficient which may be equal to -1. Therefore one of our two reductions rules is subsequently always applicable, and so on iteratively. This ensures that our method eventually terminates with success. The formula generated is a Presburger arithmetic formula with the components of the initial marking as parameters. This yields a new proof of the fact that the reachability set for BPP-nets is a semi linear set [6]. Note that Esparza's proof makes use of the notion of "siphon", and is completely different from our method. Note also that our result is actually more general since our decomposition succeeds for BPP-nets without any assumption on the initial markings: our decomposition process shows that the relation $\overline{x} \xrightarrow{\Sigma^*} \overline{x}'$ is an existentially quantified Presburger formula having $\overline{x}$ and $\overline{x}'$ as free variables (that is, $\{\langle \overline{x}, \overline{x}' \rangle \mid \overline{x} \xrightarrow{\Sigma^*} \overline{x}'\}$ is a semilinear set (see [11]) while the result of Esparza states that $\{\overline{x}' \mid \overline{v}^0 \xrightarrow{\Sigma^*} \overline{x}'\}$ is a semilinear set, for any tuple of constants $\overline{v}^0$).

6 Comparison with Berthelot's work

As can be seen in the example, in the matrix M' corresponding to the set of cyclic sequences, the constraint $x_5 > -1$ is systematically satisfied since it is applied, by the proposition, to a point of coordinate $x_5 = 0$ and x_5 is let invariant. So an obvious optimization, for the treatment of the matrix, will be to remove the null column as well as the guard $x_5 > -1$. In terms of Petri nets, this corresponds to remove the place x_5 and to perform the "fusion" of transitions r_2, r_3, r_4 (which have x_5 as an output place) and transitions r_5, r_6 (which have x_5

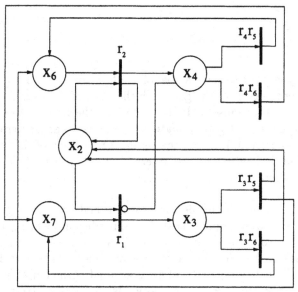

Figure 2

as an input place). The resulting Petri net is represented in figure 2. This kind of optimization can be done generally, under the preconditions of proposition 3. An analogous transformation of Petri nets is called *post-fusion* transformation by Berthelot in [2]. Our version of the cyclic decomposition can thus be seen as a variant of Berthelot's post-fusion rule. Berthelot also defined in [2] some other transformations like *pre-fusion*. It is possible to give in our framework a counterpart also for this transformation, although there is no place here to present it. The point that should be stressed here is that our cyclic decomposition rules are more general than Berthelot's rules because they apply to general programs with $\mathcal{Z}$-counters where variables take their values on $\mathcal{Z}$ (instead of $\mathcal{N}$ as in the case of Petri nets). This allows us in particular to encode 0-tests as already seen.

7 Propositional Logic Programs and BPP Nets

We show here how to simulate linear resolution via a propositional logic program π by firing transitions of an associated BPP-net. We also explain how to simulate unfolding of π by fusing transitions of the BPP-net.

7.1 Linear resolution of clauses as firing of transitions

Consider the following propositional logic program π

$$\gamma_1 : f \leftarrow a, b$$
$$\gamma_2 : a \leftarrow b, c$$

$\gamma_3 : a \leftarrow d$
$\gamma_4 : b \leftarrow$
$\gamma_5 : d \leftarrow$

Suppose that you want to solve a goal of the form $\leftarrow b, f, b$. Then you are going to match a literal, say f, of the goal with the head of a program clause, viz. γ_1, and replace it by the clause body, thus yielding the new goal $\leftarrow b, a, b, b$. This corresponds to a step of *linear resolution*. The process can be iterated. When an empty goal $\leftarrow$ is derived, it means that a linear refutation of the initial goal $\leftarrow f$ has been obtained. This can be also interpreted as a *proof by backward chaining* of the positive literal f.

Let us show that one can encode the propositional program logic π under the form of a BPP-net, and mimick linear clausal resolution by firing net transitions. The BPP-net is constructed by associating a place with each literal (of the Herbrand base) of the program, and associating a transition with each clause. For example, the net in figure 3 will be associated with clauses $\gamma_1, \gamma_2, \gamma_3, \gamma_4, \gamma_5$. Transition r_1 (resp. r_2, r_3, r_4, r_5) corresponds to clause γ_1 (resp. $\gamma_2, \gamma_3, \gamma_4, \gamma_5$).

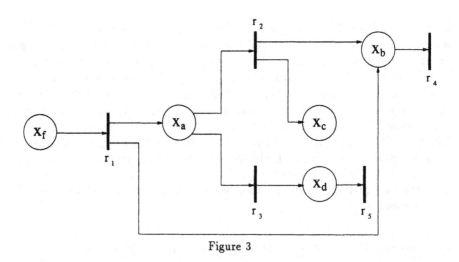

Figure 3

Places x_a, x_b, x_c, x_d, x_f correspond to literals a, b, c, d, f respectively. The head of clause γ_i is represented as an input place of the corresponding transition r_i while the literals of the body are represented as output places of r_i. The net is a BPP-net (only one input place by transition) because the clauses of the original program are definite Horn clauses (with a single literal by head). (Note the "structure sharing" among the places of the net; there is no duplication of places: for example, place x_b corresponding to the literal b, which appears twice in clauses γ_1 and γ_2, is shared as an input place of both transitions r_1 and r_2.) The reachability predicate p associated with this net is defined by the following program Σ_π:

$$\rho_1 : \ p(x_f - 1, x_a + 1, x_b + 1, x_c, x_d) \leftarrow p(x_f, x_a, x_b, x_c, x_d), x_f > 0.$$
$$\rho_2 : \ p(x_f, x_a - 1, x_b + 1, x_c + 1, x_d) \leftarrow p(x_f, x_a, x_b, x_c, x_d), x_a > 0.$$
$$\rho_3 : \ p(x_f, x_a - 1, x_b, x_c, x_d + 1) \leftarrow p(x_f, x_a, x_b, x_c, x_d), x_a > 0.$$
$$\rho_4 : \ p(x_f, x_a, x_b - 1, x_c, x_d) \leftarrow p(x_f, x_a, x_b, x_c, x_d), x_b > 0.$$
$$\rho_5 : \ p(x_f, x_a, x_b, x_c, x_d - 1) \leftarrow p(x_f, x_a, x_b, x_c, x_d), x_d > 0.$$

which is more concisely represented by the matrix:

$$
\begin{array}{rrrrr l}
-1 & 1 & 1 & 0 & 0 & x_f > 0 : \rho_1 \\
0 & -1 & 1 & 1 & 0 & x_a > 0 : \rho_2 \\
0 & -1 & 0 & 0 & 1 & x_a > 0 : \rho_3 \\
0 & 0 & 0 & 0 & -1 & x_b > 0 : \rho_4 \\
0 & 0 & 0 & 0 & -1 & x_d > 0 : \rho_5 \\
x_f & x_a & x_b & x_c & x_d &
\end{array}
$$

In this context a marking should be interpreted as a *conjunction of literals*. For example the marking $\langle 1, 0, 2, 0, 0 \rangle$ means $f \wedge b \wedge b$. With this interpretation in mind, it is easy to simulate linear resolution. For example consider the resolution of goal $\leftarrow b, f, b$ via clause γ_1, which gives the new goal $\leftarrow b, a, b, b$. This is simulated by starting with marking $\langle 1, 0, 2, 0, 0 \rangle$ on the above BPP-net, and firing transition r_1, which gives marking $\langle 0, 1, 3, 0, 0 \rangle$. Goals thus correspond to markings, and resolution via program clauses to firing of net transitions. Refuting a goal g via linear resolution corresponds to starting from the marking associated with g, and reaching the empty marking $\overline{0}$ through a certain sequence of fired transitions.

Given an initial marking $\overline{v}^0$, and letting the base clause of the program Σ_π defining the predicate p, be given by: $p(\overline{x}) \leftarrow \overline{x} = \overline{v}^0$, the atom $p(\overline{0})$, should be interpreted as: "goal $\leftarrow \overline{v}^0$ is refuted", or in a positive way as: "conjunction $\overline{v}^0$ is proved". Program Σ_π thus encodes for the *provability* via π. Each clause ρ_i of program Σ_π encodes for *backward inference* via the corresponding clause γ_i of program π. Thus, the set:

$$G = \{\overline{x} \mid \overline{x} \xrightarrow{\Sigma_\pi^*} \overline{0}\}$$

represents the set of all refutable goals.

7.2 Unfolding of clauses as postfusion of transitions

Let us now recall the idea of *unfolding* (we paraphrase here [12], p.147).
Suppose that we use clause $\gamma_1 : \ f \leftarrow a, b$ to replace f by $a \wedge b$ within a goal. We can only get an answer to the goal by subsequently eliminating a. This must be done using one of the clauses:

$$\gamma_2 : \ a \leftarrow b, c$$
$$\gamma_3 : \ a \leftarrow d$$

so the same result could be achieved in one step using one of the unfolded clauses:

$$\gamma_1' : f \leftarrow b, c, b$$
$$\gamma_2' : f \leftarrow d, b$$

So, the effect of unfolding is to short circuit (and hence shorten) the derivation. We are going to show that such an unfolding step on propositional Horn clauses can be simulated by a post-fusion step on the program Σ_π associated with program π.

Consider the program Σ_π associated with program $\pi : \{\gamma_1, \gamma_2, \gamma_3, \gamma_4, \gamma_5\}$. Its incrementation matrix is:

$$
\begin{array}{ccccc}
-1 & 1 & 1 & 0 & 0 \\
0 & -1 & 1 & 1 & 0 \\
0 & -1 & 0 & 0 & 1 \\
0 & 0 & 0 & 0 & -1 \\
0 & 0 & 0 & 0 & -1 \\
x_f & x_a & x_b & x_c & x_d
\end{array}
\quad
\begin{array}{l}
x_f > 0 : \rho_1 \\
x_a > 0 : \rho_2 \\
x_a > 0 : \rho_3 \\
x_b > 0 : \rho_4 \\
x_d > 0 : \rho_5
\end{array}
$$

One can apply post-fusion on place x_a to this matrix. This gives:

$$
\begin{array}{ccccc}
-1 & 0 & 2 & 1 & 0 \\
-1 & 0 & 1 & 0 & 1 \\
0 & 0 & 0 & 0 & -1 \\
0 & 0 & 0 & 0 & -1 \\
x_f & x_a & x_b & x_c & x_d
\end{array}
\quad
\begin{array}{l}
x_f > 0 : \rho_1\rho_2 \\
x_f > 0 : \rho_1\rho_3 \\
x_b > 0 : \rho_4 \\
x_d > 0 : \rho_5
\end{array}
$$

The fused net can be represented as in figure 4.

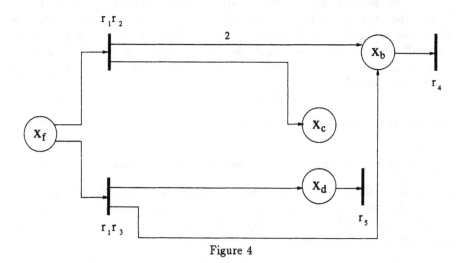

Figure 4

(Note that place x_b is shared here not only among distinct transitions, but also within a same transition by means of an input arc with weight equal to 2).

Clause $\rho_1\rho_2$ encodes for (backward inference via) a clause having f as a head, and b, b, c as a body, i.e.: $f \leftarrow b, b, c$. Clause $\rho_1\rho_3$ encodes for (backward inference via) a clause having f as a head and b, d as a body, i.e.: $f \leftarrow b, d$. One thus retrieves the two clauses γ_1' and γ_2' of the unfolded program.

We have thus shown on this little example that post-fusion on the program Σ_π encoding provability via the propositional logic program π, simulates unfolding of π. More precisely, let a be some literal of π, and π' the result of unfolding clauses of π on to a. Let Σ' be the program obtained from Σ_π by postfusing Σ_π on to x_a, then Σ' coincides, up to the order of clauses and literals, with the program $\Sigma_{\pi'}$ encoding for provability via π'.

8 Final Remarks

We have an experimental implementation in PROLOG of our reduction method, and have successfully experimented our method on a number of small examples of the literature where some places were assigned initially a parametric number of tokens (as illustrated here on a readers-writers protocol). Our method fails when, at some point of the reduction process, none of the two rules applies. It is, of course, of interest to develop some other reduction rules. This is also a topic of our ongoing research [9]. We plan to further explore the links between reduction of Petri-nets and unfolding of logic programs. In particular we are interested in simulation of unfolding of *first order* programs when the Herbrand universe is finite.

References

1. M. Ajmone Marsan, G. Balbo, G. Conte, S. Donatelli and G. Franceschinis. *Modelling with Generalized Stochastic Petri Nets*, John Wiley & Sons, Chichester,1995.
2. G. Berthelot. "Transformations and Decompositions of Nets". *Advances in Petri Nets*, LNCS 254, Springer-Verlag, 1986, pp. 359-376.
3. G.W. Brams. *Réseaux de Petri: Théorie et Pratique*, Masson, Paris, 1983.
4. S. Christensen. *Decidability and Decomposition in Process Algebras*. Ph.D. Thesis, University of Edinburgh, CST-105-93, 1993.
5. J. Esparza and M. Nielsen. "Decidability Issues for Petri Nets". Bulletin of the EATCS, Number 52, Feb. 1994.
6. J. Esparza. "Petri Nets, Commutative Context-Free Grammars, and Basic Parallel Processes". *Proc. of Fundamentals of Computer Theory '95*, LNCS 965, 1995, pp. 221-232.
7. J. Jaffar and J.L. Lassez. "Constraint Logic Programming", *Proc. 14th ACM Symp. on Principles of Programming Languages*, 1987, pp. 111-119.
8. P. Kanellakis, G. Kuper and P. Revesz. "Constraint Query Languages". Internal Report, November 1990. (Short version in *Proc. 9th ACM Symp. on Principles of Database Systems*, Nashville, 1990, pp. 299-313).

9. L. Fribourg and H. Olsén. *Datalog Programs with Arithmetical Constraints: Hierarchic, Periodic an Spiralling Least Fixpoints.* Technical Report LIENS-95-26, Ecole Normale Supérieure, Paris, November 1995.

10. L. Fribourg and H. Olsén. *A Decompositional Approach for Computing Least Fixed-Points of Datalog Programs with Z-counters.* Technical Report LIENS-96-12, Ecole Normale Supérieure, Paris, July 1996 (available by anonymous ftp on ftp.ens.fr in /pub/reports/liens or on http://www.dmi.ens.fr/dmi/preprints).

11. S. Ginsburg and E.H. Spanier. "Semigroups, Presburger formulas and languages". *Pacific Journal of Mathematics 16*, 1966, pp. 285-296.

12. J. C. Shepherdson, "Unfold/fold transformations of logic programs". *Math. Struct. in Comp. Science*, 1992, vol. 2, pp. 143-157

Inferring Argument Size Relationships with CLP($\mathcal{R}$)

Florence Benoy and Andy King

Computing Laboratory,
University of Kent at Canterbury, CT2 7NF, UK.
{p.m.benoy, a.m.king}@ukc.ac.uk

Abstract. Argument size relationships are useful in termination analysis which, in turn, is important in program synthesis and goal-replacement transformations. We show how a precise analysis for inter-argument size relationships, formulated in terms of abstract interpretation, can be implemented straightforwardly in a language with constraint support like CLP($\mathcal{R}$) or SICStus version 3. The analysis is based on polyhedral approximations and uses a simple relaxation technique to calculate least upper bounds and a delay method to improve the precision of widening. To the best of our knowledge, and despite its simplicity, the analysis derives relationships to an accuracy that is either comparable or better than any existing technique.

1 Introduction

Termination analysis is important in program synthesis, goal-replacement transformations and is also likely to be useful in off-line partial deduction. Termination analysis is usually necessary in synthesis since synthesis often only guarantees semantic or model-theoretic correctness. Termination analysis is often necessary in transformation because termination usually must be preserved wrt. the initial program and transformed goals. Termination is typically proved by showing that a well-founded ordering exists between a goal and its sub-goals. In the case of the Qs/2 program, termination is (basically) asserted by showing that the recursive Qs(1, s1) and Qs(g, sg) goals operate on lists that are strictly smaller than [x|xs]. (For the definition of the Ap/2 and Pt/4 predicates see appendix A.) For programs like Qs/2 which are not structurally recursive this, in turn, requires the derivation of inter-argument relationships. In the case Qs/2, for instance, it is necessary to infer that both 1 and g in the recursive calls are smaller than [x|xs]. This can only be inferred by deducing an inter-argument relation for Pt/4, that is, that neither the third nor fourth argument are larger than the second argument.

```
Qs([], []).                 Qs^A(0, 0).
Qs([x|xs], s) <-            Qs^A(1+xs, s) <-
    Pt(x, xs, 1, g) &          Pt^A(_, xs, 1, g) &
    Qs(1, s1) & Qs(g, sg) &    Qs^A(1, s1) & Qs^A(g, sg) &
    Ap(s1, [x|sg], s).         Ap^A(s1, 1+sg, s).
```

Note that Gödel notation is used throughout: variables are denoted by identifiers beginning with a lower case letter and constants by identifiers beginning with an upper case letter.

Once an appropriate measure of term size (norm) like list length, is deduced [12, 23], the problem of inferring argument relationships is essentially reduced to that of inferring invariants of a CLP($\mathcal{R}$) program [14]. $\mathtt{Qs}^A/2$ for example, an abstraction of $\mathtt{Qs/2}$, is a form of abstract program [14] that is obtained by a syntactic transformation in which each term in the first program is replaced by its size wrt. list length. An analysis for inferring invariants between the variables of the second program [9, 20] can then be re-interpreted as an analysis for deducing the size invariants (inter-argument relationships) of the first program [8, 31]. For example, one invariant in the second program is that the third and fourth arguments of $\mathtt{Pt/4}$ sum to the second argument. Thus, in the first program, the sum of the lengths of the third and fourth arguments of $\mathtt{Pt/4}$ must be coincident with the length of the second argument.

In broad terms, analyses for inferring invariants have either been built around affine sub-spaces [14, 20, 31], or in terms of (closed) polyhedral convex sets [8, 18, 30]. (The difference equation approach [11] to inferring inter-argument relationships, although potentially useful, requires computer algebra machinery to manipulate and solve the difference equations and therefore is probably too complicated for most partial deduction systems.) In the affine approach, invariants are represented by affine subspaces, basically points, lines or hyper-planes in $\mathbb{R}^n$, which can be represented and manipulated using matrices. The affine approach is attractive because, although is cannot express inequalities between variables, the approximation is Noetherian and therefore the termination of the analysis is not an issue.

The convex set approach characterises argument relationships as sets of conjoined linear inequalities [18, 30]. To be precise, linear inequalities represent a collection of closed half-spaces the intersection of which, defines a polyhedral convex set. In [30], a suite of transformations are defined, formulated in terms of matrices, for mechanising the derivation of argument relationships. This approach is promising because inequalities are more expressive than equalities since every affine sub-space is polyhedral.

```
Sp([], [], []).              Sp^A(0, 0, 0).
Sp([x|xs], [x|os], es) <-    Sp^A(1+xs, 1+os, es) <-
    Sp(xs, es, os).              Sp^A(xs, es, os).
```

To illustrate the expressiveness of inequalities, consider the $\mathtt{Sp/3}$ predicate [27] of merge sort in which the elements at the odd and even positions in a list are separated into two lists. The query $\mathtt{<- Sp([A, B, C], o, e)}$. will succeed with the answer $\{\mathtt{e = [B], o = [A, C]}\}$. Polyhedral approximations are expressiveness enough to even describe the invariants of $\mathtt{Sp/3}$, that is,

$$\left\{ \langle x, y, z \rangle \in \mathbb{R}^3 \;\middle|\; \begin{array}{l} z = (-y) + x \;\wedge\; y - x \leq 0 \;\wedge \\ z \leq y \leq z + 1 \;\wedge\; (-y) \leq 0 \end{array} \right\}$$

The polyhedral work of [30] is incomplete, however, because the iterative process required to compute argument relationships for recursive predicates may not converge in finitely many steps. Cousot and Cousot explain, however, how to rectify this problem with widening [8]. Widening essentially trades precision for finiteness by weakening inequality constraints to obtain stability of the iterates.

Our contribution is to show how a precise analysis based on polyhedra (rather than affine sub-spaces [14]) can be implemented straightforwardly in a language with constraint support like CLP($\mathcal{R}$) or SICStus version 3. In fact the initial prototype is less than 200 clauses and took just two person weeks to code and debug. Specifically, we adopt a relaxation technique used in disjunctive constraint programming [10] to compute convex hulls. With the use of the solver and projection machinery of CLP($\mathcal{R}$) and the clp(Q,R) libraries of SICStus, it has not been necessary to manipulate matrices, like [20, 30, 31]; or frames, like [9, 15]; or implement the Chernikova conversion mechanism, like [32].

Convergence of the iterates is enforced by widening and it is our observation that precision can be improved by delaying widening for a few (typically one or two) iterations. This simple approach seems to achieve comparable or better results to the more sophisticated widening of [8], without loss of precision. The principal advantage is in the simplicity in the implementation.

The applications of inferring argument relationships extend well beyond partial deduction. Argument relationships are useful for planning the evaluation of queries in deductive databases [29], optimising database queries [21], and play an important role in time-complexity analysis [11]. Horspool [18] proposed the use of argument relationships for improving the memory management of cdr-coded lists. Also, in Reform compilation [25], where bounded iteration (the for loop) is used to implement recursion to avoid the overheads of run-time unfolding, argument relationships can extend the scope for parallelisation by recognising predicates that are defined by structural recursion. Intuitively, this means that the compiler can deduce the recursion bound by just looking at the input arguments [26].

The exposition is structured as follows. Section 2 outlines the analysis with a worked example. Section 3 present some theory and notation to aid the presentation. Sections 4 and 5 cover the convex hull calculation and widening operation. Section 6 outlines the implementation and finally Sections 7 and 8 present the related and future work. The table in appendix 8 summaries some interesting analysis results obtained by our analyser.

2 Worked Example

Consider an argument size analysis for the predicate Ap/3. As with Qs/2, analysis is performed on an abstract program, here denoted $Ap^{\mathcal{A}}/3$. The arguments of each predicate in the abstract program represent the sizes of the arguments of the corresponding predicate in the concrete program. Therefore the relationships that hold between arguments of $Ap^{\mathcal{A}}/3$ exist as inter-argument size relationships for Ap/3 the concrete program.

```
Ap([], s, s).                    Ap^A(0, s, s).
Ap([x|xs], s, [x|t]) <-          Ap^A(1 + r, s, 1 + t) <-
    Ap(xs, s, t).                    Ap^A(r, s, t).
```

Analysis iterates to a fixpoint that characterises the inter-argument relationships. We denote the ith iterate by I_i. Each iteration in the fixpoint calculation takes an I_i as input and generates an I_{i+1} as output. I_0, the bottom element, is $\emptyset$. Generally, to compute I_{i+1}, the body atoms of each clause of the program are unified with the atoms in I_i. Since I_0 is empty, however, I_1 will abstract only those relationships embodied in the unit clause of $Ap^A/3$, that is,

$$I_1 = \{\langle r, s, t \rangle \in \mathbb{R}^3 \mid r \leq 0 \wedge -r \leq 0 \wedge s - t \leq 0 \wedge t - s \leq 0\}$$

Note that I_1 is expressed in terms of a set of inequalities. Thereafter, at each iteration, there will be a set of inequalities that describe the inter-argument relationships for each predicate. The number of atoms can grow at each iteration and therefore, to keep the size of the iterate small, the sets of inequalities for each predicate are collected and approximated by an over-estimate, a convex hull. The convex hull can itself be expressed as a single set of inequalities so that it is necessary only to maintain one set of inequalities for each predicate in the program. The convex hull derives a succinct expression of the disjunction of spaces with a minimal loss of information. The convex hull operation denoted $\overline{U}$, is used to compute I_2 and the ensuing iterates.

$$
\begin{aligned}
I_2 &= \{\langle r, s, t \rangle \in \mathbb{R}^3 \mid r = 0 \wedge s = t\} \overline{U} \{\langle 1 + r, s, 1 + t \rangle \in \mathbb{R}^3 \mid r = 0 \wedge s = t\} \\
&= \{\langle r, s, t \rangle \in \mathbb{R}^3 \mid r = 0 \wedge s = t\} \overline{U} \{\langle r, s, t \rangle \in \mathbb{R}^3 \mid r = 1 \wedge s = t - 1\} \\
&= \{\langle r, s, t \rangle \in \mathbb{R}^3 \mid 0 \leq r \wedge r \leq 1 \wedge t = r + s\}
\end{aligned}
$$

The equalities denote pairs of inequalities for brevity. Although the convex hull operation computes an approximation, useful relationships are still preserved since the convex hull corresponds to the smallest convex space enclosing the spaces represented by the sets of inequalities. Note too, the convex hull calculation effectively generates inter argument relationships, like $t = r + s$, that are common to both clauses of the predicate.

One problem with the linear inequality representation, however, is that arbitrarily large sets of inequalities can arise as the analysis proceeds. This can impede termination. Widening is therefore employed to constrict the growth of the sets and enforce convergence of the iterates to those inequalities that are common to all iterations. To be precise, $I_3 = I_2 \triangledown I_3'$ where

$$
\begin{aligned}
I_3' &= \{\langle r, s, t \rangle \in \mathbb{R}^3 \mid r = 0 \wedge s = t\} \overline{U} \\
&\quad \{\langle 1 + r, s, 1 + t \rangle \in \mathbb{R}^3 \mid 0 \leq r \wedge r \leq 1 \wedge t = r + s\} \\
&= \{\langle r, s, t \rangle \in \mathbb{R}^3 \mid r = 0 \wedge s = t\} \overline{U} \\
&\quad \{\langle r, s, t \rangle \in \mathbb{R}^3 \mid 1 \leq r \wedge r \leq 2 \wedge t = r + s\} \\
&= \{\langle r, s, t \rangle \in \mathbb{R}^3 \mid 0 \leq r \wedge r \leq 2 \wedge t = r + s\}
\end{aligned}
$$

The widening $I_2 \triangledown I_3'$ basically derives those inequalities that are common to both I_2 and I_3'. More precisely, it selects those inequalities of I_2 that hold for I_3'.

Each iteration will generate a space that is described by the set of inequalities. Until the widening is initiated, successive iterations will typically yield a space that both includes and extends the previous space. Intuitively, the invariant condition will be an expression of those spatial boundaries that are common between iterations. Those inequalities that are excluded, by widening, will be those that relate to variables whose size increases with each iteration and, in this case, represents the unconstrained growth of an argument that is a list. Once widening commences, termination follows since the set of inequalities at each iteration cannot grow any further. For this iteration, $I_3 = I_2 \bigtriangledown I_3' = \{\langle r, s, t \rangle \in \mathbb{R}^3 \mid 0 \leq r \wedge t = r + s\}$. Similarly, it can be shown that $I_4 = \{\langle r, s, t \rangle \in \mathbb{R}^3 \mid 0 \leq r \wedge t = r + s\}$, and hence the iteration sequence converges.

3 Preliminaries

3.1 Concrete Semantics

To express the widening and explain the implementation it is helpful to clarify the semantics. The semantics of the abstract program (and the concrete program) can be expressed in an s-style semantics for constraint logic programs [5]. The semantics is parameterised over an algebraic structure, C, of constraints. We write $c \models c'$ iff c entails c' and $c = c'$ iff $c \models c'$ and $c' \models c$. The interpretation base B_C for the language defined by a program P is the set of unit clauses of the form $p(\mathbf{x}) \leftarrow c$ quotiented by equivalence. Equivalence, $\sim$, is defined by: $p(\mathbf{x}) \leftarrow c \sim p(\mathbf{x}') \leftarrow c'$ iff $c \uparrow var(\mathbf{x}) = (c' \wedge (\mathbf{x} = \mathbf{x}')) \uparrow var(\mathbf{x})$ where $\uparrow$ denotes projection. When C corresponds to the Herbrand universe $Herb$, for example, $\sim$ is variance. The fixpoint semantics $\mathcal{F}_C$ is defined, as usual, in terms of an immediate consequences operator like so: $\mathcal{F}_C[\![P]\!] = lfp(T_P)$.

Definition 1 fixpoint s-semantics for CLP. The immediate consequences operator $T_P : B_C \to B_C$ is defined by:

$$T_P(I) = \left\{ [p(\mathbf{x}) \leftarrow c']_\sim \left| \begin{array}{ll} w \in P & \wedge\ w = p(\mathbf{t}) \leftarrow c, p_1(\mathbf{t}_1), \ldots, p_n(\mathbf{t}_n) \wedge \\ [w_i]_\sim \in I \wedge w_i = p_i(\mathbf{x}_i) \leftarrow c_i & \wedge \\ \forall i.var(w) \cap var(w_i) = \emptyset & \wedge \\ \forall i \neq j.var(w_i) \cap var(w_j) = \emptyset & \wedge \\ c' = \wedge_{i=1}^n (\mathbf{x}_i = \mathbf{t}_i \wedge c_i) \wedge (\mathbf{x} = \mathbf{t}) \wedge c \end{array} \right. \right\}$$

$\square$

3.2 Abstract Semantics

Ordering A preorder is a preordered set L ($\sqsubseteq$) where the relation $\sqsubseteq$ is reflexive and transitive. A poset is a preorder L ($\sqsubseteq$) where $\sqsubseteq$ is also antisymmetric. A cpo is a complete poset, that is, any $\mathbb{N}$-termed increasing chain $x_i \in L$ has a least upper bound $\sqcup_{i=1} x_i \in L$.

Polyhedral Domains Let Lin denote the set of finite sets of implicitly conjoined non-strict inequalities. Lin $(\models)$ is a preorder but lifts to a cpo $Lin/= (\models)$ with quotienting. Let $Poly^n$ denote the set of (closed) polyhedral convex sets in $\mathbb{R}^n$. $Poly^n(\subseteq)$ is also a cpo. Given a finite, ordered set of variables $X = \{x_1, \ldots, x_n\}$, there is a natural mapping from $Lin/=$ to $Poly^n$ that is $poly_X([c]_=) = \{\mathbf{x}' \in \mathbb{R}^n \mid (\bigwedge_{i=1}^n x_i = x_i') \models c\}$.

The preordering on inequalities lifts to interpretations to define a preorder $\wp(B_{Lin})$ $(\subseteq)$ where $I \subseteq I'$ iff $\forall [p(\mathbf{x}) \leftarrow c]_\sim \in I \ . \ \exists [p(\mathbf{x}) \leftarrow c']_\sim \in I' \ . \ c \models c'$. The preorder defines an equivalence relation: $I \approx I'$ iff $I \subseteq I'$ and $I' \subseteq I$ which, in turn, defines the poset $\wp(B_{Lin})/\approx (\subseteq)$ where $[I]_\approx \subseteq [I']_\approx$ iff $I \subseteq I'$. In fact $\wp(B_{Lin})/\approx (\subseteq)$ is a cpo. T_P lifts to $\wp(B_{Lin})/\approx (\subseteq)$ by $T_P([I]_\approx) = [T_P(I)]_\approx$ and is continuous.

Abstract Interpretation Rather than adopt the Galois connection approach to abstract interpretation [8] we require widening to obtain stability of our fixpoint calculation, because the domain does not satisfy the ascending chain property.

Definition 2 widening. A widening $\triangledown$ on the preorder L $(\subseteq)$ is an operator $\triangledown : L \times L \to L$ such that: $\forall x, y \in L \ . \ x \subseteq x \triangledown y$ and $\forall x, y \in L \ . \ y \subseteq x \triangledown y$ and for all increasing chains $x_0 \subseteq x_1 \subseteq \ldots$, the increasing chain defined by $y_0 = x_0, \ldots, y_{i+1} = y_i \triangledown x_{i+1}, \ldots$ is not strictly increasing, that is, $y_{l+1} \subseteq y_l$ for some l. $\qquad\square$

To improve precision we adapt the widening strategy of [8] and only apply the operator after a bounded number of iterations.

Proposition 3 adapted from [8]. If L $(\subseteq, \sqcup)$ is a cpo, $F : L \to L$ is continuous, $\bot \in L$ is such that $\bot \subseteq F(\bot)$, $\triangledown \in L \times L \to L$ is a widening, then the upward iteration sequence with widening x_i where $i, k \in \mathbb{N}$ is defined thus:

$$\begin{aligned} x_0 &= \bot \\ x_{i+1} &= x_i && \text{if } F(x_i) \subseteq x_i \\ x_{i+1} &= F(x_i) && \text{else if } i \le k \\ x_{i+1} &= x_i \triangledown F(x_i) && \text{else if } i > k \end{aligned}$$

will converge and its limit $\mathcal{A}$ is such that $lfp(F) \subseteq \mathcal{A}$ and $F(\mathcal{A}) \subseteq \mathcal{A}$. $\qquad\square$

3.3 Argument Size Analysis

A concretisation mapping is used to clarify the relationship between a concrete and abstract program in terms of a norm $|t|$ that measures the size of a term t.

Definition 4 γ. Concretisation $\gamma(I) : \wp(B_{Lin}) \to \wp(B_{Herb})$ is defined by:

$$\gamma(I) = \left\{ [p(\mathbf{x}) \leftarrow \bigwedge_{i=1}^n (x_i = t_i)]_\sim \ \middle| \ \begin{array}{l} [p(\mathbf{x}) \leftarrow c]_\sim \in I \quad \wedge \\ (\bigwedge_{i=1}^n x_i = |t_i|) \models c \end{array} \right\}$$

$\qquad\square$

A program P over $Herb$ is safely abstracted by abstract program $P^{\mathcal{A}}$ over Lin iff $\mathcal{F}_{Herb}[\![P]\!] \subseteq \gamma(\mathcal{F}_{Lin}[\![P^{\mathcal{A}}]\!])$.

4 Convex Hull Calculation

Previous approaches [9, 15, 16, 22, 32] to computing the convex hull of polyhedra rely on the frame representation. Specifically, the polyhedra are represented as a system of generators, that is, two finite sets, V and R, of vertices and rays:

$$P = \left\{ \sum_{v_i \in V} \lambda_i.v_i + \sum_{r_j \in R} \mu_j.r_j \,\middle|\, \lambda_i \geq 0 \wedge \mu_j \geq 0 \wedge \sum_i \lambda_i = 1 \right\}$$

The convex hull P of two polyhedra P_1 and P_2, respectively represented by $\langle V_1, R_1 \rangle$ and $\langle V_2, R_2 \rangle$, is then given by $\langle V, R \rangle$ where $V = V_1 \cup V_2$ and $R = R_1 \cup R_2$

Example 1. Consider the point P_1 and the line P_2. The convex hull of P_1 and P_2 is the space P_C. Both the constraint and frame representations of P_1, P_2 and P_C are given below followed by two graphs that depict the polyhedra.

$$P_1 = \left\{ \langle x, y \rangle \in \mathbb{R}^2 \,\middle|\, \begin{matrix} x \leq 0 \wedge \\ 0 \leq x \wedge \\ y \leq 1 \wedge \\ 1 \leq y \end{matrix} \right\} \qquad V_1 = \left\{ \begin{bmatrix} 0 \\ 1 \end{bmatrix} \right\} \qquad R_1 = \emptyset$$

$$P_2 = \left\{ \langle x, y \rangle \in \mathbb{R}^2 \,\middle|\, \begin{matrix} x \leq y \wedge \\ y \leq x \wedge \\ -x \leq 0 \end{matrix} \right\} \qquad V_2 = \left\{ \begin{bmatrix} 0 \\ 0 \end{bmatrix} \right\} \qquad R_2 = \left\{ \begin{bmatrix} 1 \\ 1 \end{bmatrix} \right\}$$

$$P_C = \left\{ \langle x, y \rangle \in \mathbb{R}^2 \,\middle|\, \begin{matrix} x - y \leq 0 \wedge \\ y - x \leq 1 \wedge \\ -x \leq 0 \end{matrix} \right\} \qquad V_C = \left\{ \begin{bmatrix} 0 \\ 1 \end{bmatrix}, \begin{bmatrix} 0 \\ 0 \end{bmatrix} \right\} \qquad R_C = \left\{ \begin{bmatrix} 1 \\ 1 \end{bmatrix} \right\}$$

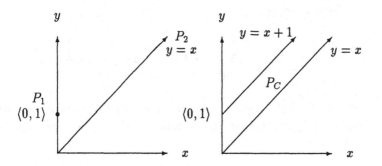

□

Usually the constraints and frame are represented together and the Chernikova algorithm is used to convert between them. For example to compute an over approximation of the convex hull, V_C and R_C are computed and then the

Chernikova algorithm is used to generate P_C. Both representations are used simultaneously as "experience shows that this redundant representation is much less expensive than the frequent use of conversions" [9]. It is interesting to note that it is the closure of the convex hull that is returned by both methods, that is the smallest polyhedral convex set that includes the convex hull.

By using a different approach to computing the convex hull, it is possible to use a single representation, namely a set of linear inequalities. $\mathrm{CLP}(\mathcal{R})$ provides the projection and solver machinery for manipulating sets of inequalities and thus allows us to implement the convex hull in an efficient but relatively simple way. The naive approach to the calculating the convex hull in $\mathrm{CLP}(\mathcal{R})$ can lead to floundering. Floundering occurs because non-linear constraints may be indefinitely postponed. Suppose that two arbitrary polyhedra, P_1 and P_2, are represented in standard form, that is,

$$P_1 = \{\mathbf{X} \in \mathbb{R}^n \mid A_1\mathbf{X} \le \mathbf{B}_1\}, \quad P_2 = \{\mathbf{X} \in \mathbb{R}^n \mid A_2\mathbf{X} \le \mathbf{B}_2\}$$

The convex hull of $P_1 \cup P_2$, P, is then defined by:

$$P_C = \left\{ \mathbf{X} \in \mathbb{R}^n \;\middle|\; \begin{array}{ll} \mathbf{X} = \sigma_1\mathbf{X}_1 + \sigma_2\mathbf{X}_2 \wedge \sigma_1 + \sigma_2 = 1 \wedge \\ A_1\mathbf{X}_1 \le \mathbf{B}_1 \quad \wedge A_2\mathbf{X}_2 \le \mathbf{B}_2 \wedge \\ -\sigma_1 \le 0 \quad \wedge \quad -\sigma_2 \le 0 \end{array} \right\}$$

The equation $\sigma_1\mathbf{X}_1 + \sigma_2\mathbf{X}_2 = 1$, however, is non-linear and in a constraint language that delays non-linear constraints the worst case can result in an infinite loop [17]. Following [10], however, equations can be reformulated by putting $\mathbf{Y}_1 = \sigma_1\mathbf{X}_1$ and $\mathbf{Y}_2 = \sigma_2\mathbf{X}_2$ so that

$$\mathbf{X} = \mathbf{Y}_1 + \mathbf{Y}_2, \quad A_1\mathbf{Y}_1 \le \sigma_1\mathbf{B}_1, \quad A_2\mathbf{Y}_2 \le \sigma_2\mathbf{B}_2$$

so that P_C is also defined by:

$$P_C = \left\{ \mathbf{X} \in \mathbb{R}^n \;\middle|\; \begin{array}{l} \mathbf{X} = \mathbf{Y}_1 + \mathbf{Y}_2 \wedge \ \sigma_1 + \sigma_2 = 1 \ \wedge \\ A_1\mathbf{Y}_1 \le \sigma_1\mathbf{B}_1 \wedge A_2\mathbf{Y}_2 \le \sigma_2\mathbf{B}_2 \wedge \\ -\sigma_1 \le 0 \quad \wedge \quad -\sigma_2 \le 0 \end{array} \right\}$$

Example 2. To illustrate the method, we refer to our earlier example. Substituting for the matrices A_1 and A_2, and the vectors B_1 and B_2, the above system of equations is as follows:

$$P_C = \left\{ \mathbf{X} \in \mathbb{R}^n \;\middle|\; \begin{array}{l} \mathbf{X} = \mathbf{Y}_1 + \mathbf{Y}_2 \qquad \wedge \qquad \sigma_1 + \sigma_2 = 1 \qquad \wedge \\ \begin{bmatrix} 1 & 0 \\ -1 & 0 \\ 0 & 1 \\ 0 & -1 \end{bmatrix} \mathbf{Y}_1 \le \sigma_1 \begin{bmatrix} 0 \\ 0 \\ 1 \\ -1 \end{bmatrix} \wedge \begin{bmatrix} 1 & -1 \\ -1 & 1 \\ -1 & 0 \end{bmatrix} \mathbf{Y}_2 \le \sigma_2 \begin{bmatrix} 0 \\ 0 \\ 0 \end{bmatrix} \wedge \\ -\sigma_1 \le 0 \qquad \wedge \qquad -\sigma_2 \le 0 \end{array} \right\}$$

Note that $\mathbf{X} = \langle x^1, x^2 \rangle$ and $\mathbf{Y}_i = \langle y_i^1, y_i^2 \rangle$,

$$
P_C = \left\{ \mathbf{X} \in \mathbb{R}^2 \left| \begin{array}{lll}
x^1 = y_1^1 + y_1^2 \wedge & \sigma_1 + \sigma_2 = 1 \wedge \\
x^2 = y_2^1 + y_2^2 \wedge & -\sigma_1 \leq 0 \wedge \\
y_1^1 \leq 0 & \wedge & -\sigma_2 \leq 0 \wedge \\
-y_1^1 \leq 0 & \wedge & y_2^1 - y_2^2 \leq 0 \wedge \\
y_1^2 \leq \sigma_1 & \wedge & -y_2^1 + y_2^2 \leq 0 \wedge \\
-y_1^2 \leq -\sigma_1 & \wedge & -y_2^1 \leq 0
\end{array} \right. \right\}
$$

and hence P_C can be derived through projection. $\qquad\square$

In terms of implementation, the chief technicality is in constructing the equations $A_i \mathbf{Y}_i \leq \sigma_i \mathbf{B}_i$ from $A_i \mathbf{X}_i \leq \mathbf{B}_i$. In fact each $A_i \mathbf{Y}_i \leq \sigma_i \mathbf{B}_i$ can be generated by a single recursive pass over the ground representation of $A_i \mathbf{X}_i \leq \mathbf{B}_i$ which basically collects and then scales the numeric constants. Once the equations are setup, a projection onto $\mathbf{X}$ then gives P_C encoded in a ground representation.

5 Widening Operation

Widening is required to enforce the convergence of the iterates. Essentially it trades precision for finiteness by weakening inequality constraints to obtain stability of the iterates. Since T_P is continuous on the cpo $\wp(B_{Lin})/\approx (\sqsubseteq)$, $\perp \sqsubseteq T_P(\perp)$ where $\perp = [\emptyset]_\approx$, by Proposition 3 it only remains to define a suitable ∇ operator for $\wp(B_{Lin})/\approx$ and to select an appropriate k. The widening $[I]_\approx \nabla [I']_\approx$ is basically an adaption of the widening of [9] lifted to interpretations. Since I and I' both contain at most one set of inequalities for each predicate symbol, the widening lifts in a straightforward way.

Definition 5.

$$
[I]_\approx \nabla [I']_\approx = [\{[p(\mathbf{x}) \leftarrow c \nabla c']_\sim \mid [p(\mathbf{x}) \leftarrow c]_\sim \in I \wedge [p(\mathbf{x}) \leftarrow c']_\sim \in I'\}]_\approx
$$

$$
\text{where } c \nabla c' = \{i \in c \mid c' \models i\}
$$

$\qquad\square$

The widening $c \nabla c'$ relaxes the constraint c by selecting those inequalities i of c which are entailed by c'. Since c, c' are encoded in the ground representation, the test for entailment amounts to scanning the list of constraints representing c and then testing each i in the list against c' with entailment. Termination follows since the widening stops the set (list) representing c' including new inequalities. (Interestingly, we have found that the naive widening $c \nabla c' = c \cap c'$ can work well if the constraints always appear in the same syntactic form.) The main subtlety in widening is choosing a useful k, that is, deciding *when* to widen. Sections 5.1, 5.2 and 5.3 explain how k affects the precision for different classes of predicate.

5.1 Widening with Uniform Increments

Consider the $\text{Ap}^{\mathcal{A}}/3$ program of Section 2 listed below.

```
Ap^A(0, s, s).
Ap^A(1 + r, s, 1 + t) <- Ap^A(r, s, t).
```

Each iteration of the analysis generates an atom $\text{Ap}^{\mathcal{A}}(x, y, z) \leftarrow c$ where the variables x and z are both incremented by 1 relative to the previous iterate. To be more precise, the ith iteration of the analysis, $[I_i]_{\approx}$, takes the form $I_i = \{[\text{Ap}^{\mathcal{A}}(x, y, z) \leftarrow c_i]_{\sim}\}$ where each c_i defines a polyhedral convex set in $\mathbf{R}^3$ by $poly_{\{x,y,z\}}(c_i) = p_i$. For example

$$p_1 = \{\langle x, y, z \rangle \mid x = 0, y = z\}, \quad p_2 = \{\langle x, y, z \rangle \mid 0 \leq x, x \leq 1, z = x + y\}$$

More generally $\text{Ap}^{\mathcal{A}}/3$ defines $p_{i+1} = p_i \,\overline{\cup}\, \{\langle 1+x, y, 1+z \rangle \mid \langle x, y, z \rangle \in p_i\}$ so that the space p_{i+1} extends and includes that of p_i. Each p_{i+1} can be obtained from p_i in a predictable way since p_{i+1} differs from p_i by uniform increments in the first and third dimensions. Although inter-argument relationships $0 \leq x, z = x + y$ are implicit in p_1, they are not explicit until p_2 and the ensuing p_i. Widening can therefore be performed to obtain the third iterate, that is $k = 2$, without loss of significant information. The invariant condition is then confirmed in the third iteration to obtain $p_3 = \{\langle x, y, z \rangle \mid 0 \leq x, z = x+y\}$. Widening prematurely looses information. We conjecture that for a directly recursive predicate with uniform increment, all of the common invariants can be found within three iterations.

5.2 Widening within a Hierarchy

Consider the $\text{Qs}^{\mathcal{A}}$ program of section 8. The program consists of a hierarchy of several predicates, where the top level predicate $\text{Qs}^{\mathcal{A}}$ has calls in its body to other predicates, the auxiliaries $\text{Pt}^{\mathcal{A}}$ and $\text{Ap}^{\mathcal{A}}$. Each I_i therefore will consist of possibly many $[p(\mathbf{x}) \leftarrow c]_{\sim}$, at most one for each predicate symbol p. I_{i+1} can only include $[\text{Qs}^{\mathcal{A}}(\mathbf{x}) \leftarrow c]_{\sim}$, however, provided I_i includes $[\text{Pt}^{\mathcal{A}}(\mathbf{x}) \leftarrow c]_{\sim}$ and $[\text{Ap}^{\mathcal{A}}(\mathbf{x}) \leftarrow c]_{\sim}$. $\text{Pt}^{\mathcal{A}}$ and $\text{Ap}^{\mathcal{A}}$ are directly recursive with uniform increment and therefore can be widened with $k = 2$. In general, however, precision can be lost if a predicate is widened before its auxiliaries are widened and thus stable. By inspecting the clauses of a program, the call graph and its Strongly Connected Components can be computed. The SCCs of the $\text{Qs}^{\mathcal{A}}$ program, for example, are the clause sets $\{\{\text{Ap}^{\mathcal{A}}/1\}, \{\text{Ap}^{\mathcal{A}}/2\}, \{\text{Pt}^{\mathcal{A}}/1\}, \{\text{Pt}^{\mathcal{A}}/2, \text{Pt}^{\mathcal{A}}/3\}, \{\text{Qs}^{\mathcal{A}}/1\}, \{\text{Qs}^{\mathcal{A}}/2\}\}$ where the p/m notation abbreviates the mth clause defining the predicate p. SCCs can be used to compute the fixpoint in a bottom-up fashion by considering the SCCs in (reverse) topological order. See Figure 1. Analysis begins with the base cases of the deepest predicates, and progressing upwards to derive fixpoints for $\text{Pt}^{\mathcal{A}}$ and $\text{Ap}^{\mathcal{A}}$, before moving on to $\text{Qs}^{\mathcal{A}}$. A complete analysis for $\text{Qs}^{\mathcal{A}}$ is given in the table.

Interpretation	Step
$I_1 = \{[\text{Ap}^A(x, y, z) \leftarrow x = 0, y = z]_\sim\}$	base
$I_2 = \{[\text{Ap}^A(x, y, z) \leftarrow 0 \leq x \leq 1, z = y + x]_\sim\}$	recurse
$I_3 = \{[\text{Ap}^A(x, y, z) \leftarrow z = y + x, (-x) \leq 0]_\sim\}$	widen
$I_4 = \{[\text{Ap}^A(x, y, z) \leftarrow z = y + x, (-x) \leq 0]_\sim\}$	stabilise
$I_5 = I_4 \cup \{[\text{Pt}^A(w, x, y, z) \leftarrow x = 0, y = 0, z = 0]_\sim\}$	base
$I_6 = I_4 \cup \{[\text{Pt}^A(w, x, y, z) \leftarrow x = z + y, 0 \leq y \leq 1, y - x \leq 0]_\sim\}$	recurse
$I_7 = I_4 \cup \{[\text{Pt}^A(w, x, y, z) \leftarrow x = z + y, y \leq x, (-y) \leq 0]_\sim\}$	widen
$I_8 = I_4 \cup \{[\text{Pt}^A(w, x, y, z) \leftarrow x = z + y, y \leq x, (-y) \leq 0]_\sim\}$	stabilise
$I_9 = I_8 \cup \{[\text{Qs}^A(x, y) \leftarrow x = 0, y = 0]_\sim\}$	base
$I_{10} = I_8 \cup \{[\text{Qs}^A(x, y) \leftarrow y = x, 0 \leq x \leq 1]_\sim\}$	recurse
$I_{11} = I_8 \cup \{[\text{Qs}^A(x, y) \leftarrow y = x, (-x) \leq 0]_\sim\}$	widen
$I_{12} = I_8 \cup \{[\text{Qs}^A(x, y) \leftarrow y = x, (-x) \leq 0]_\sim\}$	stabilise

Note that whilst other topological orderings are possible, this particular ordering minimises the size of the interpretations and thus simplifies the presentation. Widening each SCC separately also improves the efficiency. Since a predicate will not be referenced until its auxiliaries have been analysed, fewer computations will lead to failure. (Interestingly, the difference equation approach of [11] is unable to infer useful inter-argument relations for divide and conquer methods like Qs^A in the way our approach does.)

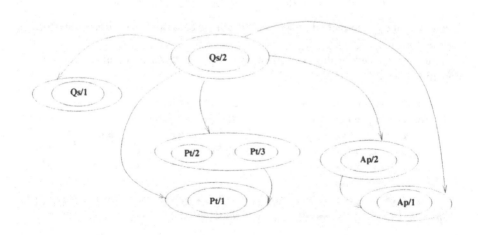

Fig. 1. Dependencies between SCCs of the Qs^A program

5.3 Widening with Non-uniform Increments

However under certain conditions all pertinent information may not be found in three iterations even when the SCCs are considered one by one. Through experimentation with our analyser, we have identified two classes of predicate that require a more intelligent widening strategy. Consider the $\text{Sp}^A/3$ predicate introduced in Section 1.

```
SpᴬA(0, 0, 0).
SpᴬA(1+xs, 1+os, es) <- SpᴬA(xs, es, os).
```

Here elements of the first list are placed alternately in the second and third lists. Thus $\text{Sp}^A/3$ defines

$$p_{i+1} = p_i \, \overline{\cup} \, \{\langle 1 + x, 1 + z, y\rangle \mid \langle x, y, z\rangle \in p_i\},$$
$$p_{i+2} = p_i \, \overline{\cup} \, \{\langle 2 + x, 1 + y, 1 + z\rangle \mid \langle x, y, z\rangle \in p_i\}$$

so that $\text{Sp}^A/3$ has a bi-modal incrementation behaviour where a uniform increment of 2, 1 and 1 in the first, second and third dimensions occurs in every second iteration. Consequently the invariant condition cannot be confirmed until the fifth iteration. Put another way, $k = 4$ is required. An analysis for Sp^A is shown below where $I_i = \{[\text{Sp}^A(x, y, z) \leftarrow c_i]_\sim\}$. The constraints in sans serif type are those that comprise the invariant condition.

c_1	$x = 0$	$y = 0$	$z = 0$			
c_2	$x \leq 1$	$-x \leq 0$	$z = 0$	$y - x = 0$		
c_3	$x - y - z = 0$	$-y \leq 0$	$x - 2y \leq 0$	$y - x \leq 0$	$y \leq 1$	
c_4	$x - y - z = 0$	$-y \leq 0$	$x - 2y \leq 0$	$2y - x \leq 1$	$y - x \leq 0$	$x - y \leq 1$
c_5	$x - y - z = 0$	$-y \leq 0$	$x - 2y \leq 0$	$2y - x \leq 1$	$y - x \leq 0$	

The widening as described in [8] would converge after three iterations having only deduced $x - y - z = 0$.

Another related problem is illustrated by the $\text{St}/3$ predicate, expressing a step function, listed below.

```
St(0, 0).                    StᴬA(0, 0).
St(x + 1, 0) <-              StᴬA(x + 1, 0) <-
   x =< 2, St(x, y).            x =< 2, StᴬA(x, y).
St(x + 1, 1) <-              StᴬA(x + 1, 1) <-
   2 < x, St(x, y).            2 < x, StᴬA(x, y).
```

The abstract version St^A is coincident with $\text{St}/3$ when the norm is size of an integer. An analysis for St^A is shown below where $I_i = \{[\text{St}^A(x, y) \leftarrow c_i]_\sim\}$.

c_1	$x = 0$	$y = 0$	
c_2	$0 \leq x$	$x \leq 1$	$y = 0$
c_3	$0 \leq x$	$x \leq 2$	$y = 0$
c_4	$0 \leq x$	$x \leq 3$	$0 \leq y$	$y \leq 1$
c_5	$0 \leq x$	$0 \leq y$	$y \leq 1$

Note that third clause of St^A is only selected in the fourth iteration so premature widening leads to loss of precision. More generally, precision may be lost when the selection of a clause is postponed until a threshold is reached. It is therefore apparent that the moment at which to apply the widening is when the iterations have captured all the invariant relationships. As shown above, however, detecting this moment may present some difficulties and therefore the current implementation permits the user to vary k. The problem of choosing when to widen relates to the usual trade-off between cost and accuracy.

6 Implementation

6.1 Ground (and Non-ground) Representation

A ground representation is used in combination with a non-ground representation. This simplifies the meta-interpreter as atoms can be looked up in the interpretation without inducing aliasing. The interpretations are ground whereas the programs are non-ground.

6.2 Bottom-up Interpreter

The bottom-up analyser is basically a simplified version of the meta-interpreter listed in [6]. The main difference between the two analysers is that our interpretations are ground and therefore variance (goal renaming) is not an issue. For a given clause, the interpreter essentially unifies each (non-ground) body atom in the definition of the clause with a matching (ground) atom in the interpretation, and then projects onto the head. Builtins are solved directly. The task of unifying a body atom with an atom in the interpretation basically reduces to decoding the ground representation of constraints. For example, if the body atom is p(U, V, W) and the interpretation contains atom(p, 3, [less(plus(var(1), var(2)), 0)]) then the call to decode from the ground representation

decode([less(plus(minus(var(1)), var(2)), 0)], 3, [U, V, W])

imposes the constraint V < U on the constraint store. The constraints on the head variables are then projected using meta-programming builtins to obtain an output in a ground form. Polyhedral abstractions from each of the clauses of a predicate are then combined incrementally as a convex hull. The convex hull operation is binary so for a predicate of say three clauses yielding the polyhedra p_1, p_2, p_3, the hull can be calculated by $(p_1 \,\overline{\cup}\, p_2) \,\overline{\cup}\, p_3$ with no loss of precision since the operation is both associative and commutative. Projection is used to eliminate the slack variables introduced in the convex hull calculation.

6.3 Entailment in CLP($\mathcal{R}$) and SICStus 3

The widening operation identifies those constraints that are invariant between iterations. At the implementation level this involves a test for entailment which is based upon the premise that for a linear constraint c to be entailed by a set of constraints C it is sufficient to show that $C \wedge \neg c$ has no solution [7].

6.4   Projection in CLP($\mathcal{R}$)

The constraints on the head variables are projected using the CLP($\mathcal{R}$) meta-programming built-in dump/3 [17] and the projection is output in a ground form. For example, with the constraint store X = 4 + Y, Z < X, the call

dump([X, Y], [var(1), var(2)], Cons)

instantiates Cons to [var(2) = var(1) - 4] which corresponds to a ground representation of the projection onto X and Y. To improve portability dump/3 is the only meta-programming facility that was utilised in CLP($\mathcal{R}$).

6.5   Projection in SICStus 3

The call_residue/2 built-in in SICStus has a similar role to dump/3 in CLP($\mathcal{R}$). Apart from small syntactic differences, the projection machinery is the main place where the CLP($\mathcal{R}$) and SICStus 3 analysers differ. In SICStus, projection is rather more complex as inequalities and equalities have to be dealt with separately. call_residue/2 accesses the residual constraints, that is, those constraints that are not satisfiable at the time of calling. For example, the call

call_residue({X = Y + Z, X = P}, Cons)

instantiates Cons to [[Z]-Z = P-Y]. Note, however, that Cons excludes the equality relationship between X and P. Since call_residue/2 is called with a goal, the program is dynamically modified with the call

assert(dummy(Target_Vars))

where Target_Vars are the variables that are the projection target. A dummy/1 goal is then passed to call_residue/2 to retrieve the constraints. A final post-processing phase assembles the residual constraints with the equality constraints.

6.6   Arithmetic in CLP($\mathcal{R}$) and SICStus 3

The coefficients of variables within the inequalities are represented as real numbers so, for example, the inequality $2x \leq 3y$ may sometimes be stored as $x - 1.5y \leq 0$ and as $x - 1.499999999999y \leq 0$ in another iteration. Although the widening ensures that termination is not compromised, roundoff errors can lead to some interesting relationships being lost. Roundoff is not a problem in the CLP($\mathcal{R}$) implementation since CLP($\mathcal{R}$) uses an small ϵ as slack in its numerical comparisons. Roundoff, however, lost relationships in the Trd/3 problem (see Appendix 8) in the initial SICStus 3 clp(R) implementation and this hastened the port to clp(Q).

7 Related Work

Most Specific Generalisation (msg) Approximations Argument size analysis can be specified by defining an appropriate pre-interpretation and by using *msg* approximations [13]. *msg* approximations are formed by taking most specific generalisations of sets of atoms. With the aid of query-answer transforms, the analysis of [13] can infer that the length of the first argument of naive reverse `rev/2` is the same as the length of the second argument. Inequalities are not supported.

Affine Approximations In the affine approach [14, 20, 31], invariants are represented by affine subspaces, basically points, lines or hyper-planes in $\mathbb{R}^n$, which can be represented and manipulated using matrices. The affine approach is attractive because, although it cannot infer inequalities between variables, the approximation is Noetherian and therefore the termination of the analysis is not an issue.

Simple Section Approximations Although developed for imperative languages, we suspect that simple sections [4] could be used to express simple inter-argument relationships. Simple sections characterise spaces that are bounded by hyper-planes of the form $x = c$, $x + y = c$ or $x - y = c$ where x and y are points on two different co-ordinate axes and c is a constant (or a special $-\infty$ or $+\infty$ symbol [8]). Simple sections can potentially reduce the complexity of convex hull calculations, can be implemented easily without CLP($\mathcal{R}$) support, but are likely to sacrifice a lot of precision. Moreover, the representation is likely to become intractable for predicates of larger arity.

Interval Approximations CHINA [1, 2, 3] is an analyser for CLP($\mathcal{R}$) and CLP($\mathcal{FD}$) that approximates conjunctions of constraints with bounding boxes. Bounding boxes are rectangular regions with sides parallel to the axes that are obtained by projecting variables onto their axes in order to represent each variable with the interval that results from the projection. Interval widening is required for termination and constraints are solved by propagating constraints around a constraint network [1, 2]. The bounding box approximation has been chosen for tractability, but our work suggests that, with some thought, it is not difficult to implement a more precise analysis with polyhedral approximations. To be fair, however, CHINA [2] introduces some nice ideas like, for example, the way constraints are compiled into finite concurrent constraint agents over a product of domains to trace the behaviour of builtins.

An interval analysis for CLP($\mathcal{R}$), not dissimilar to that used in CHINA, is described in [19]. The analysis is coupled to GAIA, is implemented in C, and uses narrowing to recover some of the precision lost in widening interval approximations. Finally, although not implemented, the paper explains how intervals can be coupled with groundness descriptions.

Polyhedral Approximations In [24] a Prolog III program is presented for checking the invariants of the CLP($\mathcal{Q}$) program to partially mechanise the derivation of inter-argument relationships. The proof method is neither a decision procedure (it is not complete) nor is it automatic since "its main drawback comes from the fact that the user has to provide the linear inter-argument relation to be proven".

In [30], an analysis for inferring linear inequalities is proposed with a suite of matrix transformations for mechanising the derivation of the inequalities. One flaw of [30], however, is that the iterative process required to compute inequalities may not converge in finitely many steps. Therefore Van Gelder proposes "an heuristic [for finding fixpoints] which often works" [30] and otherwise has recourse to human intervention, noting that useful fixpoints are not easy to find.

A widening for polyhedra is reported in [15, 16] that refines a widening first proposed in [9]. Originally used for overflow and array bounds checking, these widenings essentially remove inequalities from the first polyhedron that are not satisfied by the second. So that less information is lost the widening of [15, 16] reformulates the representation of the first polyhedron in order to maximise the number of common constraints. For example, to calculate $P_1 \bigtriangledown P_2$ where $P_1 = \{\langle x, y\rangle \in \mathbb{R}^2 \mid x = 0, y = 0\}$ and $P_2 = \{\langle x, y\rangle \in \mathbb{R}^2 \mid 0 \leq y \leq x \leq 1\}$, P_1 is re-expressed as $P_1 = \{\langle x, y\rangle \in \mathbb{R}^2 \mid 0 \leq y \leq x \leq 0\}$, yielding a result $P_1 \bigtriangledown P_2 = \{\langle x, y\rangle \in \mathbb{R}^2, \mid 0 \leq y \leq x\}$ rather than $\{\langle x, y\rangle \in \mathbb{R}^2 \mid 0 \leq x, 0 \leq y\}$. An algorithm for reformulating P_1 is detailed in [15].

Cousot and Cousot [8] address the termination problem of [30] by employing a widening to enforce convergence of the iterates. The widening builds on those reported in [9, 15, 16]. Given two polyhedral sets, $P_i \bigtriangledown P_{i+1}$, is computed from two sets of inequalities, S_i and S_{i+1}, that define P_i and P_{i+1}. First, the widening selects those inequalities of S_i that hold for all the points in P_{i+1}. This subset of S_i is denoted by S_i'. Second, the widening finds those inequalities which hold for P_i and P_{i+1} and yet are not explicit in S_i. For example, if $S_i = \{x = 1, y = 1\}$ and $S_{i+1} = \{x = y\}$, then $x = y$ holds for P_i and P_{i+1} but $x = y \notin S_i$. The widening thus selects those inequalities of S_{i+1}, like $x = y$, that can be swapped with an inequality of S_i, like $x = 1$, without altering the space P_i. This subset of S_{i+1} is denoted by S_{i+1}'. The widening $P_i \bigtriangledown P_{i+1}$ is taken to be the polyhedron defined by $S_i' \cup S_{i+1}'$. The widening uses the frame representation [9].

The argument size analysis of [28] builds on the matrix transforms of [30] but also uses a so-called affine widening to ensure termination. The widening, however, looses much of the expressiveness of polyhedral approximations and it "cannot infer relationships in the form of inequality" [28]. To improve the precision (and avoid widening) an unfolding transform is proposed for the special class of linearly recursive programs. A frame representation is used to check for a fixpoint and the representation also seems to be used in the convex union calculation [28, Section 2].

8   Future Work

In terms of efficiency, we believe that it might be possible, under certain conditions, to simplify the convex hull operation. In terms of precision, the widening can sometimes be improved by a single narrowing step $P_1 \triangle P_2 = P_1 \wedge P_2$. Future work will quantify the usefulness of this refinement. Future work will also investigate how the shapes of successive polyhedra can be used to deduce the propitious moment to widen and characterise the class of predicates that can be widened quickly without losing precision. We will also investigate how SCCs relate to chaotic iteration with widening [8]. We also intend to examine how the analysis can be ported to other systems with the (meta-programming) facilities offered by other languages, for example, Gödel, CHIP and IF/Prolog.

Acknowledgements

We should like to extend special thanks to Christian Holzbaur, for tirelessly and promptly coping with our queries regarding SICStus 3#3. Also, we gratefully acknowledge John Gallagher, Alain Kerbrat, Kung-Kiu Lau, Pedro Lopez Garcia, Jon Martin, Håkan Millroth, Julian Richardson, and Jan Smaus for their useful discussions. This work was generously supported by the Nuffield grant SCI/180/94/417/G and a Brian Spratt bursary.

Appendix A

To compare the usefulness of our implementation with previously proposed analyses [30], we list some programs which have traditionally proved difficult to analyse, complete with the results of our analysis.

Leq/2 The Leq(x, y) predicate, adapted from [30, pp. 55], holds if x is less or equal to y. Non-negative integers are encoded in successor notation. The size of Succ(t) is taken to be the size of the term t plus one. The Leq(x, y) predicate illustrates a class of predicate which for the analysis of [30] does *not* terminate. In [8] a related predicate is analysed in a finite number of iterations through widening. The widening refines those proposed in [9, 18] and is precise enough, like ours, to infer $x \leq y$. For comparison with [8], the sizes of terms are asserted to be non-negative.

Trd/2 The affine approach [14, 20, 31] cannot deduce any information for the Trd(x, y) predicate of [31, pp. 308]. By way of contrast, our combination of polyhedral sets and widening can infer some interesting results. Note that the non-negativity of x and y follows from $\frac{2}{3}x \leq y$ and $y \leq \frac{3}{2}x$. The norm in this and the following examples is taken to be list length. Note that since the prototype analyser is implemented in CLP($\mathcal{R}$) the analysis actually outputs $0.666667x \leq y \wedge y \leq 1.5x$.

`Perm/2` The `Perm(l,p)` predicate enumerates all the permutations `p` of the list `l`. To deduce termination,it is necessary to infer that `l` in the recursive call is smaller than `[h|t]`. This can only be inferred by deducing an inter-argument relation for `Del/3` - that its third argument is smaller than the second argument. This is inferred.

`Sp/3` The invariants for the `Sp/3` predicate listed in section 1 were inferred automatically, but were re-arranged for reasons of clarity. `Sp/3` is structurally recursive but has a subtle twist in that the recursive call switches the last two arguments around. The relationships that can be deduced for the three arguments are that the second and third sum to the first and that the second will either be the same size as or, at most 1 element larger than the third.

<table>
<tr><th>Program</th><th>Abstract program</th><th>Inter-argument relationships</th></tr>
<tr><td>Leq(x,x).
Leq(x,Succ(y)) <-
   Leq(x,y).</td><td>$\texttt{Leq}^{\mathcal{A}}$(x,x) <-
   $0 \leq$ x.
$\texttt{Leq}^{\mathcal{A}}$(x,1+y) <-
   $0 \leq$ x &
   $0 \leq$ y &
   $\texttt{Leq}^{\mathcal{A}}$(x,y).</td><td>$\texttt{Leq}^{\mathcal{A}}(x,y)$ <-
   $x \leq y$ &
   $(-x) \leq 0$ &
   $(-y) \leq 0$.</td></tr>
<tr><td>Trd([],[]).
Trd([_,_|x],[_,_,_|y]) <-
   Trd(x,y).
Trd([_,_,_|z],[_,_|t]) <-
   Trd(z,t).</td><td>$\texttt{Trd}^{\mathcal{A}}$(0,0).
$\texttt{Trd}^{\mathcal{A}}$(2+x,3+y) <-
   $\texttt{Trd}^{\mathcal{A}}$(x,y).
$\texttt{Trd}^{\mathcal{A}}$(3+z,2+t) <-
   $\texttt{Trd}^{\mathcal{A}}$(z,t).</td><td>$\texttt{Trd}^{\mathcal{A}}(x,y)$ <-
   $\frac{2}{3}x \leq y$ &
   $y \leq \frac{3}{2}x$.</td></tr>
<tr><td>Perm([],[]).
Perm([h|t],[a|p]) <-
   Del(a,[h|t],l) &
   Perm(l,p).

Del(x,[x|y],y).
Del(u,[y|z],[y|w]) <-
   Del(x,z,w).</td><td>$\texttt{Perm}^{\mathcal{A}}$(0,0).
$\texttt{Perm}^{\mathcal{A}}$(1+t,1+p) <-
   $\texttt{Del}^{\mathcal{A}}$(_,1+t, l) &
   $\texttt{Perm}^{\mathcal{A}}$(l,p).

$\texttt{Del}^{\mathcal{A}}$(_,1+y,y).
$\texttt{Del}^{\mathcal{A}}$(_,1+z,1+w) <-
   $\texttt{Del}^{\mathcal{A}}$(_,z,w).</td><td>$\texttt{Perm}^{\mathcal{A}}(x,y)$ <-
   $y = x$ &
   $(-x) \leq 0$.

$\texttt{Del}^{\mathcal{A}}(x,y,z)$ <-
   $z = y + 1$.</td></tr>
<tr><td>Sp([],[],[]) <-
Sp([x|xs],[x|os],es) <-
   Sp(xs,es,os).</td><td>$\texttt{Sp}^{\mathcal{A}}$(0,0,0) <-
$\texttt{Sp}^{\mathcal{A}}$(1+xs,1+os,es) <-
   $\texttt{Sp}^{\mathcal{A}}$(xs,es,os).</td><td>$\texttt{Sp}^{\mathcal{A}}(x,y,z)$ <-
   $z = -y + x$ &
   $y - x \leq 0$ &
   $y - \frac{1}{2}x \leq \frac{1}{2}$ &
   $(-y) + \frac{1}{2}x \leq 0$ &
   $(-y) \leq 0$.</td></tr>
</table>

References

1. R. Bagnara. On the detection of implicit and redundant numeric constraints in CLP programs. In *GULP-PRODE'94*, pages 312–326, 1994.

2. R. Bagnara. A hierarchy of constraint systems for data-flow analysis of constraint logic-based languages. Technical Report TR-96-10, Dipartimento di Informaticá, Universita di Pisa corso Italia 40, 56125 Pisa, Italy, 1996.

3. R. Bagnara, R. Giacobazzi, and G. Levi. Static Analysis of clp Programs over Numeric Domains. In *WSA'92*, 1992.

4. V. Balasundaram and K. Kennedy. A Technique for Summarizing Data Access and Its Use in Parallelism Enhancing Transformations. In *PLDI'89*, pages 41–53. ACM Press, 1989.

5. A. Bossi, M. Gabbrielli, G. Levi, and M. Martelli. The s-semantics approach: theory and applications. *Journal of Logic Programming*, 1991.

6. M. Codish and V. Lagoon. Persistant Type Analysis using a Non-Ground Domain. Technical report, Dept of Maths and Computer Science, Ben-Gurion University of the Negev, Israel, 1995.

7. A. Colmerauer. An Introduction to Prolog III. In *CACM*, volume 33, pages 70–90, July 1990.

8. P. Cousot and R. Cousot. Comparing the Galois Connection and Widening/Narrowing Approaches to Abstract Interpretation. Technical Report LIENS-92-16, Laboratoire d'Informatique de l'Ecole Normale Superiéure, 45 Rue d'Ulm, 75230 Paris Cédex 05, France, 1992.

9. P. Cousot and N. Halbwachs. Automatic Discovery of Linear Restraints among Variables of a Program. In *POPL'78*, pages 84–97, 1978.

10. B. De Backer and H. Beringer. A CLP language handling disjunctions of linear constraints. In *ICLP'93*, pages 550–563. MIT Press, 1993.

11. S. Debray and N. Lin. Cost Analysis for Logic Programs. *ACM Transactions on Programming Languages and Systems*, July 1992.

12. S. Decorte, D. De Schreye, and M. Fabris. Automatic Inference of Norms: a Missing Link in Automatic Termination Analysis. In *ICLP'93*, pages 420–436, 1993.

13. J. Gallagher, D. Boulanger, and Y. Saglam. Practical Model-Based Static Analysis for Definite Logic Programs. Technical Report CSTR-95-011, Department of Computer Science, University of Bristol, June 1995.

14. R. Giacobazzi, S. Debray, and G. Levi. Generalised Semantics and Abstract Interpretation for Constraint Logic Programs. Technical report, Dipartimento di Informatica, Universitá di Pisa, 1992.

15. N. Halbwachs. Détermination automatique de relations linéaires vérifiées par les variables d'un programme. Universit'e scientifique et médicale de Grenoble, 1979. Thèse de 3 ème d'informatique.

16. N. Halbwachs, Y.E. Proy, and P. Raymond. Verification of linear hybrid systems by means of convex approximations. In *First International Static Analysis Symposium*. Springer Verlag, September 1994.

17. N. C. Heintze, J. Jafar, S. Michaylov, P. J. Stuckey, and R. H. C. Yap. *The CLP(R) Programmer's Manual Version 1.2*, 1992.

18. R. N. Horspool. Analyzing List Usage in Prolog Code. University of Victoria, March 1990.

19. G. Janssens, M. Bruynooghe, and V. Englebert. Abstracting numeric values in CLP(H,N). In *PLILP'94*, pages 400–414. Springer-Verlag, 1994.

20. M. Karr. Affine Relationships Among Variables of a Program. *Acta Informatica*, 6:133–151, 1976.

21. D. B. Kemp and P. J. Stuckey. Analysis Based Constraint Query Optimisation. In *ICLP'93*, pages 666–682, 1993.

22. A. Kerbrat. Personal Communication on Polyhedral library polyhedra.tar. October, 1993.

23. J. Martin, A. King, and P. Soper. Typed Norms for Typed Logic Programs. In *LOPSTR'96*. Springer-Verlag, 1996.

24. F. Mesnard and J.-G. Ganascia. CLP(Q) for Proving Interargument Relations. In *META'92*, pages 308–320, Uppsala, Sweden, 1992. Springer-Verlag.

25. H. Millroth. *Reforming Compilation of Logic Programs*. PhD thesis, Computing Science Department, Uppsala University, 1990.

26. H. Millroth. Personal Communication on the rôle of Argument Relationships in Reform. October, 1993.

27. L. Plümer. *Termination Proofs for Logic Programs*. Springer-Verlag, 1990.

28. K. Sohn. Constraints among Argument Sizes in Logic Programs. In *PODS'94*, pages 68–74. ACM Press, 1994.

29. J. D. Ullman. Implementation of Logical Query Languages for Databases. *ACM Transactions on Database Systems*, 10(3):289–321, 1985.

30. A. Van Gelder. Deriving constraints among argument sizes in logic programs. *Annals of Mathematics and Artifical Intelligence*, (3), 1991.

31. K. Verschaetse and D. De Schreye. Derivation of Linear Size Relations by Abstract Interpretation. In *PLILP'92*, pages 296–310. Springer-Verlag, 1992.

32. D. Wilde. A Library for doing Polyhedral Operations. Technical Report PI-785, Institut de Recherche en Informatique et Systemes Aleatoires, Campus Universitaire de Beaulieu, 35042 Rennes Cedex, France, 1993.

Typed Norms for Typed Logic Programs

Jonathan C. Martin[1], Andy King[2] and Paul Soper[1]

[1] Department of Electronics and Computer Science, University of Southampton,
Southampton, SO9 5NH, UK. {jcm93r, pjs}@ecs.soton.ac.uk
[2] Computing Laboratory, University of Kent at Canterbury,
Canterbury, CT2 7NF, UK. a.m.king@ukc.ac.uk

Abstract. As typed logic programming becomes more mainstream, system building tools like partial deduction systems will need to be mapped from untyped languages to typed ones. It is important, however, when mapping techniques across that the new techniques should exploit the type system as much as possible. In this paper, we show how norms, which play a crucial role in termination analysis, can be generated from the prescribed types of a logic program. Interestingly, the types highlight restrictions of earlier norms and suggest how these norms can be extended to obtain some very general and powerful notions of norm which can be used to measure any term in an almost arbitrary way. We see our work on norm derivation as a contribution to the termination analysis of typed logic programs which, in particular, forms an essential part of offline partial deduction systems.

1 Introduction

Such is the complex nature of termination that ad hoc methods for its automatic detection in logic programs are giving way to techniques more firmly based on theory. Many of these approaches relate to the early theoretical result [3] which showed that a logic program terminates for *bounded* goals, using any computation rule, if and only if it is *recurrent*. Definitions of recurrency and boundedness are formulated in terms of level mappings which assign natural numbers, or levels, to ground atoms.

A predicate is recurrent with respect to some level mapping if the level of its head is greater than the level of each of its body atoms. The termination of bounded goals, whose level cannot increase, then follows from the well-foundedness of the natural numbers.

Level mappings are often defined in terms of *norms* which measure the size of terms. For example, the norm $|.|_{\text{list-length}}$ defined to measure the length of a list, can be used as the basis for a level mapping for the Delete/3 predicate below. Comparing the size of the second argument in the head of the recursive clause with the size of the second argument in the recursive call, and using list length as a measure for size, we see that the size of this argument decreases by one on each recursive call. Thus the predicate is recurrent with respect to the level mapping $|.|$ defined by $|\text{Delete}(t_1, t_2, t_3)| = |t_2|_{\text{list-length}}$ and terminates for all goals bounded with respect to $|.|$. Note that the predicate is also recurrent with respect to other level mappings and indeed termination can be proved for other goals by choosing a different mapping.

Delete(x, [x|y], y).
Delete(x, [y|z], [y|w]) ←
    Delete(x, z, w).

Deducing termination for programs which are not structurally recursive is more complex, requiring the derivation of inter-argument relationships [2]. Inter-argument relationships express how the sizes of an atom's arguments are related. In the case of Delete/3, for example, the length of the second argument is one plus the length of the third argument. The Perm/2 predicate defined below is one example where an inter-argument relationship is needed to prove termination.

Perm([], []).
Perm([h|t], [a|p]) ←
    Delete(a, [h|t], l) ∧
    Perm(l, p).

In fact it can be shown that this program is not recurrent and will not terminate for all ground queries – recurrency implies that a program terminates for *all* computation rules and here there exists a computation rule which selects non-ground Delete/3 goals which lead to infinite derivations. It can be shown however to be *acceptable* [1], an analogous concept to recurrency for programs executed using a left-to-right computation rule. A key step in the proof is to show that the size of the first argument in the head of the recursive clause is strictly greater than the size of the first argument in the recursive call, that is $||l||_{\text{list-length}} < ||[h|t]||_{\text{list-length}}$. This can only be inferred by deducing the inter-argument relationship for Delete/3 given above.

Choosing the right norm is crucial in deducing termination and deriving inter-argument relationships. Furthermore, different norms are often needed for each case. As an example, consider the predicate FlattenAndLength/3 defined below which flattens a list of lists and computes the length of the original list. The norm which sums the lengths of the sublists of the first argument can be used to deduce termination and is also needed to infer a useful inter-argument relationship between the first and second arguments. To derive a precise relationship between the first and third arguments, however, the norm $|.|_{\text{list-length}}$ is also needed for the first argument.

FlattenAndLength([], [], 0).
FlattenAndLength([e|x], r, Succ(z)) ←
    Append(e, y, r) ∧
    FlattenAndLength(x, y, z).

Early work on termination relied on the user to provide the necessary norms. As this had limited usefulness a method to automatically generate norms from a program was proposed in [6]. The approach focuses on deriving norms from type graphs that have previously been inferred by an analysis of the program.

The technique is effective in generating norms for proving termination of many of the programs found in the termination literature. The approach is clearly inappropriate, however, in the context of a typed language such as Gödel [11] when the types are already known.

As typed logic programming becomes more mainstream, system building tools like partial deduction systems will need to be mapped from untyped languages to typed ones. SAGE [9] is one example of a partial deduction system developed for the typed language Gödel. Although SAGE does well to demonstrate the effectiveness of self-application and how the overheads of the ground representation in meta-programs can be removed, there is much potential for improvement [10]. Its main weakness lies in a rather rudimentary termination analysis which would benefit considerably from the well developed techniques found in the termination literature. Inevitably, norms will play a crucial role in such an analysis. It is important, however, when mapping techniques across from the untyped setting that the new techniques should exploit the new type system as much as possible. In the case of automatic norm derivation the approach in [6] clearly would not take advantage of the prescribed types. As a result of this and since "any state-of-the-art approach to termination analysis needs to take type information into account" [7], new techniques are needed to derive norms directly from these types and avoid the overhead of type graph generation. We present one such technique.

In this paper we show how norms can be generated from the prescribed types of a program written in a language which supports parametric polymorphism, e.g. Gödel [11]. Interestingly, the types highlight restrictions of earlier norms and suggest how these norms can be extended to obtain some very general and powerful notions of norm which can be used to measure any term in an almost arbitrary way. We see our work on norm derivation as a contribution to the termination analysis of typed logic programs which, in particular, forms an essential part of offline partial deduction systems such as SAGE.

The paper is structured as follows. The next section introduces polymorphic, many-sorted languages and programs. Section 3 defines linear, semi-linear and hierarchical typed norms and discusses the problem of rigidity in a polymorphic many-sorted context. Section 4 describes how to infer the norms of section 3 from the prescribed types of a program. Related work is addressed in the penultimate section and we conclude with some directions for future work.

2 Theoretical foundations

2.1 Polymorphic many-sorted languages

Let Σ_τ (resp. Σ_f) be an alphabet of type constructor (resp. typed function) symbols which includes at least one base (resp. constant) and let Σ_p be an alphabet of typed predicate symbols. Let U denote a countably infinite set of type parameters so that the term structure $T(\Sigma_\tau, U)$ represents the set of parametric types. Let $V = \{V_\tau \mid \tau \in T(\Sigma_\tau, U)\}$ denote a family of countably infinite, disjoint sets of variables for polymorphic (and monomorphic) formulae, where each $v_\tau \in V_\tau$ has type τ. Variables will be denoted by the letters v, w, x, y, and z, whereas parameters will be denoted by the letter u. Each $f_\sigma \in \Sigma_f$ (resp. $p_\sigma \in \Sigma_p$) is assigned a unique[3] type (modulo renaming) $\sigma = \langle \tau_1 \ldots \tau_n, \tau \rangle$ (resp. $\sigma = \tau_1 \ldots \tau_n$) where $\tau_1 \ldots \tau_n \in T(\Sigma_\tau, U)^*$ and $\tau \in T(\Sigma_\tau, U) \setminus U$. We call τ the range type of $f_{\langle \tau_1 \ldots \tau_n, \tau \rangle} \in \Sigma_f$ when $n > 0$. Types are unique in the sense that if $f_{\langle \sigma_1 \ldots \sigma_n, \sigma \rangle}$, $f_{\langle \tau_1 \ldots \tau_n, \tau \rangle} \in \Sigma_f$ (resp. $p_{\sigma_1 \ldots \sigma_n}$, $p_{\tau_1 \ldots \tau_n} \in \Sigma_p$) then $\sigma_i = \tau_i$ and $\sigma = \tau$. A symbol will often be written without its type if it is clear from the context. The triple $L = \langle \Sigma_p, \Sigma_f, V \rangle$ defines a polymorphic many-sorted first-order language.

Terms, atoms and formulae are defined in the usual way [11]. We denote by $\mathsf{var}(o)$ (resp. $\mathsf{par}(o)$) the set of variables (resp. parameters) in a syntactic object o. The set of term (resp. type) substitutions is denoted by Sub (resp. Sub_τ). The set of all instances of Σ_f is denoted by $\Sigma_f^\dagger = \{ f_{\psi(\sigma)} | f_\sigma \in \Sigma_f \wedge \psi \in \mathsf{Sub}_\tau \}$.

2.2 Polymorphic many-sorted programs

Let $P = \langle \Delta, S \rangle$ be a polymorphic many-sorted logic program where Δ is a triple $\langle \Delta_\tau, \Delta_f, \Delta_p \rangle$ of type declarations and S is a set of statements of the form $\forall (a \leftarrow w)$ where a is an atom and w is either absent or a polymorphic many-sorted formula. The type declarations Δ_τ, Δ_f and Δ_p define respectively Σ_τ, Σ_f and Σ_p.

Each function declaration $f : \tau_1 \times \ldots \times \tau_n \to \tau \in \Delta_f$ (resp. constant declaration $c : \tau \in \Delta_f$) where $\tau_1, \ldots, \tau_n \in T(\Sigma_\tau, U)$ and $\tau \in T(\Sigma_\tau, U) \setminus U$ implies $f_{\langle \tau_1 \ldots \tau_n, \tau \rangle} \in \Sigma_f$ (resp. $c_{\langle \epsilon, \tau \rangle} \in \Sigma_f$). Similarly, each predicate declaration $p : \tau_1 \times \ldots \times \tau_n \in \Delta_p$ (resp. proposition declaration $p \in \Delta_p$) where $\tau_1, \ldots, \tau_n \in T(\Sigma_\tau, U)$ implies $p_{\tau_1 \ldots \tau_n} \in \Sigma_p$ (resp. $p_\epsilon \in \Sigma_p$). Δ_f (resp. Δ_p) is assumed to be universal, that is, each symbol has exactly one declaration in Δ_f (resp. Δ_p) so that Σ_f (resp. Σ_p) is well-defined.

Given a language $L = \langle \Sigma_p, \Sigma_f, V \rangle$ defined by a program P, we define a family of extended Herbrand domains as follows. Each ED_τ is the least set such that if $v_\tau \in V_\tau$ then $v_\tau \in \mathsf{ED}_\tau$; if $f_{\langle \epsilon, \sigma \rangle} \in \Sigma_f$ and $\tau = \psi(\sigma)$ then $f_{\langle \epsilon, \psi(\sigma) \rangle} \in \mathsf{ED}_\tau$; and if $f_{\langle \sigma_1 \ldots \sigma_n, \sigma \rangle} \in \Sigma_f$ and $t_i \in \mathsf{ED}_{\tau_i}$ with $\mathsf{par}(\sigma_i) \cap \mathsf{par}(\tau_j) = \emptyset$ for all i, j and $\mathsf{par}(\tau_j) \cap \mathsf{par}(\tau_k) = \emptyset$ for all $j \neq k$ and ψ is a unifier (not necessarily the most general) of $\{ \sigma_1 = \tau_1, \ldots, \sigma_n = \tau_n \} \cup \{ \rho_i = \rho_j \, | \, v_{\rho_i} \in \mathsf{var}(t_i) \wedge v_{\rho_j} \in \mathsf{var}(t_j) \}$ then $\psi(f(t_1, \ldots, t_n)) \in \mathsf{ED}_{\psi(\sigma)}$.

3 Norms for typed logic programs

A norm is a mapping that measures the size of a term. The norm list length, for example, might typically count the number of Cons symbols that occur in a list.

Example 1. The length of a list of integers can be expressed as

$$|\mathsf{Nil}| = 0$$
$$|\mathsf{Cons}(t_1, t_2)| = 1 + |t_2| \hspace{2cm} \square$$

---

[3] For overloaded symbols, for example +, we assume the symbol is uniquely renamed for each of its types.

The mapping is partial since it is only defined for closed, i.e. Nil-terminated, lists. To define norms as total mappings we introduce the alphabets $\Sigma_\tau = \{\text{Lin}\}$ and $\Sigma_f = \{+_{(\text{Lin.Lin,Lin})}, 0_{(\epsilon,\text{Lin})}, 1_{(\epsilon,\text{Lin})}\}$ so that ED_{Lin} represents the class of linear expressions on V_{Lin} where terms such as $x_{\text{Lin}} + y_{\text{Lin}} + y_{\text{Lin}} + 1_{(\epsilon,\text{Lin})} + 1_{(\epsilon,\text{Lin})} + 1_{(\epsilon,\text{Lin})}$ are abbreviated to $x + 2y + 3$.

It is usually too restrictive to use a single norm to measure the size of any term in a program. Different terms need to be measured according to their structure or, equivalently, according to their type. This motivates the introduction of a typed norm $|.|_\tau$ which only measures terms of type τ.

Definition 1 typed norm I. A *typed norm* for a polymorphic type τ is a mapping $|.|_\tau : \text{ED}_\tau \to \text{ED}_{\text{Lin}}$. □

Example 2. The typed norm $|.|_{\text{List(Int)}} : \text{ED}_{\text{List(Int)}} \to \text{ED}_{\text{Lin}}$ defined below measures the length of both open and closed lists of integers.

$$|v|_{\text{List(Int)}} = v$$
$$|\text{Nil}|_{\text{List(Int)}} = 0$$
$$|\text{Cons}(t_1, t_2)|_{\text{List(Int)}} = 1 + |t_2|_{\text{List(Int)}}$$

□

It is appropriate at this point to review the important concept of rigidity. This idea was originally introduced in [5] in order to prove termination for a class of goals with possibly non-ground terms. A rigid term is one whose size, as determined by a norm, is not affected by substitutions applied to the term. In the following, ϕ denotes the variable assignment which binds all variables in a term to the term 0_{Lin}.

Definition 2 rigid term. Let $|.|_\tau$ be a typed norm for τ and t be a term of type τ. Then t is *rigid* with respect to $|.|_\tau$ iff $\forall \theta \in \text{Sub}, |t|_\tau \phi = |t\theta|_\tau \phi$. □

Example 3. The term $\text{Cons}(x, \text{Cons}(y, \text{Nil}))$ is rigid wrt the norm $|.|_{\text{List(Int)}}$ of example 2 since for every substitution $\{x \mapsto t_1, y \mapsto t_2\}$ where t_1 and t_2 are terms $|\text{Cons}(t_1, \text{Cons}(t_2, \text{Nil}))| = 2$. □

By defining level mappings in terms of norms, it is possible to define a class of bounded goals [3] in terms of rigidity. More precisely, an atom is bounded with respect to a level mapping if each argument of the atom whose size is measured in the level mapping is rigid. A problem arises, however, with the typed norms used in level mappings. In measuring the level of an atom, a norm $|.|_\tau$, which can only measure terms of type τ may be applied to a term of type σ, where $\sigma = \psi(\tau)$ for some $\psi \in \text{Sub}_\tau$.

Example 4. Let $\Sigma_\tau = \{\text{Int}, \text{List}\}$, $\Sigma_f = \{\text{Nil}_{(\epsilon,\text{List}(u))}, \text{Cons}_{(u.\text{List}(u),\text{List}(u))}\}$, $\Sigma_p = \{\text{Traverse}_{\text{List}(u)}\}$ and $S = \{\text{Traverse(Nil)}., \text{Traverse}(\text{Cons}(x, y)) \leftarrow \text{Traverse}(y).\}$ then the norm $|.|_{\text{List}(u)}$ defined by

$$|v|_{\text{List}(u)} = v$$
$$|\text{Nil}|_{\text{List}(u)} = 0$$
$$|\text{Cons}(t_1, t_2)|_{\text{List}(u)} = 1 + |t_2|_{\text{List}(u)}$$

can be used to define a level mapping $|.|$ for the Traverse/1 predicate as follows

$$|\text{Traverse}(t)| = |t|_{\text{List}(u)}$$

The problem is that in trying to prove recurrency with respect to the level mapping $|.|$ for Traverse/1, the level mapping can be applied to atoms such as Traverse(Cons(1, Nil)), yet the type of the argument of Traverse/1 in this instance, List(Int), is not the type List(u) for which the mapping is defined. $\square$

This problem arises due to the polymorphism in our typed language and is not difficult to remedy. The domain of the norm must be changed and a constraint imposed to ensure that the rigidity property still holds.

Definition 3 typed norm II. A *typed norm* for a polymorphic type τ is a mapping $|.|_\tau : \cup_{\psi \in \text{Sub}_\tau} \text{ED}_{\psi(\tau)} \to \text{ED}_{\text{Lin}}$ where

$$\forall \psi \in \text{Sub}_\tau, |f_{(\tau_1 \ldots \tau_n, \tau)}(t_1, \ldots, t_n)|_\tau = |f_{(\psi(\tau_1)\ldots\psi(\tau_n),\psi(\tau))}(t_1, \ldots, t_n)|_\tau \quad \square$$

To see why the constraint is required, suppose that the term t is rigid wrt the type II norm $|.|_\tau$, then, by the definition of rigidity

$$\forall \theta \in \text{Sub}, |t|_\tau \phi = |t\theta|_\tau \phi \tag{1}$$

Now applying a variable substitution to a term often has the effect of further instantiating the type of the term. For example the type of the term Cons(x, Nil) is List(u), but the type of Cons(x, Nil)$\{x \mapsto 1\}$ = Cons(1, Nil) is List(Int). Hence we constrain the equations defining $|.|_\tau$ so that equation (1) holds.

We would like to define our norms in such a way that we can obtain a syntactic characterisation of rigid terms. We impose the two following conditions on the way norms are defined and then give a simple, syntactic check for terms which are rigid with respect to norms defined under these conditions.

Definition 4 linearity property. A typed norm $|.|_\tau$ satisfies the linearity property if

1. $|t|_\tau = c_0 + c_1 v_1 + \ldots + c_n v_n \; \forall t \in \text{ED}_\tau$ where $c_0, n \geq 0$ and $c_1, \ldots, c_n > 0$, and
2. $|t|_\tau = c_0 + c_1 v_1 + \ldots + c_n v_n$ implies $|t\theta|_\tau = c_0 + c_1 |v_1'\theta|_{\tau_1} + \ldots + c_n |v_n'\theta|_{\tau_n} \; \forall t \in \text{ED}_\tau, \forall \theta \in \text{Sub}$ where $|v_i'|_{\tau_i} = v_i \; \forall i$. $\square$

Definition 5 non-zero dependent typed norm. A typed norm $|.|_\tau$ is *non-zero* if $|t|_\tau \neq 0 \; \forall t \in \text{ED}_\tau \setminus V_\tau$. A typed norm is *non-zero dependent* if its definition depends only on non-zero typed norms. $\square$

Proposition 6 rigid term. Let $|.|_\tau$ be a non-zero dependent typed norm which satisfies the linearity property and t be a term of type τ. Then t is *rigid* with respect to $|.|_\tau$ iff $\text{var}(|t|_\tau) = \emptyset$. $\square$

Proof. (i) If $\text{var}(|t|_\tau) = \emptyset$ then by the linearity property, $|t|_\tau = |t\theta|_\tau \; \forall \theta \in \text{Sub}$. (ii) Now suppose that t is rigid with respect to $|.|_\tau$ and $|t|_\tau = c_0 + c_1 v_1 + \ldots + c_n v_n$. Then $|t|_\tau \phi = c_0 = |t\theta|_\tau \phi = c_0 + c_1 |v_1'\theta|_{\tau_1} \phi + \ldots + c_n |v_n'\theta|_{\tau_n} \phi \; \forall \theta \in \text{Sub}$, where $|v_i'|_{\tau_i} = v_i \; \forall i$ by the linearity property. Since $c_1, \ldots, c_n > 0$ and $|t|_\tau \not< 0 \; \forall t, \tau$ and as $|v_i'\theta|_{\tau_i} \phi \neq 0 \; \forall i, \theta \in \text{Sub}$, as $|.|_\tau$ is non-zero dependent, $\text{var}(|t|_\tau) = \emptyset$. $\quad\square$

Throughout the remainder of this paper we will only be concerned with type II norms. Henceforth $|.|_\tau$ will only denote a type II norm whose domain is unambiguously defined by definition 3. In view of the constraint on type II norms, we will write $|f(t_1, \ldots, t_n)|_\tau$ where f represents $f_{\langle \psi(\tau_1) \ldots \psi(\tau_n), \psi(\tau) \rangle}$ for all $\psi \in \text{Sub}_\tau$. Although each norm is annotated with its type, the following example illustrates that several norms may exist for the same type.

Example 5. The typed norm $|.|^{\text{len}}_{\text{List(List(Int))}}$ measures the length of a list whose elements are lists of integers. The typed norm $|.|^{\text{sum}}_{\text{List(List(Int))}}$ sums the lengths of the elements of such a list.

$$|v|^{\text{len}}_{\text{List(List(Int))}} = v$$
$$|\text{Nil}|^{\text{len}}_{\text{List(List(Int))}} = 0$$
$$|\text{Cons}(t_1, t_2)|^{\text{len}}_{\text{List(List(Int))}} = 1 + |t_2|^{\text{len}}_{\text{List(List(Int))}}$$

$$|v|^{\text{sum}}_{\text{List(List(Int))}} = v$$
$$|\text{Nil}|^{\text{sum}}_{\text{List(List(Int))}} = 0$$
$$|\text{Cons}(t_1, t_2)|^{\text{sum}}_{\text{List(List(Int))}} = |t_1|^{\text{sum}}_{\text{List(Int)}} + |t_2|^{\text{sum}}_{\text{List(List(Int))}}$$

where $|.|^{\text{sum}}_{\text{List(Int)}}$ is equal to the norm $|.|_{\text{List(Int)}}$ of example 2. Note that the norm $|.|^{\text{len}}_{\text{List(List(Int))}}$ is characterised by a weight of 1 in its recursive equation and the selection of the second argument position only, whereas the norm $|.|^{\text{sum}}_{\text{List(List(Int))}}$ is characterised by a weight of 0 in its recursive equation and the selection of both argument positions. $\quad\square$

To uniquely characterise a norm we introduce a pair $s = \langle w_s, I_s \rangle$ of partial mappings where $w_s : \Sigma_f^\dagger \to \mathbb{N}$ assigns a weight to each function symbol and $I_s : \Sigma_f^\dagger \to \wp(\mathbb{N})$ selects a subset of the argument positions for each function symbol. The definition of a norm for a type τ depends on s and therefore we denote the norm by $|.|_\tau^s$.

Example 6. In example 5 $\text{len} = \langle w_{\text{len}}, I_{\text{len}} \rangle$ where

$$w_{\text{len}} = \{\text{Nil} \mapsto 0, \; \text{Cons} \mapsto 1\}$$
$$I_{\text{len}} = \{\text{Nil} \mapsto \{\}, \; \text{Cons} \mapsto \{2\}\}$$

$\quad\square$

We are now in a position to define a notion of linear and semi-linear norms [4, 13] for typed programs.

Definition 7 linear typed norm. A typed norm $|.|_\tau^s$ is *linear* iff

$$\forall \psi \in \mathsf{Sub}_\tau, \forall v \in V_{\psi(\tau)} \qquad |v|_\tau^s = v$$
$$\forall f_{(\tau_1 \ldots \tau_n, \tau)} \in \Sigma_f^\dagger \qquad |f(t_1, \ldots, t_n)|_\tau^s = w_s(f_{(\tau_1 \ldots \tau_n, \tau)}) + \sum_{i \in I_s(f_{(\tau_1 \ldots \tau_n, \tau)})} |t_i|_\tau^s$$

where $I_s(f_{(\tau_1 \ldots \tau_n, \tau)}) = \{1, \ldots, n\}$. □

Note that the types highlight an inherent restriction of linear norms, that is, these norms are only defined when $\tau_i = \tau$ for $i = 1, \ldots, n$. Such norms have limited applicability.

Example 7. Given $\Sigma_\tau = \{\mathsf{Tree}\}$ and $\Sigma_f = \{\mathsf{Leaf}_{(\epsilon, \mathsf{Tree})}, \mathsf{Node}_{(\mathsf{Tree.Tree,Tree})}\}$, the linear typed norm for Tree that counts the number of function symbols in a term is defined by

$$|v|_{\mathsf{Tree}}^{\mathsf{size}} = v$$
$$|\mathsf{Leaf}|_{\mathsf{Tree}}^{\mathsf{size}} = 1$$
$$|\mathsf{Node}(t_1, t_2)|_{\mathsf{Tree}}^{\mathsf{size}} = 1 + |t_1|_{\mathsf{Tree}}^{\mathsf{size}} + |t_2|_{\mathsf{Tree}}^{\mathsf{size}}$$

□

The following definition generalises that of linear typed norms by allowing $I_s(f_{(\tau_1 \ldots \tau_n, \tau)}) \subseteq \{1, \ldots, n\}$. In the special case when $I_s(f_{(\tau_1 \ldots \tau_n, \tau)}) = \{1, \ldots, n\}$ the two definitions are equivalent.

Definition 8 semi-linear typed norm. A typed norm $|.|_\tau^s$ is *semi-linear* iff

$$\forall \psi \in \mathsf{Sub}_\tau, \forall v \in V_{\psi(\tau)} \qquad |v|_\tau^s = v$$
$$\forall f_{(\tau_1 \ldots \tau_n, \tau)} \in \Sigma_f^\dagger \qquad |f(t_1, \ldots, t_n)|_\tau^s = w_s(f_{(\tau_1 \ldots \tau_n, \tau)}) + \sum_{i \in I_s(f_{(\tau_1 \ldots \tau_n, \tau)})} |t_i|_\tau^s$$

where $I_s(f_{(\tau_1 \ldots \tau_n, \tau)}) \subseteq \{1, \ldots, n\}$. □

Example 8. If $\Sigma_\tau = \{\mathsf{Int}, \mathsf{List}\}$ and $\Sigma_f = \{\mathsf{Nil}_{(\epsilon, \mathsf{List}(u))}, \mathsf{Cons}_{(u.\mathsf{List}(u), \mathsf{List}(u))}\}$, then the norm $|.|_{\mathsf{List}(\mathsf{List}(\mathsf{Int}))}^{\mathsf{len}}$ defined in example 5 is semi-linear. □

Semi-linear norms are not expressive enough to measure the sizes of terms that can be defined in a typed language such as Gödel. To quote [4, pp. 72, paragraph 2] "The recursive structure of a semi-linear norm gets into the term structure by only one level. Moreover so far it is not defined how different semi-linear norms can be linked to work together. The definition of a semi-linear norm is recursively based only onto itself and it is easy to understand that this is a severe restriction." Again the types highlight where the essential problem lies: the norm applied to t_i is $|.|_\tau$ whereas the type of t_i is τ_i. The following definition overcomes this limitation of semi-linear norms.

Definition 9 hierarchical typed norm. A typed norm $|.|_\tau^s$ is *hierarchical* iff

$$\forall \psi \in \mathsf{Sub}_\tau, \forall v \in V_{\psi(\tau)} \qquad |v|_\tau^s = v$$
$$\forall f_{(\tau_1 \ldots \tau_n, \tau)} \in \Sigma_f^\dagger \qquad |f(t_1, \ldots, t_n)|_\tau^s = w_s(f_{(\tau_1 \ldots \tau_n, \tau)}) + \sum_{i \in I_s(f_{(\tau_1 \ldots \tau_n, \tau)})} |t_i|_{\tau_i}^s$$

where $I_s(f_{(\tau_1 \ldots \tau_n, \tau)}) \subseteq \{1, \ldots, n\}$ and $|t_i|_{\tau_i}^s$ are hierarchical typed norms. □

Example 9. With Σ_τ and Σ_f as defined in example 8, the norm $|.|^{\text{sum}}_{\text{List(List(Int))}}$ defined in example 5 is hierarchical and, in fact, cannot be expressed as a semi-linear norm. □

Note that definition 9 is closely related to definition 4.5 of [6]. Both generalise the definition of a type norm proposed in [13]. In [6] the relationship between typed norms and semi-linear norms is not made explicit, but our presentation makes the relationships between the various norms clear. In particular, we see that every linear typed norm is semi-linear and every semi-linear typed norm is hierarchical. The following proposition is needed to establish a syntactic characterisation of rigidity with respect to hierarchical typed norms.

Proposition 10. Let $|.|_\tau$ be a hierarchical typed norm. Then $|.|_\tau$ satisfies the linearity property. □

Although hierarchical norms allow us to inspect the structure of terms at a deeper level than in the semi-linear case, the pair of mappings s maps a functor of a given type to the same pair of values regardless of its depth in the term. In certain (pathological) circumstances this can impede the detection of a well-founded ordering.

Example 10. With Σ_τ and Σ_f as defined in example 7, consider the hierarchical typed norm $|.|^s_{\text{Tree}}$ defined by

$$|v|^s_{\text{Tree}} = v$$
$$|\text{Leaf}|^s_{\text{Tree}} = w_s(\text{Leaf})$$
$$|\text{Node}(t_1, t_2)|^s_{\text{Tree}} = w_s(\text{Node}) + \sum_{i \in I_s(\text{Node})} |t_i|^s_{\text{Tree}}$$

There is no definition of s which will satisfy the inequality

$$|\text{Node}(\text{Node}(w, \text{Node}(x, y)), z)|^s_{\text{Tree}} > |\text{Node}(\text{Node}(\text{Node}(w, x), y), z)|^s_{\text{Tree}} \quad (2)$$

needed to prove recurrency for the predicate Shift/1 defined by

```
Shift(Node(Node(_, Leaf), Leaf)).
Shift(Node(Node(w, Node(x, y)), z)) ←
    Shift(Node(Node(Node(w, x), y), z)).
```

The following table illustrates that for all values of $I_s(\text{Node})$ and $w_s(\text{Node})$ and for every variable assignment for w, x, y, z the left-hand side is always less than or equal to the right-hand side.

$I_s(\text{Node})$	$\lvert\text{Node}(\text{Node}(w, \text{Node}(x, y)), z)\rvert^s_{\text{Tree}}$	$\lvert\text{Node}(\text{Node}(\text{Node}(w, x), y), z)\rvert^s_{\text{Tree}}$
$\{1,2\}$	$3w_s(\text{Node}) + w + x + y + z$	$3w_s(\text{Node}) + w + x + y + z$
$\{1\}$	$2w_s(\text{Node}) + w$	$3w_s(\text{Node}) + w$
$\{2\}$	$w_s(\text{Node}) + z$	$w_s(\text{Node}) + z$
$\{\}$	$w_s(\text{Node})$	$w_s(\text{Node})$

The inequality can be satisfied, however, by substituting in (2) the norm $|.|_{\text{Tree}}^{\text{left}}$ defined by

$$|v|_{\text{Tree}}^{\text{left}} = v \qquad\qquad |v|_{\text{Tree}}^{\text{right}} = v$$
$$|\text{Node}(t_1, t_2)|_{\text{Tree}}^{\text{left}} = 1 + |t_1|_{\text{Tree}}^{\text{right}} \qquad |\text{Node}(t_1, t_2)|_{\text{Tree}}^{\text{right}} = 1 + |t_2|_{\text{Tree}}^{\text{right}} \qquad\qquad \square$$

The definition of a hierarchical typed norm can be generalised further to accommodate such examples by replacing $|t_i|_{\tau_i}^s$ in the definition with $|t_i|_{\tau_i}^{s_i}$ where each s_i is a new pair of mappings. This additional expressiveness allows a term to be measured in a very flexible way, though in practice it is unlikely that such generality will be needed and besides which the complexity introduced is mind-boggling.

4 Automatic generation of norms

We show how the typed norms of the previous section can be derived directly from the prescribed types of a program. For a program P, we require a finite set of norms which will enable us to measure the size of any term occurring in P. The norms needed will be determined by the types that can occur in P. In the following we consider two types to be equivalent if one is a renaming of the other.

Definition 11 argument types. Let P define the language $\langle \Sigma_p, \Sigma_f, V \rangle$. The set of argument types for P denoted by $T_{\text{arg}} = \{\tau_i \mid p_{\tau_1 \ldots \tau_n} \in \Sigma_p \wedge 1 \leq i \leq n\}$. $\square$

The set T_{arg} represents the types of all terms occurring as arguments of atoms in P, in that if the type of an argument of some atom is τ, then either $\tau \in T_{\text{arg}}$ or $\exists \psi \in \text{Sub}_\tau$, $\exists \sigma \in T_{\text{arg}}$ such that $\tau = \psi(\sigma)$. The following definition captures the types of subterms of arguments.

Definition 12 argument subtypes. For each $\tau \in T_{\text{arg}}$ we define T_{sub}^τ the set of subtypes of τ to be the least set such that $\tau \in T_{\text{sub}}^\tau$ and if $\sigma \in T_{\text{sub}}^\tau$, $f_{\langle \rho_1 \ldots \rho_n, \rho \rangle} \in \Sigma_f$ and $\sigma = \psi(\rho)$, then $\psi(\rho_i) \in T_{\text{sub}}^\tau$, for all $i = 1, \ldots, n$. $\square$

Example 11. Given the alphabets $\Sigma_f = \{\text{Nil}_{\langle \epsilon, \text{List}(u) \rangle}, \text{Cons}_{\langle u.\text{List}(u), \text{List}(u) \rangle}\}$ and $\Sigma_p = \{P_{\text{List}(\text{List}(u))}, Q_{\text{List}(u)}\}$, then $T_{\text{arg}} = \{\text{List}(\text{List}(u)), \text{List}(u)\}$, $T_{\text{sub}}^{\text{List}(\text{List}(u))} = \{\text{List}(\text{List}(u)), \text{List}(u), u\}$ and $T_{\text{sub}}^{\text{List}(u)} = \{\text{List}(u), u\}$. $\square$

By defining a norm $|.|_\tau$ for each $\tau \in T_{\text{arg}}$, we are able to measure the size of any argument occurring in the program. The sets $T_{\text{sub}}^{\tau_i}$ are used to facilitate the definitions of these norms. It will often be the case that some of the arguments in a program have the same type and different norms may be required to measure the sizes of such arguments. We thus define for each $\tau \in T_{\text{arg}}$ a norm parameterised by a pair s as in the preceding section. Later, s can be defined for individual arguments.

Before defining the induction process we first make an important observation which has an effect on the definition of the norms. We first note that the type of a constant or the range type of a function must be either a base type or a type with a top-level constructor. A consequence of this is that any term whose type is a parameter is a variable. The term structure of any term assigned to this variable cannot be accessed or altered in any way within the local computation, since if it could, the type of the term would be known and thus the variable would be of a more specific type. Thus the term (and its size measured wrt to any norm) never changes and hence has no effect on termination at the local level. This means that when defining the norm $|.|_u$ where $u \in U$, the value of $|t|_u$ for any term t should be constant. To simplify the definition we assume the constant value is zero. Furthermore, the norm $|.|_u$ can be removed from any definition which depends on it.

Definition 13 induced typed norm. For each $\tau \in T_{arg}$ we define the hierarchical typed norm $|.|_\tau^s : \cup_{\psi \in \mathsf{Sub}_\tau} \mathsf{ED}_{\psi(\tau)} \to \mathsf{ED}_{\mathsf{Lin}}$ as the least set of equations E_τ^s as follows. If $\tau \in U$ then $E_\tau^s = \{|.|_\tau^s = 0\}$, else

$$E_\tau^s = \{\, |v|_\nu^s = v \mid \nu \in T_{sub}^\tau \,\} \cup$$
$$\left\{ |f(t_1,\ldots,t_n)|_\nu^s = w_s(f_{\psi(\sigma)}) + \sum_{i \in I_s(f_{\psi(\sigma)})} |t_i|_{\psi(\rho_i)}^s \;\middle|\; \begin{array}{l} \nu \in T_{sub}^\tau \wedge f_\sigma \in \Sigma_f \wedge \\ \sigma = \langle \rho_1 \ldots \rho_n, \rho \rangle \wedge \\ \nu = \psi(\rho) \wedge \psi \in \mathsf{Sub}_\tau \end{array} \right\}$$

A pair $s = \langle w_s, I_s \rangle$ is partially defined for each $\tau \in T_{arg}$ as follows. For each $\nu \in T_{sub}^\tau$ and $f_\sigma \in \Sigma_f$, $\sigma = \langle \rho_1 \ldots \rho_n, \rho \rangle$ such that $\nu = \psi(\rho)$ for some $\psi \in \mathsf{Sub}_\tau$, we add the mapping $f_{\psi(\sigma)} \mapsto w \in \mathbb{N}$ to w_s and the mapping $f_{\psi(\sigma)} \mapsto I \subseteq \{1,\ldots,n\}$ to I_s with the constraint that $i \notin I$ for all $\rho_i \in U$. □

Note that due to the definition of T_{sub}^τ each $|.|_{\psi(\sigma_i)}^s$ is defined in E_τ^s. Thus each E_τ^s is well defined pending a complete definition of the pair $s = \langle w_s, I_s \rangle$.

Example 12. Given T_{arg} as defined in example 11, we partially define a pair $\mathsf{p} = \langle w_\mathsf{p}, I_\mathsf{p} \rangle$ for the type $\mathsf{List}(\mathsf{List}(u))$ and a pair $\mathsf{q} = \langle w_\mathsf{q}, I_\mathsf{q} \rangle$ for the type $\mathsf{List}(u)$ as follows:

$$w_\mathsf{p} = \left\{ \begin{array}{l} \mathsf{Nil}_{\langle \epsilon, \mathsf{List}(\mathsf{List}(u)) \rangle} \mapsto w_1, \; \mathsf{Cons}_{\langle \mathsf{List}(u).\mathsf{List}(\mathsf{List}(u)), \mathsf{List}(\mathsf{List}(u)) \rangle} \mapsto w_2, \\ \mathsf{Nil}_{\langle \epsilon, \mathsf{List}(u) \rangle} \mapsto w_3, \quad\;\; \mathsf{Cons}_{\langle u.\mathsf{List}(u), \mathsf{List}(u) \rangle} \mapsto w_4 \end{array} \right\}$$
$$I_\mathsf{p} = \left\{ \begin{array}{l} \mathsf{Nil}_{\langle \epsilon, \mathsf{List}(\mathsf{List}(u)) \rangle} \mapsto \{\}, \; \mathsf{Cons}_{\langle \mathsf{List}(u).\mathsf{List}(\mathsf{List}(u)), \mathsf{List}(\mathsf{List}(u)) \rangle} \mapsto I_1 \subseteq \{1,2\} \\ \mathsf{Nil}_{\langle \epsilon, \mathsf{List}(u) \rangle} \mapsto \{\}, \quad\;\; \mathsf{Cons}_{\langle u.\mathsf{List}(u), \mathsf{List}(u) \rangle} \mapsto I_2 \subseteq \{2\} \end{array} \right\}$$
$$w_\mathsf{q} = \left\{ \mathsf{Nil}_{\langle \epsilon, \mathsf{List}(u) \rangle} \mapsto w_5, \mathsf{Cons}_{\langle u.\mathsf{List}(u), \mathsf{List}(u) \rangle} \mapsto w_6 \right\}$$
$$I_\mathsf{q} = \left\{ \mathsf{Nil}_{\langle \epsilon, \mathsf{List}(u) \rangle} \mapsto \{\}, \mathsf{Cons}_{\langle u.\mathsf{List}(u), \mathsf{List}(u) \rangle} \mapsto I_3 \subseteq \{2\} \right\}$$

where $w_1, w_2, w_3, w_4, w_5, w_6 \in \mathbb{N}$.

Choosing for example $w_1 = w_2 = w_3 = w_5 = 0, w_4 = w_6 = 1, I_1 = \{1,2\}$ and $I_2 = I_3 = \{2\}$ we derive the following equation sets

$$E^P_{\mathsf{List(List}(u))} = \left\{ \begin{array}{ll} |v|^P_{\mathsf{List(List}(u))} & = v, \\ |\mathsf{Nil}|^P_{\mathsf{List(List}(u))} & = 0, \\ |\mathsf{Cons}(t_1, t_2)|^P_{\mathsf{List(List}(u))} & = |t_1|^P_{\mathsf{List}(u)} + |t_2|^P_{\mathsf{List(List}(u))}, \\ |v|^P_{\mathsf{List}(u)} & = v, \\ |\mathsf{Nil}|^P_{\mathsf{List}(u)} & = 0, \\ |\mathsf{Cons}(t_1, t_2)|^P_{\mathsf{List}(u)} & = 1 + |t_2|^P_{\mathsf{List}(u)} \end{array} \right\}$$

$$E^q_{\mathsf{List}(u)} = \left\{ \begin{array}{ll} |v|^q_{\mathsf{List}(u)} & = v, \\ |\mathsf{Nil}|^q_{\mathsf{List}(u)} & = 0, \\ |\mathsf{Cons}(t_1, t_2)|^q_{\mathsf{List}(u)} & = 1 + |t_2|^q_{\mathsf{List}(u)} \end{array} \right\}$$

□

Note that the sets of terms for which the norms are defined are not disjoint. For example, the domain of the norm $|.|^P_{\mathsf{List(List}(u))}$ of example 12 is a subset of the domain for the norm $|.|^q_{\mathsf{List}(u)}$. There is no confusion, however, when deciding which norm to use on a particular argument of an atom since the choice is determined by the atom's predicate symbol.

Example 13. Consider the atom $Q_{\mathsf{List}(u)}(\mathsf{Cons}(\mathsf{Cons}(1, \mathsf{Nil}), \mathsf{Nil}))$ which may appear as part of a goal for the predicate $Q_{\mathsf{List}(u)}$. Although the type of the atom's argument is $\mathsf{List(List(Int))}$, the correct norm to use would be $|.|^q_{\mathsf{List}(u)}$ for some t since the type of the predicate is $\mathsf{List}(u)$. □

All that remains now to complete the definitions of our derived norms is to define suitable weight and index functions. This in itself is a non-trivial problem.

4.1 Defining the weight and index functions

Most of the approaches to termination analysis based on norms essentially use a simple generate-and-test method for deducing termination. Norms are generated (either automatically or otherwise) and used to form level mappings which are then applied to the program for which a termination proof is sought. Inequalities are then derived whose solubility indicates the success or failure of the termination proof.

The main difficulty with this approach is the potentially infinite number of norms that can be generated. To reduce the complexity of this problem a number of heuristics can be used. Decorte et al. [6], for example, propose the following (adapted) heuristics for deriving typed norms.

1. A weight of one is assigned to all functors of arity $n > 0$.
2. A weight of zero is assigned to all constants.
3. Any argument position whose type is not a parameter is selected.

Applying these heuristics to our partially derived norms allows us to obtain the same norms that would be derived by [6] given the same type information in the form of a type graph. Although this approach works well on a large number of examples, there are occasions when it will fail to generate norms that can be used in a termination proof. The naive reverse program with an accumulating parameter [6] is one example where a reduced number of arguments needs to be selected. In that paper a solution to this problem is sketched using *symbolic norms* which effectively define an argument index function through an exhaustive search. Also, below we give an example of where constants must be assigned weights other than zero.

Example 14. If each constant occurring in the program below is assigned a weight of zero then the interargument relation derived for Path(x, y) would be $|x| = |y| = 0$. With this relationship, termination cannot be proved since we require that $|x| > |z|$ in the recursive TransitiveClosure/2 clause. To prove termination each constant must take on a different value.

TransitiveClosure(x, y) ← Path(x, y).
TransitiveClosure(x, y) ← Path(x, z) ∧ TransitiveClosure(z, y).

Path(A, B).
Path(B, C).   □

This example seems to suggest that the determination of weights must take place as an integral part of a termination analysis – the variety of the weights occurring indicates the futility of a generate and test approach in this instance.

In summary, we see that there are several approaches to the problem of deriving the weight and index functions. We do not advocate any particular method here since it is necessary to further investigate and compare suitable methods. We believe that the open-ended definitions of our derived norms should facilitate such a study.

5 Related work

One weakness of [6] is that its norms are derived from type graphs. Type graph analyses, however, have not always been renowned for their tractability. Even for small programs, the prototype analyser of [12], used in [6], is typically 15 times slower than the optimising PLM compiler [15]. Recently, type graph analysis has been shown to be practical for *medium*-sized Prolog programs [14] when augmented with an improved widening and compacting procedure. In addition, Gallagher and de Waal have shown how type graphs can be efficiently represented as unary logic programs in [8]. Clearly, however, any approach which avoids the costs of inferring type graphs is preferable.

Bossi et al. [4] define a very general concept of norm in terms of type schemata which describe structural properties of terms. Their typed norms for termination analysis are very similar to the ones presented in this paper, though they are able to define some norms which cannot be inferred using our present framework.

Example 15. Consider the following program from [4]

Check(Cons(x, xs)) ← Check(xs).
Check(Cons(x, Nil)) ← Nat(x).
Nat(Succ(x)) ← Nat(x).
Nat(0).

We would like to define a norm $|.|_{\mathsf{List(Nat)}}$ so that we can prove termination for goals ← Check(x) where x is rigid wrt $|.|_{\mathsf{List(Nat)}}$. The following norm adapted from [4] satisfies this criterion.

$$|v|_{\mathsf{List(Nat)}} = v \qquad\qquad |v|_{\mathsf{Nat}} = v \qquad\qquad |v|_{\mathsf{Empty}} = v$$
$$|\mathsf{Cons}(t_1, t_2)|_{\mathsf{List(Nat)}} = 1 + |t_2|_{\mathsf{List(Nat)}} \qquad |0|_{\mathsf{Nat}} = 0 \qquad\qquad |\mathsf{Nil}|_{\mathsf{Empty}} = 0$$
$$|\mathsf{Cons}(t_1, t_2)|_{\mathsf{List(Nat)}} = |t_1|_{\mathsf{Nat}} + |t_2|_{\mathsf{Empty}} \quad |\mathsf{Succ}(t)|_{\mathsf{Nat}} = 1 + |t|_{\mathsf{Nat}}$$

This norm cannot be inferred automatically using our method (nor that of [6]) since it is necessary for the functor Cons to have two distinct types, namely $\langle \mathsf{Nat.List(Nat), List(Nat)} \rangle$ and $\langle \mathsf{Nat.Empty, List(Nat)} \rangle$, but this is forbidden in languages like Gödel where the declarations are universal. Note that this is not a limitation of our framework but rather a limitation of the type system on which it is based. Given a more flexible system it would be possible to infer such norms as the above directly from the prescribed types. □

We note that the typed norms of [4] are not derived automatically. By contrast, our norms, are simple enough to be easily derived using only the type declarations of a program.

6 Conclusions and future work

In this paper, we have presented a flexible method for inferring a number of norms from the type declarations of a program which are sufficient to measure the size of any Herbrand term occurring in the program in an almost arbitrary way. The norms are intended for use in termination analysis and the derivation of inter-argument relationships, though we believe that their applicability is not restricted to these areas. The definition of each derived norm is parameterised by a weight function and an argument index function. This open-ended definition allows the norms to be incorporated into a wide range of analyses which define these functions in different ways. We believe that defining weight and index functions in an efficient and intelligent way is a non-trivial problem in itself. Our definitions of norms provide a useful framework in which to study this problem.

It is our intention to examine exactly how these norms can be integrated into a termination analysis for typed logic programs. With a working termination analysis we will be able to assess the usefulness of the prescribed types in inferring norms. In particular, it would be interesting to quantify how much faster the typed (Gödel) approach is against the untyped (Prolog) approach. We will investigate how to define the weight and index functions such that a minimal number of useful norms are generated and we suspect that analysis can be used to achieve this.

Acknowledgements

We gratefully acknowledge Florence Benoy, John Gallagher, Corin Gurr, John Lloyd, Peter Holst Andersen and David Sands for their stimulating and useful discussions. We would also like to thank the anonymous referees for their constructive comments. This work was supported, in part, by the Nuffield grant ref. no. SCI/180/94/417/G. Jonathan Martin was supported by EPSRC studentship ref. no. 93315269.

References

1. K.R. Apt and D. Pedreschi. Studies in pure Prolog: Termination. In *Proceedings Esprit symposium on computational logic*, pages 150–176, Brussels, November 1990. Springer-Verlag.
2. F. Benoy and A. King. Inferring argument size relations with CLP($\mathcal{R}$). In *LOPSTR'96*. Springer-Verlag, 1996.
3. M. Bezem. Characterizing termination of logic programs with level mappings. In Ewing L. Lusk and Ross A. Overbeek, editors, *Proceedings of the North American Conference on Logic Programming*, pages 69–80, Cleveland, Ohio, USA, 1989.
4. A. Bossi, N. Cocco, and M. Fabris. Typed norms. In *ESOP'92*, pages 73–92, 1992.
5. A. Bossi, N. Cocco, and M. Fabris. Norms on terms and their use in proving universal termination of a logic program. *Theoretical Computer Science*, 124:297–328, 1994.
6. S. Decorte, D. de Schreye, and M. Fabris. Automatic inference of norms: A missing link in automatic termination analysis. In *ILPS'93*, pages 420–436, 1993.
7. S. Decorte, D. de Schreye, and M. Fabris. Exploiting the power of typed norms in automatic inference of interargument relations. Technical report, Dept. computer science, K.U.Leuven, 1994.
8. J. Gallagher and A. de Waal. Fast and precise regular approximations of logic programs. In *ICLP'94*, pages 599–613, 1994.
9. C. Gurr. *A Self-Applicable Partial Evaluator for the Logic Programming Language Gödel.* PhD thesis, University of Bristol, January 1994.
10. C. Gurr. Personal communication on the literature on termination analyses. September 1995.
11. P. M. Hill and J. W. Lloyd. *The Gödel Programming Language.* MIT Press, 1994.
12. G. Janssens and M. Bruynooghe. Deriving descriptions of possible values of program variables by means of abstract interpretation. *J. Logic Programming*, 13:205–258, 1992.
13. L. Plümer. *Termination Proofs for Logic Programs.* Springer-Verlag, 1990.
14. P. Van Hentenryck, A. Cortesi, and B. Le Charlier. Type Analysis of Prolog Using Type Graphs. In *PLDI'94*, pages 337–348. ACM Press, 1994.
15. P. Van Roy. A Prolog Compiler for the PLM. Master's thesis, Computer Science Division, University of California, Berkeley, 1984.

Partial Deduction in the Framework of Structural Synthesis of Programs

Mihhail Matskin, Jan Komorowski, John Krogstie
Department of Computer Systems
Norwegian University of Science and Technology
N-7033 Trondheim, Norway
{misha, janko}@idt.unit.no, john.krogstie@ac.com

Abstract. The notion of *partial deduction* known from logic programming is defined in the framework of *Structural Synthesis of Programs* (SSP). Partial deduction for unconditional computability statements in SSP is defined. Completeness and correctness of partial deduction in the framework of SSP are proven. Several tactics and stopping criteria are suggested.

1 Introduction

The main motivation for this work is to provide incremental formal program development in the framework of the proof-as-programs approach [3, 13]. In our case, it is Structural Synthesis of Programs [16, 20] (hence abbreviation SSP). In SSP, a specification at hand is transformed into a set of formulae of a logical language complete with respect to intuitionistic propositional logic. A problem to be solved is formulated as a theorem to be proven in this logic. A program is then extracted from the proof of the theorem. This approach has been implemented (see, for instance, [21]) and commercialized. It can be further strengthened by applying a principle similar to Partial Deduction as known in logic programming [7, 12, 9].

In this paper, we formulate the principle of partial deduction for SSP and prove its correctness and completeness in the new framework.

The rest of the paper is organized as follows. A brief informal introduction to SSP is given in Sect. 2. The next section presents partial deduction in SSP. Stopping criteria and tactics are discussed in Sect. 4. Concluding remarks are given in Sect. 5, where the use of partial SSP is briefly discussed. It is assumed that the reader is acquainted with partial deduction in logic programming.

2 Introduction to Structural Synthesis of Programs (SSP)

A formal foundation of SSP was developed by Mints and Tyugu [16, 20] and applied in a number of programming systems [21]. Here we give a brief introduction to the method and define notions which will be used later in the paper. First, the *LL* language of SSP is defined. Then inference rules are formulated using sequent notation. Program extraction is discussed next. It is obtained by extending the LL language.

2.1 Logical language (LL)

The logical language of SSP has only the following kinds of formulae:

1. Propositional variables: A, B, C ....
   A propositional variable A corresponds to an object variable a from the source problem, and it expresses the fact that a value of the object variable can be computed. A propositional variable will be termed an *atom* in the following.
2. Unconditional computability statements:

$$A_1 \& \ldots \& A_k \to B$$

This expresses computability of the value of the object variable b corresponding to B from values of $a_1 \ldots a_k$ corresponding to $\underline{A}$ ($\underline{A}$ is an abbreviation for $A_1 \& \ldots \& A_k$). $\underline{A}$ will be termed the body of the statement, whereas B is termed the head. Thus $body(\underline{A} \to B) = \underline{A}$ and $head(\underline{A} \to B) = B$.

3. Conditional computability statements

$$(\underline{A}^1 \to B^1) \& \ldots \& (\underline{A}^n \to B^n) \to (\underline{C} \to D)$$

A conditional computability statement such as $(A \to B) \to (C \to D)$ expresses computability of d from c depending on the computation of b from a. We also use $(\underline{A} \to B)$ as an abbreviation for $(\underline{A}^1 \to B^1) \& \ldots \& (\underline{A}^n \to B^n)$. In the statement $(\underline{A} \to B) \to (\underline{C} \to D)$, $(\underline{A} \to B)$ will be termed the body of the statement, whereas $(\underline{C} \to D)$ will be termed the head. The functions *head* and *body* are defined as above, whereas $body(body((A \to B) \to (C \to D))) = A$ etc.

2.2 Structural Synthesis Rules (SSR)

A sequent notation is used for the derivation rules. A sequent $\Gamma \vdash X$, where Γ is a list of formulae and X is a formula, means that the formula X is derivable from the formulae appearing in Γ. Axioms have a form of $\Gamma, X \vdash X$.

The SSR inference rule are as follows.

- 1. ($\to$ -)

$$\frac{\vdash \underline{A} \to V; \Gamma \vdash \underline{A}}{\Gamma \vdash V}$$

where $\Gamma \vdash \underline{A}$ is a set of sequents

- 2. ($\to$ +)

$$\frac{\Gamma, \underline{A} \vdash B}{\Gamma \vdash \underline{A} \to B}$$

– 3. $(\rightarrow --)$

$$\frac{\vdash (\underline{A} \rightarrow B) \rightarrow (\underline{C} \rightarrow V); \Gamma, \underline{A} \vdash B; \underline{\Delta} \vdash C}{\Gamma, \underline{\Delta} \vdash V}$$

where $\Gamma, \underline{A} \vdash B$ and $\underline{\Delta} \vdash C$ are sets of sequents.

It is somewhat surprising but LL with simple implicative formulae is equivalent to the intuitionistic propositional calculus. The intuitionistic completeness of SSR was proven [16]. In addition, an experiment with a programming system based on SSR was done [22]. In this experiment, all intuitionistic propositional theorems (about 100 formulae) contained in [6] were proven automatically.

2.3 Program extraction

In order to be able to extract programs from proofs, the language LL is extended as follows.

We write

$$\underline{A} \underset{f}{\rightarrow} B$$

where f is a term representing the function which computes b from $a_1, \ldots, a_n$. Analogously, we write

$$(\underline{A} \underset{g}{\rightarrow} B) \rightarrow (\underline{C} \underset{F(\underline{g},\underline{c})}{\longrightarrow} D)$$

where g is a term representing function which is synthesized in order to compute B from A and F is a term representing computation of D from C depending on g and $\underline{c}$ ($\underline{g}$ is a tuple of terms).

Following the notation in [20], $A(a)$ means that a is a term whose evaluation gives the value of the object variable corresponding to logical variable A. In the logical axioms which are written as $\Gamma, X(x) \vdash X(x)$, x is a variable or a constant.

The resulting language is termed $LL1$.

The modified inference rules (SSR1) are as follows:

– 1. $(\rightarrow -)$

$$\frac{\vdash \underline{A} \underset{f}{\rightarrow} V; \underline{\Gamma} \vdash A(\underline{a})}{\underline{\Gamma} \vdash V(f(\underline{a}))}$$

– 2. $(\rightarrow +)$

$$\frac{\Gamma, \underline{A} \vdash B(b)}{\Gamma \vdash \underline{A} \underset{\lambda \underline{a}.b}{\longrightarrow} B}$$

– 3. $(\rightarrow --)$

$$\frac{\vdash (\underline{A} \underset{g}{\rightarrow} B) \rightarrow (\underline{C} \underset{F(\underline{g},\underline{c})}{\longrightarrow} V); \Gamma, \underline{A} \vdash B(b); \underline{\Delta} \vdash C(c)}{\underline{\Gamma}, \underline{\Delta} \vdash V(F(\lambda \underline{a}.b, \underline{c}))}$$

A problem to be solved is formulated as a theorem to be proven. An example theorem and its proof are given in the next section.

2.4 A Specification Level

Whereas the $LL1$ language specifies the internal language for structural synthesis, higher level languages are defined for expressing problem specifications. One of these, the NUT language [21], is used in the sequel. It is an object-oriented language where methods and structural relations can be translated into formulae of the $LL1$ language.

The working example in this paper is a definition of the **inverter**, **and**-port and **nand**-port of logical circuits.

ELEMENT
>   **var** Delay:<u>numeric</u>;

INVERTER
>   <u>super</u> ELEMENT;
>   <u>vir</u> InINV, OutINV: <u>bool</u>;
>   <u>rel</u> inv: InINV -> OutINV
>   {OutINV := <u>not</u> InINV}

INVERTER is a subclass of **ELEMENT**, having two virtual boolean primitive type specifiers InINV and OutINV. Virtual components can be used in computations, but their values are not contained in the value of the object. The method inv specifies computations of OutINV from InINV which are performed by sequence of statements (body of the method) in the curly brackets. Actually, we can consider this method as a language construction for $InINV \xrightarrow[f]{} OutINV$ where f refers to the body of the method, i. e. to {OutINV := <u>not</u> InINV}.

AND
>   <u>super</u> ELEMENT;
>   <u>vir</u> InAND1, InAND2, OutAND: <u>bool</u>;
>   <u>rel</u> and: InAND1,InAND2->OutAND
>   {OutAND:=InAND1 & InAND2}

NAND
>   <u>super</u> INVERTER;
>   <u>super</u> AND;
>   <u>vir</u> InNAND1, InNAND2, OutNAND: <u>bool</u>;
>   <u>rel</u> InAND1 = InNAND1; InAND2 = InNAND2;
>   OutNAND = OutINV; InINV = OutAND;
>   nand: InNAND1, InNAND2 -> OutNAND{<u>specification</u>}

Symbol "=" denotes equality methods which are transformed into two formulae of $LL1$. For example, InAND1 = InNAND1 is transformed into $InAND1 \xrightarrow[asg]{} InNAND1$ and $InNAND1 \xrightarrow[asg]{} InAND1$, where asg is the name of the standard function performing assignment. **specification** in the last method indicates that a function for the **nand** method has not been developed yet.

The interested reader can find a full description of NUT in [23].

The description of the class **NAND** can be now transformed into the following set of logical formulae (called problem-oriented axioms), where *and*, *inv* and *asg* indicate methods which implement the corresponding formulae:

$$\vdash InINV \xrightarrow[inv]{} OutINV; \vdash InAND1 \& InAND2 \xrightarrow[and]{} OutAND;$$

$$\vdash InAND1 \xrightarrow[asg]{} InNAND1; \vdash InNAND1 \xrightarrow[asg]{} InAND1;$$

$$\vdash InAND2 \xrightarrow[asg]{} InNAND2; \vdash InNAND2 \xrightarrow[asg]{} InAND2;$$

$$\vdash OutNAND \xrightarrow[asg]{} OutINV; \vdash OutINV \xrightarrow[asg]{} OutNAND;$$

$$\vdash InINV \xrightarrow[asg]{} OutAND; \vdash OutAND \xrightarrow[asg]{} InINV;$$

The theorem to be proven is $\vdash InNAND1, InNAND2 \to OutNAND$. Using the set of formulae and the inference rules from Sect. 2.2, the following proof can be made:

$$InNAND1(in1) \vdash InNAND1(in1); \vdash InNAND1 \xrightarrow[asg]{} InAND1;$$

$$\underline{InNAND2(in2) \vdash InNAND1(in2); InNAND2 \xrightarrow[asg]{} InAND2}_{(\to -)}$$
$$InNAND2(in2) \vdash InAND(asg(in2))$$

$$InNAND1(in1) \vdash InAND1(asg(in1))$$

$$\underline{\vdash InAND1 \& InAND2 \xrightarrow[and]{} OutAND}_{(\to -)}$$
$$InNAND1(in1), InNAND2(in2) \vdash OutAND(and(asg(in1), asg(in2)))$$

$$\underline{\vdash OutAND \xrightarrow[asg]{} InINV;}_{(\to -)}$$
$$InNAND1(in1), InNAND2(in2) \vdash InINV(asg(and(asg(in1), asg(in2))))$$

$$\underline{\vdash InINV \xrightarrow[inv]{} OutINV;}_{(\to -)}$$
$$InNAND1(in1), InNAND2(in2) \vdash OutINV(inv(asg(and(asg(in1), asg(in2)))))$$

$$\underline{\vdash OutINV \xrightarrow[asg]{} OutNAND}_{(\to -)}$$
$$InNAND1(in1), InNAND2(in2) \vdash OutNAND(asg(inv(asg(and(asg(in1), asg(in2))))))$$

$$\underline{\vdash InNAND1 \& InNAND2 \xrightarrow[\lambda in1\ in2.asg(inv(asg(and(asg(in1), asg(in2)))))]{} OutAND}_{(\to +)}$$

Q.E.D.

The extracted program is as follows

$$\lambda in1\ in2.asg(inv(asg(and(asg(in1), asg(in2)))))$$

or in a simplified form

$$\lambda in1\ in2.inv(and(in1, in2))$$

The example considered here is, of course, very small. The approach is, however, scalable. Problem specifications containing thousands of variables and computability statements have been developed [17].

3 Partial deduction in SSP

Partial deduction (a.k.a. partial evaluation in logic programming) is a specialization principle related to the law of syllogism [12, 8]. Our motivation for transferring Partial Deduction (PD) to the framework of SSP is based on the following observations:

- PD provides a specialization of logic programs. The most important features of PD is that more efficient programs can be generated. Efficiency for a residual program can be discussed in terms of the size of derivation trees.

  The same observation is true for SSP. Residual program specification can be more efficient in terms of synthesis of programs.

- Our experience with the NUT system shows that users are not always able to specify completely goals such as $\underline{A} \to G$. In many cases, the user knows/ remembers only the input parameters of the problem and s/he does not care about the output parameters. In this case, s/he is satisfied with result that everything that is computable from inputs is computed. For example, the user may know that inputs of the problem are values for InNAND1 and InNAND2 of the NAND element and s/he would like to know which other values can be computed. This feature is supported by the program statement compute, e.g. NAND.compute(InNAND1, InNAND2). This problem arises especially for specifications containing a large number of variables (very large circuits). These goals are hardly expressible in $LL1$. The problem is that one would take into account a set of all variables of the specification and all subsets of this set. Additionally, an order over the subsets has to be defined and possible output parameters considered as a disjunction of the subsets. This is a very inefficient approach.

  On the other hand PD allows us to make efficient derivations even if the output parameters of the problem are unknown. This issue will be discussed in Sect. 4.

- A problem similar to the above mentioned one, but with another type of incompleteness, may also arise. Consider a situation in which the user knows outputs of problem but s/he is not able to specify inputs. Actually, this relates mostly to debugging of specifications. If the original problem is not solvable, what should be added into the problem specification in order to make it solvable?

  Also in this case PD provides a good framework for making assumptions.

  It is possible to apply PD at different levels in the framework of SSP:

- At the $LL1$ specification.
- At the resulting functional expressions.
- At the meta-specification.

Here we consider the first of the above cases and, in particular, the unconditional computability statements of $LL1$. The second case has been studied elsewhere and by numerous authors, see, for instance, [2, 1, 5]. Work has also been done on applying PD at the meta-specification level [4, 15].

Before moving further on we formalize the notion PD in the SSP framework.

3.1 Partial deduction of $LL1$ specifications

It is natural to informally express PD of unconditional computability statements as follows.

Let A, B and C be propositional variables and $A \underset{f}{\to} B, B \underset{h}{\to} C, C \underset{g}{\to} D$ be unconditional computability statements. Some possible partial deductions are the following: $A \xrightarrow{\lambda a.h(f(a))} C, A \xrightarrow{\lambda a.g(h(f(a)))} D, B \xrightarrow{\lambda b.g(h(b))} D$. It is easy to notice that the first partial deduction corresponds to forward chaining (from inputs to outputs), the third one corresponds to backward chaining (from outputs to inputs) and the second one to either forward or backward chaining.

The main difference between our definition of PD and the ones considered in [12, 8, 9] are: (i) the use of logic specifications rather then logic programs and (ii) the use of intuitionistic (propositional) logic rather then classical (first order) logic.

Definition 1 ($LL1$ specification) *Let $\mathcal{U}$ be a set of unconditional computability statements $\underline{A} \underset{f}{\to} B$ and $\mathcal{S}$ be a set of conditional computability statements $(\underline{A} \underset{g}{\to} B) \to (\underline{C} \xrightarrow{F(\underline{g},\underline{c})} D)$ then $P = \mathcal{U} \cup \mathcal{S}$ is called a $LL1$ specification.*

Definition 2 ($LL1$ unconditional resultant) *An $LL1$ **unconditional resultant** is an unconditional computability statement $\underline{A} \xrightarrow{\lambda \underline{a}.f(a)} G$ where f is a term representing the function which computes G from potentially composite functions over $a_1, \ldots, a_n$*

The assumption that G is an atom can be relaxed by transformation of $A \underset{f}{\to} G$ into $\{\underline{A} \underset{f}{\to} G_1, \ldots, \underline{A} \underset{f}{\to} G_m\}$ and vice versa.

In our definitions we use the notion of computation rule (or selection function) from logic programming [11].

Definition 3 (Derivation of an $LL1$ unconditional resultant) *Let $\mathfrak{R}$ be a fixed computation rule. A **derivation of a $LL1$ unconditional resultant** R_0 is a finite sequence of $LL1$ resultants: $R_0 \Rightarrow_{\mathfrak{R}} R_1 \Rightarrow_{\mathfrak{R}} R_2 \Rightarrow_{\mathfrak{R}} \ldots$, where,*

(1) for each j, R_j is an unconditional computability statement of the form

$$\underline{B_1 \& \ldots \& B_i \& \ldots \& B_n} \xrightarrow{\lambda \underline{b_1} \ldots \underline{b_i} \ldots \underline{b_n}.f(b_1,\ldots,b_i,\ldots,b_n)} G$$

and R_{j+1} (if any) is of the form:

$$\underline{B_1 \& ... \& \underline{C} \& ... \& B_n} \xrightarrow{\quad \lambda \underline{b_1}...\underline{c}...\underline{b_n}.f(\underline{b_1},...,h(\underline{c}),...\underline{b_n}) \quad} G$$

if

- *the $\Re$-selected atom in R_j is B_i and*
- *there exists an unconditional computability statement $\underline{C} \xrightarrow{h} B_i \in P$*

called the matching computability statement. B_i is called the matching atom.

(2) for each j, R_j is an unconditional computability statement of the form

$$\underline{A_1 \& ... \& A_i \& ... \& A_m} \xrightarrow{\quad \lambda \underline{a_1}...\underline{a_i}...\underline{a_m}.f(\underline{a_1},...,\underline{a_i},...,\underline{a_m}) \quad} F$$

and R_{j+1} (if any) is of the form:

$$\underline{A_1 \& ... \& A_i \& ... \& A_m} \xrightarrow{\quad \lambda \underline{a_1}...\underline{a_i}...\underline{a_m}.h(\underline{a_i},f(\underline{a_1},...,\underline{a_i},...,\underline{a_m})) \quad} H$$

if

- *the $\Re$-selected atoms in R_j are $\underline{A_i}$ and/or $\underline{F}$. $\underline{F}$ denotes a conjunction of F (heads of computability statements) from resultants $R_0,...,R_j$.*
- *there exists an unconditional computability statement $\underline{A_i} \& \underline{F} \xrightarrow{h} H \in P$ called the matching computability statement. A_i, F are called the matching atoms.*

(3) If R_{j+1} does not exist, R_j is called a leaf resultant.

Definition 3 gives two ways of derivating resultants. (1) corresponds to backward derivations and (2) corresponds to forward derivations. We will use terms derivation form (1) and derivation form (2), correspondingly.

Definition 4 (Partial deduction of a propositional goal) *A partial deduction of a propositional goal $\underline{A} \to G$ in a specification P is the set of leaf resultants derived from $G \to G$ (derivation form (1) and in this case $\underline{A}$ cannot be selected atoms) or from $\underline{A} \to$ (derivation form (2) and in this case G cannot be selected atom).*

The assumption that G is an atom can be relaxed to allow a conjunction of atoms, $\underline{A} \to \underline{G}$, and a partial deduction of $\underline{A} \to \underline{G}$ in P is the union of partial deductions of $\mathbf{G} = \{\underline{A} \to G_1, ..., \underline{A} \to G_m\}$ in P. These partial deductions are called *residual unconditional computability statements*.

Definition 5 (Partial deduction of an $LL1$ specification) *A partial deduction of a $LL1$ specification P wrt $\mathbf{G}$ is a specification P' (also called a residual $LL1$ specification) obtained from P by replacing computability statements having G_i in their heads (derivation form (1)) or only variables from $\underline{A}$ in their bodies (derivation form (2)) by corresponding partial deductions.*

The notions of correctness and completeness are defined as follows. Let P be a $LL1$ specification, $\underline{A} \to G$ a propositional goal, and P' a partial deduction of P wrt to $\underline{A} \to G$.

Definition 6 (Correctness of partial deduction of $LL1$ specification) *The function (or its computational equivalent) for the computation of $\underline{A} \to G$ is derivable (can be extracted from a proof of $\underline{A} \to G$) from P if it is derivable from P'.*

Completeness is the converse:

Definition 7 (Completeness of partial deduction of $LL1$ specifications) *The function (or its computational equivalent) for the computation of $\underline{A} \to G$ is derivable (can be extracted from a proof of $\underline{A} \to G$) from P' if it is derivable from P.*

Our definitions of correctness and completeness require only derivation of a function which implements the goal (all functions which satisfy this criteria are computational equivalents). This may correspond, for example, to the following case. Let an $LL1$ *specification* contains computability statements $\underline{C} \underset{h}{\to} B$ and $\underline{C} \underset{f}{\to} B$. Then functions f and h are computational equivalents.

The notions of correctness and completeness are defined with respect to the possibility of proving the goal and extracting a function from the proof [10]. Our proof of correctness and completeness is based on proving that derivation of $LL1$ unconditional resultant is a derivation (proof + program extraction) in a calculus corresponding to the $LL1$ language.

Lemma 1 *Derivation form (1) of $LL1$ unconditional resultants is a derivation by SSR1 inference rules.*

Proof Consider the case, when

$$R_j = \underline{B_1 \& ... \& B_i \& ... \& B_n} \xrightarrow{\lambda \underline{b_1}...\underline{b_i}...\underline{b_n}.f(\underline{b_1},...,\underline{b_i},...,\underline{b_n})} G$$

or in a short form

$$R_j = \underline{B_1 \& B_2 \& B_3} \xrightarrow{\lambda \underline{b_1}b_2\underline{b_3}.f(\underline{b_1},b_2,\underline{b_3})} G$$

and the matching computability statement is $\underline{C} \underset{h}{\to} B_2$

According to **Definition 3** the $LL1$ unconditional resultant will be

$$\underline{B_1 \& C \& B_3} \xrightarrow{\lambda \underline{b_1}c\underline{b_3}.f(\underline{b_1},h(\underline{c}),\underline{b_3})} G$$

R_j and the matching computability statement have the form of the following problem-oriented axioms in the calculus for $LL1$ language:

$$\vdash \underline{B_1 \& B_2 \& B_3} \xrightarrow{\lambda \underline{b_1}b_2\underline{b_3}.f(\underline{b_1},b_2,\underline{b_3})} G$$

$$\vdash \underline{C} \underset{h}{\to} B_2$$

Given these axioms, the following derivation is obtained by SSR1 inference rules:

$$\frac{C(c) \vdash C(c); \quad B_1(b_1) \vdash B_1(b_1); \quad B_3(b_3) \vdash B_3(b_3); \quad \underline{C} \underset{h}{\to} B_2;}{C(c) \vdash B_2(h(\underline{c})); \quad \vdash \underline{B_1} \& B_2 \& B_3 \xrightarrow[\lambda \underline{b_1} b_2 \underline{b_3}.f(\underline{b_1}, b_2, \underline{b_3})]{} G;} (\to -)$$

$$\frac{}{B_1(b_1), \underline{C}(c), B_3(b_3) \vdash G((\lambda \underline{b_1} b_2 \underline{b_3}.f(\underline{b_1}, b_2, \underline{b_3}))(\underline{b_1}, h(\underline{c}), \underline{b_3}))} (\to -)$$

$$\frac{}{\vdash \underline{B_1} \& \underline{C} \& B_3 \xrightarrow[\lambda \underline{b_1} c \underline{b_3}.((\lambda \underline{b_1} b_2 \underline{b_3}.f(\underline{b_1}, b_2, \underline{b_3}))(\underline{b_1}, h(\underline{c}), \underline{b_3}))]{} G} (\to +)$$

After a simplification of the λ-expression under the arrow in the last sequent we end up with:

$$\underline{B_1} \& \underline{C} \& B_3 \xrightarrow[\lambda \underline{b_1} c \underline{b_3}.f(\underline{b_1}, h(\underline{c}), \underline{b_3})]{} G$$

which is equal to the $LL1$ unconditional resultant.

The above derivation is a derivation of the inference rule which corresponds to the PD step:

$$\frac{\vdash \underline{B_1} \& B_2 \& B_3 \xrightarrow[\lambda \underline{b_1} b_2 \underline{b_3}.f(\underline{b_1}, b_2, \underline{b_3})]{} G; \quad \vdash \underline{C} \underset{h}{\to} B_2}{\vdash \underline{B_1} \& \underline{C} \& B_3 \xrightarrow[\lambda \underline{b_1} c \underline{b_3}.f(\underline{b_1}, h(\underline{c}), \underline{b_3})]{} G}$$

If the unconditional computability statements are in the form of resultants and matching statements (see **Definition 3**), then a derivation in the calculus corresponding to the LL1 language will be done in accordance to the derived inference rule.

Q.E.D.

Lemma 2 *Derivation form (2) of LL1 unconditional resultants is a derivation by SSR1 inference rules.*

Proof The proof of **Lemma 2** is analogous to the proof of **Lemma 1**. The only difference is in the derivation of the inference rule for PD. We describe only the essential part of the proof and omit the part of the proof which is common with the previous proof.

R_j and matching computability statements in calculus for $LL1$ language have the form of the following problem-oriented axioms:

$$\vdash \underline{A_1} \& \underline{A_2} \& A_3 \xrightarrow[\lambda a_1 a_2 a_3.f(a_1, a_2, a_3)]{} F$$

$$\vdash \underline{A_2} \& F \underset{h}{\to} H$$

Hence, the following derivation is obtained by SSR1 inference rules:

$$A_1(a_1) \vdash A_1(a_1); \ A_2(a_2) \vdash A_2(a_2); \ A_3(a_3) \vdash A_3(a_3);$$

$$\cfrac{\cfrac{A_1 \& A_2 \& A_3 \xrightarrow[\lambda a_1 a_2 a_3 . f(a_1, a_2, a_3)]{} F}{A_1(a_1), A_2(a_2), A_3(a_3) \vdash F((\lambda a_1 a_2 a_3 . f(a_1, a_2, a_3))(a_1, a_2, a_3)); \vdash A_2 \& F \xrightarrow[h]{} H}(\rightarrow -)}{\cfrac{A_1(a_1), A_2(a_2), A_3(a_3) \vdash H(h(a_2, (\lambda a_1 a_2 a_3 . f(a_1, a_2, a_3))(a_1, a_2, a_3)))}{\vdash A_1 \& A_2 \& A_3 \xrightarrow[\lambda a_1 \lambda a_2 \lambda a_3 \ h(a_2, (\lambda a_1 a_2 a_3 . f(a_1, a_2, a_3))(a_1, a_2, a_3)))]{} F}(\rightarrow +)}(\rightarrow -)$$

A simplification of the λ-expression in the last sequent leads to

$$A_1 \& A_2 \& A_3 \xrightarrow[\lambda a_1 a_2 a_3 . h(a_2, f(a_1, a_2, a_3))]{} F$$

which is equal to the $LL1$ unconditional resultant.

The above derivation is a derivation of the inference rule which corresponds to the PD step:

$$\cfrac{\vdash A_1 \& A_2 \& A_3 \xrightarrow[\lambda a_1 a_2 a_3 . f(a_1, a_2, a_3)]{} F; \ \vdash A_2 \& F \xrightarrow[h]{} H}{\vdash A_1 \& A_2 \& A_3 \xrightarrow[\lambda a_1 a_2 a_3 . h(a_2, f(a_1, a_2, a_3))]{} H}$$

In case of a conjunction F in the matching computability statement, a set of resultants R_j $(0 > j > j+1)$ for all F_i from F is considered.

Q.E.D.

Theorem 1 (Correctness and Completeness of PD in $LL1$ specification)
Partial Deduction of a LL1 specification is correct and complete.

Proof of the theorem immediately follows from **Lemma 1** and **Lemma 2**. Since PD is a proof by SSR1 inference rules proof of $A \rightarrow G$ in P' is a subproof of $A \rightarrow G$ in P where paths to resultants are replaced by the derived resultants themselves. It means that both specifications P and P' are equal with respect to derivation of the goal and extraction of a program.

3.2 Partial deduction of conditional computability statements

Until now we have considered only unconditional computability statements as sources for PD. In case of conditional computability statements, the main framework for definitions is the same. However, particular definitions become more complicated. Here we do not consider all definitions for PD of conditional statements but rather point out most important moments.

Definition 8 (*LL1* conditional resultant) *A* **LL1 conditional resultant** *is a conditional computability statement* $\underline{(D \to E)} \to A \xrightarrow{\lambda \underline{ag}.F(\underline{a},\underline{g})} G$ *where F is a term representing the function which computes G from potentially composite functions over* $a_1, \dots, a_n, g_1, \dots, g_n$ *(*$g_1, \dots, g_n$ *are terms for all* $\underline{(D \to E)}$*)*.

We would like to notice that the main difference in this case is the treatment of nested implications.

There are several possibilities to apply conditional computability statements in PD. Conditional resultant can be a matching statement for derivation of unconditional resultant as follows.

Definition 9 (Derivation of an *LL1* unconditional resultant) *[with conditional computability statements]. Let $\Re$ be a fixed computation rule. A* **derivation of an *LL1* unconditional resultant** R_0 **with conditional computability statements** *is a finite sequence of LL1 resultants:* $R_0 \Rightarrow_\Re R_1 \Rightarrow_\Re R_2 \Rightarrow_\Re \dots$, *where,*

(4) if R_j is an unconditional computability statement of the form

$$\underline{B_1} \& \dots \& B_i \& \dots \& B_n \xrightarrow{\lambda \underline{b_1} \dots \underline{b_i} \dots \underline{b_n}.f(\underline{b_1}, \dots, \underline{b_i}, \dots, \underline{b_n})} G$$

then R_{j+1} (if any) is of the form:

$$\underline{(D \to E)} \to (\underline{B_1} \& \dots \& \underline{C} \& \dots \& B_n \xrightarrow{\lambda \underline{gb_1} \dots \underline{c} \dots \underline{b_n}.f(\underline{b_1}, \dots, h(\underline{g},\underline{c}), \dots, \underline{b_n})} G)$$

if

- *the $\Re$-selected atom in R_j is B_i and*
- *there exists a conditional computability statement*

$$\underline{(D \xrightarrow{g} E)} \to (C \xrightarrow{h(\underline{g},\underline{c})} B_i) \in P$$

called the matching computability statement. B_i is called the matching atom.

(5) if R_j is an unconditional computability statement of the form

$$\underline{A_1} \& \dots \& \underline{A_i} \& \dots \& \underline{A_m} \xrightarrow{\lambda \underline{a_1} \dots \underline{a_i} \dots \underline{a_m}.f(\underline{a_1}, \dots, \underline{a_i}, \dots, \underline{a_m})} F$$

then R_{j+1} (if any) is of the form:

$$\underline{(D \to E)} \to (\underline{A_1}, \dots, \underline{A_i}, \dots, \underline{A_m} \xrightarrow{\lambda \underline{ga_1} \dots \underline{a_i} \dots \underline{a_m}.h(\underline{g},\underline{a_i},f(\underline{a_1}, \dots, \underline{a_i}, \dots, \underline{a_m}))} H)$$

if

- *the $\Re$-selected atoms in R_j are $\underline{A_i}$ and/or $\underline{F}$. $\underline{F}$ denotes a conjunction of F (heads of computability statements) from resultants $R_0, ..., R_j$*
- *there exists a conditional computability statement*

$$(\underline{D \underset{g}{\to} E}) \to (\underline{A_i}, \underline{F} \xrightarrow{\quad h(\underline{g}, \underline{a_i}, f) \quad} H) \in P$$

called the matching computability statement. A_i, F are called the matching atoms.

Derivation of conditional resultants by unconditional computability statements can be considered as separate derivations of the head and body of conditional statements. Derivation of heads is similar to derivations of unconditional resultants. However, derivation of bodies is more complicated. We remind that bodies of conditional statements describe a function (program) to be synthesized. Actually, they are subgoals of a general goal. In our case, PD of a goal (subgoal) does not make sense (c.f. Definition 4 where $\underline{A}$ and G cannot be selected atoms in derivations form (1) and (2) correspondingly). The only way to apply PD in this case is to have an ordered set of derivations with respect to the goal and the subgoals.

This is not the only problem with PD of bodies of conditional statements. Assumptions from the head of the conditional statement can be used during derivation of subgoals. For example, if we have a conditional resultant

$$(\underline{D \to E}) \to (\underline{A_1} \& ... \& \underline{A_i} \& ... \& \underline{A_m} \xrightarrow{\quad \lambda \underline{ga_1}...\underline{a_i}...\underline{a_m}.h(\underline{g}, \underline{a_i}, f(\underline{a_1}, ..., \underline{a_i}, ..., \underline{a_m})) \quad} H)$$

then the proof of $(\underline{D \to E})$ may use $\underline{A_1}, ..., \underline{A_i}, ..., \underline{A_m}$ as assumptions. This causes a more complex form of resultants.

Unfortunately, derivation of conditional resultants with conditional computability statements cannot be defined in our framework. In this case we would have come up with more then one level of nested implications in the resulting formulae. This is out of the scope of the language defined in the Sect. 2.

Correctness and completeness for derivations of resultants with conditional computability statements are defined similarly to those in Sect. 3., this subject is out of the scope of this paper.

4 Partial Deduction tactics

PD is a very simple principle and its practical value is limited without defining appropriate strategies. These are called tactics and refer to the selection and stopping criteria. We describe them informally.

4.1 Selection criteria

Selection functions (computation rules) define which formula should be tried next for derivation of resultant. We consider the following possible selection criteria.

1. *Unconditional computability statements are selected first and if there is no unconditional computability statements that can be applied to derivation of resultant then a conditional statement (if any) is selected.*

   This is the main selection criterion which is implemented in the NUT system. This criterion keeps simplicity of derivation when it is possible. However it does not say which unconditional/conditional statement to choose next if more then one statement is applicable at the same time.

2. *Priority based selection criteria.*

   These criteria require binding priorities to computability statements. They should be done by user. Synthesis with priorities was considered in some work on SSP. The most reasonable base for priorities is an estimated computational cost of function/program which implements computations specified by computability statements. Whenever it is possible to obtain such costs, the criterion allows to synthesize more efficient program. This criterion allows to make decision when the same objects can be computed by different functions. Until now the criterion was implemented only experimentally.

3. *Only a specified set of computability statements is used in the derivation.*

   This criterion requires partitioning of the set of statements. It is not realistic to ask the user to point out particular computability statements which could be used in derivation. However, such partitioning can be done on the level of the specification language. For example, the user can specify that s/he would like to perform computations on objects of class NAND only and then only computability statements derived from this class description are considered for the derivations. This criterion is implemented and widely used in the NUT system and it is a feature of object-orientation rather than of the logical part of the system (message sending to an object means that the context of computations/ derivations is restricted by this object).

4. *A mixture of forward and backward derivations.*

   This is quite interesting but a less investigated criterion. The idea is to develop derivation forms (1) and (2) (see Sect. 2) concurrently or in parallel. It means that computability statements are selected to support derivations of both resultants in some order. It can be strict alteration or some other criterion. We think that such criteria should be investigated in more detail in the context of distributed computations. Another application of this approach was investigated in the context of debugging of specifications [14].

We would like to notice that the above criteria are not mutually exclusive but rather complementary to each other.

4.2 Stopping criteria

Stopping criteria define when to stop derivation of resultants. They can be combined freely with all the selection criteria above. We suggest the following stopping criteria.

1. *Stepwise*: The user is queried before each derivation which of the possible derivations s/he wants to perform. Actually, this stopping criterion can be of interest in debugging and providing the user with traces of the derivation process.
2. *Restricted*: A goal is given together with an indicator of the maximum depth of the derivation. This criteria is of a similar virtue as the previous one.
3. *Goal-based:* A derivation stops when resultant is equal to the goal. This criterion allows to synthesize a program when the goal is completely defined. A more interesting case is specialization of this criterion to a mixture of forward and backward derivations. In this case, a derivation can stop when bodies of resultants of derivation form (1) (backward derivation) are included in the union of bodies and heads of resultants of derivation form (2) (forward derivation).
4. *Exhaustive:* A derivation stops when no new resultants are available. This is the case when goals are not specified completely (Sect. 3) or when problem is not solvable (derivation of the goal can not be done).

The last stopping criteria is very important for PD and makes possible deriving programs from incompletely specified goals. Notice that the *Goal − based* criterion allows to derive programs in case of completely specified goals.

5   Concluding remarks

The notion of partial deduction has been transferred from logic programming to the framework of SSP. Our main results are a definition of partial deduction in this framework, a proof of completeness and correctness of PD in the framework and a set of selection criteria for utilizing them together with a set of stopping criteria.

In addition to the theoretical interest partial SSP defines a method for synthesis of programs in the case of incompletely specified goal. One specific application of the partial deduction technique in connection with SSP is to support debugging of $LL1$-specifications. In case of a non-solvable problem (a propositional goal cannot be derived) PD of an $LL1$ specification contains the set of all possible derivations and is a good starting point for reasoning about possible inconsistency and/or incompleteness of the specification [14].

This paper has focused on partial deduction of the unconditional computability statements. We have only pointed out how the approach can be extended to the case of conditional computability statements. This and tactics supporting a mixture of backward and forward derivations of resultants will be investigated in future.

References

1. M. Z. Ariola and Arvind. A syntactic approach to program transformation. In *Proceedings of the symposium on Partial Evaluation and Semantics-Based Program Manipulation (PEPM'91)*, pages 116–129. ACM press, 1991.

2. D. Bjørner, A. P. Ershov, and N. D. Jones, editors. *Partial Evaluation and Mixed Computation*, Gammel Avernæs, October 18–24 1987. North-Holland.

3. R.L. Constable, S.F. Allen, H.M. Bromley et al. Implementing mathematics with the Nurpl Proof development system Prentice-Hall, 1986.

4. H-M. Haav and M. Matskin. Using partial deduction for automatic propagation of changes in OODB. In H. Kangassalo et al, editor, *Information Modeling and Knowledge Bases IV*, pages 339–352. IOS Press, 1993.

5. N. D. Jones, C. K. Gomard, and P. Sesoft. *Partial Evaluation and Automatic Program Generation*. Prentice Hall, Englewood Cliffs, NJ, 1993.

6. S. Kleene. Introduction to metamathematics. Amsterdam, North-Holland, 1952.

7. J. Komorowski. *A Specification of An Abstract Prolog Machine and Its Application to Partial Evaluation*. PhD thesis, Department of Computer and Information Science, Linköping University, Linköping, Sweden, 1981.

8. J. Komorowski. Partial evaluation as a means for inferencing data structures in an applicative language: a theory and implementation in the case of Prolog. Proc. of the ACM Symp. Principles of Programming Languages, ACM, pp. 255–267, 1982.

9. J. Komorowski. A Prolegomenon to partial deduction. *Fundamenta Informaticae*, 18(1):41–64, January 1993.

10. I. Krogstie and M. Matskin. Incorporating partial deduction in structural synthesis of program. Technical Report 0802-6394 5/94, IDT, NTH, Trondheim, Norway, June 1994.

11. J. W. Lloyd. Foundations of logic programming. Springer Verlag, second edition, 1987.

12. J. W. Lloyd and J. C. Shepherdson. Partial evaluation in logic programming. , Journal of Logic Programming, 1991:11:217-242, also: Technical Report CS-87-09 (revised 1989), University of Bristol, England, July 1989.

13. Z. Manna, R. Waldinger. A Deductive approach to program synthesis. ACM Trans. on Programming Languages and Systems, 2(1):294:327, Jan, 1980.

14. M. Matskin. Debugging in programming systems with structural synthesis of programs (in Russian). *Software*, 4:21–26, 1983.

15. M. Matskin and J. Komorowski. Partial deduction and manipulation of classes and objects in an object-oriented environment. In *Proceedings of the First Compulog-Network Workshop on Programming Languages in Computational Logic*, Pisa, Italy, April 6-7 1992.

16. G. Mints and E. Tyugu. Justification of structural synthesis of programs. *Science of Computer Programming*, 2(3):215–240, 1982.

17. J. Pahapill. Programmpaket zur modeliering der hydromachinen systeme. 6. Fachtagung Hydraulik und Pneumatik, Magdeburg, pp. 609-617, 1985.

18. D. A. Schmidt. Static properties of partial evaluation. In Bjørner et al. [2], pages 465–483.

19. E. Tyugu. The structural synthesis of programs. In *Algorithms in Modern Mathematics and Computer Science*, number 122 in Lecture Notes in Computer Science, pages 261–289, Berlin, 1981. Springer-Verlag.

20. E. Tyugu. *Knowledge-Based Programming*. Turing Institute press, 1988.

21. E. Tyugu. Three new-generation software environments. *Communications of the ACM*, 34(6):46–59, June 1991.

22. B. Volozh, M. Matskin, G. Mints, E. Tyugu. Theorem proving with the aid of program synthesizer Cybernetics, 6:63-70, 1982.

23. T. Uustalu, U. Kopra, V. Kotkas, M. Matskin and E. Tyugu. The NUT Language Report. The Royal Institute of Technology (KTH),TRITA-IT R 94:14, 51 p., 1994.

Extensible Logic Program Schemata

Timothy S. Gegg-Harrison

Department of Computer Science
Winona State University
Winona, MN 55987, USA
tsg@vax2.winona.msus.edu

Abstract. Schema-based transformational systems maintain a library of logic program schemata which capture large classes of logic programs. One of the shortcomings of schema-based transformation approaches is their reliance on a large (possibly incomplete) set of logic program schemata that is required in order to capture all of the minor syntactic differences between semantically similar logic programs. By defining a set of extensible logic program schemata and an associated set of logic program transformations, it is possible to reduce the size of the schema library while maintaining the robustness of the transformational system. In our transformational system, we have defined a set of extensible logic program schemata in λProlog. Because λProlog is a higher-order logic programming language, it can be used as the representation language for both the logic programs and the extensible logic program schemata. In addition to the instantiation of predicate variables, extensible logic program schemata can be extended by applying standard programming techniques (e.g., accumulating results), introducing additional arguments (e.g., a second list to append to the end of the primary list), combining logic program schemata which share a common primary input, and connecting logic program schemata which are connected via a result of one schema being an input to the other schema. These extensions increase the robustness of logic program schemata and enhance traditional schema-based transformational systems.

1 Introduction

Schema-based transformational systems maintain a library of logic program schemata which capture large classes of logic programs. One of the shortcomings of schema-based transformation approaches is their reliance on a large (possibly incomplete) set of logic program schemata that is required in order to capture all of the minor syntactic differences between semantically similar logic programs. By defining a set of extensible logic program schemata and an associated set of logic program transformations, it is possible to reduce the size of the schema library while maintaining the robustness of the transformational system. Our schema-based approach to logic program transformation is similar to the schema-based transformations of Fuchs and his colleagues [6,16]. The main difference is that their schema language which was developed for representing Prolog schemata in a tutoring system [7,8] is not the same as their object language which is Prolog. We propose using a higher-order logic programming language to represent the logic programs and the set of extensible logic program schemata.

Logic program schemata have proven useful in teaching recursive logic programming to novices [8,9], debugging logic programs [10], transforming logic programs [5,6,16], and synthesizing logic programs [3,4]. A number of researchers have looked into various approaches to meta-languages which support logic program schemata, including our work on basic Prolog schemata [7,8], the work by Brna and his colleagues on Prolog programming techniques [2], Barker-Plummer's work on Prolog clichés [1], the work of Marakakis and Gallagher on program design schemata [14], Flener's work on logic algorithm schemata [3,4], and the work by Hamfelt and Fischer Nilsson on metalogic programming techniques [12]. An alternative approach to using a meta-language to represent program schemata is to have a set of general Prolog programs which can be extended by adding arguments and subgoals to produce other programs within the class. This is the approach taken by Sterling and his colleagues with their Prolog skeletons that are extended with programming techniques [13]. The present proposal attempts to merge both of these approaches by using a higher-order logic programming language as both the object language and the meta-language. Like Sterling's skeletons, extensible logic program schemata capture well-understood control flow patterns in logic programs and can be extended by applying programming techniques. Like traditional logic program schemata, extensible logic program schemata are higher-order logic programs that contain predicate variables which can be instantiated to produce logic programs with the same basic structure. Thus, extensible logic program schemata combine the strengths of both approaches.

2 Logic Program Schemata

λProlog is a higher-order logic programming language that extends Prolog by incorporating higher-order unification and λ-terms [15]. The syntactic conventions of λProlog are mostly the same as those of Prolog. In addition to λProlog's support of predicate variables and λ-terms, the most notable difference between the syntax of the Prolog and λProlog is that λProlog uses a curried notation. The Prolog program sum/2:

```
sum([],0).
sum([H|T],B) :- sum(T,R), B is H + R.
```

which finds the summation of all the elements in its input list would be written in λProlog's curried form as:

```
sum [] 0.
sum [H|T] B :- sum T R, B is H + R.
```

We can rewrite sum/2 as a single clause using disjunction:

```
sum A B :-  (A = [], B = 0);
            (A = [H|T], sum T R, B is H + R).
```

which enables us to write sum/2 in λProlog is as a λ-term:

```
sum A B :- (X\Y\(sigma H\(sigma T\(sigma R\(
            (X = [], Y = 0);
            (X = [H|T], sum T R, Y is H + R)
            ))))) A B.
```

λ-terms are used in λProlog to represent predicate application and anonymous predicates. Predicate application is denoted in λProlog by juxtaposition. Anonymous predicates are denoted with λ-abstractions which have the form λx.ρ(x) in λ-calculus and the form (X\(ρ(X)) in λProlog and represents an anonymous predicate that has a single argument X which succeeds if ρ(X) succeeds where ρ(X) is an arbitrary set of λProlog subgoals. In addition to supporting λ-terms, λProlog also permits existential quantifiers. λProlog uses the keyword sigma to represent the existential quantifier ∃ so the λ-term λx.λy.∃z.(p x y z) would be coded in λProlog as (X\Y\(sigma Z\(p X Y Z))) and represents an anonymous predicate that has two arguments X and Y which succeeds if p X Y Z succeeds for some Z.

Another important difference between Prolog and λProlog is that λProlog is a typed language. λProlog has several built-in types, including types for *int*, *bool*, *list*, and *o* (the type of propositions). If τ_1 and τ_2 are types then $(\tau_1 \rightarrow \tau_2)$ is a type corresponding to the set of functions whose domain and range are given by τ_1 and τ_2, respectively. The application of T_1 to T_2 is represented as $(T_1\ T_2)$ and has the type τ_1 if T_1 is a term of type $(\tau_2 \rightarrow \tau_1)$ and T_2 is a term of type τ_2. If X is a variable and T is a term of type τ', then the abstraction $(X : \tau \setminus T)$ is a term of type $\tau \rightarrow \tau'$. λProlog has a built-in type inference mechanism which gives its programmers the illusion that they are programming in a typeless language. Thus, the type system of λProlog serves as an aid to the programmer rather than an added layer of syntax. Lists and integers are handled the same way in λProlog as they are in Prolog. Unlike Prolog, however, λProlog supports separate types for propositions and booleans. The type *o* captures propositions and has the values true and fail and operations for conjunction, disjunction, and implication of propositions. The type *bool* captures boolean expressions and has the values truth and false and operations for conjunction and disjunction of booleans, and relationship comparisons (<, =<, >, >=). Note that because booleans are distinct from propositions, it is necessary to have the λProlog subgoal truth is X < Y in place of the Prolog subgoal X < Y.

We have identified several logic program schemata that serve as prototype logic programs for list processing [11]. Each of these schemata has two arguments, an input list and a result. Although many logic programs can be used with various modes, we assume a given mode for each of our logic programs. In addition to recursive list processing schemata, it is also possible to define a set of recursive natural number programs which also have two arguments. One of the largest classes of list processing programs is the class of global list processing programs which includes all those list processing programs that process all elements of the input list (i.e., the entire input list is reduced). Global list processing programs are captured by the reduceList/2 schema:

```
reduceList [] Result :-
    Base Result.
reduceList [H|T] Result :-
    reduceList T R, Constructor H R Result.
```

Global natural number processing programs are captured by the `reduce-Number/2` schema:

```
reduceNumber 0 Result :-
    Base Result.
reduceNumber N Result :-
    M is N - 1, reduceNumber M R,
    Constructor N R Result.
```

The `reduceList/2` and `reduceNumber/2` schemata can be generalized to include all singly-recursive reduction programs by incorporating the termination condition with the base case value computation and permitting an arbitrary destructor:

```
reduce Input Result :-
    Base Input Result.
reduce Input Result :-
    Destructor Input H T, reduce T R,
    Constructor H R Result.
```

Some explanation of the `reduce/2` schema is in order. It has two arguments and contains three predicate variables. The first argument is the primary input and the second argument is the primary output. The primary input and output can be either simple or structured terms, but they are both first-order terms. The three predicate variables represent arbitrary λProlog predicates. The predicate variable `Destructor` defines the process for destructing the input. The predicate variable `Constructor` defines the process for constructing the output. The other predicate variable, `Base`, is used to define the terminating condition, defining both the process to identify the terminating condition and the process which defines how to construct the output for the terminating condition. An example should help clarify `reduce/2`.

Consider the `factorial/2` program. For an arbitrary query `factorial A B`, the primary input is A and primary output is B. The destructor predicate decrements the input by one. This process can be defined with the anonymous predicate `(X\Y\Z\ (Z is X - 1, Y = X))`. The constructor predicate for `factorial/2` multiplies the current input by the factorial of one less than the current input and can be defined with the anonymous predicate `(X\Y\Z\(Z is X * Y))`. As can be seen in the base case clause of the definition of `factorial/2`, the terminating condition occurs whenever the input becomes one and the terminating output value should be one in this case. This process can be defined with the anonymous predicate `(X\Y\(X = 0, Y = 1))`. Combining all this together, we can produce a program for `factorial/2` by instantiating the predicate variables in `reduce/2`:

```
factorial N Result :-
    (X\Y\(X = 0, Y = 1)) N Result.
factorial N Result :-
    (X\Y\Z\(Z is X - 1, Y = X)) N C M,
    factorial M R,
    (X\Y\Z\(Z is X * Y)) C R Result.
```

Furthermore, since `factorial/2` is a global natural number processing program, it is also possible to produce a program for it by instantiating the predicate variables in `reduceNumber/2`:

```
factorial 0 Result :-
    (X\(X = 1)) Result.
factorial N Result :-
    M is N - 1, factorial M R,
    (X\Y\Z\(Z is X * Y)) N R Result.
```

Now consider `sum/2` again. For an arbitrary query `sum A B`, the primary input is A and primary output is B. The destructor predicate decomposes the input into the head element and the tail of the list. This process can be defined with the anonymous predicate `(X\Y\Z\(X = [Y|Z]))`. The constructor predicate for `sum/2` computes the summation by adding the current element to the sum of the rest of the list and can be defined with the anonymous predicate `(X\Y\Z\(Z is X + Y))`. As can be seen in the base case clause of the definition of `sum/2`, the terminating condition occurs whenever the input list becomes empty and the terminating output value should be 0. This process can be defined with the anonymous predicate `(X\Y\(X = [], Y = 0))`. Combining all this together, we can produce a program for `sum/2` by instantiating the predicate variables in `reduce/2`:

```
sum List Result :-
    (X\Y\(X = [], Y = 0)) List Result.
sum List Result :-
    (X\Y\Z\(X = [Y|Z])) List H T, sum T R,
    (X\Y\Z\(Z is X + Y)) H R Result.
```

Furthermore, since `sum/2` is a global list processing program, it is also possible to produce a program for it by instantiating the predicate variables in `reduceList/2`:

```
sum [] Result :-
    (X\(X = 0)) Result.
sum [H|T] Result :-
    sum T R, (X\Y\Z\(Z is X + Y)) H R Result.
```

In order to capture programs like `position/3` which simultaneously reduce both a list and a natural number, we need to introduce another logic program schemata. The `reduceLN/3` schema captures programs which simultaneously reduce a list and a number. In addition to capturing `position/3`, the `reduceLN/3` schema also captures programs like `take/3` and `drop/3` which keep or remove the first n elements, respectively. The reduceLN/3 schema looks like:

```
reduceLN [] N Result.
reduceLN L N Result :-
    L = [H|T], M is N - 1, reduceLN T M R,
    ((N = 0, Base L Result); Constructor H R Result).
```

An example of reduceLN/3 schema is the position/3 program:

```
position 0 [E|T] E.
position N [H|T] E :- M is N - 1, position M T E.
```

If we instantiate Base to (X\Y\(sigma Z\(X = [Y|Z]))) and Constructor to (X\Y\Z\(Z = Y)) then we can produce position/3 from reduceLN/3 assuming that the case of requesting the nth element from a list of less than n elements is a ill-posed query:

```
position [] N E.
position L N E :-
    L = [H|T], M is N - 1, position T M R,
    ((N = 0, (X\Y\(sigma Z\(X = [Y|Z]))) L E);
    (X\Y\Z\(Z = Y)) H R E).
```

The class of reduction programs presented so far share a common destructor. As such, we can refer to the schemata defined so far as *destructor-specific* schemata. It is also possible to have *constructor-specific* schemata. Two of the most popular higher-order programming programs are map/3 and filter/3. Mapping and filtering programs are a subclass of reduction programs that also share a common constructor. Rather than reducing a list by combining each element with the result of reducing the remainder of the list, sometimes it is desirable to map a function predicate across all the elements of a list. For example, we may want to double all of the elements in a list. In order to double all of the elements of a list, we must first apply a function predicate that doubles each element and then put the doubled element in the front of the list produced by doubling all the elements in the remainder of the list. In general, the predicate map/3 can be used to apply an arbitrary binary function predicate to each element of a list:

```
map [] [] P.
map [H|T] Result P :-
    map T R P,
    (X\Y\Z\(sigma W\(P X W, Z = [W|Y]))) H R Result.
```

We can write doubleAll/2 using this map/3 predicate:

```
doubleAll List Result :-
    map List Result (X\Y\(Y is 2 * X)).
```

The predicate filter/3 takes a unary predicate and a list and filters out all elements from the list that do not satisfy the predicate. For example, we may want to filter out all non-positive numbers from a list of numbers. We can write `filter/3` in λProlog as follows:

```
filter [] [] P.
filter [H|T] Result P :-
    filter T R P,
    (X\Y\Z\((P X, Z = [X|Y]); Z = Y)) H R Result.
```

We can write `positivesOnly/2` using this `filter/3` predicate:

```
positivesOnly List Result :-
    filter List Result (X\(truth is X > 0)).
```

It is possible to consider the mapping constructor and the filtering constructor as special cases of the following constructor:

```
(P X XX, Z = [XX|Y]); Z = Y
```

Notice that this constructor has the additional disjunctive subgoal (`Z = Y`) which is never invoked for mapping programs and it only captures filtering constructors if we rewrite the filtering constructor to add an additional argument to its filtering predicate:

```
(A\B\(P A, A = B))
```

which represents the mapped element. Now we can define the following special case of `reduceList/2` for mapping/filtering programs:

```
mapList [] [].
mapList [H|T] Result :-
    mapList T R,
    ((P H XX, Result = [XX|R]); Result = R).
```

It is important to note that the schemata presented in this section are very robust, capturing a large class of programs which also includes `reverse/2`, `insertion-sort/2`, `product/2`, `prefix/2`, and many others. We can extend each of these schemata to capture additional logic programs. For example, we can extend `reduce/2` to capture other programs like `append/3` and `count/3`. This is described in the next section.

3 Extensions to Logic Program Schemata

The `reduce/2` schema captures a large group of logic programs, but there is still a large group of logic programs that it is unable to capture. One of the major differences between logic programs is the number of arguments. In addition to instantiating predicate variables in logic program schemata to produce logic programs, it is also possible to extend program schemata to include additional arguments. Vasconcelos and Fuchs [16] handle this in their enhanced schema language by introducing argument vectors and having positional indicators to ensure specified arguments occur in the same position across terms. We propose handling varying number of arguments by extending our logic program schemata. There are several types of argument extension that can be applied to the reduce/2 schema, corresponding to adding arguments to the predicate variables in reduce/2. We can extend the reduce/2 schema to add an additional argument to the Base predicate:

```
reduceB List Result ArgBase :-
    Base List Result ArgBase.
reduceB List Result ArgBase :-
    Destructor List H T,
    reduceB T R ArgBase,
    Constructor H R Result.
```

An example of this type of extension is the creation of append/3 from prefix/2:

```
prefix [] L.
prefix [H|T] [H|L] :- prefix T L.
```

The prefix/2 predicate succeeds if its primary list is a prefix of its other list. The prefix/2 predicate can be extended by the adding a new argument which represents the second list (i.e., the list that is to be appended to the primary list). If we make the new Base predicate unify its arguments then we get append/3:

```
append [] L List :- (X\Y\(X = Y)) L List.
append [H|T] [H|L] List :- append T L List.
```

Another argument extension that can be applied to the reduce/2 schema is to add an argument to the Constructor predicate:

```
reduceC [] Result ArgCons :-
    Base List Result.
reduceC List Result ArgCons :-
    Destructor List H T,
    reduceC T R ArgCons,
    Constructor H R Result ArgCons.
```

An example of this type of extension is the creation of count/3 from length/2:

```
length [] 0.
length [H|T] L :- length T X, L is X + 1.
```

If we make the new Constructor predicate increment the count only when the head of the list satisfies a predicate given by the newly added argument then we can produce count/3:

```
count [] 0 P.
count [H|T] C P :-
    count T R P,
    (W\X\Y\Z\(P W, Y is X + 1); Y = X) H R C P.
```

Note that the additional argument on the Constructor for count/3 serves as a "filter" which tests the appropriateness of the input element. For such programs, it would be possible incorporate the "filter" into the Destructor (i.e., it is possible to extend reduce/2 by adding an additional argument to the Destructor predicate):

```
count [] 0 P.
count List C P :-
    (W\X\Y\Z\(remove W X Y Z)) List H T P,
    count T R P, C is R + 1.

remove [A|B] A B P :- P A.
remove [H|T] A B P :- remove T A B P.
```

which is an example of the use of reduceD/3:

```
reduceD [] Result ArgDest :-
    Base List Result.
reduceD List Result ArgDest :-
    Destructor List H T ArgDest,
    reduceD T R ArgDest,
    Constructor H R Result.
```

The purpose of these semantics-altering extensions that enable the addition of arguments is to widen the applicability of the semantics-preserving schema transformations. Any transformation that is applicable to reduce/2 is also applicable to reduceB/3, reduceC/3, and reduceD/3. There are two types of semantics-preserving extensions that can be applied to logic program schemata to produce equivalent logic program schemata: application of programming techniques and combination (or merging) and connection of logic program schemata. The first type of semantics-preserving extension is the application of programming techniques to logic program schemata. Programming techniques have been studied fairly extensively and a number of commonly occurring programming practices have been identified. One popular programming technique is the introduction of an accumulator, enabling the composition of the output from the right rather than from the left. Given that a program unifies with the reduce/2 schema, we can transform the program by instantiating the following reduceAcc/2 schema with the same Base and Constructor predicates:

```
reduceAcc Input Result :-
    Base Dummy Acc,
    reduceAcc2 Input Result Acc.
reduceAcc2 Input Result Result :-
    Base Input Dummy.
reduceAcc2 Input Result Acc :-
    Destructor Input H T, Constructor Acc H A,
    reduceAcc2 T Result A.
```

as long as `Constructor` is an associative predicate. As an example, consider `sum/2` again. We can produce the more efficient (tail recursive) accumulator implementation of `sum/2` by instantiating this `reduceAcc/2` schema:

```
sum List Result :-
    (X\(X = 0)) Acc, sum2 List Result Acc.
sum2 [] Result Result.
sum2 [H|T] Result Acc :-
    (X\Y\Z\(Z is X + Y)) Acc H A, sum2 T Result A.
```

A similar type of transformation is possible for programs captured by the `reduceLN/3` schema. The `reduceLN/3` is a forward processing schema which reduces its list from the front and reduces its integer from some maximum value down to 0. An equivalent backward processing schema which continues to reduce its list from the front but reduces its integer up from 0 to the maximum rather than from the maximum down to 0 looks like:

```
reduceUpLN L N Result :-
    Max = (X\(X = N)),
    reduceUpLN2 L 0 Max Result.
reduceUpLN2 [] N Max Result.
reduceUpLN2 L N Max Result :-
    L = [H|T], M is N + 1, reduceUpLN2 T M Max R,
    ((Max N, Base L Result); Constructor H R Result).
```

As an example, consider `position/3` again. We can transform the standard forward processing program given in the previous section to a backward processing program using the `reduceLN/3` → `reduceUpLN/3` transformation producing the following implementation of `position/3`:

```
position L N E :-
    Max = (X\(X = N)),
    position2 L 0 Max E.
position2 [] N Max Result.
position2 L N Max E :-
    L = [H|T], M is N + 1, position2 T M Max R,
    ((Max N, (X\Y\(sigma Z\(X = [Y|Z]))) L E);
    (X\Y\Z\(Z = Y)) H R E).
```

The second type of semantics-preserving logic program extension is the combination (or merging) of logic program schemata. The idea is to merge two logic program schemata whenever they have a common argument. Combination schema transformations are listed in the following table.

Initial Schemata		Combination Schema
mapList/2	reduceList/2	mapReduceList/2
reduceList/2	reduceList/2	reduceListList/3
reduceLN/3	reduceLN/3	reduceLNLN/4
reduceListAcc/2	reduceUpLN/3	reduceConnect/2
reduceListAcc/2	reduceUpLNLN/4	reduceConnect/3

Probably the most obvious combination schema transformation is to combine logic program schemata which have a common primary input. The reduceList/2 + reduceList/2 → reduceListList/3 transformation combines two reduceList/2 schemata that have a common primary input.

```
reduceList [] Result1 :-        reduceList [] Result2 :-
  Base1 Result1.                  Base2 Result2.
reduceList [H|T] Result1 :-     reduceList [H|T] Result2 :-
  reduceList T R,                 reduceList T R,
  Constructor1 H R Result1.       Constructor2 H R Result2.
```

⇓

```
reduceListList [] Result1 Result2 :-
  Base1 Result1, Base2 Result2.
reduceListList [H|T] Result1 Result2 :-
  reduceListList T R1 R2,
  Constructor1 H R1 Result1,
  Constructor2 H R2 Result2.
```

An example of the use of the reduceList/2 + reduceList/2 → reduceListList/3 transformation is the creation of a singly-recursive implementation of the average/2 predicate from the following straightforward solution:

```
average List Average :-
    length List Length,
    sum List Sum,
    Average is Sum / Length.

length [] 0.
length [H|T] Length :- length T R, Length is R + 1.

sum [] 0.
sum [H|T] Sum :- sum T R, Sum is R + H.
```

Applying the reduceList/2 + reduceList/2 → reduceListList/3 transformation to this program produces the following implementation of average/2:

```
average List Average :-
    average2 List Length Sum,
    Average is Sum / Length.
average2 [] 0 0.
average2 [H|T] Length Sum :-
    average2 T L S, Length is L + 1, Sum is S + H.
```

Because the reduceListList/3 schema was created by combining two global list processing schemata which share a common primary input and have distinct outputs, the same process can also be used to combine two accumulated implementations of global list processing schemata (or even one of each). It is also possible to combine two reduceLN/3 schemata with the reduceLN/3 + reduceLN/3 → reduceLNLN/4 transformation.

```
reduceLN [] N Result1.                  reduceLN [] N Result2.
reduceLN L N Result1 :-                  reduceLN L N Result2 :-
L = [H|T], M is N - 1,                   L = [H|T], M is N - 1,
reduceLN T M R,                          reduceLN T M R,
((N = 0, Base1 L Result1);               ((N = 0, Base2 L Result2);
Constructor1 H R Result1).               Constructor2 H R Result2).
```

⇓

```
reduceLNLN [] N Result1 Result2.
reduceLNLN L N Result1 Result2 :-
L = [H|T], M is N - 1,
reduceLNLN T M R1 R2,
((N = 0, Base1 L Result1, Base2 L Result2);
 (Constructor1 H R1 Result1),
  Constructor2 H R2 Result2)).
```

An example of the use of the reduceLN/3 + reduceLN/3 → reduceLNLN/4 transformation is the splitting of a list into two sublists, one sublist which contains the first n elements of the list and a second sublist which contains all but the first n elements of the list. This task can be accomplished using the well-known take/3 and drop/3 predicates:

```
takedrop List N FirstPart ButFirstPart :-
    take List N FirstPart, drop List N ButFirstPart.

take [] N [].
take L N Result :-
    L = [H|T], M is N - 1, take T M R,
    ((N = 0, (X\Y\(Y = []))) L Result);
    (X\Y\Z\(Z = [X|Y])) H R Result).

drop [] N [].
drop L N Result :-
    L = [H|T], M is N - 1, drop T M R,
    ((N = 0, (X\Y\(Y = X))) L Result);
    (X\Y\Z\(Z = Y)) H R Result).
```

Applying the reduceLN/3 + reduceLN/3 → reduceLNLN/4 transformation to takedrop/4 produces the following implementation:

```
takedrop [] N [] [].
takedrop L N Res1 Res2 :-
    L = [H|T], M is N - 1, takedrop T M R1 R2,
    ((N = 0,
      (X\Y\(Y = [])) L Res1, (X\Y\(Y = X)) L Res2);
     (X\Y\Z\(Z = [X|Y])) H R1 Res1),
     (X\Y\Z\(Z = Y)) H R2 Res2)).
```

The reduceLN/3 + reduceLN/3 → reduceLNLN/4 transformation has a corresponding reduceUpLN/3 + reduceUpLN/3 → reduceUpLNLN/4 transformation which enables the combination of two backward processing reduce-LN/3 programs. Although the transformational system of Vasconcelos and Fuchs [16] supports the combination of logic program schemata which share a common input, their system currently does not support any transformations which connect two logic programs where the output of one schema is the input to another schema. We can support such transformations by connecting mapList/2 and reduceList/2 where the mapping/filtering program maps a predicate across the elements of the input list and this mapped list is then reduced. The mapList/2 + reduceList/2 → mapReduce-List/2 transformation combines the mapList/2 schema with the reduceList/2 schema where the list that is produced by the mapping/filtering program is the input to the reduction program.

`mapList [] [].`
 `mapList [H|T] TempRes :-`
 ` mapList T R,`
 ` ((P H XX, TempRes = [XX|R]);`
 ` TempRes = R).`
	`reduceList [] Result :-`
	 ` Base Result.`
	 `reduceList [H|T] Result :-`
	 ` reduceList T R,`
	 ` Constructor H R Result.`

$$\Downarrow$$

```
mapReduceList [] Result :-
 Base Result.
mapReduceList [H|T] Result :-
 mapReduceList T R,
 ((P H XX, Constructor XX R Result); Result = R).
```

As an example, consider the following straightforward solution to counting the number of positive elements in a list by filtering out the non-positive elements (using positivesOnly/2) and then counting the number of elements in the filtered list (using length/2):

```
positiveCount List Result :-
    positivesOnly List X, length X Result.
```

```
positivesOnly [] [].
positivesOnly [H|T] Result :-
    positivesOnly T R,
    ((truth is H > 0, XX = H, Result = [XX|R]);
    Result = R).

length [] 0.
length [H|T] L :- length T X, L is X + 1.
```

Applying the mapList/2 + reduceList/2 ⇒ mapReduceList/2 transformation to this positiveCount/2 program produces the following implementation:

```
positiveCount [] 0.
positiveCount [H|T] Result :-
    positiveCount T R,
    (((truth is H > 0, XX = H), Result is R + 1);
    Result = R).
```

Another class of combination schema transformations enable the connection of two logic program schemata that share a common primary input and the result of one schema is an additional input to the other schema. We have identified two schema transformations for this type of combination schema transformation: reduceListAcc/2 + reduceUpLN/2 ⇒ reduceConnect/2 and reduceListAcc/2 + reduceUpLNLN/3 ⇒ reduceConnect/3.

```
reduceListAcc L N :-            reduceUpLN L N Result :-
 Base1 A,                        Max = (X\(X = N)),
 reduceListAcc2 L N A.           reduceUpLN2 L 0 Max Result.
reduceListAcc2 [] N N.          reduceUpLN2 [] N Max Result.
reduceListAcc2 L N A :-         reduceUpLN2 L N Max Result :-
 L = [H|T],                      L = [H|T], M is N + 1,
 Constructor1 A H B,             reduceUpLN2 T M Max R,
 reduceListAcc2 T N B.           ((Max N, Base2 L Result);
                                  Constructor2 H R Result).
```

$$\Downarrow$$

```
reduceConnect List Result :-
 Base1 Acc, Max = (X\(X = C)),
 reduceC2 List Acc A 0 Max Result.
reduceC2 [] Acc Acc N Max Result :-
 Connect Acc C, Max = (X\(X = C)).
reduceC2 List Acc RL N Max Result :-
 List = [H|T], M is N + 1, Constructor1 Acc H A,
 reduceC2 T A RL M Max R,
 ((Max N, Base2 List Result); Constructor2 H R Result).
```

As an example of the reduceAccList/2 + reduceUpLN/2 ⇒ reduceConnect/2 transformation, consider finding the middle element in an arbitrary list.

A straightforward solution to this problem is to count the number of elements in the list (using length/2), divide this count by two, and then use this value to find the middle element (using position/3):

```
middle List Middle :-
    length List Length, Half is (Length + 1) div 2,
    position List Half Middle.

length [] 0.
length [H|T] Length :- length T R, Length is R + 1.

position [] N E.
position L N E :-
    L = [H|T], M is N - 1, position T M R,
    ((N = 0, (X\Y\(sigma Z\(X = [Y|Z]))) L E);
    (X\Y\Z\(Z = Y)) H R E).
```

The first step in the transformation of middle/2 is to transform length/2 to an accumulated implementation using the reduce/2 → reduceAcc/2 tranformation producing the following implementation of length/2:

```
length List Length :- Acc = 0, length2 List Length Acc.
length2 [] Len Len.
length2 [H|T] Len Acc :- A is Acc + 1, length2 T Len A.
```

The next step is to transform position/3 from a forward processing program to a backward processing program using the reduceLN/3 → reduceUpLN/3 transformation producing the following implementation of position/3:

```
position L N E :-
    Max = (X\(X = N)),
    position2 L 0 Max E.
position2 [] N Max Result.
position2 L N Max E :-
    L = [H|T], M is N + 1, position2 T M Max R,
    ((Max N, (X\Y\(sigma Z\(X = [Y|Z]))) L E);
    (X\Y\Z\(Z = Y)) H R E).
```

The final step in the transformation is to apply the reduceListAcc/2 + reduceUpLN/3 → reduceConnect/2 transformation to combine length/2 and position/3 to produce the following implementation of middle/2:

```
middle List Middle :-
    Acc = 0, Max = (X\(X = Half)),
    middle2 List Acc Length 0 Max Middle.
middle2 [] Length Length AH Max Middle :-
    Half is (Length + 1) div 2, Max = (X\(X = Half)).
middle2 [H|T] AL Length AH Max Middle :-
    NL is AL + 1, NH is AH + 1,
    middle2 T NL Length NH Max Mid,
    ((Max AH, Middle = H); Middle = Mid).
```

The final combination schema transformation that we consider is the `reduce-ListAcc/2 + reduceUpLNLN/4 → reduceConnect/3` transformation.

```
reduceListAcc L N :-           reduceUpLNLN L N R1 R2 :-
  Base1 A,                       Max = (X\(X = N)),
  reduceListAcc2 L N A.          reduceUpLNLN2 L 0 Max R1 R2.
reduceListAcc2 [] N N.         reduceUpLNLN2 [] N Max R1 R2.
reduceListAcc2 L N A :-        reduceUpLNLN2 L N Max R1 R2 :-
  L = [H|T],                     L = [H|T], M is N + 1,
  Constructor1 A H B,            reduceUpLNLN2 T M Max S1 S2,
  reduceListAcc2 T N B.          ((Max N, Base21 L R1, Base22 L R2);
                                 (Constructor21 H S1 R1),
                                  Constructor22 H S2 R2)).
```

⇓

```
reduceConnect List R1 R2 :-
  Base1 Acc, Max = (X\(X = C)),
  reduceC2 List Acc A 0 Max R1 R2.
reduceC2 [] Acc Acc N Max R1 R2 :-
  Connect Acc C, Max = (X\(X = C)).
reduceC2 List Acc RL N Max R1 R2 :-
  List = [H|T], M is N + 1, Constructor1 Acc H A,
  reduceC2 T A RL M1 M2 Max S1 S2,
  ((Max N, Base21 List R1, Base22 List R2);
   (Constructor21 H S1 R1), Constructor22 H S2 R2)).
```

As an example of the `reduceListAcc/2 + reduceUpLNLN/4 → reduceConnect/3` transformation, consider the task of splitting a list of elements in half. We can do this in λProlog by invoking three reduction programs:

```
splitlist List FirstHalf LastHalf :-
    length List N, M is N div 2,
    take List M FirstHalf, drop List M LastHalf.

length [] 0.
length [H|T] Length :- length T R, Length is R + 1.

take [] N [].
take L N Result :-
    L = [H|T], M is N - 1, take T M R,
    ((N = 0, (X\Y\(Y = []))) L Result);
     (X\Y\Z\(Z = [X|Y])) H R Result).

drop [] N [].
drop L N Result :-
    L = [H|T], M is N - 1, drop T M R,
    ((N = 0, (X\Y\(Y = X)) L Result);
     (X\Y\Z\(Z = Y)) H R Result).
```

In order to apply the `reduceUpLN/3 + reduceUpLN/3 → reduceUp-LNLN/4` transformation to `take/3` and `drop/3` we must first transform them from forward processing programs to backward processing programs using the `reduceLN/3`

→ reduceUpLN/3 transformation:

```
take L N Result :-
    Max = (X\(X = N)),
    take2 L 0 Max Result.
take2 [] N Max [].
take2 L N Max Result :-
    L = [H|T], M is N + 1, take2 T M Max R,
    ((Max N, (X\Y\(Y = []))) L Result);
     (X\Y\Z\(Z = [X|Y])) H R Result).

drop L N Result :-
    Max = (X\(X = N)),
    drop2 L 0 Max Result.
drop2 [] N Max [].
drop2 L N Max Result :-
    L = [H|T], M is N + 1, drop2 T M Max R,
    ((Max N, (X\Y\(Y = X)) L Result);
     (X\Y\Z\(Z = Y)) H R Result).
```

Now we can combine take/3 and drop/3 by applying the reduceUpLN/3
+ reduceUpLN/3 → reduceUpLNLN/4 transformation:

```
takedrop L N Res1 Res2 :-
    Max = (X\(X = N)),
    takedrop2 L 0 Max Res1 Res2.
takedrop2 [] N Max [] [].
takedrop2 L N Max Res1 Res2 :-
    L = [H|T], M is N + 1,
    takedrop2 T M Max R1 R2,
    ((Max N,
      (X\Y\(Y = []))) L Res1, (X\Y\(Y = X)) L Res2));
     (X\Y\Z\(Z = [X|Y])) H R1 Res1),
      (X\Y\Z\(Z = Y)) H R2 Res2)).
```

After transforming length/2 to its accumulated implementation as we did in the
previous example, we can apply the reduceListAcc/2 + reduceUpLNLN/4 →
reduceConnect/3 transformation producing the following implementation of
splitlist/3:

```
splitlist L Res1 Res2 :-
    Acc = 0, Max = (X\(X = Half)),
    splitlist2 L Acc N 0 Max Res1 Res2.
splitlist2 [] Length Length N Max [] [] :-
    Half is (Length + 1) div 2, Max = (X\(X = Half)).
splitlist2 L AL Length AH Max Res1 Res2 :-
    L = [H|T], NL is AL + 1, NH is AH + 1,
    splitlist2 T NL Length NH Max R1 R2,
    ((Max AH, (X\Y\(Y = []))) L Res1,
      (X\Y\(Y = X)) L Res2);
     ((X\Y\Z\(Z = [X|Y])) H R1 Res1,
      (X\Y\Z\(Z = Y)) H R2 Res2)).
```

Logic program schemata and logic program schema transformations can be used to help in program development by enabling the programmer to produce a simple straightforward solution to the problem and then transform that solution into an efficient one by applying a set of program transformations.

4 Conclusion

We have proposed an extensible schema-based logic program transformation system as an improvement to the traditional schema-based meta-language approaches. In this system, we have defined a set of extensible logic program schemata in λProlog. Because λProlog is a higher-order logic programming language, it can be used as the representation language for both the logic programs and the extensible logic program schemata. In addition to the instantiation of predicate variables, extensible logic program schemata can be extended by applying standard programming techniques (e.g., accumulating results), introducing additional arguments (e.g., a second list to append to the end of the primary list), combining logic program schemata which share a common primary input, and connecting logic program schemata which are connected via a result of one schema being an input to the other schema. These extensions increase the robustness of logic program schemata and enhance traditional schema-based transformational systems.

References

[1]   D. Barker-Plummer. Cliché Programming in Prolog. In M. Bruynooghe, editor, *Proceedings of the 2ⁿᵈ Workshop on Meta-Programming in Logic*, Leuven, Belgium, pages 247-256, 1990.

[2]   P. Brna, A. Bundy, A. Dodd, M. Eisenstadt, C. Looi, H. Pain, D. Robertson, B. Smith, and M. van Someren. Prolog Programming Techniques. *Instructional Science*, 20: 111-133, 1991.

[3]   P. Flener. *Logic Program Synthesis from Incomplete Information*. Kluwer Academic Publishers, 1995.

[4]   P. Flener and Y. Deville. Logic Program Synthesis from Incomplete Specifications. *Journal of Symbolic Computation*, 15: 775-805, 1993.

[5]   P. Flener and Y. Deville. Logic Program Transformation Through Generalization Schemata. In M. Proietti, editor, *Proceedings of the 5ᵗʰ International Workshop on Logic Program Synthesis and Transformation*, Utrecht, The Netherlands, pages 171-173, Springer-Verlag, 1995.

[6]   N.E. Fuchs and M.P.J. Fromhertz. Schema-Based Transformations of Logic Programs. In T.P. Clement and K. Lau, editors, *Proceedings of the 1ˢᵗ International Workshop on Logic Program Synthesis and Transformation*, Manchester, England, pages 111-125, Springer-Verlag, 1991.

[7] T.S. Gegg-Harrison. *Basic Prolog Schemata.* Technical Report CS-1989-20, Department of Computer Science, Duke University, Durham, North Carolina, 1989.

[8] T.S. Gegg-Harrison. Learning Prolog in a Schema-Based Environment. *Instructional Science*, 20: 173-190, 1991.

[9] T.S. Gegg-Harrison. Adapting Instruction to the Student's Capabilities. *Journal of Artificial Intelligence in Education*, 3: 169-181, 1992.

[10] T.S. Gegg-Harrison. Exploiting Program Schemata in an Automated Program Debugger. *Journal of Artificial Intelligence in Education*, 5: 255-278, 1994.

[11] T.S. Gegg-Harrison. Representing Logic Program Schemata in λProlog. In L. Sterling, editor, *Proceedings of the 12th International Conference on Logic Programming*, Kanagawa, Japan, pages 467-481, MIT Press, 1995.

[12] A. Hamfelt and J. Fischer Nilsson. Declarative Logic Programming with Primitive Recursive Relations on Lists. In M. Maher, editor, *Proceedings of the 13th Joint International Conference and Symposium on Logic Programming*, Bonn, Germany, pages 230-243, MIT Press, 1996.

[13] M. Kirschenbaum and L.S. Sterling. Applying Techniques to Skeletons. In J. Jacquet, editor, *Constructing Logic Programs*, pages 127-140, MIT Press, 1993.

[14] E. Marakakis and J.P. Gallagher. Schema-Based Top-Down Design of Logic Programs using Abstract Data Types. In L. Fribourg and F. Turini, editors, *Proceedings of the 4th International Workshops on Logic Program Synthesis and Transformation and Meta-Programming in Logic*, Pisa, Italy, pages 138-153, Springer-Verlag, 1994.

[15] G. Nadathur and D. Miller. An Overview of λProlog. In R.A. Kowalski and K.A. Bowen, editors, *Proceedings of the 5th International Conference and Symposium on Logic Programming*, Seattle, Washington, pages 810-827, MIT Press, 1988.

[16] W.W. Vasconcelos and N.E. Fuchs. An Opportunistic Approach for Logic Program Analysis and Optimisation Using Enhanced Schema-Based Transformations. In M. Proietti, editor, *Proceedings of the 5th International Workshop on Logic Program Synthesis and Transformation*, Utrecht, The Netherlands, pages 174-188, Springer-Verlag, 1995.

Specialising Meta-level Compositions of Logic Programs

Antonio Brogi and Simone Contiero

Dipartimento di Informatica, Università di Pisa
Corso Italia 40, 56125 Pisa, Italy
{brogi,contiero}@di.unipi.it

Abstract. Meta-level compositions of object logic programs are naturally implemented by means of meta-programming techniques. Meta-interpreters defining program compositions however suffer from a computational overhead that is due partly to the interpretation layer present in all meta-programs, and partly to the specific interpretation layer needed to deal with program compositions. We show that meta-interpreters implementing compositions of object programs can be fruitfully specialised w.r.t. meta-level queries of the form Demo(E,G), where E denotes a program expression and G denotes a (partially instantiated) object level query. More precisely, we describe the design and implementation of a declarative program specialiser that suitably transforms such meta-interpreters so as to sensibly reduce — if not to completely remove — the overhead due to the handling of program compositions. In many cases the specialiser succeeds in eliminating also the overhead due to meta-interpretation.

1 Introduction and Motivations

A simple, yet powerful, extension of logic programming consists of introducing a set of meta-level operations for composing separate object programs. The introduction of program composition operations enhances the expressive power and knowledge representation capabilities of logic programming by supporting a wealth of applications (e.g., see [4, 7]) ranging from software engineering applications, such as modular programming, to artificial intelligence applications, such as hierarchical and hypothetical reasoning.

Meta-level compositions of object programs are naturally implemented by meta-programming. As shown in [7, 9], several operations over definite logic programs can be implemented by extending the so-called *vanilla* meta-interpreter [41]. In this paper, we will consider an extended vanilla meta-interpreter M_π that supports a number of program composition operations over a collection π of object programs. In particular, we will refer to an existing implementation of the meta-interpreter in the system COMPOSE [5], a logic programming system written in the programming language Gödel [22].

The meta-interpreter M_π can be exploited to prove meta-level queries of the form Demo(E,G), where E denotes a composition of object programs and G an object level query. Unfortunately, M_π suffers from a computational overhead which is due partly to the interpretation layer present in all meta-programs, and partly to the specific interpretation layer needed to deal with program compositions.

The main objective of this paper is to eliminate, or at least to reduce, such an overhead. It is well-known that partial evaluation [13] (also referred to as partial deduction [24] in logic programming) can be exploited to specialise programs so as to improve their efficiency. In particular, the application of partial evaluation techniques for reducing the interpretation overhead in meta-programs has been studied by many authors (e.g., [10, 14, 24, 37, 43]). Other authors have pointed out the effectiveness of combining partial evaluation with other program transformation techniques [14, 38, 39].

We will describe the design, implementation and application of a program specialiser, built according to the following requirements:

(1) The specialiser should be targeted to improving the efficiency of the meta-interpreter M_π. Rather than aiming at designing a general specialiser for logic programs, our objective is to build an *ad hoc* specialiser to be suitably integrated with the system COMPOSE [5].

(2) The specialiser should be written in a *declarative* programming style. As pointed out in [3, 21, 22], dynamic meta-programming applications (such as program specialisation) require the adoption of a so-called *ground* representation of object programs in order to encompass declarativeness.

(3) Finally, we would like to prove the correctness of the program specialiser by applying, as much as possible, general results from the theory of partial evaluation in logic programming [31]. Rather than extending the basic results of partial evaluation to the extension considered, as done for instance in [11], we would like to reduce our application to a special instance of the general case of partial evaluation in logic programming.

Several program specialisers for logic programs have been developed (e.g., [15, 39, 43]). The majority of them is written in Prolog and employs extra-logical features of the language, such as the cut operator and built-in predicates like **var**, **nonvar**, **assert**, **retract**, and **copy_term**. Unfortunately this spoils declarativeness, which is one of the distinguishing features of logic programming, allowing programmers to specify *what* programs compute without specifying *how* they do it [3, 22].

As mentioned before, our objective is to build a program specialiser targeted to improving the efficiency of the meta-interpreter M_π. Since the currently available implementation of M_π in the system COMPOSE is written in Gödel, the first obvious solution is to try to apply SAGE [19], an existing partial evaluator for Gödel programs. Even if SAGE is in principle applicable to any Gödel program, it has been primarily designed for a special class of meta-programs, which does not include our meta-interpreter M_π. Unfortunately, as we will discuss thoroughly in Sect. 5, SAGE does not offer a substantial speed-up when specialising M_π. This led us to implement in Gödel a specialiser targeted for the extended meta-interpreter M_π. Besides directly ensuring the integration with COMPOSE, this choice was also suggested by the wide support offered by Gödel for developing meta-programming applications using the ground representation of object programs.

The overall specialisation process may be described in two phases. In the first phase, given the extended vanilla meta-interpreter M_π and a query of the form Demo(E,x), a new program M_π^s specialised w.r.t. queries of the form Demo(E,x) is produced by applying standard partial evaluation techniques based on unfolding. There are two main reasons for partially evaluating M_π w.r.t. an unbound object level goal. First, when using the meta-interpreter M_π, the same program expression E will be in general employed to query many different object goals. It is therefore convenient to obtain a partially evaluated meta-interpreter that can be used to query any object level goal on a program expression E. Moreover, general existing techniques can be employed to further specialise the obtained meta-interpreter w.r.t. partially instantiated object queries G. The correctness of the partial evaluation phase is established (see [6]) by proving the equivalence between the meta-interpreter M_π and its partially evaluated version M_π^s.

The second phase consists of applying program transformation techniques to the meta-program M_π^s thus obtaining a new program New_M_π. Two alternative techniques are applied to M_π^s, depending on the structure of the given program expression E. In one case, the program transformation eliminates from M_π both the overhead due to the interpretation layer and the overhead due to the specific interpretation layer needed to deal with program compositions. In the other case, a simple transformation (based on introducing new predicates) is applied, which still sensibly reduces the second type of overhead. The equivalence between M_π^s and New_M_π is proved in both cases.

The paper is organised as follows. In Sect. 2 we introduce the extended vanilla meta-interpreter M_π defining a set of program composition operations. In Sect. 3 we recall some background results from the theory of partial evaluation in logic programming. Section 4 presents the design and implementation of our program specialiser, as well as the equivalence results. Section 5 contains an assessment of the overall approach, while Sect. 6 discusses related work. Finally, Section 7 contains some concluding remarks and directions for future work. All proofs are omitted and can be found in [6].

2 Meta-level Compositions of Object Programs

Four basic operations for composing definite logic programs are introduced: Union (denoted by Union), intersection (Inters), encapsulation (Enc), and import (Import). These operations have been thoroughly described in [4, 7, 9], where their semantics, implementation, and a wide range of programming examples are presented.

We recall here the implementation of program composition operations by means of meta-programming, as described in [5]. Let us first introduce a simple extension of the *vanilla* meta-interpreter [41], where a two-argument predicate Demo is used to denote provability[1].

---

[1] In the following we will adhere to the syntactic conventions used in the Gödel lan-

```
(1) Demo(e,Empty).
(2) Demo(e,(y And z)) <- Demo(e,y) & Demo(e,z).
(3) Demo(e,y) <- Clause(e,y If z) & Demo(e,z).
```

The procedural reading of the above clauses is the following. Clause (1) states that the Empty goal is solved in any object program. Clause (2) deals with conjunctive goals: To solve a conjunction y And z, solve both y and z. Finally, clause (3) addresses the case of goal reduction: To solve an atomic goal y, choose a clause from the program e (whose clauses are represented at the meta-level by means of the predicate Clause) such that its head unifies with y, and recursively solve its body z.

The vanilla meta-interpreter can be employed to interpret compositions of object programs by extending the definition of Clause to represent program compositions, and by introducing a predicate Statement to represent (collections of) object programs. Each program composition operation is represented at the meta-level by a functor whose meaning is defined by means of the Clause predicate:

```
(4) Clause(e1 Union e2, z If w) <-  Clause(e1, z If w).
(5) Clause(e1 Union e2, z If w) <-  Clause(e2, z If w).
(6) Clause(e1 Inters e2, z If (w And u)) <-  Clause(e1, z If w) &
                                             Clause(e2, z If u).
(7) Clause(Enc(e), z If Empty) <-  Demo(e,z).
(8) Clause(e1 Import e2, z If w) <-  Clause(e1, z If (w And u)) &
                                     Demo(e2, u).
(9) Clause(Pr(p), z If w) <-  Statement(p, z If w).
```

Clauses (4) and (5) define the Union operation. Namely, a clause belongs to the meta-level representation of the composition e1 Union e2 if it belongs either to the meta-level representation of e1 or to the meta-level representation of e2. Clause (6) states that a clause z If (w And u) belongs to the meta-level representation of e1 Inters e2 if there are two clauses, one in e1 and the other in e2, such that their heads unify in z and the conjunction of their bodies, suitably instantiated, equals (w And u). The meta-level representation of an encapsulated program Enc(e) — clause (7) — consists of assertions of the form Clause(Enc(e), z If Empty) where z is provable in e. In this way, the code of e is hidden to other programs, which may only refer to the set of sentences provable in e. Clause (8) defines the Import operation. The clauses in e1 Import e2 are obtained from the clauses of e1 by dropping calls to hidden predicates in the original clause body, provided that they are provable in the private part e2 (and possibly instantiating the public calls). Finally clause (9) states that the definition of predicate Clause resorts to the definition of Statement when its first argument, Pr(p), denotes a single object program.

Object level programs are represented by means of the Statement predicate. For instance, the simple program Plus:

---

guage [22]: Identifiers of variables start with lower case letters, while identifiers of non-variables start with upper case letters.

```
Plus(Zero,x,x).
Plus(S(x),y,S(z)) <- Plus(x,y,z).
```

has the following meta-level representation:

```
Statement(Plus, Plus(Zero,x,x) If Empty).
Statement(Plus, Plus(S(x),y,S(z)) If Plus(x,y,z)).
```

The extended vanilla meta-interpreter described so far employs the *non-ground* representation of object programs, in which object level variables are denoted by variables at the meta-level. An alternative, equivalent formulation of the extended meta-interpreter using the ground representation of object programs is described in [5]. A thorough discussion of the relative merits of the two representations is outside the scope of this paper and can be found in [5, 20, 21, 33]. However, since the extended vanilla meta-interpreter does not modify the object programs, the use of a non-ground representation of object programs is preferable since the resulting meta-interpreter has a natural declarative semantics [9], is simpler and more efficient.

The operations Union, Inters, Enc, and Import define the following class Exp of program expressions:

$$\text{Exp} ::= \text{Exp Union Exp} \mid \text{Exp Inters Exp} \mid \text{Enc(Exp)} \mid$$
$$\text{Exp Import Exp} \mid \text{Pr(P)}$$

where P is (the name of) a definite object program. From now onwards, we will refer to the elements of Exp by E, F (possibly subscripted), and we will denote by M_π the meta-interpreter consisting of clauses (1)—(9), together with the meta-level representation of a set π of object programs.

3 Background: Partial evaluation in Logic Programming

This section is devoted to briefly recall some basic definitions and theoretical foundations of partial evaluation in logic programming, taken from [31]. The interested reader may also refer to [38] for an introduction to program transformation in logic programming. We adopt the definitions of SLD(NF) derivation, SLD(NF) refutation, and SLD(NF) tree given in [31], which slightly generalise the corresponding definitions introduced in [30][2].

Definition 1. Let P be a program, A an atom, and T an $SLD(NF)$ tree for $P \cup \{\leftarrow A\}$. Let $G_1, \ldots, G_r$ be (non-root) goals in T chosen so that each non-failing branch in T contains exactly one of them. Let R_i $(i = 1, \ldots, r)$ be the resultant of the derivation from $\leftarrow A$ down to G_i, given by the branch leading to G_i. Then the set of clauses $R_1, \ldots, R_r$ is called a *partial evaluation* of A in P.

---

[2] In [31] SLD(NF) trees may contain *incomplete* derivations, i.e. at any point in a derivation we are allowed to simply not select any literal and terminate the derivation. Correspondingly, a non-failing branch of an (incomplete) SLD(NF) tree is any successful or incomplete derivation.

If $\mathbf{A} = \{A_1, \ldots, A_k\}$ is a finite set of atoms, then a *partial evaluation of* $\mathbf{A}$ *in* P *is the union of partial evaluations of* $A_1, \ldots, A_k$ *in* P.

Definition 2. A *partial evaluation* of P w.r.t. a finite set of atoms $\mathbf{A}$ is a program obtained from P by replacing the set of clauses of P whose head contains one of the predicate symbols appearing in $\mathbf{A}$ (called the *partially evaluated predicates*) with a partial evaluation of $\mathbf{A}$ in P.

Moreover, a partial evaluation of P w.r.t. $\mathbf{A}$ *using SLD-trees* is a partial evaluation in which all the SLDNF-trees used for the partial evaluation are actually SLD-trees. Two general conditions, called *closedness* and *independence*, are introduced in [31] to establish the equivalence between the original program and its partial evaluations.

Definition 3. Let S be a set of first order formulas and $\mathbf{A}$ a finite set of atoms. We say that S is $\mathbf{A}$-*closed* if each atom in S containing a predicate symbol occurring in an atom in $\mathbf{A}$ is an instance of an atom in $\mathbf{A}$.

Definition 4. Let $\mathbf{A}$ be a finite set of atoms. We say $\mathbf{A}$ is *independent* if no pair of atoms in $\mathbf{A}$ have a common instance.

We finally recall one of the main equivalence results presented in [31].

Proposition 5. *Let P be a (normal) program, G a (normal) goal, $\mathbf{A}$ a finite, independent set of atoms, and P' a partial evaluation of P w.r.t. $\mathbf{A}$ using SLD-trees such that $P' \cup \{G\}$ is $\mathbf{A}$-closed. Then the following hold:*

(i) $P' \cup \{G\}$ has an SLD-refutation with computed answer ϑ iff $P \cup \{G\}$ does, and

(ii) $P' \cup \{G\}$ has a finitely failed SLD-tree iff $P \cup \{G\}$ does.

According to the above proposition, from now onwards we will consider two programs equivalent if and only if they have the same computed answers and finite failures w.r.t. a set of given queries.

4 A Program Specialiser for Meta-level Compositions of Object Programs

We now present the design and implementation of a program specialiser for the extended vanilla meta-interpreter $\mathbf{M}_\pi$ introduced in Sect. 2. We first describe the partial evaluation phase, and then the program transformation phase. The actual implementation of the whole specialiser is discussed at the end of the section. An assessment of the program specialiser is contained in Sect. 5.

4.1 Phase I: Partial evaluation

Given the extended meta-interpreter $\mathbf{M}_\pi$ and a program expression $\mathbf{E}$, the partial evaluation phase should yield a new, specialised meta-program $\mathbf{M}_\pi'$ equivalent to $\mathbf{M}_\pi$ w.r.t. queries of the form $\mathtt{Demo(E,G)}$, for any object query $\mathbf{G}$.

In order to specialise M_π w.r.t. queries of the form Demo(E,x), we shall partially evaluate M_π w.r.t. (atoms with) predicate Clause. Indeed, the very structure of M_π shows that the definition of Demo relies on the definition of Clause to perform each reduction step. Actually, the extra interpretation layer needed to deal with program compositions relies on predicate Clause. We will show that, since the program expressions we consider are fully specified, the unfolding of Clause is an effective way of specialising M_π.

Equivalence Result. In order to show when a partial evaluation of the meta-interpreter M_π, obtained by unfolding the predicate Clause, is equivalent to M_π, it is necessary to determine the set of atoms A w.r.t. which the meta-interpreter M_π will be partially evaluated. Since Clause is defined recursively on the structure of program expressions, the unfolded definition of an atom like Clause(E,x) may contain, in some body, atoms of the form Clause(F,y), with F sub-expression of E. By definition of partial evaluation (Definition 2), Clause(F,y) does not unify with any statement in the specialised program M'_π, that is M'_π is not closed w.r.t. {Clause(E,x)}. Indeed M'_π will not be in general equivalent to M_π, since M'_π will fail on queries on which M_π will succeed.

In order to specialise M_π w.r.t. a query of the form Demo(E,x), we will therefore consider a partial evaluation of M_π w.r.t. the set of atoms A= {Clause(E, x), Clause(E$_1$,x),...,Clause(E$_n$,x)} where {E, E$_1$,...,E$_n$} is the set Γ^*(E) of all the sub-expressions of E, which can be inductively defined as follows.

Definition 6. Let E, F be program expressions. Then:

$$
\begin{aligned}
\Gamma^*(\text{E Union F}) &= \{\text{E Union F}\} \cup \Gamma^*(\text{E}) \cup \Gamma^*(\text{F}) \\
\Gamma^*(\text{E Inters F}) &= \{\text{E Inters F}\} \cup \Gamma^*(\text{E}) \cup \Gamma^*(\text{F}) \\
\Gamma^*(\text{Enc(E)}) &= \{\text{Enc(E)}\} \cup \Gamma^*(\text{E}) \\
\Gamma^*(\text{E Import F}) &= \{\text{E Import F}\} \cup \Gamma^*(\text{E}) \cup \Gamma^*(\text{F}) \\
\Gamma^*(\text{Pr(P)}) &= \{\text{Pr(P)}\}
\end{aligned}
$$

We can now state the main equivalence result we are interested in.

Proposition 7. *Let E be a program expression and let* A={Clause(F,x) | F ∈ Γ^*(E)}. *Let* M'_π *be a partial evaluation of* M_π *w.r.t.* A. *Then, for any object level query* G, *the following hold:*
(i) M'_π ∪{← Demo(E,G)} *has an SLD-refutation with computed answer* ϑ *iff* M_π ∪{← Demo(E,G)} *does, and*
(ii) M'_π ∪{← Demo(E,G)} *has a finitely failed SLD-tree iff* M_π ∪{← Demo(E,G)} *does.*

Unfortunately, Proposition 7 is not a direct corollary of Proposition 5 (Sect. 3). Indeed, the specialised program M'_π in Proposition 7 does not satisfy the closedness condition w.r.t. the set A={Clause(F,x) | F ∈ Γ^*(E)}, since the definition of Demo in M'_π (the same as in M_π) contains the clause
    (3) Demo(e,y) <- Clause(e,y If z) & Demo(e,z).
where Clause(e, y If z) is not an instance of any atom in A.

One way of directly applying Proposition 5 is to consider the partial evaluation of M_π w.r.t. the above set of atoms A extended with the set of atoms $\{\text{Demo}(F, x) \mid F \in \Gamma^*(E)\}$. This would enforce the closedness condition at the cost of generating a larger code for M_π'. This solution is not quite convenient since the new clauses for Demo increase the size of the code of the meta-interpreter without really increasing its degree of specialisation and thus negatively affect the performances of the program.

It is instead possible to prove the equivalence between M_π and M_π' by considering a third program M_π'' and by proving that M_π'' is equivalent — by virtue of Proposition 5 — both to M_π and to M_π'. Namely, given a program expression E, we consider the two sets of atoms $A_1 = \{\text{Clause}(F, x) \mid F \in \Gamma^*(E)\}$, and $A_2 = \{\text{Demo}(F, x) \mid F \in \Gamma^*(E)\}$. The proof of Proposition 7 is then partitioned in three parts:

(i) We first show that every partial evaluation of M_π performed in two stages, first w.r.t. A_1, and then w.r.t. A_2, can be equivalently performed in a single step w.r.t. the set $A_1 \cup A_2$.

(ii) We then show that every partial evaluation M_π'' of M_π w.r.t. $A_1 \cup A_2$ is equivalent to M_π as far as queries of the form Demo(E,G) are concerned.

(iii) Finally we show that, given a partial evaluation M_π' of M_π w.r.t. A_1, every partial evaluation M_π'' of M_π' w.r.t. A_2 is equivalent to M_π' as far as queries of the form Demo(E,G) are concerned.

Then, by transitivity of equivalence, Proposition 7 holds (for a complete proof, see [6]).

Partial Evaluation Strategy. In the previous section we have stated (Proposition 7) that *any* partial evaluation of the meta-interpreter M_π w.r.t. the set of atoms $A = \{\text{Clause}(F, x) \mid F \in \Gamma^*(E)\}$ is equivalent to M_π as far as queries of the form Demo(E,G) are concerned. However, Proposition 7 gives no clues either on *which* partial evaluation to choose or on *how* to actually build it.

According to Definition 1 (Sect. 3), the profile of a partial evaluation of a program w.r.t. an atom depends on two choices:

(i) Which computation rule is employed in the construction of the SLD tree (the computation rule is implicit in Definition 1), and

(ii) Which set of nodes $G_1, \ldots, G_r$ is chosen to build the set of clauses defining the specialised program.

In order to design our partial evaluation strategy, we have therefore to fix these two choices. As far as choice (i) is concerned, we consider any computation rule that "gives priority" to predicates Clause and Statement. Simply stated, for each goal G, we consider rules that always select an atom with predicate Clause or Statement, if any. If there is no such atom in G, then no constraint is imposed and the rule is free to choose any atom in G. We will denote by $\mathcal{R}_{CS}$ any computation rule that satisfies the above constraint. Intuitively speaking, such a constraint reflects the idea of first unfolding the "promising" atoms (i.e., those which can be specialised by unfolding), while postponing the unfolding of all other atoms.

Consider now choice (ii). Let T be an SLD-tree for $M_\pi \cup \{\leftarrow \texttt{Clause(F,x)}\}$. The set of nodes $G_1, \ldots, G_r$ is chosen as the set of all (non-root) nodes G_j in T such that:

(S_1) For each proper ancestor N of G_j: $Pred(\mathcal{R}_{CS}(N)) \in$ CS, and

(S_2) G_j is either a success leaf of T, or a non-leaf node of T such that $Pred(\mathcal{R}_{CS}(G_j)) \notin$ CS

where CS $= \{\texttt{Clause,Statement}\}$, and $Pred(\mathcal{R}_{CS}(N))$ denotes the predicate symbol of the atom selected by $\mathcal{R}$ in N.

Summing up, our strategy of partial evaluation for M_π consists of: (i) adopting any computation rule $\mathcal{R}_{CS}$ in the construction of SLD trees, and (ii) selecting the nodes in the SLD trees according to rules (S_1) and (S_2). We then call any partial evaluation adopting such a strategy a (R_{CS},S_1,S_2)-*partial evaluation*. As shown in [6], every (R_{CS},S_1,S_2)-partial evaluation of M_π w.r.t. $A = \{\texttt{Clause(F,x)} \mid F \in \Gamma^*(E)\}$ *is* a partial evaluation according to Definition 1.

It is worth noting that the notion of (R_{CS},S_1,S_2)-partial evaluation allows us to shrink the set of atoms A w.r.t. which the partial evaluation of the meta-interpreter M_π is performed, thus directly reducing the size of the code of the specialised program. Indeed, for any program expression E, it is sufficient to consider only the set of atoms of the form $\texttt{Clause(F,x)}$ such that F is either E itself or some "critical" sub-expression of E. Namely, given E, the set of its critical sub-expressions $\Gamma(E)$ contains every sub-expression F_i of E that is either encapsulated ($\texttt{Enc(F}_i)$) or imported by some other expression (F_j $\texttt{Import}$ F_i). Indeed these are the cases in which the definition of predicate $\texttt{Clause}$ resorts to predicate $\texttt{Demo}$ in the meta-interpreter M_π. (Formally $\Gamma(E)$ can be inductively defined by refining Definition 6, as done in [6].)

We will then consider (R_{CS},S_1,S_2)-partial evaluations of the meta-interpreter M_π w.r.t. the reduced set of atoms $A' = \{\texttt{Clause(F,x)} \mid F \in (\Gamma(E) \cup \{E\})\}$. It is important to observe [6] that the equivalence result established in Proposition 7 continues to hold.

Independence of the Computation Rule. As pointed out in [31], it is interesting to analyse the role of computation rules in the equivalence results concerning partial evaluations of logic programs.

Proposition 7 holds for all computation rules used in obtaining the partial evaluation M'_π of M_π. As far as the equivalence of M'_π and M_π w.r.t. goals is concerned, Proposition 7 states that, for instance, "if $M'_\pi \cup \{\leftarrow \texttt{Demo(E,G)}\}$ has a refutation with computed answer ϑ using some computation rule, then $M_\pi \cup \{\leftarrow \texttt{Demo(E,G)}\}$ has a refutation with computed answer ϑ, which may use another, possibly different computation rule". Indeed, since M_π and M'_π are both definite programs, from the independence of the computation rule theorem [30], part (i) of Proposition 7 (concerning refutations) can be stated for any three computation rules, one to be used in the partial evaluation, another for M'_π, and a third for M_π. In particular, this means that the same computation rule can be used throughout. Notice that, as pointed out in [31], the same independence result does not hold for failures, that is, for part (ii) of Proposition 7. Namely a goal may have, using the same computation rule, a finitely failed SLD-tree in $\mathbf{M}'_\pi$ and an infinite derivation in $\mathbf{M}_\pi$. However, as observed in [31], part (ii) of Proposition 7 holds for any *fair* computation rule, by the completeness result of negation as failure for definite programs [30].

Similar considerations apply to the equivalence result between $\mathbf{M}_\pi$ and its (R_{CS}, S_1, S_2)-partial evaluation $\mathbf{M}^s_\pi$. Namely the result holds for any pair of fair computation rules to be used for $\mathbf{M}_\pi$ and $\mathbf{M}^s_\pi$, and for any R_{CS} computation rule employed in obtaining $\mathbf{M}^s_\pi$.

4.2 Phase II: Program Transformation

We now describe how program transformation techniques can be applied to further optimise the meta-interpreter $\mathbf{M}^s_\pi$ obtained at the end of the partial evaluation phase.

A first optimisation step consists of deleting from $\mathbf{M}^s_\pi$ the clauses defining predicate Statement. Such a transformation does not affect the equivalence between $\mathbf{M}_\pi$ and $\mathbf{M}^s_\pi$, since the predicate Statement is *totally* evaluated by a (R_{CS}, S_1, S_2)-partial evaluation. Namely, Statement is neither connected to Demo nor to Clause in the dependency graph of $\mathbf{M}^s_\pi$.

We will now show how an analysis of the given program expression E (used during the partial evaluation phase) can support more dramatic optimisations.

Meta-level Elimination. Let us consider first the cases in which the given program expression E does not contain Enc or Import operations. It is easy to observe that in such cases the set $\Gamma(E)$ is empty, and hence a (R_{CS}, S_1, S_2)-partial evaluation of $\mathbf{M}_\pi$ w.r.t. $\mathbf{A}' = \{\texttt{Clause}(\mathbf{F}, \mathbf{x}) \mid \mathbf{F} \in (\Gamma(E) \cup \{E\})\}$ is simply a (R_{CS}, S_1, S_2)-partial evaluation of $\mathbf{M}_\pi$ w.r.t. the set $\{\texttt{Clause}(E, \mathbf{x})\}$. Therefore, in these cases, the partial evaluation phase returns a meta-interpreter $\mathbf{M}^s_\pi$ of the form:

```
Demo(e,Empty).
Demo(e,(y And z)) <- Demo(e,y) & Demo(e,z).
Demo(e,y) <- Clause(e,y If z) & Demo(e,z).
Clause(E, H1 If B1).
...
Clause(E, Hn If Bn).
```

It is important to observe that the above program corresponds to a standard vanilla meta-interpreter for a single object program, in which the first argument (viz., the program expression) of both Demo and Clause can be removed altogether. The equivalence between the vanilla meta-interpreter and the interpreted object program [9, 33] supports a major optimisation step: The specialised meta-program $\mathbf{M}^s_\pi$ can be transformed into an equivalent *object* program of the form:

```
H1 <- B1.
...
Hn <- Bn.
```

Therefore, in these cases the specialisation process eliminates not only the overhead due to the handling of program compositions but also the whole meta-interpretation layer overhead.

Program Expression Argument Elimination. Let us consider the cases in which the given program expression E contains Enc or Import operations. Differently from the cases analysed in the previous subsection, the set $\Gamma(E)$ is not empty and a (R_{CS}, S_1, S_2)-partial evaluation of M_π w.r.t. A' = {Clause(F, x) | F $\in (\Gamma(E) \cup \{E\})$} will contain some definition of Clause which does not consist of unit clauses only. Hence, in these cases, the specialised meta-interpreter M_π^s cannot be directly transformed into an equivalent object program.

It is however possible to optimise M_π^s by applying a standard program transformation technique for eliminating predicate arguments. Namely, the program expression argument (viz., the first argument) can be eliminated from both predicates Demo and Clause. As described in [6], the transformation consists of introducing two new predicates Demo_i and Clause_i for each program expression Fi $\in (\Gamma(E) \cup \{E\})$. Then each atom of the form Clause(Fi, t) (resp., Demo(Fi, t)) in the definition of Clause is replaced by an atom of the form Clause_i(t) (resp., Demo_i(t)). Finally, the definition of Demo is replaced by the definition of m+1 predicates Demo_0, Demo_1, ..., Demo_m, each of them defined as in the standard vanilla meta-interpreter.

The above transformation defines a standard argument filtering technique that sensibly reduces the execution time needed to perform unifications [17, 39]. Indeed, even though the transformation slightly increases the size of the code, it provides a considerable performance improvement, as we will discuss in Sect. 5. The correctness of the transformation is ensured by the one-to-one correspondence between the derivations in M_π' and the derivations in the transformed program [6].

4.3 Implementation

The program specialiser described in the previous sections, given the meta-interpreter M_π and a program expression E, builds a specialised version New_M_π of M_π by performing first a partial evaluation phase and then a program transformation phase.

The whole program specialiser has been written in Gödel [22]. The choice of using Gödel was motivated by two different considerations. First, one of our objectives was to build a program specialiser to be integrated with the existing system COMPOSE [5], which is written in Gödel. Second, Gödel offers considerable support for the development of meta-programming applications, such as program transformers, adopting a declarative programming style [3, 5, 19].

It is worth observing that both kinds of representations of object level programs — ground and non-ground — are employed in our specialiser. Indeed the meta-interpreter M_π defining meta-level compositions of programs employs a *non-ground* representation of object programs. On the other hand, the meta-program defining the program specialiser employs a *ground* representation of the object program (which is in turn the meta-interpreter M_π).

5 Assessment

The specialiser described in the previous sections, given a meta-interpreter M_π and a program expression E, always returns a specialised program New_M_π that is more efficient than M_π. We will now briefly compare M_π and New_M_π as far as memory occupation and execution times are concerned.

Memory occupation is an important aspect of program transformation, since a typical risk of applying unfolding techniques is code explosion [2, 10, 29]. In our case, as shown in [6], our program specialisation strategy ensures that the size of the optimised program New_M_π is approximately the same of M_π.

The performance speed-ups supported by our program specialiser have been analysed by considering some standard benchmark examples. The results of these experiments are reported in Table 1.

The first column (Query) contains a representation of an object level query G. The second column (Prog_Exp) specifies the program expression E — where U stands for Union, ∩ for Inters, * for Enc and ◁ for Import — w.r.t. which the meta-interpreter M_π is specialised. The third column (M_π) contains the execution times for the query Demo(E,G) in the initial meta-interpreter M_π. The fourth column (New_M_π) contains the execution times, for the same query, of the meta-interpreter New_M_π obtained by specialising M_π w.r.t. E. The fifth column (Rate) explicitly shows the rate between the third and the fourth column, that is, the performance speed-up yielded by the specialisation process. Finally, the last column (SAGE(M_π)) contains the execution times of the program obtained by specialising M_π by means of SAGE [19], a partial evaluator for Gödel programs.

The first benchmark example is Quicksort, consisting of three object programs: Quick defining the kernel of the standard quicksort algorithm, Split defining the process of partitioning a list into two sub-lists, and the well-known program Append for concatenating two lists. The second example is the Hanoi problem, represented by means of an object program Hanoi, defining the solution strategy and by the Append program. The third example concerns the problem of finding acyclic paths on a graph whose nodes represent cities and whose arcs represent train connections between cities. Program Path defines acyclic paths on a graph described by Train, while Lib defines standard auxiliary predicates and IC represents constraints over the arcs forming paths.

Execution times have been calculated using the (Bristol) Gödel 1.4 module Statistics and are expressed in milliseconds.

The experimental results highlight that when the given program expression E does not contain Enc or Import operations, then our program specialiser pro-

Query	Prog_Exp	M_π	New_M_π	Rate	SAGE(M_π)
Quicksort	Quick ∪ Append ∪ Split	106	9	11.7	117
	(Quick ∪ Append) ◁ Split	191	122	1.5	245
Hanoi	Hanoi ∪ Append	291	23	12.6	265
	Hanoi ∪ (Append)*	187	91	2.0	177
Ac_Path	Path ∪ Lib ∪ (Train ∩ IC)	782	10	78.2	76
	Path ∪ (Lib)* ∪ (Train ∩ IC)	513	370	1.3	79

Table 1. Experimental results.

duces an object level program thus yielding a speed-up factor greater than 10. This factor may grow further if E contains Inters operations, which can sensibly reduce the size of the specialised program. When instead E contains Enc or Import operations, the specialised meta-interpreter cannot be flattened down to the object level, and therefore the corresponding speed-up factor is considerably smaller, between 1.3 and 2.

The last column of Table 1 shows that the execution times of the specialisations of M_π produced by SAGE are close to the execution times of the initial meta-interpreters. The main reason for this behaviour is that, although SAGE can be applied to any Gödel program, it is primarily targeted to optimise (meta-)programs using the ground representation of object programs. Moreover, SAGE performs a static analysis of the initial program in order to distinguish *safe* predicates, whose unfolding is always terminating and which will be specialised, from *unsafe* predicates which will be only partly specialised. In the case of the meta-interpreter M_π for the first two examples, predicates Clause and Demo are marked unsafe by SAGE, while only Statement is marked safe and unfolded. Therefore, the specialised program is similar to the initial one, and presents similar performances. The third example (Ac_Path) is instead a case in which SAGE supports a very good speed-up. Namely, the very last row indicates a speed-up greater than 6, while the speed-up given by our strategy is 1.3. The reason of this result is that while our strategy inhibits the unfolding of Demo, SAGE recognises in this case the possibility of a safe unfolding and performs it. This example also highlights how the structure of the program expression E employed to construct the query affects both the execution times of M_π and the results of the partial evaluation process. Indeed, if Lib is not encapsulated then our specialiser yields a speed-up that is around seven times better than what SAGE does.

Our specialisation technique addresses the problem of specialising the meta-interpreter M_π w.r.t. queries of the form Demo(E,x), where the object level query x is not specified. As pointed out in Sect. 1, general existing program specialisation techniques can be employed to further specialise the obtained program New_M$_\pi$ w.r.t. partially instantiated object queries. In this perspective, we tried to combine our program specialiser with Mixtus [39], a partial evaluator for full Prolog, and with SP [15], a system that is able to specialise declarative logic programs, written in Prolog's syntax. In order to evaluate the effectiveness of such a combination, we have compared the specialised programs obtained, respectively: (I) By applying our program specialiser to M_π w.r.t. a program expression E, by converting the specialised (definite) program New_M$_\pi$ from the Gödel syntax into the Prolog syntax, and by specialising it by means of Mixtus (or SP) w.r.t. some partially instantiated object query G, or (II) By employing only Mixtus (or SP) to specialise M_π first w.r.t. to E, and then w.r.t. G.

Experiments on the benchmark examples described in this section showed the effectiveness of such a combination. In particular the examples highlight that the use of our program specialiser together with Mixtus (or SP) — approach (I) — generally gives better speed-ups than using Mixtus (or SP) alone — approach (II). More precisely, when our program specialiser succeeds in transforming the meta-interpreter M_π into an equivalent object level program, the obtained speed-up is definitively higher than the overall speed-up supported by approach (II). When, instead, our program specialiser cannot produce an object level program, then the two approaches yield very similar results.

Notice that, if we consider only the first stage of the specialisation process (i.e., the specialisation w.r.t. E) then Mixtus and SP may give better results than our specialiser. This is due to the fact that Mixtus and SP employ more sophisticated program specialisation techniques than our simple (and partial) unfolding. However, also in these cases, after Mixtus or SP have been applied to perform the second stage of the specialisation process (w.r.t. G), the combined approach (I) offers a similar speed-up as using only Mixtus or SP (II). A disadvantage of combining our specialiser with Mixtus or SP concerns declarativeness. Namely, the declarative style of our program specialiser — using Gödel's ground representation of object programs — is not supported by Mixtus and SP — which employ Prolog's non-declarative features.

6 Discussion

In the previous sections we have presented a program specialisation technique targeted to specialising the extended meta-interpreter M_π. We have shown that the proposed technique ensures correctness, termination, and effectiveness.

Gallagher identified in [16] two levels of control in the specialisation process. The *local* control deals with the construction of SLD(NF) trees for individual atoms, while the *global* control determines the set of atoms for which partial evaluations should be computed. Starting from [16], considerable progress has been made on the control issues during the last few years (e.g., [27, 28, 32, 35]).

The partial evaluation phase of our program specialiser (Sect. 4.1) can be expressed in terms of global and local control strategies as follows. Our local control strategy defines an unfolding rule that promotes (by employing R_{CS} computation rules) the unfolding of predicates Clause and Statement w.r.t. the unfolding of predicate Demo. Moreover our global control strategy just considers the program expression arguments in order to abstract the set of atoms for which the partial evaluations are to be computed. As previously discussed, termination is ensured at both levels of control (local and global).

An intriguing question is whether other control strategies may yield better results than our when applied to the meta-interpreter M_π. As pointed out in [23], several approaches to local control have been proposed, based on determinacy, well-founded measures, and homeomorphic embedding.

Determinacy [15, 18] only (except once) selects atoms that match a single clause head. This strategy does not guarantee termination and seems often too conservative (even including "look ahead") [23]. It is easy to verify that these limitations carry over to the case of our meta-interpreters.

Imposing well-founded orders [10, 34] ensures local termination and provides a higher degree of specialisation. Bruynooghe et al. [10] point out that special care must be taken when employing well-founded measures for partially evaluating meta-interpreters. They observe that, in the case of the vanilla meta-interpreter, one almost never wants to stop the unfolding of atoms of the form Demo(A And B) or Demo(Empty). On the other hand, the control on the unfolding of atoms of the form Demo(P(t)) should rely on the properties of P(t) (viz., of the object level atom). Our meta-interpreter M_π extends the standard vanilla meta-interpreter by introducing an extra argument (E) denoting the program expression in which goals are queried. A well-founded measure should therefore take into account *also* the first argument (E) of Demo and Clause in order to control their unfolding. Indeed our local partial evaluation strategy exploits the structure of E to guide the unfolding of Clause and to ensure its termination. This strategy can be expressed by means of a well-founded measure that takes into account *only* the first argument (E) of Demo and Clause.

On the other hand, the definition of suitable measures taking into account both arguments of Demo and Clause (viz., the program expression and the object level goal) is not as straightforward. For instance, the adoption of standard "norm-based" well-founded measures [10] on both arguments does not increase (and often worsen) the degree of specialisation obtained by employing a well-founded measure on the first argument only. Bruynooghe et al. [10] suggested the unfolding of atoms of the form Demo(P(t)) when P is a non-recursive predicate in the object level program. In our setting, since predicate definitions are spread over different modules, one should suitably extend the definition of recursive predicate. (For instance, a predicate which is non-recursive in an object program P may become recursive in a program expression containing P.) Moreover, the partial evaluation of the vanilla meta-interpreter starts with queries of the form Demo(A) where A is a partially instantiated object-level atom. In contrast, the partial evaluation of the extended meta-interpreter M_π starts with queries of the form Demo(E,x) where the object-level query is not specified. In such cases the unfolding process will in general instantiate x (by exploiting Clause and Statement) and this should not always stop the unfolding process.

Another approach for specifying local control relies on homeomorphic embedding [27, 40]. Homeomorphic embedding consists of employing well-quasi orders rather than well-founded orders on selected atoms, and it seems to define in general more sophisticated local control strategies than well-founded orders. In our case, however, the observation on the unboundness of the object-level goal x in the initial query Demo(E,x) continues to hold.

It is important to observe that our program specialisation technique can be exploited to deal with other significant extensions of the multi program setting described in Sect. 2. Namely, the specialisation technique described in this paper has been also applied [6] to meta-level compositions of object programs written in an extended syntax. As shown in [8], allowing object level programs to contain formulae of the form G In E, where G is an object level goal and E is a program expression, notably increases the expressive power of the language of program expressions, for instance by supporting forms of context-switching and message-passing. The meaning of the meta-annotation In is defined by adding the following clause to the extended vanilla meta-interpreter M_π:

(3') Demo(e, (g In e1)) <- Demo(e1, g).

The only change needed to apply our specialisation technique to this extension concerns the set of program expressions w.r.t. which M_π must be partially evaluated. Namely, given a program expression E, the set of "critical" program expressions includes — in addition to the set $\Gamma(E) \cup \{E\}$ — all program expressions occurring in the object programs in E and their critical sub-expressions.

It is worth noting that general local control strategies (like those based on well founded measures and homeomorphic embedding) are not able to exploit the special structure of meta-programs containing In formulae, and perform overly eager unfolding without increasing the degree of specialisation. The problem is that general local control strategies unfold the statements of all object programs in M_π independently of whether or not these programs will be involved in the computations associated with the given program expression E. Our strategy instead takes advantage of the (a priori) knowledge of the special structure of the meta-interpreter M_π. Indeed, our ad hoc analysis of E is able to identify the subset of the object programs in M_π that are actually involved in the computations associated with E, and hence supports a more appropriate specialisation of M_π.

It is worth observing that the introduction of the In feature is a classical example of use of meta-programming techniques for defining language extensions. This example confirms the intuition that the more particular the structure of the meta-interpreter the less effective is the application of general program specialisation techniques. More generally, this example seems to suggest that at least some classes of meta-programs require ad hoc specialisation techniques for properly dealing with their structure.

We now briefly discuss other related work. Levi and Sardu [29] made one of the first experiments of applying partial evaluation techniques to multiple logic program settings. They describe the realisation of a partial evaluator for a knowledge base management system, where separate Prolog programs can be combined by means of inheritance operators. Their partial evaluator is based on controlled unfolding and is targeted to handle object programs written in full Prolog, including built-ins and cuts. The experimental results reported in [29] show that the partial evaluator is able to yield very good speed-ups for the examples considered. On the other hand, the correctness of the partial evaluation strategy employed is not discussed at all.

Bugliesi, Lamma and Mello [11] also studied the problem of applying partial evaluation techniques to specialising compositions of object logic programs in the contextual logic programming setting [36]. Their approach neatly differs from ours in that all the definitions and results for partial evaluation in logic programming presented in [31] are extended in [11] to deal with the extended multi-program setting[3]. Conversely, a meta-programming definition of composition operations over logic programs (like the one considered in this paper) has several advantages. First, the considered extension can be directly expressed from within logic programming itself, so that for instance a standard logic programming interpreter can be exploited to query meta-level composition of programs. Second, it is not necessary to extend the theory of partial evaluation in logic programming, since the whole extension is expressed in terms of standard logic (meta-)programs and the results of [31] can be directly exploited, as shown in Sect. 4.

The issue of partially evaluating meta-programs interpreting a single object program has been studied by many authors. Several efforts [3, 16, 19, 26] have been devoted to specialising meta-programs using the ground representation of object programs rather than meta-programs using the non-ground representation (like the meta-interpreter M_π considered in this paper). Other works [37, 39, 43] address the problems of handling Prolog's non-logical features in the specialisation of Prolog meta-programs.

Several general issues in the specialisation of meta-programs have been studied for instance in [10, 14, 20]. Gallagher [14] showed how meta-interpreters defining control strategies can be specialised by compiling the control strategy into the object program. He also pointed out that partial evaluation is only a part of the specialisation process, and that it is in general convenient to apply also other program transformation techniques (like predicate addition/deletion). Bruynooghe et al. [10] suggested that meta-programs should be specialised in an *ad hoc* way, and pointed out the problem of how to automatically recognise meta-interpreters.

The specialisation of (meta-)interpreters has a strong relation with standard compilation techniques, as it was originally illustrated by Futamura [13] (*first Futamura projection*) and others [14, 20, 42]. In our setting, program specialisation relates the meta-logical implementation of program composition operations with their compilation-oriented implementation described in [4]. Hill and Gallagher

---

[3] Definitions of extended resultant, extended SLD-tree, and so on, are introduced, and the basic results given in [11] are proved in the new setting.

[20] thoroughly discussed the relation between meta-programming and program specialisation, as well as some promising applications of meta-programming specialisation such as implementing other languages, expert systems, and enhanced language interpreters.

7 Concluding Remarks

We have presented a specialisation technique for handling meta-interpreters defining compositions of object programs. The correctness of the transformation has been proved by resorting to standard results of partial evaluation in logic programming. The program specialiser has been implemented in Gödel by using meta-programming and a ground representation of the object program (i.e., the extended vanilla meta-interpreter M_π), so that the whole program specialiser is written in a declarative way. The effectiveness of the approach has been demonstrated by comparing the speed-up offered by our program specialiser with the speed-up offered by SAGE, as well as by other existing specialisers.

An interesting direction for future work is the use of different representations of object programs for implementing program specialisers. Leuschel and Martens [26], for instance, have recently pointed out the disadvantages of writing partial evaluators by employing a ground representation of object programs in which (the representation of) substitutions must be explicitly handled. They have therefore proposed a new ground representation for object (Prolog) programs in which the representation of substitutions is hidden at the meta-level. The results reported in [26] indicate such a representation as very promising, at least for some applications.

Another interesting direction is the study of more sophisticated strategies of global (and local) control for specialising our meta-interpreters. A further (even more) promising direction is to introduce reflection mechanisms [1, 12, 25] in order to integrate meta-level and object level computations in the specialised programs. This would allow considerable speed-ups even when the specialised program cannot be directly converted into an equivalent object level program.

Acknowledgements

We would like to thank the anonymous referees for their helpful comments on the first version of this paper. This work has been partly supported by the INTAS project 93-1702 on "Efficient Symbolic Computing".

References

1. J. Barklund. Metaprogramming in Logic. In A. Kent and J.G. Williams, editors, *Encyclopedia of Computer Sciene and Technology*, chapter 33, pages 205–227. Marcel Dekker, 1995.
2. K. Benkerimi and J.W. Lloyd. A Partial Evaluation Procedure for Logic Programs. In S. Debray and M. Hermenegildo, editors, *Logic Programming: Proceedings of the 1990 North American Conference*, pages 343–358. The MIT Press, 1990.

3. A. F. Bowers and C. A. Gurr. Towards Fast and Declarative Meta-Programming. In K. Apt and F. Turini, editors, *Meta-Logics and Logic Progamming*, chapter 2, pages 137–166. The MIT Press, 1995.

4. A. Brogi. *Program Construction in Computational Logic*. PhD thesis, Department of Computer Science, University of Pisa, 1993.

5. A. Brogi and S. Contiero. Composing logic programs by meta-programming in Gödel. In K. Apt and F.Turini, editors, *Meta-programming and Logic Programming*, chapter 7, pages 167–194. The MIT Press, 1995.

6. A. Brogi and S. Contiero. A Program Specialiser for Meta-level Compositions of Logic Programs. TR 96-20, Dpt. of Computer Science, University of Pisa, 1996.

7. A. Brogi, P. Mancarella, D. Pedreschi, and F. Turini. Modular Logic Programming. *ACM Transactions on Programming Languages and Systems*, 16(4):1361–1398, 1994.

8. A. Brogi, C. Renso, and F. Turini. Amalgamating Language and Meta-Language for Composing Logic Programs. In M. Alpuente, R. Barbuti, and I. Ramos, editors, *Proc. of the GULP-PRODE'94 Joint Conference*, vol.2, pages 408–422, 1994.

9. A. Brogi and F. Turini. Meta-Logic for Program Composition: Semantics Issues. In K.R. Apt and F. Turini, editors, *Meta-logics and Logic Programming*, chapter 4, pages 83–110. The MIT Press, 1995.

10. M. Bruynooghe, D. De Schreye, and B. Martens. A General Criterion for Avoiding Infinite Unfolding during Partial Evaluation. *New Generation Computing*, 11(1):47–79, 1992.

11. M. Bugliesi, E. Lamma, and P. Mello. Partial Deduction for Structured Logic Programming. *Journal of Logic Programming*, 16(1, 2):89–122, 1993.

12. S. Costantini, P. Dell'Acqua, and G. A. Lanzarone. Extending Horn Clauses Theories by Reflection Principles. In M. MacNish, D. Pearce, and L. M. Pereira, editors, *Logics in Artificial Intelligence*, LNAI 838, pages 400–413. Springer-Verlag, 1994.

13. Y. Futamura. Partial Computation of Programs. In J. Hartmanis and G. Goos, editors, *RIMS Symp. on Software Science and Engineering*, LNCS 147, pages 1–35. Springer-Verlag, 1982.

14. J. Gallagher. Transforming Logic Programs By Specialising Interpreters. In *ECAI-86*, pages 313–326, 1986.

15. J. Gallagher. A System For Specialising Logic Programs. Technical Report 91-32, University of Bristol, 1991.

16. J. Gallagher. Tutorial on Specialisation of Logic Programs. In *Proceedings PEPM93, ACM SIGPLAN Symposium on Partial Evaluation and Semantics-Based Program Manipulation*, pages 88–98. ACM Press, 1993.

17. J. Gallagher and M. Bruynooghe. Some Low-Level Source Transformations for Logic Programs. In M. Bruynooghe, editor, *Proceedings of the Second Workshop on Meta-Programming in Logic, Leuven, Belgium*, pages 229–244, 1990.

18. J. Gallagher and M. Bruynooghe. The Derivation of an Alghoritm for Program Specialisation. *New Generation Computing*, 9(3-4):305–333, 1991.

19. C.A. Gurr. *A Self-Applicable Partial Evaluator for the Logic Programming Language Gödel*. PhD thesis, University of Bristol, 1994.

20. P. Hill and J. Gallagher. Metaprogramming in Logic programming. In A. Robinson and C. Hogger, editors, *Handbook of Logic in Artificial Intelligence and Logic Programming*, chapter 5. Oxford University Press, 1996.

21. P.M. Hill and J.W. Lloyd. Analysis of metaprograms. In H.D. Abramson and M.H. Rogers, editors, *Metaprogramming in Logic Programming*, pages 23–52. The MIT Press, 1989.

22. P.M. Hill and J.W. Lloyd. *The Gödel Programming Language*. The MIT Press, 1994.

23. J. Jørgensen, M. Leuschel, and B. Martens. Conjunctive Partial Deduction. In J. Gallagher (editor) *Pre-proceedings of LOPSTR-96*, pages 46–62, 1996.

24. J. Komorowski. An Introduction to Partial Deduction. In A. Pettorossi, editor, *Meta-Programming in Logic*, LNCS 649, pages 49–69. Springer-Verlag, 1996.

25. E. Lamma, P. Mello, and A. Natali. Reflection Mechanisms for Combining Prolog Databases. *Software: Practice and Experience*, 21(6):603–624, 1991.

26. M. Leuschel and B. Martens. Partial Deduction of the Ground Representation and its Application to Integrity Checking. In John Lloyd, editor, *Proceedings of ILPS'95*, pages 495–509. The MIT Press, 1995.

27. M. Leuschel and B. Martens. Global Control for Partial Deduction through Characteristic Atoms and Global Trees. In *Proceedings of the 1996 Dagstuhl Seminar on Partial Evaluation, LNCS 1110*, pages 263–283, 1996.

28. M. Leuschel and D. De Schreye. An Almost Perfect Abstract Operation for Partial Deduction Using Characteristic Trees. In *Technical Report CW 215*, October 1995.

29. G. Levi and G. Sardu. Partial Evaluation of Metaprograms in a "Multiple Worlds" Logic Language. *New Generation Computing*, 6(2,3):227–247, 1988.

30. J.W. Lloyd. *Foundations of logic programming*. Springer-Verlag, 2nd, 1987.

31. J.W. Lloyd and J.C. Shepherdson. Partial evaluation in logic programming. *Journal of Logic Programming*, 11:217–242, 1991.

32. B. Martens and J. Gallagher. Ensuring Global Termination of Partial Deduction while Allowing Flexible Polyvariance. In L. Sterling, editor, *Proceedings of ICLP95*, pages 597–611. The MIT Press, 1995.

33. B. Martens and D. De Schreye. Why untyped non-ground meta-programming is not (much of) a problem. *Journal of Logic Programming*, 22(1):47–99, 1995.

34. B. Martens and D. De Schreye. Automatic Finite Unfolding using Well-Founded Measures. In *Journal of Logic Programming*, 1996 (to appear).

35. B. Martens, D. De Schreye, and T. Horváth. Sound and Complete Partial Deduction with Unfolding Based on Well-Founded Measures. *Theoretical Computer Science*, 122(1-2):97–117, 1995.

36. L. Monteiro and A. Porto. Contextual logic programming. In G. Levi and M. Martelli, editors, *Proceedings Sixth ICLP*, pages 284–302. The MIT Press, 1989.

37. S. Owen. Issues in the Partial Evaluation of Meta-Interpreters. In H. Abramson and M.H. Rogers, editors, *Meta-Programming in Logic Programming*, pages 319–340. The MIT Press, 1989.

38. A. Pettorossi and M. Proietti. Transformations of logic programs: Foundations and techniques. *The Journal of Logic Programming*, 19 & 20:261–320, 1994.

39. D. Sahlin. *An Automatic Partial Evaluator for Full Prolog*. PhD thesis, KTH, Dpt. of Telecommunications and Computer Systems, Stockolm, Sweden, 1991.

40. M. Sørensen and R. Glück. An Algorithm of Generalization in Positive Supercompilation. In John Lloyd, editor, *Proceedings of ILPS'95, the International Logic Programming Symposium*, pages 465–479. The MIT Press, 1995.

41. L. Sterling and E. Shapiro. *The Art of Prolog*. The MIT Press, 1986.

42. A. Takeuchi. Affinity between meta interpreters and partial evaluation. In H.-J. Kugler, editor, *Information Processing 86*, pages 279–282. North-Holland, 1986.

43. A. Takeuchi and K. Furukawa. Partial evaluation of Prolog programs and its application to meta-programming. In H.-J. Kugler, editor, *Information Processing 86*, pages 415–420. North-Holland, 1986.

Forms of Logic Specifications:
A Preliminary Study[*]

Kung-Kiu Lau[1] and Mario Ornaghi[2]

[1] Department of Computer Science
University of Manchester, Manchester M13 9PL, United Kingdom
kung-kiu@cs.man.ac.uk
[2] Dipartimento di Scienze dell'Informazione
Universita' degli studi di Milano, Via Comelico 39/41, Milano, Italy
ornaghi@dsi.unimi.it

Abstract. There is no universal agreement on exactly what form a specification should take, what part it should play in synthesis, and what its precise relationship with the specified program should be. In logic programming, the role of specification is all the more unclear since logic programs are often used as executable specifications. In this paper we take the view that specifications should be set in the context of the problem domain, which we call a *framework*. We conduct a preliminary study of two useful forms of logic specifications: *if-and-only-if* and *partial* specifications. First we set up a three-tier formalism for synthesis, the top-tier being a framework. Then within this formalism we define these two forms of specifications, and discuss their roles in synthesis.

1 Introduction

The purpose of program synthesis is to derive programs that are correct wrt to their (formal or informal) specifications. There is no universal agreement, however, on exactly what form a specification should take, what part it should play in synthesis, and what its precise relationship with the specified program should be. In logic programming, the role of specification is all the more unclear because a logic program itself is a Horn clause theory ([11]), and as such can double as a definition or specification. Indeed logic programs are often used as executable specifications, for instance in rapid prototyping.

In our work in deductive synthesis of logic programs (see e.g. [17, 18]), we maintain a strict distinction between specifications and programs. We take the view that program synthesis should take place in a three-tier formalism (with model-theoretic semantics). At the bottom level, we have *programs*, for computing (specified) relations. In the middle, we have *specifications* for defining

---

[*] Part of this work was done during the first author's visit to Computing Science Department, Uppsala University, Sweden, supported by the European Union HCM project on Logic Program Synthesis and Transformation, contract no. 93/414. He wishes to thank Jonas Barklund for his invitation and hospitality.

or specifying new relations (and functions). At the top, we have a *framework* that embodies an axiomatisation of (all the relevant knowledge of) the problem domain, that provides an unambiguous semantic underpinning for specifications and programs, as well as the correctness relationship between them.

In such a three-tier structure, a specification can serve two purposes: (i) to define new relation symbols, and (ii) to provide a starting point for, as well as help with, program synthesis. Furthermore, a specification can define relation symbols at two levels: (a) it can define symbols that can be used at the top level, i.e. relation symbols that expand the (language of the) framework; (b) it can define relation symbols that can be used at the bottom level, i.e. relation symbols that appear only in programs. Of course, symbols introduced at the framework level can also be used in programs. However, the converse is strictly not true.

In this paper, we first motivate a three-tier formalism for synthesis (Section 2), and then define and discuss two forms of specifications, viz. *if-and-only-if*, and *partial* specifications (Sections 4 and 5) in the context of a framework $\mathcal{F}$. We shall show that if-and-only-if specifications can be used to define symbols at both the framework and the program level, whereas partial specifications can define only program level symbols. However, as we shall show by means of examples, the latter specifications provide much more help than the former for practical program derivation.

We believe that a study and a classification of different forms of specifications is interesting, and could offer new possibilities to program synthesis. This paper is a preliminary step towards this goal.

2 A Three-tier Formalism

In this section, we use so-called *executable specifications*, to motivate a three-tier formalism for program synthesis. In logic programming, executable specifications are of course just logic programs. However, it is not clear exactly what the meaning of a logic program P is as an executable specification. Is it just the minimum Herbrand model of P? Is it the completion $Comp(P)$ of P? Or is it something else?

We would argue that the meaning of P as an executable specification is only well-defined in the context of the underlying problem domain, or *framework*. For example, consider the following Prolog program (in [22]) for *subset*:

```
member(X, [X|_]).
member(X, [_|Xs]) :- member(X, Xs).
  subset([], _).
subset([X|Xs], Ys) :- member(X, Ys), subset(Xs, Ys).
```
(1)

As a program, the meaning of (1) is of course completely defined, for example, by the usual minimum model semantics. However, as a specification, it is not at all clear that (1) specifies the *subset* relation (on sets), since it uses only lists. More precisely, (1) uses one particular representation of sets by lists, namely unordered lists possibly with duplicates. Clearly there are alternative programs/specifications for *subset* that use other list representations of sets. Sets can be represented by lists in various ways, since equality on sets differs from equality on lists. For example, $\{a, b\} = \{b, a\}$, whereas $a.b.nil \neq b.a.nil$. However, this information, as well as the definition of the chosen set representation by lists, is not (cannot be) contained in (1) itself; it can only be in the underlying framework.

For this reason, the intended meaning S of a program P used as an executable specification, needs to be specified separately. For instance, S for (1) might be the following informal specification (also in [22]):

$$\text{``subset(X, Y) is to be true if: X and Y are two lists of integers} \atop \text{and the set X represents is a subset of the set that Y represents.''} \quad (2)$$

Now, (2) uses the abstract data types of finite sets, lists, and integers, but it does not contain such theories. Therefore, its full and precise meaning is only defined in the the framework $\mathcal{F}$ of finite sets and lists of integers. For example, $\mathcal{F}$ contains the knowledge that the elements of a set can be listed in any order and the list may contain duplicates. This knowledge is assumed by (2).

This example therefore shows that to reason about synthesis, we need to have a three-tier formalism in which the meaning of a program P, at the *bottom* level, is defined by a specification S, at the *middle* level, while the meaning of S is in turn defined in the framework (in question), at the *top* level.

Thus we maintain a strict distinction between programs and specifications. In particular, by definition, so-called executable specifications do not provide a starting point for program synthesis, and so we do not regard them as proper specifications for this purpose. Rather, they are really programs that can and should be derived formally, especially if we want to know precisely what their (intended) meaning is.

It might seem that if we used a typed programming language such as Gödel ([10]), then the framework could be 'encoded' in executable specifications, and this would invalidate our view that executable specifications by themselves are not well-defined. However, other than *computational* knowledge, i.e. programs (typed or untyped), a framework also contains all the *non-computational* knowledge, e.g. induction principles, that is necessary for reasoning about programs. This allows us to write down specifications in a declarative style, and to derive from the same specification different (correct) programs.

3 Frameworks and Their Models

In this section, we briefly discuss frameworks and their model-theoretic semantics. This will set the scene for introducing specifications later.

A framework is an axiomatisation of a problem domain. It has

- a (many-sorted) signature of

- sort symbols;
- function declarations, for declaring constant and function symbols;
- relation declarations, for declaring relation symbols.
- a set of first-order axioms for the declared symbols.

A framework $\mathcal{F}$ is thus a full first-order logical theory. $\mathcal{F}$ has an intended model, viz. its *isoinitial model I*.

Definition 1. An *isoinitial model I* of $\mathcal{F}$ is a reachable model[3] such that for any relation r defined in $\mathcal{F}$, ground instances $r(t)$ or $\neg r(t)$ are true in I iff they are true in all models of $\mathcal{F}$.

Example 1. For example, we can define a framework $\mathcal{SET}(Int)$ for sets as lists of integers as follows:

Framework $\mathcal{SET}(Int)$;

IMPORT: $\mathcal{LIST}(Int)$;

SORTS: $Int, List, Set$;

FUNCTIONS: $\{\ \} : List \rightarrow Set$;

RELATIONS: $\in : (Int, Set)$;

AXIOMS: $\forall L : List, x : Int . x \in \{L\} \leftrightarrow mem(x, L)$;
$\forall A, B : Set . A = B \leftrightarrow \forall x : Int . x \in A \leftrightarrow x \in B$

$\mathcal{SET}(Int)$ imports a framework $\mathcal{LIST}(Int)$ (defined in Example 2 below) for lists of integers, which is the standard theory of lists (of integers) with the usual list operations, in particular the 'list membership' relation *mem*. The sort symbol *Int* stands for the standard (pre-defined) integer type. The sort *Set* is constructed by the *constructor* $\{\ \}$. The relation $\in$ is the usual 'set membership' relation. The first axiom defines $\in$ in terms of *mem*, while the second axiom defines set equality in terms of $\in$.

The isoinitial model of $\mathcal{SET}$ is the usual structure of lists of integers in which sets are represented as lists, i.e. the sort *Set* is interpreted as the set of finite sets of integers.

Note that the syntax of a framework is similar to that used in algebraic abstract data types (e.g. [24]).[4] However, algebraic abstract data types are usually defined by equational or Horn axioms, whereas frameworks are defined by full first-order axioms. Therefore, an algebraic abstract data type is an *initial* model of its specification, whereas a framework has an *isoinitial* model. Both initial and isoinitial theories enjoy the properties of 'no junk' and 'no confusion' ([8]), but only isoinitial theories handle negation properly.

The existence of an isoinitial model is not always guaranteed though. Indeed, we distinguish between two kinds of frameworks:

---

[3] That is a model where each element (of the domain) can be represented by a ground term.

[4] Or in typed logic programming languages such as Gödel [10].

– *Closed Frameworks.*

A closed framework $\mathcal{F}$ is a theory that has an isoinitial model. This means that the axioms completely characterise the intended meaning (namely the interpretation in the isoinitial model) of the sort, function and relation symbols of the signature. It can be shown that if $\mathcal{F}$ has at least one reachable model, and for every ground atomic A, either A or $\neg A$ is provable in $\mathcal{F}$, then there exists an isoinitial model I of $\mathcal{F}$. Moreover, if $\mathcal{F}$ is a (possibly infinite) recursive set of axioms, then in I relation symbols are interpreted by decidable relations, and function symbols are interpreted by total computable functions.

– *Open Frameworks.*

When an isoinitial model does not exist for a framework $\mathcal{F}$, we say that $\mathcal{F}$ is an *open* framework. In this case, the absence of I means that the axioms of $\mathcal{F}$ leave open the interpretation of some of the symbols of $\mathcal{F}$'s signature. Open frameworks are very useful in that they allow us to introduce parameters, and to deal with incomplete information that can be supplied via parameters (see [19]).

For simplicity, in this paper we will consider only specifications within closed frameworks. Such frameworks can be constructed incrementally, starting from a simple framework with an obvious isoinitial model, e.g. the term model generated by the constructor symbols (see e.g. [19]).

Example 2. A typical closed framework is (first-order) Peano arithmetic $\mathcal{NAT}$:[5]

> **Framework** $\mathcal{NAT}$;
>
> SORTS: Nat;
>
> FUNCTIONS: 0 $: \rightarrow Nat$;
> s $: Nat \rightarrow Nat$;
> $+, * : (Nat, Nat) \rightarrow Nat$;
>
> AXIOMS: $\neg 0 = s(x) \wedge s(a) = s(b) \rightarrow a = b$;
> $x + 0 = x$;
> $x + s(y) = s(x + y)$;
> $x * 0 = 0$;
> $x * s(y) = x + x * y$;
> $H(0) \wedge (\forall i . H(i) \rightarrow H(s(i))) \rightarrow \forall x . H(x)$.

The isoinitial model $I_{\mathcal{NAT}}$ of $\mathcal{NAT}$ is the term model generated by its constructors 0 (zero) and s (successor), $+$ is the usual sum and $*$ is the usual product.

Finite structures, like integers with a fixed precision, or characters, can be axiomatised as well.[6] Now, suppose $\mathcal{INT}$ is a framework axiomatising integers. Then we can use $\mathcal{NAT}$ and $\mathcal{INT}$ to introduce the framework $\mathcal{LIST}(Int)$ for lists of integers:[7]

---

[5] We will omit the most external universal quantifiers from now on.

[6] By categorical axiomatisations where all the models are isomorphic.

[7] The sorts of the variables can be inferred from the context.

Framework $\mathcal{LIST}(Int)$;

IMPORT: $\mathcal{NAT},\mathcal{INT}$;

SORTS: $Nat, Int, List$;

FUNCTIONS: $nil\ :\ \to List$;
$\qquad\qquad\ \ .\ :(Int, List) \to List$;
$\qquad\qquad nocc :(Int, List) \to Nat$;

RELATIONS: $elemi :(List, Nat, Int)$;

AXIOMS: $\neg nil = a.B \wedge a_1.B_1 = a_2.B_2 \to a_1 = a_2 \wedge B_1 = B_2$;
$\qquad\qquad H(nil) \wedge \forall a, J\ .\ H(J) \to H(a.J) \to \forall L\ .\ H(L)$;
$\qquad\qquad nocc(x, nil) = 0$;
$\qquad\qquad a = b \to nocc(a, b.L) = s(nocc(a, L))$;
$\qquad\qquad \neg a = b \to nocc(a, b.L) = nocc(a, L)$;
$\qquad\qquad elemi(L, 0, a) \leftrightarrow \exists B\ .\ L = a.B$;
$\qquad\qquad elemi(L, s(i), a) \leftrightarrow \exists b, B\ .\ L = b.B \wedge elemi(B, i, a)$;

Lists can be constructed from the term model generated by the constructors $\cdot$ and nil. It can be shown that an isoinitial model $I_{\mathcal{LIST}}$ of $\mathcal{LIST}(Int)$ is an expansion of $I_{\mathcal{NAT}}$ and $I_{\mathcal{INT}}$. Indeed $I_{\mathcal{LIST}}$ is the usual structure (the term model generated by the constructors nil and $\cdot$) of lists of integers, where the function $nocc(a, L)$ gives the number of occurrences of a in L, and the relation $elemi(L, i, a)$ means a occurs at position i in L.

$\mathcal{LIST}(Int)$ contains $\mathcal{NAT}$, $nocc(a, L)$ and $elemi(L, i, a)$, and induction on lists, in order to provide a kernel with a sufficiently strong language and set of axioms. This kernel can be expanded mainly through if-and-only-if specifications, as we will see in the next Section.

Finally, since a framework introduces types, programs in a framework are typed.

4 If-and-only-if Specifications

In a given framework, as shown in the incremental construction of $\mathcal{SET}$ (and $\mathcal{LIST}$ and $\mathcal{NAT}$), we can define new (total computable) functions and (decidable) relations, by adding axioms which we call if-and-only-if specifications. In this section, we define and discuss such specifications. They are proper specifications, and they can also be used for constructing frameworks incrementally.

Definition 2. An *if-and-only-if specification* (or *iff specification* for short) S of a new *relation* r in a framework $\mathcal{F}$ consists of a definition of the form

$$r(x) \leftrightarrow R(x)$$

where $R(x)$ is any formula of the language of $\mathcal{F}$.

If $R(x)$ contains the defined symbol r, then we say that S is a *recursive* iff specification.

Recursive iff specifications have to be used with great care, since they may be ill-defined. For example, $r(x) \leftrightarrow \neg r(x)$ is logically inconsistent, whilst $r(x) \leftrightarrow r(x)$, though logically valid, does not characterise any specific intended interpretation of r (any interpretation satisfies it).

In contrast, non-recursive iff specifications are always consistent. In logic they are known as *explicit definitions*, and they have a clear declarative semantics:

Let $\mathcal{F}$ be a framework and D_r be an explicit definition of a new relation r. Then, for every model M of the framework $\mathcal{F}$, there is a unique r-expansion M_r of M such that in M_r, r is interpreted according to D_r, whereas the old symbols are interpreted as in M.

For this reason, we will use mainly non-recursive iff specifications.

Thus, given a framework $\mathcal{F}$ and a (non-recursive) iff specification D_r, there is a unique r-expansion of the isoinitial model I of $\mathcal{F}$ that satisfies D_r. In other words, a relation defined by D_r has a unique interpretation in I. This is illustrated in Figure 1.

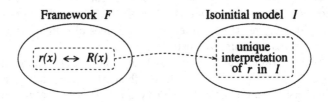

Fig. 1. Model-theoretic semantics of (non-recursive) *iff* specifications.

Example 3. In $\mathcal{SET}$, we can specify *subset* by the iff specification:

$$subset(A, B) \leftrightarrow \forall x \,.\, x \in A \rightarrow x \in B \tag{3}$$

In the sequel, instead of $subset(A, B)$ we will write $A \subseteq B$, for the sake of clarity. Since sets are represented by lists in $\mathcal{SET}$, we can specify *sublist* by:

$$sublist(X, Y) \leftrightarrow \{X\} \subseteq \{Y\} \tag{4}$$

(in (3) A and B are sets, whereas in (4) X and Y are lists.)

In the isoinitial model of $\mathcal{SET}$, *subset* and *sublist* have a unique interpretation each.

Iff specifications are the most widely used form of specifications in logic program synthesis, e.g. [9, 5, 12, 17, 18]. In these papers,[8] various techniques are described for systematically deriving standard logic programs ([9, 5, 12,

---

[8] More details of these, and related papers, can be found in [6].

17]) or constraint logic programs ([18]). However, it should be noted that in e.g. [9, 5, 12], there is no (explicit) use of frameworks, or of model-theoretic semantics of iff specifications as described here, but they do make use of recursive iff specifications.

Iff specifications provide a starting point for program synthesis. For example in $\mathcal{SET}$ it is easy to see how we can derive the following program from (4):

$$
\begin{aligned}
&sublist(nil, Z) \leftarrow \\
&sublist(x.Y, Z) \leftarrow mem(x, Z), sublist(Y, Z) \\
\\
&mem(x, x.Z) \leftarrow \\
&mem(x, y.Z) \leftarrow mem(x, Z)
\end{aligned}
\tag{5}
$$

(5) of course corresponds to the program (executable specification) (1) in Section 2. However, (5) has been (formally) derived from the specification (4) in $\mathcal{SET}$.

Besides synthesis, iff specifications can also be used to expand (the language of) a framework $\mathcal{F}$ by new symbols, since they have unique interpretations in the isoinitial model I of $\mathcal{F}$. However, for this purpose, we must use only *adequate* definitions D, viz. those that give rise to expansions of I which are also isoinitial models of the theory $\mathcal{F} \cup D$. Indeed, since D is of the form $\forall x . r(x) \leftrightarrow R(x)$, where R is any formula of the language, it may happen that the axioms of $\mathcal{F}$ are too weak to completely characterise the meaning of the new symbol r. For example, let $R(x)$ be a formula of $\mathcal{NAT}$ such that $\mathcal{NAT} \not\vdash R(0)$ and $\mathcal{NAT} \not\vdash \neg R(0)$ (such a formula exists); then the meaning of $r(0)$ is left open. Non-adequacy means that, starting from a closed framework $\mathcal{F}$, we get a framework containing an open symbol r. In model-theoretic terms, there is no longer an isoinitial model in the class of r-expansions of the models of $\mathcal{F}$.

A useful criterion for adequacy is the existence of a program P for computing the specified relation, such that P existentially terminates and the completion of P can be proved in the framework $\mathcal{F}$, enriched by the iff specifications of the predicates in P (see [16]). In other words, program synthesis can actually be used to expand $\mathcal{F}$ with adequate iff specifications.

Expansions of frameworks by new function symbols are equally important:

Definition 3. An (adequate) *iff specification* of a new *function* f in a framework $\mathcal{F}$ consists of a definition of the form

$$
\forall x, y . y = f(x) \leftrightarrow r(x, y)
$$

where $r(x, y)$ is a relation introduced by an (adequate) iff specification S_r, such that $\mathcal{F} \cup S_r \vdash \forall x . \exists! y . r(x, y)$.

An (adequate) iff specification S_f of a function introduces a new closed function symbol f, i.e. the (unique) f-expansion of the isoinitial model remains isoinitial and the meaning of f is completely characterised by the axioms of $\mathcal{F} \cup S_f$.

By adding new (closed) symbols, we can build up a framework for the problem domain in a natural and purely declarative way.

Example 4. We can expand $\mathcal{LIST}(Int)$ by adding the following (commonly used) functions and relations defined by iff specifications:

FUNCTIONS: $l : List \rightarrow Int$;
$\quad\quad\quad\quad\quad | : (List, List) \rightarrow List$;

RELATIONS: $mem \quad : (Int, List)$;
$\quad\quad\quad\quad len \quad : (List, Nat)$;
$\quad\quad\quad\quad concat : (List, List, List)$;
$\quad\quad\quad\quad perm \quad : (List, List)$;
$\quad\quad\quad\quad ord \quad : (List)$;

AXIOMS: $mem(e, L) \leftrightarrow \exists i . elemi(L, i, e)$;
$\quad\quad\quad len(L, n) \leftrightarrow \forall i . i < n \leftrightarrow \exists a . elemi(L, i, a)$;
$\quad\quad\quad n = l(L) \leftrightarrow len(L, n)$;
$\quad\quad\quad concat(A, B, L) \leftrightarrow (\forall i, a . i < l(A) \rightarrow$
$\quad\quad\quad\quad\quad\quad\quad\quad\quad\quad\quad (elemi(A, i, a) \leftrightarrow elemi(L, i, a)))\wedge$
$\quad\quad\quad\quad\quad\quad\quad\quad\quad\quad\quad (\forall j, b . elemi(B, j, b) \leftrightarrow$
$\quad\quad\quad\quad\quad\quad\quad\quad\quad\quad\quad elemi(L, j + l(A), b))$;
$\quad\quad\quad perm(A, B) \leftrightarrow \forall e . nocc(e, A) = nocc(e, B)$;
$\quad\quad\quad C = A|B \leftrightarrow concat(A, B, C)$;
$\quad\quad\quad ord(L) \leftrightarrow \forall i . elemi(L, i, e_1) \wedge elemi(L, s(i), e_2) \rightarrow e_1 \leq e_2$.

where l and $|$ are the usual functions for length and concatenation; and *mem*, *len*, *concat*, *perm*, and *ord* are the usual 'membership', 'length', 'concatenation', 'permutation', and 'ordered' relations.

All these definitions can be shown to be adequate.

We prefer (adequate) non-recursive iff specification for framework construction since they enable us to have a purely declarative specification language, i.e. to define the meaning of new symbols in a non-recursive way in terms of symbols that are already defined. For example, in $\mathcal{LIST}(Int)$ using the above additional definitions, we can specify sorting, declaratively as follows:

$$sort(X, Y) \leftrightarrow perm(X, Y) \wedge ord(Y)$$

However, recursive axioms cannot be avoided altogether, especially for axiomatising primitive operations on data types. For example, in $\mathcal{NAT}$, $+$ and $*$ cannot be defined non-recursively.

Thus our strategy for building a framework is as follows. First we define a sufficiently strong kernel framework by using *any* kind of axioms, both recursive and non-recursive. This requires skill and care, in order to avoid inconsistencies, and to guarantee the existence of an isoinitial model. Subsequently, we use adequate non-recursive iff specifications for introducing new symbols. Of course, recursive iff specifications are not forbidden, but they require more care.

5 Partial Specifications

For the purpose of program synthesis, in particular deriving different programs from the same specification, iff specifications are often too inflexible and unhelpful. For this purpose, it is better to use weaker forms of specifications that admit multiple interpretations, which we shall call *partial specifications*. In this section we define and discuss three of them: *super-and-sub*, *conditional* and *selector* specifications. These seem to us to be the most important and useful cases in practice.

5.1 Super-and-sub Specifications

Definition 4. A *super-and-sub specification* of a new relation r in a framework $\mathcal{F}$ consists of a definition of the form

$$\forall x \,.\, (R_{sub}(x) \rightarrow r(x)) \wedge (r(x) \rightarrow R_{super}(x))$$

where $R_{sub}(x)$ and $R_{super}(x)$ are two formulas of the language of $\mathcal{F}$ such that $\mathcal{F} \vdash \forall x \,.\, R_{sub}(x) \rightarrow R_{super}(x)$.

The implication $\forall x \,.\, R_{sub}(x) \rightarrow R_{super}(x)$ is satisfied by the isoinitial model I of $\mathcal{F}$.[9] Therefore the *sub* relation $R_{sub}(x)$ in I (i.e. the set of values $\mathbf{x}$ such that $I \models R_{sub}(\mathbf{x})$) is contained in the *super* relation $R_{super}(x)$, and the specified relation r is any relation that contains R_{sub} but is contained in R_{super}. This is illustrated in Figure 2.

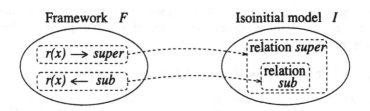

Fig. 2. Model-theoretic relation between R_{super} (*super*) and R_{sub} (*sub*).

Thus in contrast to one defined by an iff specification, a relation r defined by a super-and-sub specification S has many interpretations in the isoinitial model I of the framework $\mathcal{F}$. A *correct implementation* of S is any program P for computing r, such that the interpretation of r in P's minimum Herbrand model is a relation that contains R_{sub} and is contained in R_{super}.

It follows that a super-and-sub specification of a relation r can be implemented correctly in different ways. In particular, the relation R_{super} defines or suggests many possible implementations for r, but a correct implementation must compute a relation that contains R_{sub}. Thus R_{super} defines the search space for correct implementations, whilst R_{sub} guides the search for them. In

---

[9] It is in fact satisfied by all the models of $\mathcal{F}$, since it is a theorem of $\mathcal{F}$.

other words, R_{super} and R_{sub} delimit the search space for correct implementations. Consequently, super-and-sub specifications are very versatile and natural, and therefore helpful, for practical program synthesis.

In general, of course a partial specification is useful in practice only if we have methods to prove the correctness of programs. For super-and-sub specifications, the following theorem provides the necessary proof-theoretic characterisation of correctness:

Theorem 5. *Let S be a super-and-sub specification written as a pair of implications:*

$$r(x) \rightarrow R_{super}(x)$$
$$r(x) \leftarrow R_{sub}(x)$$

and let P be a program for computing r, $Comp^+(P)$ be the if-part and $Comp^-(P)$ be the only-if-part of the completion of P. If

(a) $\forall x . \mathcal{F} \cup \{r(x) \leftrightarrow R_{super}(x)\} \vdash Comp^+(P)$,
(b) $\mathcal{F} \cup \{\forall x . r(x) \leftrightarrow R_{sub}(x)\} \vdash Comp^-(P)$, and
(c) P existentially terminates;

then P is a correct implementation of S.

Indeed (a) guarantees that the success set is contained in R_{super}, (b) guarantees that the finite-failure set contains R_{sub}, and (c) says that the success and finite failure sets are complementary.

This theorem is not only useful for proving the correctness of an implementation wrt a super-and-sub specification, but it can also provide a basis for a synthesis method.

Example 5. Suppose we are given the following iff specifications:

$$nocc_1(L) \qquad \leftrightarrow \forall x . nocc(x, L) \leq 1$$
$$select_{super}(x, Y, H) \leftrightarrow \neg nocc_1(Y) \vee \neg x \in \{Y\} \vee nocc_1(x.H) \wedge \{x.H\} = \{Y\}$$

$nocc_1(L)$ means that L does not contain duplicates, and $select_{super}(x, Y, H)$ means that H does not contain duplicates and contains all the elements of Y except x.

Suppose for every pair (x, Y) such that $x \in \{Y\}$ and $nocc_1(Y)$ holds, we want to compute at least one H such that $select_{super}(x, Y, H)$ holds. We can specify this as $select(x, Y, H)$ by a super-and-sub specification of the form

$$select_{sub}(x, Y, H) \rightarrow select(x, Y, H) \wedge select(x, Y, H) \rightarrow select_{super}(x, Y, H) \quad (6)$$

and look for a correct program P in the search space delimited by $select_{super}$ and $select_{sub}$, by first considering $select_{super}$ and then $select_{sub}$.

Note that while considering $select_{super}$ we can even leave $select_{sub}$ unspecified, and only require that

$$select_{sub}(x, Y, H) \text{ be satisfied by at least one } H \text{ whenever } x \in \{Y\}$$
$$\text{and } nocc_1(Y) \text{ holds, and } select_{sub}(x, Y, H) \rightarrow select_{super}(x, Y, H). \quad (7)$$

In this way, we do not (over)constrain the search space unnecessarily.

Now, the most obvious candidate for P is clearly one derivable from $select_{super}$ such that we can prove condition (a) of Theorem 5. We have:

$$select(x, x.X, X) \leftrightarrow select_{super}(x, x.X, X)$$
$$\leftrightarrow \neg nocc_1(x.X) \vee \neg x \in x.X \vee nocc_1(x.X) \wedge \{x.X\} = \{x.X\}$$
$$\leftrightarrow true$$
$$select(x, y.Y, y.H) \leftrightarrow select_{super}(x, y.Y, y.H)$$
$$\leftrightarrow \neg nocc_1(y.Y) \vee \neg x \in y.Y \vee nocc_1(x.y.H) \wedge$$
$$\{x.y.H\} = \{y.Y\}$$
$$\leftarrow \neg nocc_1(Y) \vee \neg x \in Y \vee nocc_1(x.H) \wedge \{x.H\} = \{Y\}$$
$$\leftrightarrow select(x, Y, H)$$

So we have derived the program

$$select(x, x.X, X) \leftarrow$$
$$select(x, y.Y, y.H) \leftarrow select(x, Y, H) \tag{8}$$

Obviously (8) satisfies condition (a) of Theorem 5.

Next we need to establish that (8) also meets condition (b) of Theorem 5 for a suitable $select_{sub}$. Looking at (8), we might surmise the following definition of $select_{sub}$:

$$select_{sub}(x, Y, H) \leftrightarrow nocc_1(Y) \wedge nocc_1(x.H) \wedge$$
$$\exists U, V . H = U|V \wedge Y = U|x.V \tag{9}$$

This satisfies the requirement (7) above. So, if we can prove condition (b) of Theorem 5, then (9) is a suitable definition.

The proof is:

$$select(x, A, B) \leftrightarrow nocc_1(A) \wedge nocc_1(x.B) \wedge \exists U, V . B = U|V \wedge A = U|x.V$$
$$\rightarrow (\exists V . B = V \wedge A = x.V)$$
$$\vee(\exists y, Y, V . B = y.Y|V \wedge A = y.Y|x.V)$$
$$\rightarrow \exists X, Y, H . A = x.X \wedge B = X \vee A = y.Y \wedge B = y.H$$
$$select(x, y.Y, y.H) \leftrightarrow nocc_1(y.Y) \wedge nocc_1(x.y.H) \wedge$$
$$\exists U, V . y.H = U|V \wedge y.Y = U|x.V$$
$$\rightarrow nocc_1(Y) \wedge nocc_1(x.H) \wedge \exists U, V . H = U|V \wedge Y = U|x.V$$
$$\leftrightarrow select(x, Y, H)$$

Thus the program (8) is a correct implementation of the super-and-sub specification (6) where $select_{sub}$ is as defined by the iff specification (9).[10]

---

[10] Termination needs to be proved separately.

5.2 Conditional Specifications

Definition 6. A *conditional specification* of a new relation r in a framework $\mathcal{F}$ consists of a definition of the form

$$\forall x, y \,.\, IC(x) \rightarrow (r(x,y) \leftrightarrow OC(y) \wedge R(x,y))$$

where $IC(x)$ is a condition on x, $OC(y)$ is a condition on y, and $R(x,y)$ is a formula of the language of $\mathcal{F}$.

Roughly speaking, the relation $r(x,y)$ is defined if and when $IC(x)$ holds, and in this case $r(x,y)$ is defined to be $R(x,y)$ and $OC(y)$ will also hold. If we follow the pre-post-condition style of program specification (e.g. [14, 23]), then a conditional specification defines a program P to compute $r(x,y)$ in such a way that whenever $IC(x)$ is satisfied, P satisfies $OC(y) \wedge R(x,y)$. Therefore, we shall say that $IC(x)$ is an *input-* or *pre-condition* on x, $OC(y)$ is an *output condition* on y, and the formula $OC(y) \wedge R(x,y)$ is a *post-condition*.

Example 6. For example, we could specify the *sublist* relation by the following conditional specification:

$$IC(Y) \rightarrow (sublist(X,Y) \leftrightarrow OC(X) \wedge \{X\} \subseteq \{Y\}) \tag{10}$$

where $IC(Y)$ and $OC(X)$ state that Y and X do not contain duplicates. Note that here Y is the input and X the output.

The specification (10) defines $sublist(X,Y)$ to be $subset(\{X\},\{Y\})$ (and specifies that X does not contain duplicates) whenever Y does not contain duplicates.

Thus, like one defined by a super-and-sub specification, a relation defined by a conditional specification C has many interpretations in the isoinitial model I of the framework $\mathcal{F}$.

It is easy to see that a conditional specification

$$IC(x) \rightarrow (r(x,y) \leftrightarrow OC(y) \wedge R(x,y)) \tag{11}$$

can always be re-written as a pair of implications:

$$r(x,y) \rightarrow \neg IC(x) \vee (OC(y) \wedge R(x,y))$$
$$r(x,y) \leftarrow \;\; IC(x) \wedge (OC(y) \wedge R(x,y))$$

That is (11) becomes the super-and-sub specification:

$$r(x,y) \rightarrow R_{super} \leftrightarrow \neg IC(x) \vee (OC(y) \wedge R(x,y))$$
$$r(x,y) \leftarrow R_{sub} \;\;\leftrightarrow\;\; IC(x) \wedge (OC(y) \wedge R(x,y))$$

For instance, the conditional specification (10) can be re-written as:

$$sublist(X,Y) \rightarrow select_{super} \leftrightarrow \neg IC(Y) \vee (OC(X) \wedge subset(X,Y))$$
$$sublist(X,Y) \leftarrow select_{sub} \;\;\leftrightarrow\;\; IC(Y) \wedge (OC(X) \wedge subset(X,Y)) \tag{12}$$

Therefore, for synthesising programs from a conditional specification C, we can apply the same proof method for super-and-sub specifications (in the previous subsection), by re-writing C as a pair of implications. The search for correct programs, however, is now governed by the input and output conditions, IC and OC respectively. Moreover, now R_{sub} is defined *a priori*, thus making the search easier.

Example 7. Consider the conditional specification (10), or the equivalent super-and-sub specification (12).

(i) Suppose both the input and output conditions IC and OC are the relation $nocc_1$. It can be shown that if we use the specification (6) for *select* (and the corresponding program (8)), then we can derive the following program for *sublist*:

$$sublist(nil, Y) \leftarrow$$
$$sublist(x.X, Y) \leftarrow select(x, Y, H), sublist(X, H) \tag{13}$$

following the strategy outlined in Example 5, except that here $select_{sub}$ is defined *a priori*. For brevity, we omit the derivation steps.

(ii) Alternatively, if in (10) we choose both IC and OC to be *ord* defined by the iff specification:

$$ord(L) \leftrightarrow \forall i, x, y \,.\, elemi(L, i, x) \wedge elemi(L, s(i), y) \rightarrow x \leq y$$

($ord(L)$ means that L is a sorted list), and then specify *append* by the following iff specification:

$$append(X, Y, Z) \leftrightarrow X|Y = Z \tag{14}$$

we can derive the following alternative program for *sublist*:

$$append(nil, X, X) \leftarrow$$
$$append(x.X, Y, x.Z) \leftarrow append(X, Y, Z)$$
$$sublist(nil, X) \leftarrow \tag{15}$$
$$sublist(x.X, Y) \leftarrow append(W, x.Z, Y), sublist(X, Z)$$

Again, we omit the derivation steps.

5.3 Selector Specifications

Definition 7. A *selector specification* has the following form:

$$(i) \quad \forall x, y \,.\, IC(x) \wedge r(x, y) \rightarrow R(x, y) \wedge OC(y)$$
$$(ii) \quad \forall x \,.\, IC(x) \rightarrow \exists y \,.\, r(x, y)$$

where r is the new specified relation and $R(x, y)$, $IC(x)$ and $OC(y)$ are formulas of the language of the framework.

This specification says that r is any relation contained in R, such that for every input x that satisfies the input condition $IC(x)$, r picks up, or *selects*, at least one output y.

This kind of specification is useful for deriving sub-programs in hierarchical program synthesis.

Example 8. Consider the hierarchical synthesis of a program for the relation *sort* defined by:

$$sort(X, Y) \leftrightarrow perm(X, Y) \wedge ord(Y)$$

in $\mathcal{LIST}(Int)$, and an (as yet) incomplete sorting program with the following structure:

$$
\begin{aligned}
&sort(nil, nil) && \leftarrow \\
&sort(x.nil, x.nil) && \leftarrow \\
&sort(x.y.A, B) && \leftarrow split(x.y.A, I, J), \ldots
\end{aligned}
$$

where in the recursive clause the input $x.y.A$ is split into two shorter parts I and J, that can be used in various ways in the body. In this case *split* can be specified as follows:

$$
\begin{aligned}
&l(X) > 1 \wedge split(X, Y, Z) \rightarrow perm(X, Y|Z) \wedge l(Y) < l(X) \wedge l(Z) < l(X) \\
&l(X) > 1 \rightarrow \exists Y, Z \,.\, split(X, Y, Z)
\end{aligned}
$$

That is, if X has length greater than 1, then *split* has to select a pair Y and Z, among all the pairs such that $Y|Z$ is a permutation of X, with the requirement the selected lists Y and Z must be shorter than X. A trivial example of a correct program is:

$$split(x.y.A, x.nil, y.A) \leftarrow \tag{16}$$

This choice gives rise to a program for insertion sort. Other choices give rise to other sorting algorithms.

For this kind of specifications, we have the following correctness theorem:

Theorem 8. *Let S be the following selector specification:*

$$
\begin{aligned}
&(i) \quad \forall x, y \,.\, IC(x) \wedge r(x, y) \rightarrow R(x, y) \wedge OC(y) \\
&(ii) \quad \forall x \,.\, IC(x) \rightarrow \exists y \,.\, r(x, y)
\end{aligned}
$$

Let P be a program for computing r. If

(a) $\mathcal{F} \cup \{\forall x, y \,.\, r(x, y) \leftrightarrow \neg IC(x) \vee R(x, y) \wedge OC(y)\} \vdash Comp^+(P)$, *and*
(b) for every goal $\leftarrow r(g, Y)$, where g is a ground term that satisfies $IC(g)$, $P \cup \{\leftarrow r(g, Y)\}$ successfully terminates;

then P is a correct implementation of S.

Example 9. For example, consider the program for *split* (16):

(a) We can prove

$$
\begin{aligned}
split(x.y.A, x.nil, y.A) &\leftrightarrow (\neg l(x.y.A) > 1 \vee (perm(x.y.A, x.nil|y.A) \\
&\qquad \wedge l(x.nil) < l(x.y.A) \wedge l(y.A) < l(x.y.A))) \\
&\leftrightarrow true
\end{aligned}
$$

(b) The successful termination of (16) for every goal $\leftarrow split(g, X, Y)$, where g is ground and has length greater than 1, is obvious.

Hence the program (16) is a correct implementation of S.

6 Discussion and Concluding Remarks

We have presented a model-theoretic view of frameworks and specifications. The model-theoretic semantics discussed here is used in [19] to define the model-theoretic relationship between frameworks, specifications and programs, in a three-tier formalism for logic program synthesis.

The kinds of specifications presented here are intended for *deductive synthesis*, and not for *constructive synthesis* (see [6] for a survey of different approaches to logic program synthesis). Our use of frameworks distinguishes our approach to specifications from related work in deductive synthesis. Moreover, we use a model-theoretic approach whereas others predominantly adopt a proof-theoretic approach. For example, in [9, 5, 12], frameworks are not used, and iff specifications are used in a proof-theoretic way to derive logic programs, and/or to prove them correct.

Nevertheless, there are similarities between our specifications and some of their verification conditions. For example, Clark [4, Section 4] (see also [13, p.158]) uses the following *correctness sentence*:

$$\forall x, y \, . \, I(x) \rightarrow (r(x,y) \leftrightarrow O(x,y)) \tag{17}$$

where $I(x)$ and $O(x,y)$ are input and output relations, to verify the total correctness of a program P to compute r. (17) is almost identical to our conditional specification, although it is not used for specification purposes.

In general, constructive synthesis follows the 'proofs as programs' approach (e.g. [1, 20]).[11] A specification consists of an input-output theorem of the form

$$\forall x \exists y \, . \, r(x,y) \tag{18}$$

From a proof of this theorem, a program to compute r can be extracted. This kind of specification is similar to our selector specification without an input condition, i.e. for every input x there is at least one y which satisfies $r(x,y)$ and is computed by the specified (or extracted) program.

In logic programming, the connection between deductive and constructive synthesis is particularly close. For example, in the constructive synthesis method of [2], the input-output relation $r(x,y)$ in (18) is itself an iff specification. In [15, 7], program extraction is performed by proving goals of the form

$$\forall x \exists y \, . \, q(x,y) \leftarrow r(x) \tag{19}$$

using an extended Prolog execution mechanism. Here, $r(x)$ can be regarded as an input, and $q(x,y)$ as an output. Therefore, (19) is similar to a selector specification of the form:

$$r(x) \wedge q_P(x,y) \rightarrow q(x,y)$$
$$r(x) \rightarrow \exists y \, . \, q_P(x,y)$$

---

[11] Note that Manna & Waldinger uses 'deductive synthesis' to refer to what we call 'constructive synthesis' here.

where $q(x, y)$ is the relation in the specification language, and q_P is the relation computed by the (extracted) program. It is also worth noting that if for every x such that $r(x)$ holds, the program computes all the y such that $q(x, y)$, i.e. if the answers of a goal $\leftarrow q_P(g, Y)$ are all the values v such that $q(g, v)$ is true in the isoinitial model of the framework, then (19) is a conditional specification.

Conditional specifications are widely used in so-called *formal methods*, e.g. VDM [14] and Z [23], in the form of pre- and post-conditions for specifying the effects of operations on the current computational state. However, these methods use such specifications in a purely proof-theoretic way.

Super-and-sub specifications, and selector specifications may also have been used by other researchers in deriving programs, but we are not aware of any formalisation of such specifications in existing literature.

Finally, it would seem that iff specifications are best suited to the incremental construction of a framework by adding adequate definitions via the synthesis of corresponding totally correct programs. For synthesis itself, it would seem that partial specifications are the most natural and versatile.

Acknowledgements

We wish to thank Alberto Pettorossi, and the referees, for their helpful comments and suggestions.

References

1. J.L. Bates and R.L. Constable. Proofs as programs. *ACM TOPLAS* 7(1):113-136, 1985.
2. A. Bundy, A. Smaill and G. Wiggins. The synthesis of logic programs from inductive proofs. In J.W. Lloyd, editor, *Proc. Esprit Symposium on Computational Logic*, pages 135–149, Springer-Verlag, 1990.
3. C.C. Chang and H.J. Keisler. *Model Theory*. North-Holland, 1973.
4. K.L. Clark. Predicate Logic as a Computational Formalism. Tech. Rep. 79/59, Imperial College, 1979.
5. K.L. Clark. The Synthesis and Verification of Logic Programs. Tech. Rep. 81/36, Imperial College, 1981.
6. Y. Deville and K.K. Lau. Logic program synthesis. *J. Logic Programming* 19,20:321–350, 1994. Special issue: Ten years of logic programming.
7. L. Fribourg. Extracting logic programs from proofs that use extended Prolog execution and induction. In D.H.D. Warren and P. Szeredi, editors, *Proc. 7th Int. Conf. on Logic Programming*, pages 685–699, MIT Press, 1990.
8. J. Goguen and J. Meseguer. Unifying functional, object-oriented and relational programming with logical semantics. In B. Shriver and P. Wegner, editors, *Research Directions in Object-Oriented Programming*, pages 417–477, MIT Press, 1987.
9. Å. Hansson and S.-Å. Tärnlund. A natural programming calculus. In *Proc. IJCAI 79*, pages 348–355, 1979.
10. P.M. Hill and J.W. Lloyd. *The Gödel Programming Language*. MIT Press, 1994.

11. W. Hodges. Logical features of Horn clauses. In D.M. Gabbay, C.J. Hogger, and J.A. Robinson, editors, *Handbook of Logic in Artificial Intelligence and Logic Programming*, Vol 1, pages 449–503, Oxford University Press, 1993.

12. C.J. Hogger. Derivation of logic programs. *J. ACM*, 28(2):372–392, April 1981.

13. C.J. Hogger. *Introduction to Logic Programming*. Academic Press, 1984.

14. C.B. Jones. *Systematic Software Development Using VDM*. Prentice Hall, 2nd edition, 1990.

15. T. Kanamori and H. Seki. Verification of Prolog programs using an extension of execution. In E. Shapiro, editor, *Proc. 3rd Int. Conf. on Logic Programming*, *Lecture Notes in Computer Science* 225, pages 475–489, 1986.

16. K.K. Lau and M. Ornaghi. On specification frameworks and deductive synthesis of logic programs. In L. Fribourg and F. Turini, editors, *Proc. LOPSTR 94 and META 94*, *Lecture Notes in Computer Science* 883, pages 104–121, Springer-Verlag, 1994.

17. K.K. Lau, M. Ornaghi and S.-Å. Tärnlund. The halting problem for deductive synthesis of logic programs. In P. van Hentenryck, editor, *Proc. 11th Int. Conf. on Logic Programming*, pages 665–683, MIT Press, 1994.

18. K.K. Lau and M. Ornaghi. A formal approach to deductive synthesis of constraint logic programs. In J.W. Lloyd, editor, *Proc. 1995 Int. Logic Programming Symp.*, pages 543–557, MIT Press, 1995.

19. K.K. Lau and M. Ornaghi. The relationship between logic programs and specifications — the subset example revisited. To appear in *J. Logic Programming*.

20. Z. Manna and R. Waldinger. Fundamentals of deductive program synthesis. *IEEE Trans. on Soft. Eng.* 18(8):53–79, 1992.

21. P. Miglioli, U. Moscato and M. Ornaghi. Abstract parametric classes and abstract data types defined by classical and constructive logical methods. *J. Symb. Comp.* 18:41–81, 1994.

22. R.A. O'Keefe. What does subset mean? *ALP Newsletter* 8(3):10, August 1995.

23. J.M. Spivey. *Understanding Z*. Cambridge University Press, 1988.

24. M. Wirsing. Algebraic specification. In J. Van Leeuwen, editor, *Handbook of Theoretical Computer Science*, pages 675–788. Elsevier, 1990.

Synthesis of Proof Procedures for Default Reasoning

Phan Minh Dung[1], Robert A. Kowalski[2] and Francesca Toni[3]

[1] Asian Institute of Technology, Division of Computer Science
PO Box 2754, Bangkok 10501, Thailand
dung@cs.ait.ac.th
[2] Imperial College, Department of Computing
180 Queen's Gate, London SW7 2BZ, UK
rak@doc.ic.ac.uk
[3] National Technical University of Athens
Department of Electrical and Computing Engineering, Division of Computer Science
15773 Zographou, Athens, Greece
ftoni@softlab.ece.ntua.gr

Abstract. We apply logic program development technology to define abstract proof procedures, in the form of logic programs, for computing the admissibility semantics for default reasoning proposed in [2].
The proof procedures are derived from a formal specification. The derivation guarantees the soundness of the proof procedures. The completeness of the proof procedures is shown by employing a technique of symbolic execution of logic programs to compute (an instance of) a relation implied by the specification.

1 Introduction

In [2], we have shown that many default logics [13, 19, 14, 15] can be understood as special cases of a single abstract framework, based upon an abductive interpretation of the semantics of logic programming [7, 8] and its abstractions [4, 5, 1, 11], and extending Theorist [18]. Moreover, we have proposed a new semantics for default logics, more liberal than their standard semantics and generalising the admissibility semantics for logic programming [4], equivalent to the partial stable model semantics [20] (see [10]).

In this paper, we define two proof procedures for computing the abstract admissibility semantics. The second proof procedure is a computationally more efficient refinement of the first. Both procedures generalise and abstract a proof procedure [8] for logic programming, but are formulated as logic programs. The relationships of the proof procedures with other existing proof procedures for default reasoning and the relevance of the proof procedures in the field of default reasoning are discussed in an extended version of this paper [6]. In the present paper, we describe the technology used to define the abstract proof procedures. Both are derived from a formal specification by conventional techniques of deductive synthesis of logic programs (e.g. those described already in [12], Chapter 10, and, more recently, in [3]). The derivation guarantees the soundness of the proof procedures. The completeness of the proof procedures is shown via symbolic execution of the logic programs to compute (an instance of) a relation implied by the specification.

The logic programs are derived top-down in two stages: the top-most level is derived first, relative to lower-level predicates that can then be "developed". The top-level program is proved correct and complete, parametrically with respect to the lower-level predicates. (Generalised) logic programs computing the lower-level predicates are given in [6].

The rest of the paper has the following structure: Section 2 revises the main features of the abstract framework and the admissibility semantics; Section 3 introduces the top-level of the first abstract proof procedure to compute the admissibility semantics; Section 4 introduces the top-level of the more efficient proof procedure; Section 5 gives conclusions.

2 Argumentation-theoretic framework and admissibility semantics

An *argumentation-theoretic framework* consists of a set of sentences T, the *theory*, viewed as a given set of beliefs, a (non-empty) set of sentences Ab, viewed as *assumptions* that can be used to extend T, and a notion of *attack*, namely a (binary) relation between sets of assumptions.

Both theory and assumptions are formulated in some underlying language provided with a notion of derivability Th which is *monotonic*, in the sense that $T \subseteq T'$ implies $Th(T) \subseteq Th(T')$, and *compact*, in the sense that $\alpha \in Th(T)$ implies $\alpha \in Th(T')$ for some finite subset T' of T.

The notion of attack is *monotonic*, in the sense that, for any sets of assumptions $A, A', \Delta, \Delta' \subseteq Ab$, if A attacks Δ then:

- A' attacks Δ for any $A' \supseteq A$;
- A attacks Δ' for any $\Delta' \supseteq \Delta$.

Moreover, the notion of attack satisfies the property that no set of assumptions attacks the empty set of assumptions.

Theorist [18], circumscription [13], logic programming, default logic [19], autoepistemic logic [15] and non-monotonic modal logic [14] are all instances of the abstract argumentation-theoretic framework (see [2]).

A set of assumptions $\Delta \subseteq Ab$ is *closed* iff $\Delta = Ab \cap Th(T \cup \Delta)$.

An argumentation-theoretic framework is *flat* iff every set of assumptions is closed. The frameworks for logic programming and default logic are flat.

A set of assumptions Δ is

- *admissible* iff Δ is closed, Δ does not attack itself and
  for each closed $A \subseteq Ab$, if A attacks Δ then Δ attacks A.

Admissible sets of assumptions correspond to admissible scenaria for logic programming [4]. The standard semantics of scenaria in Theorist [18], extensions in default logic [19], stable expansions in autoepistemic logic [15], fixed points in non-monotonic modal logic [14] and stable models in logic programming [9] correspond to the less liberal notion of *stable* sets of assumptions, i.e. sets of assumptions which are admissible and attack every assumption they do not contain. [4]

The semantics of admissible and stable sets of assumptions are *credulous*, in the sense that a sentence δ is a *non-monotonic consequence* of a theory T iff δ belongs to *some* extension sanctioned by the semantics. Corresponding to every credulous semantics there is a *sceptical* semantics in which δ is a *non-monotonic consequence* of T iff δ belongs to *all* extensions sanctioned by the semantics. Many cases of circumscription [13] can be understood as the sceptical semantics corresponding to stable sets of assumptions.

In this paper we focus upon the computation of non-monotonic consequences using the (credulous) admissibility semantics. We define proof procedures for computing the admissibility semantics for any abstract argumentation-theoretic framework.

3 Proof procedure for admissibility

The procedure is defined in the form of a *metalevel logic program*, the top-level clauses of which define the predicate *adm*, whose specification is given as follows:

Definition 1. Let $\langle T, Ab, \text{attacks} \rangle$ be an argumentation-theoretic framework. For any sets of assumptions $\Delta_0, \Delta \subseteq Ab$
$$adm(\Delta_0, \Delta) \leftrightarrow [\Delta_0 \subseteq \Delta \wedge \Delta \text{ is admissible}].$$

Typically, the set Δ_0 will be given, such that $T \cup \Delta_0 \vdash \alpha$ for some formula $\alpha \in \mathcal{L}$, and the problem will be to generate Δ, such that $adm(\Delta_0, \Delta)$. Consequently, $T \cup \Delta \vdash \alpha$ as well, and the set Δ provides an admissible "explanation" for the query α.

This characterisation of the predicate *adm* provides a *specification* for the proof procedure. In the remainder of this section, this specification together with the definition of admissibility given earlier will be referred to as $Spec_{adm}$. The logic program providing the proof procedure will consist of top-level clauses defining *adm* and lower-level clauses, defining the predicate *defends* given later in the section, in definition 3. The predicate *adm* takes names of sets of sentences as arguments, and is therefore a metapredicate. [5]

We focus on the top-level of the program. This part of the program will be derived from $Spec_{adm}$ and from the specification (given later, in definition 3) of the lower-level predicate *defends*.

---

[4] Trivially, a set of assumptions $A \subseteq Ab$ attacks an assumption $\alpha \in Ab$ iff A attacks $\{\alpha\}$.

[5] Moreover, there is an additional, implicit argument T in *adm* and all predicates considered in these paper.

The following simple, but important, theorem provides an alternative characterisation of admissibility. By virtue of this theorem, the condition that an admissible set of assumptions Δ does not attack itself does not need to be checked explicitly. It can be shown to hold implicitly if, for all closed attacks A against Δ, we restrict attention to counter attacks against assumptions in $A - \Delta$. This restriction has the additional computational advantage of reducing the number of candidate counter attacks that need to be considered.

Theorem 2. *A set of assumptions $\Delta \subseteq Ab$ is admissible iff*
   Δ is closed, and
   for each closed $A \subseteq Ab$, if A attacks Δ then Δ attacks $A - \Delta$.

The proof of this theorem can be found in the appendix.

Definition 3. Let $\langle T, Ab, attacks \rangle$ be an argumentation-theoretic framework. For any sets of assumptions $\mathcal{D}, \Delta \subseteq Ab$,
   $defends(\mathcal{D}, \Delta) \leftrightarrow \forall A \subseteq Ab \,[[A \text{ attacks } \Delta \wedge closed(A)] \rightarrow \mathcal{D} \text{ attacks } A - \Delta]$
where $closed(A)$ means "A is closed". We also say that $\mathcal{D}$ *defends* Δ.

This definition provides a specification for the predicate $defends$. This specification together with the auxiliary definitions of attackand $closed$ and with definitions of set-theoretic operations and relationships will be referred to as $Spec_{defends}$.
   The following corollary, which follows directly from theorem 2, characterises admissibility and $Spec_{adm}$ in terms of $defends$, and will be used to prove theorems 5 and 14 below.

Corollary 4.
1. *$\Delta \subseteq Ab$ is admissible iff Δ is closed and Δ defends Δ.*
2. *The specification $Spec_{adm}$ can be expressed equivalently as*
   $adm(\Delta_0, \Delta) \leftrightarrow \Delta_0 \subseteq \Delta \wedge defends(\Delta, \Delta) \wedge closed(\Delta)$.

The proof procedure is given by the logic program

$$Prog_{adm}: \boxed{\begin{array}{l} adm(\Delta, \Delta) \leftarrow defends(\Delta, \Delta), closed(\Delta) \\ adm(\Delta, \Delta') \leftarrow defends(\mathcal{D}, \Delta), closed(\Delta \cup \mathcal{D}), adm(\Delta \cup \mathcal{D}, \Delta') \end{array}}$$

Note that, in the case of flat argumentation-theoretic frameworks, every set of assumptions is closed. Therefore, in this case, the conditions $closed(\Delta)$ and $closed(\Delta \cup \mathcal{D})$ in $Prog_{adm}$ can be omitted.
   The soundness of $Prog_{adm}$ is expressed by corollary 6 below, which is a direct consequence of the following theorem:

Theorem 5. $Spec_{adm} \wedge Spec_{defends} \models Prog_{adm}$.

Proof: We prove the theorem by deriving the program $Prog_{adm}$ from the specification. By letting $\Delta_0 = \Delta$ in $Spec_{adm}$, as formulated in corollary 4.2

$adm(\Delta_0, \Delta) \leftrightarrow \Delta_0 \subseteq \Delta \wedge defends(\Delta, \Delta) \wedge closed(\Delta)$

we immediately obtain the first clause of the program.

To obtain the second clause, we let $\Delta_0 = \Delta'_0 \cup \mathcal{D}$ in the only-if half of $Spec_{adm}$, as formulated in corollary 4.2, and observe that $\Delta'_0 \cup \mathcal{D} \subseteq \Delta$ implies $\Delta'_0 \subseteq \Delta$, obtaining

$adm(\Delta'_0 \cup \mathcal{D}, \Delta) \rightarrow [\Delta'_0 \subseteq \Delta \wedge defends(\Delta, \Delta) \wedge closed(\Delta)]$.

Then, by applying the if half of $Spec_{adm}$, by transitivity of $\rightarrow$, we obtain

$adm(\Delta'_0 \cup \mathcal{D}, \Delta) \rightarrow adm(\Delta'_0, \Delta)$

which implies

$adm(\Delta'_0 \cup \mathcal{D}, \Delta) \wedge closed(\Delta'_0 \cup \mathcal{D}) \wedge defends(\mathcal{D}, \Delta'_0) \rightarrow adm(\Delta'_0, \Delta)$.

By renaming Δ'_0 to Δ and Δ to Δ', we obtain the second clause of the program. $\square$

Note that the derivation of the program $Prog_{adm}$ from the specifications $Spec_{adm}$ and $Spec_{defends}$ is achieved by simple deductive steps (e.g. transitivity of $\rightarrow$ and or introduction) possibly exploiting properties of the relations involved (e.g., of $\subseteq$).

Corollary 6. *For all $\Delta_0, \Delta \subseteq Ab$,*
  if $Prog_{adm} \wedge Spec_{defends} \models adm(\Delta_0, \Delta)$,
  then $Spec_{adm} \wedge Spec_{defends} \models adm(\Delta_0, \Delta)$.

Namely, if, for some given $\Delta_0 \subseteq Ab$, the goal $\leftarrow adm(\Delta_0, X)$ succeeds for $X = \Delta$, with respect to $Prog_{adm}$ and assuming $Spec_{defends}$, then Δ is an admissible superset of Δ_0. As a consequence, the procedure $Prog_{adm}$ is sound. The procedure $Prog_{adm}$ is also complete in the following sense:

Theorem 7. *For all $\Delta_0, \Delta \subseteq Ab$,*
  if $Spec_{adm} \wedge Spec_{defends} \models adm(\Delta_0, \Delta)$
  then $Prog_{adm} \wedge Spec_{defends} \models adm(\Delta_0, \Delta)$.

Proof : Assume $Spec_{adm} \wedge Spec_{defends} \models adm(\Delta_0, \Delta)$. Then,
  $Spec_{defends} \models \Delta_0 \subseteq \Delta \wedge defends(\Delta, \Delta) \wedge closed(\Delta)$.
Then, by the first clause of $Prog_{adm}$
  $Prog_{adm} \wedge Spec_{defends} \models adm(\Delta, \Delta)$.
There are two cases: (1) $\Delta_0 = \Delta$ and (2) $\Delta_0 \subset \Delta$.
In the first case, $Prog_{adm} \wedge Spec_{defends} \models adm(\Delta_0, \Delta)$ immediately.
In the second case, since, trivially, any defence of a set Δ also defends any subset of Δ, i.e. for any sets of assumptions $D, \Delta, \Delta' \subseteq Ab$
  $Spec_{defends} \models defends(D, \Delta) \wedge \Delta' \subseteq \Delta \rightarrow defends(D, \Delta')$
then
  $Spec_{defends} \models defends(\Delta, \Delta_0) \wedge closed(\Delta)$.
Then, $Prog_{adm} \wedge Spec_{defends} \models adm(\Delta, \Delta) \wedge defends(\Delta, \Delta_0) \wedge closed(\Delta)$.
But $\Delta = \Delta \cup \Delta_0$. Therefore,
  $Prog_{adm} \wedge Spec_{defends} \models adm(\Delta \cup \Delta_0, \Delta) \wedge defends(\Delta, \Delta_0) \wedge closed(\Delta \cup \Delta_0)$.
But then, by the second clause of $Prog_{adm}$,
  $Prog_{adm} \wedge Spec_{defends} \models adm(\Delta_0, \Delta)$. $\square$

Namely, if Δ is an admissible superset of a given set of assumptions Δ_0, then the program $Prog_{adm}$, assuming $Spec_{defends}$, successfully computes $X = \Delta$, given the goal $\leftarrow adm(\Delta_0, X)$. Note that the proof of completeness is achieved by symbolic execution of the program $Prog_{adm}$, and by appropriately choosing defences satisfying $Spec_{defends}$.

The full proof procedure is obtained by adding to $Prog_{adm}$ a program $Prog_{defends}$ for computing $defends$, for checking $closed$ and for computing the set-theoretic constructs, $\cup, \subseteq$, etc. This program may or may not be in the form of a logic program. If such a program is sound with respect to the specification $Spec_{defends}$, then $Prog_{adm} \wedge Prog_{defends}$ is also sound, with respect to $Spec_{adm}$ and $Spec_{defends}$:

Theorem 8. *Given $Prog_{defends}$ such that, for all $\Delta, \mathcal{D} \subseteq Ab$,*
  if $Prog_{defends} \models defends(\mathcal{D}, \Delta)$ then $Spec_{defends} \models defends(\mathcal{D}, \Delta)$, and
  if $Prog_{defends} \models closed(\Delta)$ then $Spec_{defends} \models closed(\Delta)$,
then, for all $\Delta_0, \Delta \subseteq Ab$,
  if $Prog_{adm} \wedge Prog_{defends} \models adm(\Delta_0, \Delta)$
  then $Spec_{adm} \wedge Spec_{defends} \models adm(\Delta_0, \Delta)$.

The proof of this and the following theorem can be found in the appendix.

Moreover, if a given program $Prog_{defends}$ is complete with respect to the specification $Spec_{defends}$, then $Prog_{adm} \wedge Prog_{defends}$ is also complete, with respect to $Spec_{adm}$ and $Spec_{defends}$. More precisely:

Theorem 9. *Given $Prog_{defends}$ such that, for all $\Delta, \mathcal{D} \subseteq Ab$,*
  if $Spec_{defends} \models defends(\mathcal{D}, \Delta)$ then $Prog_{defends} \models defends(\mathcal{D}, \Delta)$, and
  if $Spec_{defends} \models closed(\Delta)$ then $Prog_{defends} \models closed(\Delta)$
then, for all $\Delta_0, \Delta \subseteq Ab$,
  if $Spec_{adm} \wedge Spec_{defends} \models adm(\Delta_0, \Delta)$
  then $Prog_{adm} \wedge Prog_{defends} \models adm(\Delta_0, \Delta)$.

4 More efficient proof procedure

The proof procedure given by the program $Prog_{adm}$ performs a great deal of redundant computation. When a defence for the currently accumulated set of assumptions is generated, it is added to the accumulated set, without distinguishing between old assumptions that have already been defended and new assumptions that still have to be defended. As a consequence, defences for the old assumptions are recomputed redundantly when generating a defence for the new set. Moreover, when re-defending assumptions, new defences for such assumptions might be selected, different from the ones generated before, and these may need to be defended in turn. To avoid these redundancies, it suffices to distinguish in the currently accumulated set of assumptions, $\Delta \cup \mathcal{D}$, between those assumptions Δ that are already "defended" by $\Delta \cup \mathcal{D}$ itself and those assumptions $\mathcal{D}$ that have just been added to $\Delta \cup \mathcal{D}$ and require further defence. For this purpose, we employ a variant $adm^e(\Delta_0, \mathcal{D}, \Delta)$ of the predicate $adm(\Delta_0, \Delta)$.

Definition 10. Let $\langle T,\ Ab,$ attacks$\rangle$ be an argumentation-theoretic framework. For any sets of assumptions $\Delta_0, \mathcal{D}, \Delta \subseteq Ab$,

$$adm^e(\Delta_0, \mathcal{D}, \Delta) \leftrightarrow \Delta_0 \cup \mathcal{D} \subseteq \Delta \ \wedge$$
$$[[defends(\Delta_0 \cup \mathcal{D}, \Delta_0) \wedge closed(\Delta_0 \cup \mathcal{D})] \rightarrow \Delta \text{ is admissible}].$$

We refer to this definition, together with that of admissibility, as $Spec_{adm^e}$.

The relationship between adm and adm^e is given by the following lemma, whose proof can be found in the appendix.

Lemma 11. *For all sets of assumptions Δ_0 and Δ,*

1. *if $Spec_{adm^e} \wedge Spec_{defends} \models adm^e(\emptyset, \Delta_0, \Delta) \wedge closed(\Delta_0)$*
   then $Spec_{adm} \wedge Spec_{defends} \models adm(\Delta_0, \Delta)$;
2. *if $Spec_{adm} \wedge Spec_{defends} \models adm(\Delta_0, \Delta)$*
   then $Spec_{adm^e} \wedge Spec_{defends} \models adm^e(\emptyset, \Delta_0, \Delta)$

The top-most level of a procedure which computes the predicate adm^e is given by the logic program

$$Prog_{adm^e}: \quad \boxed{\begin{array}{l} adm^e(\Delta, \emptyset, \Delta) \\ adm^e(\Delta, \mathcal{D}, \Delta') \leftarrow defends^e(\mathcal{D}', \Delta, \mathcal{D}), \\ \qquad closed(\Delta \cup \mathcal{D} \cup \mathcal{D}'), \\ \qquad adm^e(\Delta \cup \mathcal{D}, \mathcal{D}' - (\Delta \cup \mathcal{D}), \Delta') \end{array}}$$

where $defends^e$ is the variant of the predicate $defends$ specified as follows:

Definition 12. Let $\langle T,\ Ab,$ attacks$\rangle$ be an argumentation-theoretic framework. For any sets of assumptions $\Delta, \mathcal{D}, \Delta' \subseteq Ab$,

$$defends^e(\mathcal{D}', \Delta, \mathcal{D}) \leftrightarrow$$
$$\forall A \subseteq Ab\,[[A\ attacks\ \mathcal{D} \wedge closed(A)] \rightarrow \mathcal{D}' \cup \Delta \cup \mathcal{D}\ attacks\ A - (\Delta \cup \mathcal{D})].$$

We will refer to this specification together with the definitions of attack, *closed* and the set-theoretic constructs as $Spec_{defends^e}$.

The following corollary, which follows directly from theorem 2, characterises admissibility and $Spec_{adm}$ in terms of $defends^e$, and will be used to prove theorem 14.

Corollary 13.
1. Δ *is admissible iff* $defends^e(\Delta, \emptyset, \Delta)$ *and* $closed(\Delta)$.
2. $Spec_{adm^e}$ *is equivalent to*
   $$adm^e(\Delta_0, \mathcal{D}, \Delta) \leftrightarrow \Delta_0 \cup \mathcal{D} \subseteq \Delta \ \wedge$$
   $$[[defends^e(\mathcal{D}, \Delta_0, \Delta_0) \wedge closed(\Delta_0 \cup \mathcal{D})] \rightarrow \Delta \text{ is admissible}].$$

The soundness of $Prog_{adm^e}$ is given by corollary 16 below, which follows directly from lemma 11 and from the following theorem:

Theorem 14. $Spec_{adm^e} \wedge Spec_{defends^e} \models Prog_{adm^e}$.

Proof : We prove the theorem by deriving the program $Prog_{adm^e}$ from the specification. By letting $\mathcal{D} = \emptyset$ and $\Delta = \Delta_0$ in $Spec_{adm^e}$

$$adm^e(\Delta_0, \mathcal{D}, \Delta) \leftrightarrow \Delta_0 \cup \mathcal{D} \subseteq \Delta \wedge$$
$$[defends(\Delta_0 \cup \mathcal{D}, \Delta_0) \wedge closed(\Delta_0 \cup \mathcal{D}) \rightarrow \Delta \text{ is admissible}]$$

we obtain

$$adm^e(\Delta, \emptyset, \Delta) \leftrightarrow \Delta \subseteq \Delta \wedge [defends(\Delta, \Delta) \wedge closed(\Delta) \rightarrow \Delta \text{ is admissible}]$$

equivalent to the first clause of $Prog_{adm^e}$ because of corollary 4.1.

To obtain the second clause, first replace the predicate adm^e in the second clause of the program by the equivalent specification in terms of $defends^e$ given by corollary 13.2, obtaining

$$[\Delta \cup \mathcal{D} \subseteq \Delta' \wedge [[defends^e(\mathcal{D}, \Delta, \Delta) \wedge closed(\Delta \cup \mathcal{D})] \rightarrow \Delta' \text{ is admissible}]] \leftarrow$$
$$[defends^e(\mathcal{D}', \Delta, \mathcal{D}) \wedge closed(\Delta \cup \mathcal{D} \cup \mathcal{D}') \wedge \Delta \cup \mathcal{D} \cup \mathcal{D}' \subseteq \Delta' \wedge$$
$$[[defends^e(\mathcal{D}' - (\Delta \cup \mathcal{D}), \Delta \cup \mathcal{D}, \Delta \cup \mathcal{D}) \wedge closed(\Delta \cup \mathcal{D} \cup \mathcal{D}')] \rightarrow$$
$$\Delta' \text{ is admissible}]].$$

This can be rewritten in the logically equivalent form

$$[\Delta \cup \mathcal{D} \subseteq \Delta' \ \wedge \Delta' \text{ is admissible}] \leftarrow$$
$$[defends^e(\mathcal{D}, \Delta, \Delta) \wedge closed(\Delta \cup \mathcal{D}) \wedge$$
$$defends^e(\mathcal{D}', \Delta, \mathcal{D}) \wedge closed(\Delta \cup \mathcal{D} \cup \mathcal{D}') \wedge \Delta \cup \mathcal{D} \cup \mathcal{D}' \subseteq \Delta' \wedge$$
$$[[defends^e(\mathcal{D}' - (\Delta \cup \mathcal{D}), \Delta \cup \mathcal{D}, \Delta \cup \mathcal{D}) \wedge closed(\Delta \cup \mathcal{D} \cup \mathcal{D}')] \rightarrow$$
$$\Delta' \text{ is admissible}]].$$

which follows immediately from the fact that

$$\Delta \cup \mathcal{D} \subseteq \Delta' \leftarrow \Delta \cup \mathcal{D} \cup \mathcal{D}' \subseteq \Delta'$$

and from the following lemma, whose proof can be found in the appendix. $\quad\square$

Lemma 15.
$$defends^e(\mathcal{D}, \Delta, \Delta) \wedge defends^e(\mathcal{D}', \Delta, \mathcal{D}) \rightarrow defends^e(\mathcal{D}' - (\Delta \cup \mathcal{D}), \Delta \cup \mathcal{D}, \Delta \cup \mathcal{D}).$$

As for $Prog_{adm}$ given in section 3, the derivation of $Prog_{adm^e}$ from the specifications $Spec_{adm^e}$ and $Spec_{defends^e}$ consists of simple deductive steps (here presented in a backward fashion), possibly exploiting properties of the relations involved (e.g. $\subseteq$ and $defends$, as expressed by lemma 15).

Corollary 16. For all $\Delta_0, \Delta \subseteq Ab$,
   if $Prog_{adm^e} \wedge Spec_{defends^e} \models adm^e(\emptyset, \Delta_0, \Delta) \wedge closed(\Delta_0)$,
   then $Spec_{adm} \wedge Spec_{defends} \models adm(\Delta_0, \Delta)$.

Namely, if, for some given set of assumptions Δ_0, the goal $adm^e(\emptyset, \Delta_0, X)$ succeeds for $X = \Delta$, with respect to $Prog_{adm^e}$ and assuming $Spec_{defends^e}$, then Δ is an admissible superset of Δ_0. As a consequence, the proof procedure $Prog_{adm^e}$ is sound. $Prog_{adm^e}$ is also complete in the following sense:

Theorem 17. For all $\Delta_0, \Delta \subseteq Ab$,
   if $Spec_{adm} \wedge Spec_{defends} \models adm(\Delta_0, \Delta)$,
   then $Prog_{adm^e} \wedge Spec_{defends^e} \models adm^e(\emptyset, \Delta_0, \Delta)$.

Proof : Assume $Spec_{adm} \wedge Spec_{defends} \models adm(\Delta_0, \Delta)$. Then
   $Spec_{defends} \models \Delta_0 \subseteq \Delta \wedge defends(\Delta, \Delta) \wedge closed(\Delta)$, and

$Spec_{defends^e} \models \Delta_0 \subseteq \Delta \wedge defends^e(\Delta, \emptyset, \Delta) \wedge closed(\Delta)$.

Moreover, it is easy to see that

$Spec_{defends^e} \models [[\Delta_0 \subseteq \Delta \wedge defends^e(\Delta, \emptyset, \Delta)] \rightarrow defends^e(\Delta, \emptyset, \Delta_0)]$.

Therefore, (i) $Spec_{defends^e} \models defends^e(\Delta, \emptyset, \Delta_0)$.

Similarly,

$Spec_{defends^e} \models [\Delta_0 \subseteq \Delta \wedge defends^e(\Delta, \emptyset, \Delta) \rightarrow defends^e(\Delta, \Delta_0, \Delta - \Delta_0)]$.

Therefore, (ii) $Spec_{defends^e} \models defends^e(\Delta, \Delta_0, \Delta - \Delta_0)$.

To show $Prog_{adm^e} \wedge Spec_{defends^e} \models adm^e(\emptyset, \Delta_0, \Delta)$, use the following instance of the second clause of the program:

$adm^e(\emptyset, \Delta_0, \Delta) \leftarrow defends^e(\mathcal{D}', \emptyset, \Delta_0)$,
$\qquad closed(\Delta_0 \cup \mathcal{D}')$,
$\qquad adm^e(\Delta_0, \mathcal{D}' - \Delta_0, \Delta)$

Let $\mathcal{D}' = \Delta$. Then, the first condition is provable from $Spec_{defends^e}$ by (i), and the second condition is provable from $Spec_{defends^e}$ since $\Delta_0 \subseteq \Delta$ and Δ is closed. To prove the third condition, use the following instance of the second clause of the program:

$adm^e(\Delta_0, \Delta - \Delta_0, \Delta) \leftarrow defends^e(\mathcal{D}', \Delta_0, \Delta - \Delta_0)$,
$\qquad closed(\Delta \cup \mathcal{D}')$,
$\qquad adm^e(\Delta, \mathcal{D}' - \Delta, \Delta)$

Let $\mathcal{D}' = \Delta$. Then, the first condition is provable from $Spec_{defends^e}$ by (ii), and the second condition is provable from $Spec_{defends^e}$ since Δ is closed. Moreover, the third condition is provable by the first clause of $Prog_{adm^e}$. Therefore,

$Prog_{adm^e} \wedge Spec_{defends^e} \models adm^e(\emptyset, \Delta_0, \Delta)$. $\qquad \square$

As in section 3, the proof of completeness is achieved by symbolic execution of the procedure $Prog_{adm^e}$, with two calls to the specification $Spec_{defends^e}$.

The full proof procedure is obtained by adding to $Prog_{adm^e}$ a program $Prog_{defends^e}$ for computing $defends^e$, for checking $closed$ and for computing the set-theoretic constructs, $\cup, \subseteq$, etc. In [6] we give the top-most level of a (generalised) logic program for computing $defends^e$, which provides a sound but incomplete proof procedure.

5 Conclusion

We have used logic program development technology to define two proof procedures for the admissibility semantics for the abstract, argumentation-theoretic framework presented in [2].

Rather than develop new methods, we have employed existing techniques of deductive synthesis [3] to derive two small but non-trivial programs and to prove them sound, and techniques of symbolic execution to prove them complete.

The second program is an improvement of the first, obtained by adding an argument, $\mathcal{D}$, to the predicate adm, thus obtaining a predicate adm^e. The new argument plays the role of an accumulator, and gives rise to a more efficient proof procedure $Prog_{adm^e}$. This is re-synthesised from scratch from a new specification for adm^e. As a subject for future work, it would be interesting to explore the possibility of deriving $Prog_{adm^e}$ from the initial, inefficient proof procedure, $Prog_{adm}$, using standard techniques of logic program transformation (fold, unfold and so on, see [17]) and/or techniques borrowed from functional programming (e.g., see [16]).

Acknowledgements

This research was supported by the EEC activity KIT011-LPKRR. The third author was partially supported by EEC HCM Project no CHRX-CT93-00414, "Logic Program Synthesis and Transformation". The authors are grateful to the LOPSTR'96 participants for helpful comments and suggestions.

References

1. A. Bondarenko, F. Toni, R. A. Kowalski, An assumption-based framework for non-monotonic reasoning. *Proceedings of the 2nd International Workshop on Logic Programming and Non-monotonic Reasoning*, Lisbon, Portugal (1993), MIT Press (L. M. Pereira and A. Nerode, eds) 171–189
2. A. Bondarenko, P. M. Dung, R. A. Kowalski, F. Toni, An abstract, argumentation-theoretic framework for default reasoning. To appear in *Artificial Intelligence*, Elsevier.
3. Y. Deville, K.-K. Lau, Logic program synthesis. *Journal of Logic Programming* 19/20 (1994), Elsevier, 321–350
4. P. M. Dung, Negation as hypothesis: an abductive foundation for logic programming. *Proceedings of the 8th International Conference on Logic Programming*, Paris, France (1991), MIT Press (K. Furukawa, ed.) 3–17
5. P. M. Dung, On the acceptability of arguments and its fundamental role in nonmonotonic reasoning and logic programming. *Proceedings of the 13th International Joint Conference on Artificial Intelligence*, Chambery, France (1993), Morgan Kaufmann (R. Bajcsy, ed.) 852–857
6. P. M. Dung, R. A. Kowalski, F. Toni, Argumentation-theoretic proof procedures for non-monotonic reasoning. Logic Programming Section Technical Report, Department of Computing, Imperial College, London (1996)
7. K. Eshghi, R.A. Kowalski, Abduction through deduction. Logic Programming Section Technical Report, Department of Computing, Imperial College, London (1988)
8. K. Eshghi, R. A. Kowalski, Abduction compared with negation as failure. *Proceedings of the 6th International Conference on Logic Programming*, Lisbon, Portugal (1989), MIT Press (G. Levi and M. Martelli, eds) 234–254
9. M. Gelfond, V. Lifschitz, The stable model semantics for logic programming. *Proceedings of the 5th International Conference on Logic Programming*, Washington, Seattle (1988), MIT Press (K. Bowen and R. A. Kowalski, eds) 1070–1080
10. A. C. Kakas, P. Mancarella. Preferred extensions are partial stable models. *Journal of Logic Programming* 14(3,4) (1993), Elsevier, 341–348
11. A. C. Kakas, P. Mancarella, P.M. Dung, The Acceptability Semantics for Logic Programs. *Proceedings of the 11th International Conference on Logic Programming*, Santa Margherita Ligure, Italy (1994), MIT Press (P. van Hentenryck, ed.) 504–519

12. R.A. Kowalski. *Logic for problem solving.* Elsevier, New York (1979)
13. J. McCarthy, Circumscription – a form of non-monotonic reasoning. *Artificial Intelligence* 13 (1980), Elsevier, 27–39
14. D. McDermott, Nonmonotonic logic II: non-monotonic modal theories. *Journal of ACM* 29(1) (1982) 33–57
15. R. Moore, Semantical considerations on non-monotonic logic. *Artificial Intelligence* 25 (1985), Elsevier, 75–94
16. R. Paige, S. Koenig, Finite differencing of computable expressions. *ACM Transactions on Programming Languages Systems* 4(3) (1982), ACM Press, 402–454
17. A. Pettorossi, M. Proietti, Transformation of logic programs. *Journal of Logic Programming* 19/20 (1994), Elsevier, 261–320
18. D. Poole, A logical framework for default reasoning. *Artificial Intelligence* 36 (1988), Elsevier, 27–47
19. R. Reiter, A logic for default reasoning. *Artificial Intelligence* 13 (1980), Elsevier, 81–132
20. D. Saccà, C. Zaniolo, Stable model semantics and non-determinism for logic programs with negation. *Proceedings of the 9th ACM SIGACT-SIGMOD-SIGART Symposium on Principles of Database Systems*, Nashville, Tennessee (1990) ACM Press, 205–217

Appendix

Proof of theorem 2

$\Rightarrow$ Given a closed attack A against Δ, we need to prove only that Δ attacks $A - \Delta$. Since Δ is admissible, Δ attacks A. But, if Δ attacks $A \cap \Delta$, then Δ attacks itself, contradicting the hypothesis that Δ is admissible.

$\Leftarrow$ We need to prove only that Δ does not attack itself. Suppose that Δ attacks itself. Then, Δ attacks $\Delta - \Delta = \emptyset$. But, by definition of attack, no set can attack $\emptyset$.

Proof of theorem 8

Assume $Prog_{adm} \wedge Prog_{defends} \models adm(\Delta_0, \Delta)$. Then, since $Prog_{defends}$ is sound with respect to $Spec_{defends}$,
$Prog_{adm} \wedge Spec_{defends} \models adm(\Delta_0, \Delta)$.
Then, directly from corollary 6,
$Spec_{adm} \wedge Spec_{defends} \models adm(\Delta_0, \Delta)$.

Proof of theorem 9

Assume $Spec_{adm} \wedge Spec_{defends} \models adm(\Delta_0, \Delta)$. Then, directly from theorem 7,
$Prog_{adm} \wedge Spec_{defends} \models adm(\Delta_0, \Delta)$. By completeness of $Prog_{defends}$,
$Prog_{adm} \wedge Prog_{defends} \models adm(\Delta_0, \Delta)$.

Proof of lemma 11

1. First, note that, $adm^e(\emptyset, \Delta_0, \Delta) \wedge closed(\Delta_0)$ implies
$\Delta_0 \subseteq \Delta \wedge [[defends(\Delta_0, \emptyset) \wedge closed(\Delta_0)] \rightarrow \Delta$ is admissible$] \wedge closed(\Delta_0)$.
But $Spec_{defends}$ trivially implies $defends(\Delta_0, \emptyset)$. Therefore

$\Delta_0 \subseteq \Delta \ \wedge [closed(\Delta_0) \to \Delta$ is admissible$] \wedge closed(\Delta_0)$
which, in $Spec_{adm}$, implies $adm(\Delta_0, \Delta)$.

2. $adm(\Delta_0, \Delta)$ implies $\Delta_0 \subseteq \Delta \ \wedge \Delta$ is admissible.
This trivially implies
$\Delta_0 \subseteq \Delta \ \wedge [[closed(\Delta_0) \wedge defends(\Delta, \emptyset)] \to \Delta$ is admissible$]$
which, in $Spec_{adm^e}$ implies $adm^e(\emptyset, \Delta_0, \Delta)$.

Proof of lemma 15 : Assume
  (i) $defends^e(\mathcal{D}, \Delta, \Delta)$, and
  (ii) $defends^e(\mathcal{D}', \Delta, \mathcal{D})$.
Assume $A \subseteq Ab$ attacks $\Delta \cup \mathcal{D}$. We need to show that $\mathcal{D}' \cup \Delta \cup \mathcal{D}$ attacks $A - (\Delta \cup \mathcal{D})$.

- If A attacks $\mathcal{D}$ then, by (ii), $\mathcal{D}' \cup \Delta$ attacks $A - (\Delta \cup \mathcal{D})$, and thus $\mathcal{D}' \cup \Delta \cup \mathcal{D}$ attacks $A - (\Delta \cup \mathcal{D})$.
- If A attacks Δ then, by (i), $\mathcal{D} \cup \Delta$ attacks $A - \Delta$. It suffices to show that $\mathcal{D} \cup \Delta$ does not attack $\mathcal{D}$. Suppose, on the contrary, that $\mathcal{D} \cup \Delta$ attacks $\mathcal{D}$. Then, by (ii), $\mathcal{D}' \cup \Delta$ attacks $(\mathcal{D} \cup \Delta) - (\mathcal{D} \cup \Delta) = \emptyset$. But this is not possible, because, by definition of attack, there are no attacks against $\emptyset$.

Author Index

Lecture Notes in Computer Science

For information about Vols. 1–1133

please contact your bookseller or Springer-Verlag

Vol. 1171: A. Franz, Automatic Ambiguity Resolution in Natural Language Processing. XIX, 155 pages. 1996. (Subseries LNAI).

Vol. 1172: J. Pieprzyk, J. Seberry (Eds.), Information Security and Privacy. Proceedings, 1996. IX, 333 pages. 1996.

Vol. 1173: W. Rucklidge, Efficient Visual Recognition Using the Hausdorff Distance. XIII, 178 pages. 1996.

Vol. 1174: R. Anderson (Ed.), Information Hiding. Proceedings, 1996. VIII, 351 pages. 1996.

Vol. 1175: K.G. Jeffery, J. Král, M. Bartošek (Eds.), SOFSEM'96: Theory and Practice of Informatics. Proceedings, 1996. XII, 491 pages. 1996.

Vol. 1176: S. Miguet, A. Montanvert, S. Ubéda (Eds.), Discrete Geometry for Computer Imagery. Proceedings, 1996. XI, 349 pages. 1996.

Vol. 1177: J.P. Müller, The Design of Intelligent Agents. XV, 227 pages. 1996. (Subseries LNAI).

Vol. 1178: T. Asano, Y. Igarashi, H. Nagamochi, S. Miyano, S. Suri (Eds.), Algorithms and Computation. Proceedings, 1996. X, 448 pages. 1996.

Vol. 1179: J. Jaffar, R.H.C. Yap (Eds.), Concurrency and Parallelism, Programming, Networking, and Security. Proceedings, 1996. XIII, 394 pages. 1996.

Vol. 1180: V. Chandru, V. Vinay (Eds.), Foundations of Software Technology and Theoretical Computer Science. Proceedings, 1996. XI, 387 pages. 1996.

Vol. 1181: D. Bjørner, M. Broy, I.V. Pottosin (Eds.), Perspectives of System Informatics. Proceedings, 1996. XVII, 447 pages. 1996.

Vol. 1182: W. Hasan, Optimization of SQL Queries for Parallel Machines. XVIII, 133 pages. 1996.

Vol. 1183: A. Wierse, G.G. Grinstein, U. Lang (Eds.), Database Issues for Data Visualization. Proceedings, 1995. XIV, 219 pages. 1996.

Vol. 1184: J. Waśniewski, J. Dongarra, K. Madsen, D. Olesen (Eds.), Applied Parallel Computing. Proceedings, 1996. XIII, 722 pages. 1996.

Vol. 1185: G. Ventre, J. Domingo-Pascual, A. Danthine (Eds.), Multimedia Telecommunications and Applications. Proceedings, 1996. XII, 267 pages. 1996.

Vol. 1186: F. Afrati, P. Kolaitis (Eds.), Database Theory - ICDT'97. Proceedings, 1997. XIII, 477 pages. 1997.

Vol. 1187: K. Schlechta, Nonmonotonic Logics. IX, 243 pages. 1997. (Subseries LNAI).

Vol. 1188: T. Martin, A.L. Ralescu (Eds.), Fuzzy Logic in Artificial Intelligence. Proceedings, 1995. VIII, 272 pages. 1997. (Subseries LNAI).

Vol. 1189: M. Lomas (Ed.), Security Protocols. Proceedings, 1996. VIII, 203 pages. 1997.

Vol. 1190: S. North (Ed.), Graph Drawing. Proceedings, 1996. XI, 409 pages. 1997.

Vol. 1191: V. Gaede, A. Brodsky, O. Günther, D. Srivastava, V. Vianu, M. Wallace (Eds.), Constraint Databases and Applications. Proceedings, 1996. X, 345 pages. 1996.

Vol. 1192: M. Dam (Ed.), Analysis and Verification of Multiple-Agent Languages. Proceedings, 1996. VIII, 435 pages. 1997.

Vol. 1193: J.P. Müller, M.J. Wooldridge, N.R. Jennings (Eds.), Intelligent Agents III. XV, 401 pages. 1997. (Subseries LNAI).

Vol. 1194: M. Sipper, Evolution of Parallel Cellular Machines. XIII, 199 pages. 1997.

Vol. 1195: R. Trappl, P. Petta (Eds.), Creating Personalities for Synthetic Actors. VII, 251 pages. 1997. (Subseries LNAI).

Vol. 1196: L. Vulkov, J. Waśniewski, P. Yalamov (Eds.), Numerical Analysis and Its Applications. Proceedings, 1996. XIII, 608 pages. 1997.

Vol. 1197: F. d'Amore, P.G. Franciosa, A. Marchetti-Spaccamela (Eds.), Graph-Theoretic Concepts in Computer Science. Proceedings, 1996. XI, 410 pages. 1997.

Vol. 1198: H.S. Nwana, N. Azarmi (Eds.), Software Agents and Soft Computing: Towards Enhancing Machine Intelligence. XIV, 298 pages. 1997. (Subseries LNAI).

Vol. 1199: D.K. Panda, C.B. Stunkel (Eds.), Communication and Architectural Support for Network-Based Parallel Computing. Proceedings, 1997. X, 269 pages. 1997.

Vol. 1200: R. Reischuk, M. Morvan (Eds.), STACS 97. Proceedings, 1997. XIII, 614 pages. 1997.

Vol. 1201: O. Maler (Ed.), Hybrid and Real-Time Systems. Proceedings, 1997. IX, 417 pages. 1997.

Vol. 1202: P. Kandzia, M. Klusch (Eds.), Cooperative Information Agents. Proceedings, 1997. IX, 287 pages. 1997. (Subseries LNAI).

Vol. 1203: G. Bongiovanni, D.P. Bovet, G. Di Battista (Eds.), Algorithms and Complexity. Proceedings, 1997. VIII, 311 pages. 1997.

Vol. 1204: H. Mössenböck (Ed.), Modular Programming Languages. Proceedings, 1997. X, 379 pages. 1997.

Vol. 1205: J. Troccaz, E. Grimson, R. Mösges (Eds.), CVRMed-MRCAS'97. Proceedings, 1997. XIX, 834 pages. 1997.

Vol. 1206: J. Bigün, G. Chollet, G. Borgefors (Eds.), Audio- and Video-based Biometric Person Authentication. Proceedings, 1997. XII, 450 pages. 1997.

Vol. 1207: J. Gallagher (Ed.), Logic Program Synthesis and Transformation. Proceedings, 1996. VII, 325 pages. 1997.

Vol. 1208: S. Ben-David (Ed.), Computational Learning Theory. Proceedings, 1997. VIII, 331 pages. 1997. (Subseries LNAI).

Vol. 1209: L. Cavedon, A. Rao, W. Wobcke (Eds.), Intelligent Agent Systems. Proceedings, 1996. IX, 188 pages. 1997. (Subseries LNAI).

Vol. 1210: P. de Groote, J.R. Hindley (Eds.), Typed Lambda Calculi and Applications. Proceedings, 1997. VIII, 405 pages. 1997.

Vol. 1211: E. Keravnou, C. Garbay, R. Baud, J. Wyatt (Eds.), Artificial Intelligence in Medicine. Proceedings, 1997. XIII, 526 pages. 1997. (Subseries LNAI).

Vol. 1212: J. P. Bowen, M.G. Hinchey, D. Till (Eds.), ZUM '97: The Z Formal Specification Notation. Proceedings, 1997. X, 435 pages. 1997.